Seasons of the Mind

Seasons of the Mind

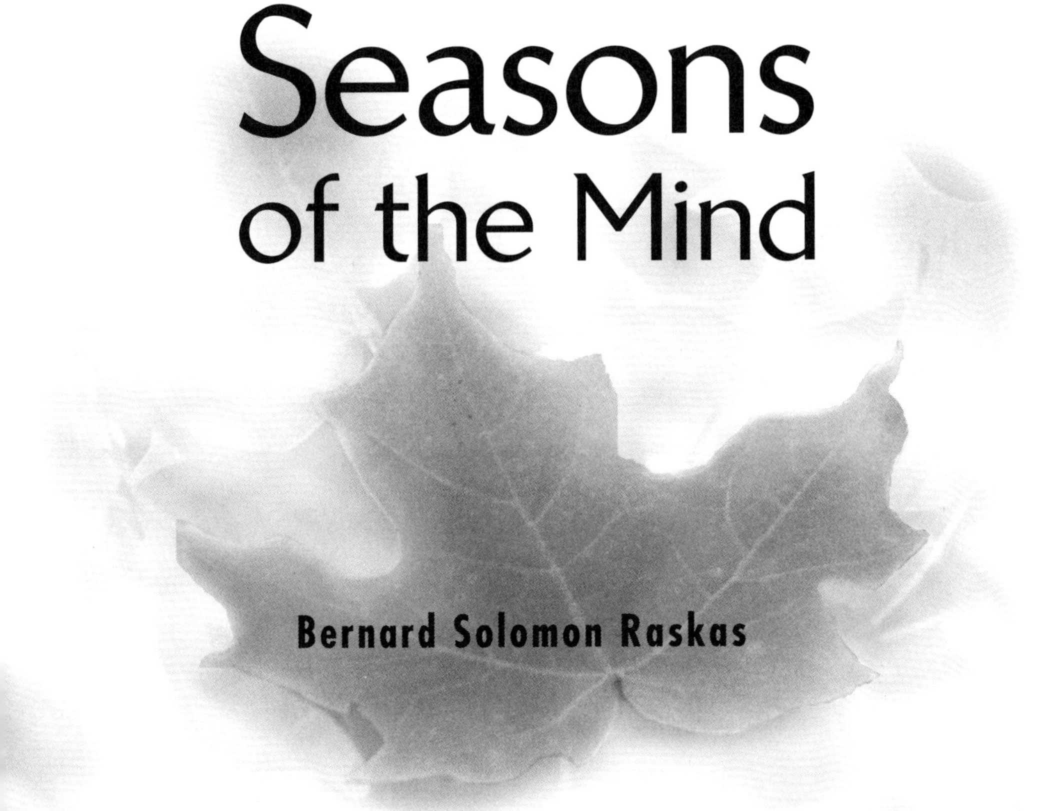

Bernard Solomon Raskas

LERNER PUBLICATIONS COMPANY / MINNEAPOLIS

This book is simultaneously published by The Jerusalem Publishing House, Ltd., 39 Tschernichovski Street, Jerusalem, Israel 91071

Lerner Publications Company
A division of Lerner Publishing Group
241 First Avenue North
Minneapolis, MN 55401 U.S.A.

Website address: www.lernerbooks.com

Library of Congress Cataloging-in-Publication Data

Raskas, Bernard S.
Seasons of the mind : Minnesota rabbi /
by Bernard Solomon Raskas.
p. cm.
Includes index.
ISBN 0-8225-4528-7 (pbk : alk paper)
1. Judaism—20th century. 2. Judaism—History. I. Title.

BM45.R2976 2001
296'.09'04—dc21 00-010278

Manufactured in the United States of America
1 2 3 4 5 6 — JR — 06 05 04 03 02 01

Table Of Contents

Section I ~ Seasons

Section II ~ Issues

Section III ~ Identity

Section IV ~ Now and Then

Section V ~ Transcendence

Dedication

In memory of

Sidney Barrows

Mensch

Only to do justice

And to love goodness

And to walk humbly with God;

Then will your name achieve respect.

Micah 6:8

Section I — Seasons

1. Rosh Hashanah: The Celebration of Life

Rosh Hashanah is the celebration of life. Its theme is found in the meaningful words and haunting melody that we chant over and over again on the High Holy Days: "Remember us that we may live, O Sovereign who delights in life. Inscribe us in the Book of Life, for Your sake, Living God."

Greeting cards wish everyone "to be inscribed in the Book of Life." The *shehecheyanu* prayer involving life is recited many times. It is the tradition to use an exotic fruit on the second night to add another *shehecheyanu* prayer. Carrot dishes are served because the Yiddish word for carrots is *mehrin,* which also means "increase"—obviously, the length of life.

After each sounding of the shofar on Rosh Hashanah we repeat the passage that begins with *hayom harat olam.* "On this day the world was born." We celebrate the beginning of the life of the universe.

The Torah reading on Rosh Hashanah deals with the birth of Isaac, and the Prophetic selection recounts the birth of Samuel. A significant prayer notes, "Your awe is upon all creation" and, therefore, "let all creation unite in revering Your name."

Following the theme of creation, the following passage from the Talmud (Sanhedrin 4:5) is most powerful: "A human was first created, a single individual to teach the lesson that whoever destroys one life, Scripture ascribes as though one destroyed the whole world, and whoever saves one life, as though one had saved the whole world."

Near Caesarea in Israel are the ruins of one of the most interesting amphitheaters in history. It was here that the Romans arranged the so-called games that pitted man against beast and, in the gladiatorial contests, man against man. The ultimate charge was: Fight unto death!

To the ancient rabbis, who taught that each person was fashioned in God's image and that saving or destroying one human life was like the salvation or destruction of the entire world, these arenas became the embodiment of evil. It was unthinkable that a Jew should ever voluntarily attend any of these games and find even the slightest pleasure in seeing one human being kill another. But Rabbi Nathan disagreed with the prevailing opinion, saying, "A Jew goes and he shouts!"

What this means is that when the victorious gladiator was about to strike the death blow, he asked the audience for advice. If they shouted, "Thumbs up!" the loser's life would be saved. Therefore, if a Jew attended and shouted "Thumbs up!" it was just possible that a life would be saved.

Indeed, it is part of Jewish thought that under threat of death a Jew may violate any commandment but must not reject monotheism, commit incest, or shed blood. This is based on the verse, "And you shall live by them" (Leviticus 18:5) "And not die by them" (Sanhedrin 74a). Out of this flow the concepts *pikuach nefesh,* "saving a life"; *tzar baaleh chaim,* "causing no pain to any living being"; *baal tashith,* "not wasting the environment."

In fact, quite the contrary. The Jerusalem Talmud teaches, "In the future a person will not enjoy that his [or her] eye saw and did not take the time to appreciate" (Kiddushin 4:12). In every Jewish prayer book there is a section known as *birchot hanayhanin,* "Blessings of enjoyment." There is a *bracha* (blessing) expressing gratitude for fragrant plants and shrubs, spices, fruit, and the first blossoming of trees. There are special *berechot* (blessings) for seeing the ocean, wonders of nature, vast deserts, high mountains, and a sunrise. Of course, one is to express gratitude upon seeing a rainbow and seeing creatures of extraordinary beauty.

Jewish tradition requires one to recite a blessing over new clothes and shoes. However, many authorities teach that it is not proper to recite a blessing if the clothes are made out of the hide of an animal killed solely for that purpose. They use the following verse to support this teaching: "God's compassion extends to all of Creation" (Psalms 145:-9).

Cherishing the life of the universe is the most basic principle of the Jewish tradition. It is appropriate that it be the very core of Rosh Hashanah, the first day, commemorating the concept of the sacredness of all life.

Following the first atomic explosion in New Mexico, observers were discussing what had gone through their minds when the "big flash" came. William L. Lawrence, the science reporter for the *New York Times,* said quietly that he thought, "This is the type of flash when God said 'Let there be light.'"

On the dawn of Rosh Hashanah there will flash the light for the first day of the new year. As the day wears on, Jews will gather in synagogues for prayer and contemplation. We face the new day and the new year. We are ready to accept what they have to offer. We have hope because of the light of love, understanding, mercy and truth.

Or, in the words of Tevye, in *Fiddler On The Roof:*

To life, to life, *L'chaim!*
One day it's honey and raisin cake,
Next day a stomach ache,
Drink *L'chaim* TO LIFE!
To us and our good fortune,
Be happy, be healthy, long life!
And if our good fortune never comes,
Here's to whatever comes.
Drink *L'chaim* TO LIFE!

May the New Year bring you more years to your life and more life to your years.—1996

2. Continuity and Renewal

Rosh Hashanah is late this year. Rosh Hashanah is early this year. Actually, Rosh Hashanah always occurs on the first day of Tishri. We can set our calendars by it.

Ever since the Jewish calendar was set centuries ago, Rosh Hashanah has been the fixed symbol of Jewish continuity and renewal. The ritual guides us in reviewing the past and preparing for the future. Rosh Hashanah is a great statement of the way that Jewish life reaffirms itself and at the same time launches us with confidence into the future.

On Rosh Hashanah the shofar has been sounded for thousands of years. On Rosh Hashanah the apples and honey remind us of our childhood. Rosh Hashanah anchors us in history and strengthens our identity.

Frederick Wilhelm, the king of Prussia, once asked his chaplain to prove the endurance of religion. "Your Majesty," the chaplain replied, "the Jews." He correctly saw that the Jews collectively and individually are the embodiment of a long and continuous history of ideas and experiences.

Rosh Hashanah makes us aware that deep within the consciousness of the Jew burns the awareness of a unique spiritual destiny. Our personal existence is bound up with the deeper meaning of history. We are not lonely individuals on an endless road.

Rosh Hashanah is also a time for renewal, for *cheshbon hanefesh,* a spiritual self-examination. If anything, this one holy day emphasizes that as a group and as individuals we can change; indeed, we must change.

This year on Rosh Hashanah we will enter synagogues that range in design from the work of Percival Goodman to Frank Lloyd Wright. We will see Torah covers that dazzle in design. Silver Torah decorations will include the contemporary designs of Wolpert, Zabari, Ofin, Greenvercel, and others. The *talitot* (prayer shawls) will reflect the work of Agam or will be tie-dyes or individual weavings. The *kipot* (skullcaps) will show stunning creativity. The music will not only include the traditional *nusach* (standard melodies) but also the contemporary work of Janowsky, Davidson, Bernstein, and even a whiff of Bob Dylan. Sermons by rabbis (men and women) will cover every conceivable topic from intermarriage to the environment to world politics to personal problems.

These forms of renewal introduce more vigor and relevance to Rosh Hashanah. The Talmud itself notes with approval the statement: "Just as his (her) ancestors left a place to create new forms, so I was left a place by my ancestors to create new forms" (Hulin 7a).

Rosh Hashanah does not record the passing of a year in simple units of time. Indeed, the more accurate assessment of a year is not the hours spent or the seconds kept, but the measure of human emotions and feelings, the joys and the tears, the hopes and the fears.

On Rosh Hashanah a person must measure himself or herself by ideas of right and wrong; of deeds done and left undone; of sin, guilt, repentance, forgiveness, and amendment of life; of community responsibility and irresponsibility. This is an opportunity to correct our spiritual statement and balance the account of living.

Rosh Hashanah, then, is the time for continuity and renewal as a human community, as Jews, and as individuals. It is time to offer gratitude in the words of the classic prayer marking milestones: "For having the opportunity of life, for having sustained and for having reached a new time."—1993

3. Here Comes the Judge

The most well-known prayer that exemplifies the High Holy Days is *Untahneh Tokef.* It seems to give voice to the essential feeling of Rosh Hashanah: "And fear and trembling takes hold of them for it is proclaimed, 'The day of judgment is here.'"

Indeed, who can contemplate the past year without fear and trembling? The incessant wrangling over nuclear proliferation deepens our anxiety, as we well know that it is five minutes before doomsday on the atomic clock. In America we puff ourselves up with celebrations in tribute to the Statue of Liberty; we're walking tall and we're Number One in world power. Yet underneath we are troubled because we have the highest debt in world history, hunger stalks us in our neighborhoods, and crime is rampant. The truth is, we're whistling in the dark.

As Jews we are concerned because there is no ease in Zion. Outside of Israel it has been estimated that Jews assimilate at the rate of 240 a day, and that is 10 per hour. In our personal lives problems are multiplying and stress is mounting.

Every generation considers its own era to be a time of fearful crisis. Our time is somewhat different because change is much more rapid. Nuclear energy, impersonal automation, and other forces delicately balanced against each other in the world only intensify the situation.

In view of this, on this day of Rosh Hashanah, it would be appropriate and helpful, if not vital, to turn to our traditions, which contain the wisdom of the ages. From this we might well learn perspective, guidance, and the will, if not to resolve our problems, at least to learn to cope with them and live the best lives possible.

There is a wonderful verse in the Talmud that can well set the tone for us: *bahodesh hidshu mahahsehchem, ubashofar shipru maasehchem,* "In this first month renew your lives and through the shofar improve your deeds, then I will consider you as having been created anew" (Leviticus Rabbah 29:6).

This is a time to renew our values and recommit ourselves to our goals. Tempered by history, we should realistically lower our expectations but not abandon our ideals. To put it another way: What we can change, we should arrange, and what we cannot cure we must learn to endure.

It is to everyone's advantage to stop nuclear proliferation and slow the arms race. The sooner we realize that a nuclear war is unwinnable, the quicker we will find the path to peace. It's time for the nations of the world to get together, to stop the destructiveness of nuclear fallout and the ridiculousness of Star Wars. It's time to believe and live the words of the Psalmist: "The heavens belong to God" (Psalms 115:16). If we can't seem to get peace on earth yet, at least let's agree to keep harmony in the heavens.

Here is where we have a particular responsibility as Americans. Somehow we seem to think if we feel good we are good. If we play games with the tax structure, if we delude ourselves with power and think we're walking tall, if we ignore the future, then everything will turn out all right. But how can it if we ignore our pressing national problems? Let us not confuse bigness with greatness. The day will come when we will have to pay the piper, when the deficit is handed down to grandchildren and the inner rot of liberty sets in.

It is time to stop the inflated rhetoric and deal with what this republic is all about: life, liberty, and the pursuit of happiness. What happens to our quality of life if we don't support the arts, education, and humanities? What happens to our liberty if the movement succeeds to deny us the right of choice and to dictate and monitor our personal morality? What kind of happiness can there be if the handicapped are not helped and children go hungry; when alcoholism, drug rehabilitation, and health care is ignored and human services are cut back?

We may thrill to the words of Captain Stephen Decatur who said, "My country, may she always be right, but my country right or wrong." However, real patriotism was better voiced by the social leader Carl Schurz: "My country, may she always be right. If right, to be kept right, if wrong, to be set right." I love America so much that I want to right every wrong I can. I want to swell with pride when I feel this is a caring nation from sea to shining sea. That, to me, is the real judgment of America.

This leads to the situation of the American Jew today. We are the largest and most powerful Jewish community in history. Yet we are not sure of ourselves, and to say that we are one is mouthing a myth. We feel a deep malaise about our Jewish educational systems. To speak honestly, we are disappointed, even embarrassed, about some things that are happening in Israel.

But before we rush to judgment on this Judgment Day, let's get a little historical perspective. Israel is comparatively young and is home to people who came from a hundred cultures. Israel has fought at least five wars to protect its freedom. America, just about 100 years after its founding, had to fight a fratricidal civil war. Israel has taken in almost 3 million refugees from oppressed lands, including starving blacks from Ethiopia. Did any other country or religious culture do that? Go visit the Hebrew University, the Technion, and Ben Gurion University and see what has been achieved in such a brief period. Spend time at Bezalel Art School, look at the high-tech industries, take a long look at the hospitals and care facilities. Forget the stories in the media; they don't matter, because they are only interested in sensationalism and improving ratings. Live with the people of Israel as Laeh and I do every year, and then you will understand what Israel has achieved despite staggering odds.

Certainly, the people and the government have made mistakes, but what country hasn't? It is time to leave the messianic expectations of Zionism and be realistic. Also, remember history and the Holocaust, when no one would take in the Jews. Look at how many young Jews remained Jewish because of Israel. History will prove, I am certain, that Israel was not the only but also the best and wisest investment of the past century of Jewish history. History will also demonstrate that one of the fundamental reasons the dream of the State of Israel became a reality was because American Jewry threw the full weight of its financial, political, and moral forces behind her.

But now it's time to tend to our own house. I am heartened when young Jewish parents come to me literally screaming about the Jewish education of their children. It hurts, but it also feels good when I hear people say: "What are we going to do about the future of our synagogue?" If people care, there is hope.

Some are worried about pledges of money going down in the Jewish community, but my concern is the lack of morale. If there is morale there will be a Talmud Torah, a Sholom Home, a Jewish Family Service—a Jewish community infrastructure. Remember, it's fine to be involved and it's fine to make observations as a Jew, but be sure you're an observant Jew.

Let me point out something to American Jews who also are Zionists but, like myself, have chosen for varying reasons to live outside Israel. The great texts of Judaism were written outside of Israel. Precisely because Jews were forced to live in the international marketplace of ideas, they had to create a survival philosophy and a pattern of living as well as intellectual excellence that would keep Judaism and its culture intact under the most challenging, adverse conditions. Some illustrations: The Bible we read every Shabbat and holy day from the Torah scroll+ was written, according to tradition, by Moses, who never put a foot in the Promised Land. The Babylonian Talmud, the masterpiece of Jewish literature, was written, obviously, in Babylonia. The commentaries of Rashi were written in France. Maimonides wrote his great works in Egypt. The great Code of Jewish Law, the Shulchan Aruch, was organized and outlined in Spain. Hasidism came out of Russia and Poland. Modern Jewish philosophy is a product of Germany. And so I predict that the next great work will come out of America. I can't prove it, but I can feel it. If we American Jews care about being Jewish we will find a way to be Jewish. It probably will be a new way, but it will be our way.

Then, finally, I would like to draw an important implication from the liturgy and theology of Rosh Hashanah. Today God is a judge—and God alone. It is not our business as human beings to pass judgment on others, particularly our friends, our family, and especially our children. Justice Holmes once wrote, "The great act of faith is when a man decides he is not God." When we realize that we are not God we have a better chance of diminishing our guilt and becoming human.

What is the point of all this? The point is that each child is a mystery, unique and totally unlike any other child that is born or ever will be born. With all the best intentions and the most devoted care and nurturing, parents can accomplish only so much with a child. There was a time when behavioral psychologists convinced us that the newborn infant is like a blank sheet of paper waiting for parents to write on. Today we know better. The child comes into the world with its basic temperament determined by the wholly accidental combination of a multitude of genes that contain not only the traits of parents but also of ancestors long forgotten.

When we acknowledge the built-in limitations of the human condition, we also avoid the destructive tendency to blame ourselves when children do not turn out as we had hoped. Deluded by a sense of omnipotence, we fall easy prey to the illusion that when children follow their own ways, which may be different from ours, it is all our fault. We do not grant them the freedom of choice and respect that they are individuals.

We forget the many other factors that go into the making of a person—not only genes but also the environment, T.V., the peer group, teachers, characters encountered in books, and the spirit of the times. While no parent has the right to abdicate responsibility, neither should the parent arrogate to himself or herself the feeling of being all powerful.

This is exactly the central message of Rosh Hashanah. We are shaped by forces beyond us, yet we do have a significant measure of choice. We can choose how to respond to circumstances and events in our lives. We can make moral choices and determine our character consciously. In fact, we must determine to establish control over our lives and live in a sane and responsible manner.

In a nutshell, our biological inheritance, our childhood experiences and our social conditions exercise a vital influence upon us. These factors are real and powerful, but the human will is no less powerful. We are not only shaped by our environment, we shape it. We are not only the result of centuries of circumstance, we create circumstance.

Our genes may determine whether our eyes are blue or brown, but whether we look upon each other with cold indifference or warm compassion is for us to choose. Our physical height may be biologically determined, but our moral stature we fashion for ourselves. Our environment determines the language we speak, but whether our words are harsh or gentle, cruel or comforting depends squarely on us. Our passions, appetites and instincts are part of our animal equipment, but whether they rule us or we rule them is left for each of us to decide. Each of us must determine the course of our life in the coming years.

A story now making the rounds was told to me by a rabbi from Johnstown, Pennsylvania, the scene of the famous Johnstown Flood. It seems when another flood years later hit the area, the rabbi climbed to the roof of the synagogue. A rowboat came by and the rabbi called back to the offer of help, "No thanks, I have faith in God. The Almighty will save me." The waves came higher so the rabbi climbed to the peak of the roof. This time a motorboat came by to save him, but the rabbi waved it off, professing his faith that God would save him.

When the waves began lapping at his feet, a helicopter swooped down and lowered a rope ladder to save him, but the rabbi refused, still depending on the Eternal One. You can guess what happened. The rabbi drowned.

When the rabbi arrived in Heaven before God, he complained, "I had such faith in You. I dedicated my whole life to serving You. Why didn't You save me?"

To which the Eternal One replied, "I sent you two boats and a helicopter!"

God has provided us with the means to save ourselves from nuclear destruction, namely cooperation. We have the opportunity if not the responsibility, through the political process, to make America great. We have the means and the talent to start a renaissance of Judaism in America. All we need is the will. We can straighten out our personal lives by living realistically, honestly, and, above all, wisely. We can and we must try. No one can guarantee results, but no one is absolved from trying. All Judaism asks is to try. No more, no less. But remember, no less.—1978

4. May One Pray for the Death of an Enemy?

On Rosh Hashanah we will gather in our synagogues to reflect on the past year and to think about the coming year. We will recall our deeds and misdeeds. We will be praying for our loved ones, the Jewish people, and for peace in the world. But even as we do all this, we will remember the times that we were hurt by individuals and hated because we were Jews. Those reflections then present us with a dilemma concerning our enemies.

Jews have had no lack of enemies. Throughout history, from Haman to Hitler, Jews have experienced *sinat chinam,* "causeless hatred." In fact, this great hatred was so unique that a new term was created to describe it: anti-Semitism.

It would be natural for Jews, like all human beings, to react with feelings of anger, outrage, pain, and retribution. This reaction raises an interesting theological question: "Is it permissible to pray for the death of an enemy?"

The Bible is filled with passages calling for the death of enemies. They range from the mild to the most violent. Perhaps they could be summarized in the prayer of the Psalmist, "May the sinners be consumed and the wicked be no more" (104:35). For a victim to feel otherwise would be unnatural.

But this attitude is countered by biblical admonitions such as "You shall not take vengeance or hate" (Leviticus 19:18), or "Do not rejoice when your enemy falls" (Proverbs 24:17). There is an obvious ambivalence in the biblical views toward an enemy. Indeed, the Bible goes beyond counsel to curb one's natural anger toward an enemy by instructing: "When you encounter your enemy's ox or ass wandering, you must take it back to him. When you see the ass of your enemy lying under its burden and would refrain from raising it, you must nevertheless raise it with him" (Exodus 23:4-5).

To forestall the possibility that one should do this out of concern for the welfare of the animal alone, the Book of Proverbs (25:21) clarifies the matter: "If your enemy be hungry give him bread to eat, and if he be thirsty give water to drink." What this seems to imply is that the enemy is human.

There is also a great measure of enlightened morality (practical wisdom) in the counsel to help an enemy. The reason is explained in rabbinic literature (Tosefta; Baba Metzia 2:26): "Aid an enemy before you aid a friend, to subdue hatred." There are very few humans who receive help who do not feel a sense of gratitude. The ultimate destruction of an enemy, where possible, would be to turn him or her into a friend.

Despite the destructive ways of the enemy, he or she is a person, a spouse, a parent, a member of a family. An enemy, though an enemy, has feelings, thoughts, and needs. An enemy may have immoral intentions or carry out evil actions or be psychologically disturbed or mentally ill, but he or she still is human.

In terms of self-defense the matter is clear. There is no turning of the cheek. Resisting active evil is expressed in the well-known principle: "If someone comes to kill you, stand up and kill him (her) first" (Sanhedrin 7a). In the face of clear and present danger, it is a responsibility, indeed, to defend one's self in the strongest and most appropriate manner.

The ambivalence of the Bible on the matter of praying for the death of an enemy is reflected in the *amidah,* the classic formulation of the essence of Jewish prayer. In one passage it is written: "Let all Your enemies soon be destroyed. May You quickly uproot and crush the arrogant."

This prayer was added to the "eighteen benedictions" as formulated by the early rabbis. Recognizing its historic context, later generations repeatedly rephrased and modified it. They apparently wanted to give it a more universal tone and leave it somewhat vague.

Perhaps that is why the parable of Mar, the son of Ravina, a prominent rabbi of the fourteenth century, was added at the conclusion of the *amidah.* The opening words read: "My God, keep my tongue from evil, my lips from guile. To those who slander me, let my soul be silent." Clearly, this insertion tends to negate the previous passage. In doing so, it permits one who prays the opportunity to determine his or her attitude toward the enemy. For, after all, was not an enemy created in the image of God?

Perhaps the issue can be even broadened by the way we see God. There are times when God is described as "a man of war" (Exodus 15:3). On other occasions, God is perceived as "merciful and compassionate and forgiving" (Exodus 34:6). Are these two sides of the same God? Are they conflicting and irreconcilable attributes? Is this a theological paradox or an impenetrable mystery? Perhaps it is a fallacy of ascribing human feelings to God.

Leaving this theological riddle to the theologians, we must deal with the matter in the daily context of reading the newspaper, hearing the radio, watching television. How do we react, how should we respond, how should we pray when innocent civilians—men, women and children—are taken hostage, wounded, and killed?

This question raises an interesting issue of definition: One person's terrorist may be another's freedom fighter. The evil empire may see the other side as an oppressor or even a great Satan. One person's murderer may be considered another's martyr. What to do?

It is precisely here that Jewish tradition offers guidance.

Once Rabbi Meir was harassed by "lawless people." He prayed that they should die. Upon hearing this prayer, his wife Beruria (using Psalms 104:35 as a theological pun) admonished him, saying, "Do not pray that the wicked be no more, but that there should be no more wickedness. Do not pray for the death of an enemy, but the death of enmity" (Berachot 10a).

This incident begins to address our concern. Referring to prayer, at least, the focus should be on eliminating hostility. Judaism, being not a pacifist but a practical religion, understands that the expression of hatred cannot and should not be ignored. But at the same time, we must keep things in perspective and filter events through the lens of moral balance.

An example of setting the issue of the hater and hatred in the proper context can be found in an extraordinary passage in the Talmud (Berachot 7a). In the neighborhood of Rabbi Joshua, son of Levi, there lived a sectarian. The sectarian used to trouble Rabbi Joshua greatly in his interpretations of the Bible.

One day the Rabbi thought, "I shall curse him." When the propitious moment for cursing arrived, Rabbi Joshua was dozing. On awakening, he said, "I see from this that my intention was improper. For it is written: 'And God's mercies are over all of God's works; and it is further written, 'Neither is it good for the righteous to punish.'"

We are human in our feelings. The enemy is human also. Somewhere in between there is a need to strike a balance. Would that it were so simple. That is why it is written in Orchot Tzaddikim (15c): "Pray for your enemy that he (she) serves God."

This very thought is reflected in a prayer on Rosh Hashanah that is 1200 years old. "May all the world come to worship You and unite in seeking that which is good for all."—1990

5. It's About Time

Rosh Hashanah, the commemoration of the creation of the universe, is a difficult concept to grasp. That is because it has to do with the idea of time. Even the essential symbol of Rosh Hashanah, the sound of the shofar, exists only in time. It cannot be seen, touched, felt, or tasted.

In the roller coaster of life, we need to understand time and the timeless. Awash in trivia, people need ceremonies to remind themselves that they are part of something important, if not mysterious. We Jews, for example, have a blessing for sighting a rainbow or the ocean, for our food, for beginnings and endings. As Kohelet put it, "there is a time for everything."

Life is precious and life is sacred. As we move about God's world, we must walk with reverence for creation. We are of the universe and are its caretakers. On Rosh Hashanah we reaffirm our responsibility to celebrate the life of the universe.

Rosh Hashanah also marks the end of the old year, teaching that there is a time for letting go. We need to let go of our children so they can grow up. We need to let go of our anger and our guilt. We need to let go of certain traumas and events of the past so we can experience the many opportunities of the present and the future.

We need to let go of material objects lest we become overly dependent on them. Letting go does not necessarily mean physically relinquishing the object. We need to overcome our dependency on it and realize that the essence of our being is not the material object.

In spiritual preparation for the coming sacred days it might be proper to read *A Brief History of Our Time* by Steven Hawkins, a towering figure in modern physics. The book has sold more than 2 million copies. Few readers realize that for many of his years Hawkins has been living with a neurological disease. As a young man of twenty-one working on his Ph.D. at Oxford, he was stricken with what is commonly known as Lou Gehrig's Disease. Since he can hardly move a muscle and cannot even feed himself, he has to use a voice synthesizer to communicate his extraordinary discoveries. About discovering his illness in his student days, he said, "When I found I could not control my body, but my mind was free, I changed my attitude. I determined that I would choose to let mind conquer matter. I would determine how I think and nothing and no one would stand in the way of my thinking."

Rosh Hashanah comes to remind us that we can do *teshuvah,* control our thinking. This in turn helps us to determine our behavior. It is a time to reassess our thoughts and our deeds.

Let us think for a minute about the purpose of religion. If religion comes to teach us anything, it comes to tell us that we as individuals can change the course of our lives. And that is central to the human concept of time.

Creation is part of everyday living. The daily wonders of God can be seen in the birth of a baby, the budding of the trees, the varieties of the birds, and the infinite glory of the growing flowers. Creation may also be reflected in the endeavors of the artist who continually seeks to add beauty to life even as the creative person desires to deepen the experience and meaning of life itself.

This thought was given fine expression by Rabbi Abraham J. Heschel in his book *The Sabbath.* "Creation, we are taught, is not an act that happened once upon a time, once and for ever. The act of bringing the world into existence is a continuous process. God called the world into being, and that call goes on."

This coming Rosh Hashanah, the sound of the shofar summons us to consider that life is all about time and its use.—1979

6. The Dawn of Conscience

The term Rosh Hashanah, literally "head" (or beginning) of the year, is found only once in the Bible (Ezekiel 40:1), and even there it does not appear to refer to the first day of the year. In the Bible it is described as *Yom Teruoh,* a day of blowing the horn. This is the basic reason that we sound the shofar on this day.

The designation commonly used is clearly enunciated in the Mishna: "The first day of Tishri is Rosh Hashanah (New Year) for the reckoning of years." By tradition Rosh Hashanah symbolizes creation and becomes the "birthday of the world" as well as the "birthday" of human beings. Unlike the New Year celebrations of some cultures, characterized by revelry and hilarity, Rosh Hashanah is observed with a solemnity that is marked by prayer, contemplation, and self-searching.

If the earth is more than four billion years old why, then, is Rosh Hashanah, the beginning of the Jewish New Year, referred to as the day when the world was created? The explanation is that the Jewish calendar is less than 5,800 years old; on Rosh Hashanah Jews celebrate the time when recorded history began.

Humans' career as cave dwellers began some 100,000 years ago; then, about 10,000 years ago, humans learned agriculture. Not until the last five-and-a-half millennia do we find human responsibility to other humans. So it is that on Rosh Hashanah, appropriately enough, we celebrate the anniversary of the dawn of conscience.

In fact, the first episode in the Bible that highlights clear moral choice and accountability for one's actions is the Cain and Abel story in which God asks Cain, "Where is Abel your brother?" Cain's reply is: "Am I my brother's keeper?" The answer of the Bible is that we are our brother's keepers, for God's reply is: "The blood of your brother is crying out to Me." This phrase represents the first statement of conscience, and with it begins the history of civilization.

The dominant theme and motif of these days is the trial. Our conscience is placed on trial. The trial image sharpens our self-awareness and judgment, flowing from the idea that we must review our deeds, both good and bad, during the past year. The trial begins on Rosh Hashanah and reaches its climax on Yom Kippur.

The uniqueness of this trial is that the verdict can be influenced by genuine contrition. Increased prayer, charity giving, and acts of repentance tend to lessen the harsh verdict or even reverse it. In Jewish theology, sincere return to noble and good living is the surest sign of genuine repentance.

The Hebrew word for "repentance" is *teshuvah.* Literally, *teshuvah* means "return." This teaches us that atonement in Judaism implies returning to the right direction in life.

A Hasidic rebbe once asked, "If you are going East and suddenly you want to travel West, how far do you have to go?" His congregants gave him many complex answers, but the rebbe himself answered his own question in this way: "If you are going East and suddenly you want go West, all you have to do is turn around. It is as simple as that."

On Rosh Hashanah we confront our conscience, and we hope to turn into finer human beings. It is the uniqueness of Judaism to have fashioned a holy day, the first day of the new year, as the proper occasion to do this. That is why Anatole Leroy-Beaulieu, the French author once wrote, "Conscience is like charity, a Semitic importation. Israel introduced it into the world." Rosh Hashanah marks the birthday of that introduction.—1981

7. The Curious Case of Kol Nidre

Kol Nidre is one of the most popular and powerful prayers to be found in Jewish liturgy. Yet, it is not a prayer but a legal formula which does not even mention the name of God. The origin of its famous melody is unknown, and its inclusion in the prayer book was strongly opposed by several prominent rabbis.

The setting of Kol Nidre, which begins the Yom Kippur service, is a Jewish court. Two people hold Torah scrolls at either side of the cantor, thus constituting a *bet din,* a court of three which is required for the legal procedure of granting dispensation from vows. The prayer is preceded by a brief paragraph invoking the Academy on High, which is the heavenly body of rabbis. Because Kol Nidre is based on court procedure, which could not be conducted on a holiday, it is recited before sunset. Since it is chanted before dark, it is the practice to put on the *tallit* (prayer shawl).

The text is a precise legal formula in which the worshipers proclaim that all personal vows and oaths that they made unwittingly, rashly, or unknowingly (and that, consequently, cannot be fulfilled) during the year should be considered null and void. However, it should be pointed out that the Talmud (Yoma 8:9) says explicitly, "Yom Kippur atones for sins against God. Yom Kippur does not atone for sins against another human being until one has placated the person offended."

In order to understand the nature and function of Kol Nidre, we must go back to biblical times, when it was common practice for people to make vows that could not possibly be honored. After the Second Temple was destroyed, this practice continued among the people. The leaders of the community were troubled, for they viewed a person's word as his or her bond. Failing to convince the people of the desirability of avoiding rash promises altogether, the rabbis of the Talmud finally created a formal ritual for annulling unkept vows.

No one knows for certain, but it is probable that it was created in about the ninth century. Rav Amram's *siddur* contains the first complete known text of Kol Nidre, quite different from the talmudic legal formula. Kol Nidre was a collective rather than an individual annulment. It is a mixture of Hebrew and the then vernacular Aramaic.

There are two other explanations for its introduction. According to Rabbi Mordecai ben Hillel (d. Germany, 1298), this formula was instituted in the thirteenth century by Rabbi Meir ben Barukh of Rothenberg (d. 1293) to permit transgressors who had been excommunicated because of their defiance of communal regulations to worship with the congregation. Toward the end of the nineteenth century, Joseph Bloch had proposed the theory that Kol Nidre arose in the seventh century when secret Jews, who had been converted to Christianity after persecution by the Visigoths (590-711) would come to the synagogue on Yom Kippur eve. According to him, Kol Nidre was their expression of overwhelming grief at their apostasy and their means of seeking absolution for vows they had been forced to make to an alien faith. Bloch claimed that in subsequent centuries, during the persecutions by the later Byzantine rulers (700-850), and still later under the Spanish Inquisition (1391-1492), Kol Nidre served a similar purpose.

When it first appeared, the prayer was condemned by many generations of rabbis on the grounds that it offered an easy means to avoid personal obligations. After all, Kol Nidre theoretically made it possible for someone to take a vow, knowing that it could be annulled next Yom Kippur. Accordingly, the rabbis clearly ruled it could not be applied to promises made to another person. In the twelfth century they changed the wording to ensure this.

Unfortunately, Kol Nidre also served as a pretext for anti-Semitic slander. During the Middle Ages in particular, Christians used the formula as an excuse for isolating Jews from participating in business, claiming that their words could not be trusted.

When the Reform movement began in nineteenth-century Germany, Kol Nidre was deleted from its liturgy. It was not until 1962 that the text appeared in the *Union Prayer Book* and now in the new *Gates of Repentance.* The spiritual power of Kol Nidre among the people resisted every challenge put to it over a period of ten centuries, and it comes down to us today as one of the most beloved liturgical elements in all Judaism.

There have been many different melodies for Kol Nidre. A popular myth advances the notion that a Spanish Marrano composed the melody we use today. Other scholars have hypothesized that the melody arose in sixteenth-century Germany. But no one knows for certain, and the music's origin remains mysterious. However, its emotional appeal remains overpowering.

A German poet, a non-Jew, found himself in a small synagogue on the eve of the Atonement Service. He wrote, "Suddenly, the Cantor, with a deeply earnest heartrending melody, rich in awe and supplication began to sing. I had to struggle with a a rare feeling of emotion. Feverishly I sighed. Hot, burning tears pouring from one's eyes cast a wondrous spell and at the same time purified. I fled into the night and came home. In that unforgettable hour, no black speck defiled my soul." He had heard that mysterious brooding melody, the Kol Nidre.

It is a song which converted a Catholic priest, Aime Pallier, to the synagogue. It brought Franz Rosenzweig back to his faith when he had already determined to leave it. A great Christian theologian wrote in the classic book, *The Idea of the Holy,* of the *Tremendum,* the sense of awe in life when he came home from a North African synagogue where he listened to the Kol Nidre. The best-known musical setting of this prayer is by a non-Jew, Max Bruch, who wrote it for cello and orchestra when commissioned by the Jewish community of Liverpool.

For us today, the Kol Nidre can symbolize the need to deepen our sensitivity toward the resolutions that we make in our finest moments of spiritual decision. Kol Nidre can serve us as a reminder that only by resolute will and self-discipline can we hope to lessen the distance between what we are and what we ought to be. The self-righteousness and smugness which stand in the way of our spiritual growth need to be dispelled by a confession in utter humility. When accompanied by such a meditation, the recital of Kol Nidre prepares us for the soul-cleansing experience of Yom Kippur.—1986

8. Yom Kippur Teaches Nobody Is Perfect

The history of Yom Kippur is long, its ritual is complicated, and its theology is complex. But, basically, it is founded on the understanding that nobody is perfect. The greater portion of the observance of this holy day is focused on the forgiveness of sins, mistakes, misunderstandings, wrongdoing, and misdirection. The thrust of Yom Kippur is found in the biblical verse, "For there is not one person on earth who does not sin" (Ecclesiastes 7:20).

But Judaism does not stop there; perhaps it even begins there, by creating many opportunities for forgiveness, atonement, and reconciliation. Although all of the Jewish liturgy is replete with these ideas, they remain focused in the popular mind on one day—Yom Kippur—and encapsulated into one word—*teshuvah.*

Teshuvah is often translated as penitence, atonement, or forgiveness, but it would be more accurate to render it as "return." This implies returning to the path of normal, healthy living and returning to God. It is best expressed in a verse from Hosea 14:12: "Return *(shuvah)* Israel to *Adonoy,* your God, for you have stumbled through your sins."

Teshuvah (repentance and returning) is both the simplest of matters and the most complex of all matters, as pointed out by the world-famous Talmudic scholar Adin Steinsaltz. In his thoughtful book, *The Strike of the Spirit,* he elaborates the rabbinic belief that each individual is constantly struggling with *yehtzer hatov,* the inclination to do good, and *yehtzer harah,* the inclination to do wrong. However, *teshuvah* doesn't require traveling great distances but only turning around to face the good and God. The way to leave sin is simply to turn one's back—literally and spiritually turn around. Sometimes this is easy; at other times, it is painfully difficult. Perhaps that is why the ancient rabbis declared that a repentant sinner is often greater than the righteous.

It is interesting to note that the Yom Kippur liturgy is always read in the plural. The classic *al chet* prayer recited on Yom Kippur always uses the word "we." This is done not to embarrass the sinner and also to understand that, as a community, we are always involved to help, to be understanding, to be compassionate.

There is a thoughtful passage in the play by Arthur Miller entitled *Incident at Vichy.* The play is a study of sin, guilt, and responsibility during the Nazi occupation of France. At the end of the play Leduc, the doctor, says: "It is not your guilt that I want, it's your responsibility that might have helped."

Jewish theology and practice have provided a classic way to atone for a sin. First is the confession and recognition of the sin. Then comes the restitution in money, in kind, or in verbally seeking forgiveness. Finally, there is redetermination to rethink good and Godly living. Judaism stresses that there is nothing in this world for which we cannot be forgiving if we have sincerity, a desire to restore the wrong, and a full assumption of responsibility.

Most of the Jewish laws on sin and repentance (returning) can be found in the classic text of Maimonides' *Mishneh Torah* under the section *hilchot teshuvah* (the laws of repentance). In Judaism there is no weighty feeling of heavy, burdensome guilt that can never be relieved. There is no sense of original sin that is pressed on the shoulders of every person. Rather, there is the recognition that each of us is human and each has our own problems and our own potential.

Once a clever young man in Posen decided to test the skill of Rabbi Akiba Eiger by creating a perfect, blemishless, but synthetic *etrog* (citron) for use in the Sukkot Festival. He brought it to Rabbi Eiger's home for examination.

The sage picked it up, examined it, inhaled its scent, and looked at it in the light. Then he put it down and began examining the other samples. This happened several times, until the rabbi chose another, less perfect *etrog.* When the young man asked why he hadn't chosen the one which seemed far superior, the sage smiled and said, "Nothing in this world is perfect."

No human being is perfect. This relieves us of the pressure of striving for unattainable perfection and helps us accept ourselves as we are. On the other hand, the recognition of our imperfection gives us the opportunity to improve and return to good living.

On one occasion two Jews fell to discussing the difference between angels and humans. One noted that angels were perfect and could do no wrong. The other remarked, "Yes, although humans can do wrong, they can also improve, and angels cannot do that."

Redressing wrongs and improving oneself is a great, exhilarating feeling. The opportunity to do that is the gift of Yom Kippur.—1979

9. What Made Jonah Run?

The Book of Jonah, a seemingly fantastic tale of a reluctant prophet swallowed by a huge fish while fleeing from God, is read publicly once a year in the synagogue late in the afternoon on Yom Kippur. Even a cursory reading of the career of this wayward, even miserable, prophet raises the inevitable question: What in Jonah's life is so important that his story is read on the holiest day of the year?

Jonah is given the charge by God to preach repentance to Nineveh, the capital of Assyria, the archenemy of the Jews. Jonah, a burning Jewish nationalist, cannot bear to bring reconciliation to this evil empire. So he flees and pays cash for a berth on a ship to one of the most remote spots of the then-known civilized world—Tarshish.

But as soon as the ship leaves port, a violent storm breaks out. Forced to lighten the load, the terrified crew throws the cargo overboard. But one man, even during the height of the storm, sleeps in the recesses of the ship—behavior which confounds the captain who expects all passengers to do their share in appeasing the gods. It is determined that Jonah is to blame for not doing his part, and he is thrown into the sea.

Jonah is swallowed by a fish, and for three nights and days he plunges into his own soul. In the end, he accepts his duty as a prophet. Lesson one: You can't run away from God.

In his attempt to escape his calling, Jonah finds himself in the belly of the fish, symbolizing the state of isolation and withdrawal from human contact and responsibility. In comparative mythology one finds similar folktales from Europe, Asia, and the Pacific Islands. The ocean is the symbol of the psyche; only the surface is exposed, while below lie the bottomless depths of the unconscious and the repression of obligation. The fish navigating the ocean represents energy that forces us to confront ourselves. Lesson two: You can't run away from responsibility.

While inside the fish Jonah mulls his relationship with God and humans, both of which he wishes to deny. While meditating alone, he is learning the meaning of *teshuvah* (return), and he renews his relationship with the most essential forces in his life. In a sense he is reborn. Eric Fromm points out that the essence of love is to be found in relationships that require constant renewal and labor. Lesson three: You must be willing to do *teshuvah* (work on relationships) if you want to find life meaningful and worthwhile.

The main thrust of the Book of Jonah is found in the episode of the gourd. The reluctant prophet leaves Nineveh and prepares a shelter for himself under the shade of a huge gourd which has miraculously sprung up overnight, and it provides him with shade and comfort. The following day a tiny worm attacks the plant and it is destroyed. Jonah is dismayed by this cruel fate and is angry and deeply disturbed.

God then instructs Jonah: If Jonah could have compassion for a simple plant, doesn't he understand the compassion God must feel toward a city of 120,000 men, women, children, and innocent animals? God teaches Jonah (and us) that the God of the Jews is the God of the entire world. The enemy is human. Lesson four: There is only one God and one humanity.

When Jonah is upset about the plant, God asks, "Are you angry?" Jonah replies, "I am so angry I could die." Perhaps this is a cry of despair. Often people in difficult circumstances will say that they are so upset that they could die. This is often an expression of depression or suicidal feelings that occurs when a person feels that the present is bad and can't imagine that things could be better.

The Book of Jonah may actually be a message to the despondent. Jonah is depressed, but by working through his problems he continues with his task. Eventually, the Assyrians do repent and they are saved. Lesson five: There is always hope.

In essence, Jonah is a tale for our time and about us. Injustice is everywhere. Some run away and some say we are doomed. Conflict is the lot of our time. Some say withdraw, others say the situation is hopeless. Some succumb to cynicism and others take flight into selfishness.

The Book of Jonah tells us that we can reorder our lives. It teaches us that we can control the forces of destruction and despair. From Jonah we can learn that a change in attitude and a redirection of purpose can improve our lives. Society is not doomed; it can be saved. Lesson six: It is never too late to change.

The Book of Jonah is read during *mincha,* the afternoon service, which, according to the rabbis, is a special hour for God's grace. Elijah was answered during the Afternoon Prayer (Berachot 6b). The *mincha* service, according to tradition, was instituted by Isaac, who was bound to the altar on the afternoon of Yom Kippur. The Zohar, the classic text of Jewish mysticism, declares that *mincha* on Yom Kippur is of greater importance than all the other days of the year.

Given all this, it is appropriate that a book reflecting God's compassion and lovingkindness should be read at this time. The forgiveness of God and the value of *teshuvah* (return, repentance) is emphasized. Not just for the saints or the pious ones, but also for the sinners and perpetrators. Most especially, there is Divine mercy for the ordinary or average person. After all, if poor, bumbling, depressed, reluctant Jonah could be understood and forgiven by God, then there is hope for the rest of us on Yom Kippur afternoon.

As the rays of the sun begin to descend and fade on the holiest day of the year, the message of Jonah is deeply moving. Meditating during these moments may very well reveal the real meaning of Yom Kippur—it is time to return to our responsibilities.—1992

10. Why Fast? Jewish Hunger for Spirituality

Beginning with a statement in the Bible (Leviticus 23:32) and reinforced by centuries of practice, the central ritual of Yom Kippur is fasting. Aside from the biblical commandment and Jewish tradition, why fast? The reasons may be grouped into four basic categories.

The first is that it is a sign of contrition for the wrongs we have done and the good we have failed to do. What better ritual is there for a Day of Atonement? It is an act of affirming one's sincerity.

While some sort of sacrifice (symbolic or real) is a sign of remorse, Judaism has taken great pains to avoid masochism. Jewish law carefully guards the method of fasting. The aged, pregnant women, small children, and the ill are specifically warned not to fast—indeed, they are forbidden to fast. In the nineteenth century, the Gaon Rabbi Hayyim of Brisk was lenient with the sick in the matter of eating on Yom Kippur. He was asked, "How is it that the master is so lenient when it comes to Yom Kippur?" Said he, "Not that I am lenient when it comes to Yom Kippur, but that I am strict when it comes to saving a life."

A rabbinical student once came to a renowned rabbi and asked to be ordained as a rabbi. The rabbi inquired about his daily conduct and the candidate replied, "I always dress in black; I only drink water; I place tacks in my shoes for self-mortification; I roll in the snow; and I order the synagogue caretaker to give me forty stripes daily on my bare back." Just then a black horse entered the courtyard, drank water and began rolling in the snow.

"Observe," said the rabbi. "This creature is black; it drinks only water; it has nails in its shoes; it rolls in the snow, and it receives more than forty stripes a day. Still it is nothing but a horse."

Judaism rejects the concept of needless self-torture as a means of attaining a high level of spirituality. That is why a whole tractate of the Talmud (Taanit) is devoted to laws of fasting. Fasting is a means to an end, not an end in itself.

The second reason for fasting is to demonstrate self-discipline. Disciplining oneself is never easy, but all religious teachers have insisted on its value. It is interesting that of the Ten Commandments, seven are negative and only three are positive. In the classic list of 613 commandments, there are 248 affirmative precepts, but there are 365 negative ones. This goes to the heart of contemporary society. We are struggling to restrain the rampant greed, the uncontained violence, and the drug abuse that are plaguing us. Our core issue today is how to control our harmful impulses, how to teach our children proper behavior, and how to transmit to society the importance of channeling one's drive into healthy avenues.

A third reason for fasting is that it is a means to focus on the spiritual. Judaism encourages the legitimate gratification of bodily instincts. However, it also emphasizes the spiritual as primary in our lives. Humans do not live by bread alone, but also by faith, values, and the dimension of the spiritual.

Rabbi Israel Salanter, the founder of the modern Jewish ethics movement, once failed to appear in the synagogue on Kol Nidre eve. His congregation waited, and when the rabbi did not appear, the members became worried and went out to search for him. After several hours of effort they found him in a neighbor's barn. It seems that on the way to the synagogue Rabbi Salanter had found a neighbor's calf that had strayed and become entangled in the brush. With great difficulty he tenderly freed it and brought it back to the barn. The members of the congregation found him tending the animal's wounds.

They protested, saying, "How could you do that? Don't you know that your first duty as a rabbi is prayer?"

He answered gently, "God is called *Rahmana,* the Merciful One. An act of mercy is a prayer, too."

The fourth reason for fasting is that it is a means of awakening compassion. By knowing what it means to go hungry, if only for a day, our hearts are moved for those who suffer. By fasting we are motivated to think of others and to alleviate their distress. In the Yom Kippur morning haftorah, (Isaiah 58:6-7), this idea is given its classic meaning:

"This is the fast I desire:
To unlock the fetters of wickedness,
And untie the cords of the yoke
To let the oppressed go free;
To break off every yoke.
It is to share your bread with the hungry,
And to take the wretched poor into your home;
When you see the naked, to clothe them."

There was a tradition that when one comes to the synagogue on the eve of Yom Kippur before the *mincha* (afternoon) service, one empties the money in one's pockets and gives it to charity. It was the practice to set out empty plates with signs of needy institutions behind them so that the donor might select appropriate charities.

This finds modern expression in the writing of a check at this time and sending it to MAZON (meaning 'food'), a remarkable Jewish agency that distributes funds to Jewish and non-Jewish causes. This past year 180 institutions benefited from it. A total of 1.6 million dollars was distributed to those in need.

At the Temple of Aaron in St. Paul, Minnesota, it is the tradition that each congregant bring a package or a can for the food shelf when they come to the synagogue for Kol Nidre services. This past year, 3,500 pounds of food were collected and distributed to the hungry. Rabbi Abraham Joshua Heschel of Apt (eighteenth to nineteenth century) used to say: "If it were in my power, I would do away with all fasts, except on the bitter day, which is the Ninth of *Av,* recalling the day of the destruction of both Temples and other Jewish calamities, for who could eat on that day? And the fast of the exalted and deeply spiritual day of Yom Kippur—for who needs to eat on that day?"

Indeed, on this day we are so satisfied with the spiritual that our physical hunger is of little importance.—1994

11. Worry, But Be Happy

Amidst our anxiety over the situation in the Persian Gulf and the Middle East generally, it would appear to be difficult to observe the commandment, this Sukkot of "You shall rejoice in your festival" (Deuteronomy 16:14). But this is precisely the time to relax our tensions somewhat, to restore our balance, and to emphasize our faith. Sukkot, this year, tells us: worry, but be happy.

The holiday of Sukkot is one of the most joyous festivals in the Jewish year. The High Holy Days and all the solemnity have just passed. Now a spirit of thanksgiving and joy should also be a part of Jewish life. The focus of the celebration traditionally shifts from the synagogue to the home.

In biblical times, Sukkot was known as *Hechag,* "the festival." From what we can gather, it was one of the most significant in the ancient Jewish world. In fact, when the Maccabees succeeded in liberating the Temple from the Syrian Greeks, they announced the delayed celebration of Sukkot, which they had not been able to observe during the actual fighting.

The festival of Sukkot marks the final harvest of the year, an event of great importance to ancient Israel, an agricultural society. Sukkot has two other names: *Chag Hassif,* the "festival of the harvest," and *Zman Simchawtaynu,* the "time of our rejoicing." It expresses thanksgiving for the harvest and rejoicing over the Torah.

The value of Sukkot and its special significance were not lost on the founding fathers of our country. The American holiday of Thanksgiving is based directly on Sukkot. If one studies both festivals, one finds many parallels.

There are several items that mark Sukkot. There is the booth, known as the *sukkah,* a temporary structure covered with leaves or corn stalks. In Christian literature it is called the "tabernacle." There are the *lulav,* palm branch, and the *etrog,* a form of citron. Also included in the decorations of the lulav are branches of willow and sprigs of myrtle.

The *lulav* and the *etrog* were identifying symbols of the Second Jewish Commonwealth, where they were used as decorations on coins. They also appear in the mosaic floors of synagogues from the early centuries. There is a particularly splendid example preserved in the Kibbutz Bet Alpha.

Students of Jewish history have always wondered why these four items, *lulav, etrog, aravah,* and *hadas* (palm, citron, willow, and myrtle) were singled out for the proper observance. Many explanations have been offered, ranging from the homiletic to the practical. The most reasonable seems to be that of Maimonides, the great Jewish sage.

Maimonides pointed out that they were plentiful and everybody could easily get them. They looked good, and two of them smelled good. He observed, "They keep fresh and green for several days, which is not the case with peaches, pomegranates, asparagus and the like." And so, he concluded, "They are the basis of the holiday of joy for fruits and flowers lift the spirit and instill joy in the heart."

The aspect of the joy of Sukkot is that of sharing. The concept of an abundant harvest includes the idea that it was not given for our own enjoyment alone. There are specific rules in the Bible outlining how the Jew is obligated to share the harvest with the less fortunate. These were translated in the centuries through the value of *tzedakah,* "concern for others."

But there is a very specific application of the idea of sharing in the joy of Sukkot in the tradition of extending an invitation to a poor person to join in a delicious Sukkot festival dinner. This tradition is based on the ceremony called *ushpizin,* which began with Isaac Luria and the followers of Jewish mysticism in Sefat in the sixteenth century. The word *ushpizin* is Aramaic for "guests." According to these Jewish students of the Kabbalah (Jewish mysticism), a different biblical guest—Abraham, Isaac, Jacob, Moses, Aaron, Joseph, and David—

comes each day to visit the *sukkah*. They correspond to the seven *Sefirot* of lovingkindness, power, beauty, victory, splendor, foundation, and sovereignty.

The origin of *ushpizin* seems to be connected to the example of hospitality by Abraham. According to tradition, the shelter of *sukkot* (huts) was available to the Israelites during the forty years of wandering in the wilderness solely as a result of Abraham's offer of hospitality to the three strangers that appeared before his tent. This scene remains as a role model during Sukkot and the rest of the year as well.

The festival of Sukkot is centered about the building of a *sukkah*. According to Jewish law, the *sukkah* must be covered with foliage, but there must be enough space between the greens so that the stars can be seen. The Talmud teaches us an important lesson in this specification, and it can be told through the following literary passage.

In a novel entitled *The Harbor* by Ernest Poole, a group of boys who lived by the side of the railroad tracks in the slums of a city became bitter and destructive. But one lad, the hero of the novel, developed the habit of wandering out to a secluded spot on a hill. He found that when he was there, even the ugly, dirty freight cars as they banged and clanged about him could be overlooked, for by lifting his eyes "he could see the stars above the freight trains." The boy became a great man.

Judaism teaches the Jew symbolically through the *sukkah* to lift his or her eyes above the present into the future. It reminds us that all we need to do is lift our eyes and we will see the stars. This is always a source of inspiration and encouragement.

That is a good reason why, on the concluding days of this festival, we observe Simhat Torah with joy and celebration. For it is the Torah that reminds us even in times of worry to remember the balancing forces of joy and hope.—1990

12. Was the Crossing of the Red Sea a Miracle?

Was the crossing of the Red Sea, also known as the Sea of Reeds, a miracle? This part of the Passover story is probably the most impressive of the Exodus narrative. What really happened?

The Biblical words read: "Then Moses held out his arm over the sea and God drove back the sea with a strong east wind all that night and turned the seas into dry ground. The waters were split. And the Israelites went into the sea on dry ground, the waters forming a wall for them on their right and their left" (Exodus 14:21-22).

There is a vast sea of differences on how this event is viewed. The literalists believe it was a miracle—that is, a supernatural interruption in the normal course of nature meant to impress a people who had been enslaved for hundreds of years. Proponents of literal interpretation cite the verse "And when the people saw the wondrous power of God they believed" (Exodus 14:31).

The opposite opinion holds that the event never occurred; it is simply a myth that evolved over the centuries to explain the liberation of the Israelites. The story of the great divide is a powerful metaphor to retain the memory of the freedom that marked the beginning of the Hebrew nation. Indeed, Benjamin Franklin suggested a picture of Israel's liberation for the reverse side of the official seal of the United States.

There are those, such as Maimonides, who have sought a natural basis for what the story clearly presents as God's intrusion into events. Periodically, scientists such as geologists, naturalists, and climatologists look for the spot where a reedy sea could be forded when tides drive waters back and forth or where sudden east winds create natural upheavals that a grateful people might see as an act of God. Many other great scholars such as the early rabbis, Saadia, Gaon, Judah Halevi, Samuel Hirsch, and Martin Buber, to mention but a few, have come up with other views. Essentially, all of these attempts are part of the effort to deal with the question of miracles.

The Hebrew terms for "miracle" are revealing: *Ot* and *nes* can be translated as "sign"; *mofayt* and *peleh* mean "wonder." The sign indicates a Divine presence in the universe. The wonder is the spirituality that the event inspires. The rabbis generally felt that the signs and wonders in the Bible served to remind people of God as a part of the historical process. Interestingly enough, however, they felt that miracles are not evidences of truth. This is clearly stated in the Talmud (Bava Metzia 59a).

In a certain debate Rabbi Eliezer called for and achieved a series of miracles to prove his view. But Rabbi Joshua rejected them disdainfully, quoting the Bible: "The Torah is not in heaven." His contrary opinion was accepted by the rule of the majority.

It is forbidden to rely upon miracles (Pesachim 64b). One cannot court danger and expect to be saved by a miracle. The rabbis were intensely practical in their view of human undertakings. They were unwilling to endorse the suspension of natural laws in the face of prudence.

However, the rabbis did go out of their way to emphasize the daily miracle of life, which expresses itself in the workings of nature. They taught that the everyday miracle of baking bread is greater than the miracle of crossing of the Red Sea. In the systems of blessings they included the natural functions of the body, the wonder of the natural world, the use of the mind, and the entire web of life. This approach to miracles is expressed in the prayer *modim* (thanksgiving), to be recited in the daily *amida.* The formula reads, "We thank You for the miracles which are daily with us, and for the wonders and benefits that are constantly with us, evening, morning, and night." The rabbis were able to see the extraordinary in the ordinary.

This same theme was central to the work of the great contemporary Jewish theologian, Abraham Joshua Heschel. He emphasized "wonder," "radical amazement," and even mystery in the events of the Bible and the daily happenings that we experience and observe. He also speaks of the "ineffable" and "unexpressible" of the daily wonder of living.

When our youngest son was a child, he would stand in front of a large picture window and watch as the sun began to set. At just the right moment he would shout, "Sunset! Sunset!" Then, we would rush and observe with him the great beauty of this natural event. On one particular occasion, the sunset was simply glorious. We stood silently and watched. Our little son uttered just one word: "Awesome." We all sensed it was a miracle.

There are mountains of marvelous commentaries on the Red (Reed) Sea crossing. One of the most appropriate is found in the Talmud (Megillah 10b). Seeing the Egyptians, who had enslaved the Israelites for hundreds of years, drowning in the returning waters, the angels wanted to rejoice. But God silenced them, saying: "The work of my hands is drowning in the sea and you desire to sing songs!"

For this reason it is the custom at the Passover Seder to spill ten drops of wine—one drop for each plague as it is mentioned.

This year there have been many commemorations to mark the 50th anniversary of the conclusion of World War II. Controversy has surrounded them all, and the ambivalence of feelings has been justifiable. It is a true sign *(nes)* of moral sensitivity that ancient Jewish tradition includes a thoughtful comment that applies to this very issue.

Was the crossing of the Red (Reed) Sea a miracle? Well, that depends on your point of view.—1993

13. Matzah - Spiritually Enriched Bread

Every Jew in every generation since the first Passover some 3,500 years ago knows that the most important symbol of Passover is matzah. Matzah dramatically proclaims the very meaning of the great festival that marks the birth of the Jewish people.

It is interesting that in all cultures bread, whether leavened or unleavened, occupies a central position. The Hindu scriptures state: "Everything is food but bread is the great mother." The bread rituals of the various civilizations are basically involved with the gods or God. They range all the way from the grain ceremonials of the American Indians to the communion wafer that is central in the Catholic mass.

By contrast, matzah in Judaism is basically associated with two unique concepts. The first is found in the beginning of the Passover *haggadah:* "Why do we eat this matzah?" And we are told that the matzah is to remind us that our ancestors left Egypt in such haste that they did not have time to let the dough of the bread rise. Hence, we eat unleavened bread to identify with Jewish history. In point of fact, the word *haggadah* itself means a retelling or the story of the Jewish people. On Passover we literally eat history and so it becomes a part of us.

What we learn from this basic ritual is that we Jews are immersed in remembering our past, even as our history gives us a sense of identity. The Jew is unique and, indeed, has survived because we never forgot who we were, how we came to be, and, therefore, what ought we to be doing in life.

It is exactly as Abraham Joshua Heschel once said: "We are a people in whom the past endures, in whom the present is inconceivable without moments gone by. The Exodus lasted a moment, a moment enduring forever. What happened once upon a time happens all the time."

The second meaning of the eating of the matzah is also told at the beginning of the *haggadah* when we say: "This is the bread of affliction." And then we add: "Let everyone who is hungry come and eat; all who are needy, come and join us." What this means is that bread generally, and matzah specifically, has ethical implications. We do not simply gather the grain, store it, bake it, and serve it to ourselves alone. We have responsibilities to others in terms of sharing food. This goes beyond the concept of thanksgiving, for it involves a sensitivity to others. It is, indeed, a very elevated religious concept.

Nicholas Berdayev, a Russian Jewish philosopher, once said it this way: "Bread for myself is a physical problem. Bread for my neighbor is a spiritual problem." Jews have always understood this. That is why the Bible told us to leave the corners of the fields and the after-gleanings for the poor. The whole concept of *tzedakah* is really an extension of this basic understanding of our responsibility to share the very substance of life with those who are needy.

Perhaps this is best illustrated in a wonderful story about Passover. A solicitor for charity went to the home of a wealthy Jew on the eve of Passover to solicit *maot hittim.* This is money for the needy who cannot afford to have a proper Passover. He rapped on the door, waking the affluent one from his afternoon siesta. Angry that his nap was disturbed, the wealthy Jew opened the door in a sour mood. His mood was translated into action when he saw the solicitor and slapped his face. The solicitor placed one hand on his face to soothe the stinging pain and extended the other hand to the wealthy man, saying: "The slap you have given me. Now, what will you give to the poor?"

On Pesach the Jew knows when he or she eats the matzah that the most important thing is to understand that it is the bread of poverty and to identify with the needy. Matzah stands for the ethical excellence of our people. It reminds us that the real purpose of our rituals is to teach us to do what is proper in life and to care about others.

A prominent rabbi in a *shtetl* (small European village) used to personally supervise the baking of the matzah. Although he was very busy, he devoted the whole week prior to Passover to oversee this important task. Once he fell ill and could not carry out his usual charge. His congregants came to him and said, "Rabbi, we are sorry that you cannot personally be present to supervise the baking of the matzah, so we will do it for you. But, is there anything special that we should be careful to observe?" And the good rabbi replied, "Yes, make sure that those employed to bake the matzah receive a fair wage."

That is the real meaning of matzah—spiritually enriched bread.—1984

14. I Love Pesach in the Springtime

Pesach always comes at the right time of the year. Its timing in our lives is superb. In the first place, Pesach always arrives as the symbol of spring. The winter is hard and the freeze lasts a long period of time. In a very real way, we are frustrated as we look out at the world.

Just when we are in this mood Pesach comes to remind us that winter is nearly over. At the Seder the use of the green parsley is a symbol of the freshness of the coming spring. On the seventh day of Passover we read from the Song of Songs: "For, lo, the winter is past, the flowers appear on the earth and the time of singing has come."

With the rebirth of nature, faith is rekindled, joy returns to our lives, and we feel like singing. The blooming of the flowers, the cheerful chirping of the birds, and the gladness of the sunshine make an irresistible message of hope and good cheer. It were as if God has performed for us another act of the drama of creation.

Spring is the easiest time of the year to believe in God as we witness the powers of recreation. Since this year Pesach occurs in April, the following poetic passage expresses this mood very well:

"For shall we not believe God lives
Thru such awakening?

Behold, how God each April gives
The miracle of Spring."

Another reason that Pesach comes at the right time is that during this season the world seems disheartened about the future of freedom. Every year at this time spirits seem to drag as we face the immense problems associated with bringing freedom to all of God's children. The fight against racism has just suffered a serious setback in Alabama, and in the North the issue becomes more tangled by the hour.

We ponder: Just where are we heading? We are becoming increasingly involved in the struggle for freedom in El Salvador. And we anxiously wonder if it will ever be over. The famines in India and Africa stir us deeply. And we ask, "Can we ever satisfy a hungry world?"

All of this would be disheartening were it not for one real fact. Pesach comes to tell us that even though a people be enslaved for hundreds of years there is a possibility for freedom and liberation. According to the most conservative historical estimates, the Hebrew people lived in concentration camps and slave labor compounds in Egypt for 210 years, and yet they were liberated.

It is also worthwhile to note the first of the Ten Commandments begins with, "I am the Lord your God who brought you out of the land of Egypt, out of the house of bondage." This is the signature of faith, for this is a God of freedom.

The point is that God does care even though God's message is slow in coming. There is a Divine concern for those who are oppressed, for those who suffer, for those who are enslaved. Pesach is proof positive that freedom is possible. Every Pesach I am once more inspired to rededicate myself to the causes of freedom. I know nothing hopeless in the affairs of men and women when it comes to compassion and justice.

The message of Pesach also comes at the right time to work its purpose. During the winter, and particularly near its end, we feel as if we are in the doldrums. Pesach literally puts us to work. Think of all the things we have to do: clean the house and change the dishes, order the matzah and wine, invite the family, make sure that the youngest knows the Four Questions, buy baby a new pair of shoes. Even the Seder makes participants of all of us. In fact, we were told this by the Talmud: "Everyone is required to participate in the drinking of four cups of wine—men and women, as well as the children."

Aside from motivating us and moving us in positive directions, Pesach teaches us an important lesson. All of us must be participants in the great drama of liberation, all of us must share in creating a better society, all of us must move from inaction into action if we are to better the world. As one wit once put it: You may be on the right track, but if you just sit there you'll be run over.

All told, Pesach is a unique festival not only in Judaism, but in the history of religion. The Seder with the serving of symbolic foods enables the Jew to relive and re-create the past. Israel Zangwill correctly said, "On Pesach the Jew eats history." He (she) literally digests the bread of affliction, and so the meaning of freedom becomes a part of the marrow of his (her) bones and the essence of his (her) body. A Jew knows what it means to suffer.

In this way the Seder ceremony literally appeals to all the senses. We hear the crackling of the matzah, we taste the *haroset,* we smell the sharpness of the horseradish, we feel the *haggadah* in our hand, and our eye takes in the entire scene. Through personal involvement, a Jew senses completely the meaning of Passover and the underlying message of freedom.

That is why every year I eagerly await Pesach. I love Pesach in the springtime, because in it I sense with my entire being that to be a Jew is to be a part of history and the drama of creation.—1982

15. It's Enough to Make Your Blood Boil

It happens every spring, because Passover and blood-libel go together. Blood-libel is the allegation that Jews murder non-Jews, especially Christians, in order to obtain blood for Passover or other rituals. It is the result of a complex of deliberate lies, fabricated accusations, and popular misbeliefs and myths about the so-called murder-lust of the Jews. Based on the monstrous falsehood of the bloodthirstiness of Jews and their alleged hatred of Christianity, this charge has brought untold suffering and misery throughout the centuries.

The blood-libel led to trials and massacres of Jews in the Middle Ages, and in modern times it was revived by the Nazis. Its origin is rooted in the ancient and primitive concepts concerning the potency and magic of blood.

The beginnings seem to be during the time of Hellenism, when it was alleged that the Jews would kidnap a Greek, fatten him for a year, sacrifice him, and then eat his flesh. According to Apion, this was told to King Antiochus Epiphanes, who no doubt used it as propaganda in order to profane the Temple in Jerusalem.

The same blood-libel charge was leveled against Christians when they were eating the holy bread of the communion, since it was felt that the divine child was hidden in the bread. Church Father Tenullian complained bitterly against this charge. Ironically enough, this charge was then deflected by Christian society to the most visible minority in opposition to its tenets.

The first recorded case of blood-libel against the Jews in the Middle Ages was that of William of Norwich in 1144. It is alleged that the Jews "bought a Christian child before Easter and tortured and hung him" in imitation of the Passion of Jesus. Absolutely no evidence was found that a murder had been committed. It seems that the boy had been merely in a cataleptic fit when found and was buried alive by his relatives.

As the blood-libel began to spread over Eastern Europe, the myth of Jewish malefactions was multiplied. It was charged that Jews used the blood of Christians for medicinal purposes. Then the motif evolved that Jews used Christian blood for Passover matzot. The maliciousness of blood-libel seems to know no limits, even accusing Jews of the use of blood for the required four cups of wine on Passover.

This, despite the fact that Jews were forbidden to offer any kind of sacrifice after the destruction of the Temple in the year 70. The dietary laws of *Kashrut* include meat-salting *(melicha),* which is designed to prevent the least drop of blood from remaining in meat. Jews were authorized very limited forms of meat to be eaten. Even the slightest speck of blood in an egg invalidates it. The use of blood in any form is abhorrent to every phase of the Jewish tradition. Indeed, it is a classic Jewish rule that *met ahsur behahnahah,* "any utilization of a dead body is forbidden" (Avodah Zarah 29b).

Yet, despite these conditions and the fact that no blood-libel has ever been substantiated, the charges have continued. Jews were tortured and massacred because of this collective madness. No less than 220 instances are recorded in which Jews were formally charged with blood-libel.

It became so horrendous that the German emperor Frederick II invited a large number of Christian scholars to study the matter. The commission published the following as its formal findings: "Neither the Old nor the New Testaments state that the Jews lust for human blood. On the contrary, it is expressly stated in the Bible, in the Laws of Moses, and in the Jewish ordinances, designated in Hebrew as the Talmud, that they should not defile themselves with blood."

However, this did not stop the blood lust of the Christian mobs, which was often stirred and incited by Christian clergy during Easter. This so embarrassed the church that Popes Innocent IV, Gregory X, Martin, and Paul III condemned the blood accusations in official papal declarations. But this did little to stop the superstitions and wild mobs.

Often blood-libels were fomented to distract the population from other current problems or for personal gain. Thus, in Bazin, Hungary, in 1529, it was charged that a nine-year-old boy had been bled to death, suffering cruel torture—and thirty Jews were publicly burned. The true facts of the case were disclosed later in Vienna, where the child was found alive. He had been stolen by the accuser, Count Wolf of Bazin, as an easy but fiendish manner of ridding himself of his Jewish creditors.

The most famous expression of blood-libel in the twentieth century was the Beilis case, a trial held in Russia between Spring 1911 and Fall 1913. A Jewish worker in a brick factory was accused of killing and mutilating a twelve-year-old boy named Andrei Yushchinsky. Leaflets distributed by the "Black Hundred," a virulent anti-Semitic organization, fomented the riots. The case attracted universal attention. In the end, the jury, composed of simple Russian peasants, after seven hours of deliberation, unanimously ruled "not guilty."

In recent times the Nazis unashamedly used the blood-libel in full force for anti-Jewish propaganda. The Nazi daily, *Der Stuermer,* devoted a special issue, horrifyingly illustrated, to the blood-libel, in which German "scientists" openly served Nazi aims. It is difficult to describe the base level of the accusations and misery, resulting in insults, torture, murder, and expulsions of Jews that followed. The cruelty, falsity, and baseless charges are a shameful chapter of that period.

Regretfully, it never ends. On February 8, 1991, a member of the Syrian delegation brought the charge of blood-libel before the United Nations Commission on Human Rights. It was in the form of a book entitled, *The Matzoh of Zion,* in Arabic. The preface was written by the Syrian Defense Minister, Major General Mustafa Tlass, who asserts the blood-libel as fact.

The cover features stereotypical Jews wearing kippot gleefully cutting the neck of a non-Jew (probably Father Thomas in the infamous Damascus blood-libel in 1840). Blood is shown pouring into a bowl. The "victim" is holding a cross or a rosary. Inside is written, "The Jew can kill you and take your blood to make Zionist bread."

The twenty-nine nations present unanimously called on the commission to issue a public condemnation of the inflammatory Syrian stand. The permanent representative of the United States to the UN in Geneva said: "Such statements, absurd and patently false, are historical incitements to prejudice and violence. We had thought that they had been relegated to the ash can of history. They offend the decorum of this body and damage the credibility of its work."

In the May 7, 1991, issue of the *Village Voice,* Nat Hentoff in three large columns documents a validation of the charge of blood-libel occurring in Chicago. He cites names, places, and quotations from the *Chicago Sun-Times.*

After so many years, at Passover time a blood-libel seems to spring up. It still happens in remote villages in South America, the countryside in Europe, and in rural areas of the United States. The only response is to state the facts, live with dignity, and preserve our Jewishness.

Ahad Haam, the great Jewish writer, expressed the Jewish attitude toward the accusations of blood-libel this way: This accusation is based on an absolute lie. Every Jew who has been brought up among Jews knows as an indisputable fact that throughout the length and breadth of Jewry there is not a single individual who drinks human blood for religious purposes. . . .

Let the world say what it will about our moral inferiority; we know that its ideas rest on popular fabrications and have no real basis in fact. . . . "But," you ask, "is it possible that everybody can be wrong, and the Jews right?" Yes, it is possible: the blood accusation proves it possible. Here, you see, the Jews are right and perfectly innocent.—1992

16. The Whole *Megillah*

A *megillah* is not necessarily the Book of Esther. The word *megillah* means simply "scroll." There are *chamesh megillot,* Five Scrolls: The Song of Songs, Ruth, Lamentations, Ecclesiastes, and Esther. However, since the Book of Esther became so overwhelmingly popular, it came to be known, from Talmudic days onward, as simply the *Megillah.* Small wonder that it has become a centuries-old best-seller. It contains drama, mystery, intrigue, splendid narrative, distinctly portrayed characters, a hero, a heroine, a villain, a chase, and even sex. There is even a treatise in the Talmud bearing that name.

The *Megillah* claims to be a historical account that took place in the fortress of Shushan or Susa. It is true that there was a Persian king named Ahashuerus, which is merely the Hebrew form of Xerxes (some say it was Artaxerxes), but this is just the beginning. Some scholars maintain that the scroll was written sometime between 486 and 465 B.C.E. Others contend it was penned in the Maccabean period. Still others argue Mordecai and Esther are derived from the Babylonian deities Marduk and Ishtar. Some believe it is totally of divine origin, while others contend it is an historical romance. Whatever it may be, it is a great and enduring book for the Jewish people and fully justifies one of the great holidays in Judaism.

It is an exact expression of the anti-Semitism that has haunted the Jews over the centuries and its inevitable failure. It contains the classic defamatory words of the anti-Semite, the accusation that, "There is a certain people, scattered and dispersed among the other peoples in all the provinces of your realm, whose laws are different from those of any other people and who do not obey the king's laws; and it is not in Your Majesty's interest to tolerate them." Haman is the archetypical anti-Semite who spans the centuries and in whose shadow Hitler falls. The danger of persecution is real, but in the end victory is snatched from the jaws of defeat, and the Jews are saved.

Dr. Solomon Goldman in his excellent commentary on the Book of Esther in the Sancino series deals with the complete absence of the name of God in the book. There are allusions to the divine presence, but the omission of a direct reference to God is clearly intentional. The reason for this can only be surmised.

Perhaps, since the *Megillah* was to be read at the annual merry-making of Purim, when considerable license was permitted, the author feared that the Divine Name might be profaned. Again, the book was written during a period when the Divine Name was used sparingly lest it be pronounced in vain. Some suggest that it might lead Jews to a feeling of triumphalism which would engender negative feelings among the populace. But, whatever the reason for the calculated omission, the Book of Esther breathes religiosity and trust in God's providential care for the Jews.

To be sure, the question of whether it should be admitted into the Jewish canon was subject to debate, as recorded in the Talmud (Megillah 7a). The question raised was whether Esther was written with the proper *ruach hakodesh,* "divine inspiration." The book was finally included in the *Ketuvim* (Holy Writings) section of the Tanach (Hebrew Bible) since it was clear that it was an expression of Divine Providence. It was translated into Greek by Lysimachus, son of Ptolemy, of Jerusalem. His translation was brought to Egypt in the "fourth year of the reign of Ptolemy and Cleopatra." Since then, it has been translated into almost every language.

Biblical scrolls are rarely illuminated. The Book of Esther is the exception. We find a remarkable color illustration in a 1238 Ashkenazic Bible depicting Esther as well as Haman and his sons on the gallows, the latter being a favorite theme of artists. In a fourteenth-century Hebrew Bible executed in Ratisbon, "Mordecai's Elevation" is depicted. Illustrating the entire Esther scroll was a popular art form, and scrolls were often given as a dowry to the bride since women were particularly obligated to listen to the reading of the book. One interesting version of the Book of Esther was done in micrographic writing in the shape of a bear, executed by Hirsch Ilya Schlimowitz, a Russian, in 1870.

The process of illustrating the *Megillah* has been carried on in modern times. Henryk Glicenstein produced a set of engravings, Arthur Szyk created a miniature set, and Marc Chagall did a series of pen-and-ink drawings. In recent times there has been a veritable explosion of printed colored versions of the book.

They range from the very contemporary drawings of Stephen Maltz in London to a richly printed illuminated text produced in connection with the Israel Museum that sells for approximately $200.

Even the case in which the *Megillah* is kept became an art form. Often it was made out of olive wood, and scenes of the Book of Esther were carved on it. Many *Megillah* holders were made out of metal, particularly silver with ornate designs. One *Megillah* case was made in the form of a fish. At times the *Megillah* was rolled as a Torah Scroll, and the cover was beautiful embroidered cloth. Today, *Megillah* cases are being made in a whole variety of experimental forms, one rivaling another.

The traditional view is that the Book of Esther should be read "like a letter" since there is a direct reference to *eggeret hapurim,* "The letter of Purim" (9:29). Therefore, as the scroll is unrolled and when a passage or two is read, it is folded back in the manner of a letter. The tempo of reading changes with the narration of sad or glad events.

Something quite beautiful and characteristic of the Jewish lifestyle is found in the *Megillah*: a shared feast. One traditionally sends homemade pastries to friends. Also one is expected to give gifts to at least two poor persons, accounting for the Talmudic interpretation of Esther 9:22.

The *Megillah* commands merry-making. This has given rise to carnivals, plays, costume balls, parades, and singing and dancing, as well as feasting. All express the joy of deliverance. Purim also comes during early spring, when there was a need to be released from the winter and to feel free at least one day from the confines of the ghetto. Most likely the Jewish commemoration of Purim was influenced by the celebrations of their neighbors.

The Talmudic treatise named *Megillah* begins with a discussion of whether the *Megillah* should be read in public or private. Must it be written on parchment or will paper suffice? Who may read the *Megillah?* Must ten persons be present? May those who cannot read Hebrew do so in another language?

Then there is the issue of whether parts of the *Megillah* may be read or the entire *Megillah.* Although this issue was debated over a period of time (perhaps centuries), it was decided that the entire *Megillah* must be read. From this comes the expression *die gantze megillah,* "The whole *Megillah,*" or the whole story.

Yes, the Book of Esther does contain the whole *Megillah* of the Jewish people, its tragedies and its triumphs, its presentation and its faith, its loyalty and its mystery, its fasting and its feasting, its fear and its fun.

In truth, Purim is *the* holiday of the Jewish people because it celebrates the miracle of Jewish survival, and that is *die gantze megillah*—the whole story of Judaism. Jews today are a continuing part of that miracle, and that is why this year Jews have a right to wish one another "A Merry Purim."—1975

17. Masks of Purim

There is a current joke in Israel that contains a bit of black humor but is relevant to Purim. The question is: "What is the difference between Haman and Saddam Hussein? The answer is: "With Haman we put on the masks afterwards, but with Hussein we put on the masks before." Implied in this *bittereh gelechter* (bitter laughter) is the implication that as Haman was destroyed so Hussein will be destroyed.

It is interesting that Purim is celebrated with donning masks. We speak of masking our feelings and, while it is very important psychologically to express our deepest anxieties and fears, it is also important to maintain a reasonable control over them. Israel's policy of *haflagah* (restraint) in the face of aggression and provocation is relevant.

In essence, Purim is a celebration of the Jewish people's overcoming anti-Semitism and persecution. A cursory glance at Jewish history indicates how many times we were faced with catastrophe and yet snatched victory from the jaws of defeat. And, even on those occasions when we suffered emotional and physical damage, we were able to recover and continue not only to persevere but also to create.

In the Jewish experience there are more than 110 Purims, instances when individual Jewish communities or families were threatened with destruction and were delivered. One example is the Basra Purim, which occurred in 1774 in Basra, Iraq, when the Jews were hard pressed. Many of them were robbed and pillaged; however, shortly thereafter, their enemies perished in a battle. The Jews of Basra at that time called it *yom ha'nes,* "The Day of the Miracle." They rejoiced and pledged that they would celebrate this event year after year for generations to come. There is a lesson to be learned directly from this special Purim.

A very basic purpose for Purim is based on the verse from the Book of Esther which tells us that "deliverance will come from another place." The Hebrew word for place is *makom. Makom* is also a euphemism for God. What this means is that one must keep one's faith.

Purim also comes to teach us perspective. The great talent of the Jew is survival. Wars and hostilities have their moments of advance and retreat. When we are faced with a difficult period we must maintain balance and perspective. The ultimate defeat of fear comes about through faith: Faith in ourselves that we can solve our problems and faith in God who has given us the resources and the hope to solve those problems. Faith is not a magical device but, rather, a sure scale against which to measure our fears. If fears are to be resolved, they must be seen in the perspective of a good God, a helpful society, and a friendly universe.

When the French tyrant Napoleon started to move his powerful armies, all of Europe was in a state of fear and trembling. In Spain an embattled army under the Duke of Wellington was trying to resist his advance. One day a young lieutenant came into the British general's tent with a map clutched in his trembling hands and declaimed in near hysteria, "Look, General, the enemy is upon us!" "Young man," the general replied, "get larger maps, and the enemy won't seem so close."

If we possess the larger map of faith, the great enemy of mankind, called fear, will not appear so close. The world has existed for millions of years and will continue to do so. People have solved their problems and will continue to do so.

What is unique about Purim is its celebration through humor, masquerades, plays, noise-making, and other such devices. This achieves two purposes. The first is to ridicule the anti-Semite and treat that person as a buffoon. On one level, Saddam Hussein is a desperate despot who deserves our contempt. He sees himself as being clever, but history will treat him as a clown. His cruelty will be seen for what it is and, rather than being lauded, he will be laughed at.

Purim also gives us the opportunity to express our anger in appropriate ways. It takes our justifiable feelings of hate and turns them into expressions of humor. It is a remarkable psychological device.

I wonder what holiday we will devise to celebrate the downfall of Saddam Hussein, and what delicacy will we create to name after him?

How and through whom the Jews have been and will be delivered might very well be called the masks of God.—1988

18. Shake, Rattle, and Roll

On Purim, Haman's name is read fifty-four times in the *Megillah* (Book of Esther), and fifty-four times the reading is interrupted with resounding noise which again erupts when the names of his ten sons are read. Noise-making at the mention of the name of Haman dates back to the earliest days, back to the time when *Megillah* reading became customary.

In Deuteronomy 25:19 we read, "You shall erase the remembrance of Amalek," who was the first enemy of the Jews after they left Egypt. According to tradition, Haman was a descendant of Amalek. This led to the custom of drawing pictures of Haman or writing his name on stones and sticks and then rubbing them together to erase what had been written or drawn. Some Jews wrote the name of Haman on a slip of paper and erased it at his mention. Others wrote it on the soles of their shoes and rubbed them to stomp it out.

Leon de Modena wrote that in Venice the Jews, while reading the *Megillah,* would "clap hands at the name of Haman as a testimony to their abhorrence and distaste." In Nuremberg the name of Haman was written on pieces of paper, then was systematically erased at the recitation of his name. In Persia (Iran) drums were beaten, and in certain parts of Italy trumpets were blown. Sometimes it was customary to break a bowl with Haman's name on it.

However, since the Middle Ages it has been the practice to use a *gragger*, a form of rattle in which a piece of wood or metal scrapes against another rigid piece of the same substance. As it was twirled it gave off a rasping noise. The faster it was twirled, the higher the pitch of the noise.

The word *gragger* comes from the Polish *grzechotka,* meaning "rattle." It was also known as *twri,* "twirler," *hamanklaper,* "Haman buster," or a *drehyer,* "a turner." In Hebrew it is known as *raashan,* simply "noisemaker." With many people, particularly children, causing a great deal of noise in the synagogue, problems of decorum often were raised.

Indeed, often synagogal regulations were enacted prohibiting any noises during the reading of the *Megillah.* In 1783, the *ma'amad* (board of trustees) of the Spanish-Portuguese congregation in London ruled that anyone making a disturbance during Purim was to be evicted from the congregation. In 1866, the *Kehilla* (congregation) of Rogasen in the province of Posen, Poland, promulgated a set of rules concerning synagogue demeanor and included the prohibition against Haman *graggers* on Purim.

However, the need to express feelings of outrage against anti-Semitism prevailed. So it was that a whole new form began, centering about *graggers.* Two excellent collections can be found in the Jewish Museum in New York and the Israel Museum in Jerusalem. One fine specimen was created by the late painter and silversmith, Ilya Schor. It is made of wood and silver and on it we see Queen Esther and King Ahashuerus, as well as a little girl with a plate of *shalach manot* (Purim goodies).

Israel has given birth to a whole new art form of *graggers.* Generally they are large. Some of them sell in the price range of $1,000. This past year they featured Sadam Hussein as Haman.

One Jerusalem craftsman named Oded Davidson is particularly inventive. He takes World War II air-raid alert sirens and turns them into silver-plated noisemakers. Whistles intended for air-raid warning are also built into rattles. Each piece is overlaid with several silver plates accompanied by quotes from the Book of Esther.

A religious Jew, Oded Davidson views his craft as more than a profession. "I try to take common items from all over the world and bring or return them to Judaism," says Oded. Guided by a concept of "double-*mitzvah,*" the artisan seeks to create things of beauty which also serve a purpose in Jewish ritual.

As a rabbinical student, I attended a Judaica auction at Sotheby's in New York. Although the prices were far beyond my capacity, I noticed a primitive *gragger* about eight inches long. When I read the description, I learned it was made in a concentration camp out of the slates of a bunker. Punched into it with a nail were Hebrew words from the *Megillah* which mean, "And they hung Haman on the tree." Fortunately, no one else noticed it and I was able to acquire it for a pittance. It is one of my most precious possessions.

Purim expresses the total range of religious and human feelings. The synagogue is shattered by an outpouring of emotion. There is tragedy and triumph, hate and humor, courage and comedy, faith and foolishness.

The story is told of a woman who was attending the dignified and decorous service at Westminster Abbey when suddenly she broke into strong, emotional expression. The proper ushers rushed up to her and said, "What is the trouble?" She answered, "I've got religion." The uptight usher replied, "Madam, this is a place of worship, one doesn't get religion here."

Purim is a festival that demonstrates that Judaism views religion in the context of all human expressions of feeling. The synagogue is a place for joy and sorrow, tears and laughter, moments of quiet, and times of noise. The synagogue is the living room of the Jewish community. Purim comes to welcome the wide range of emotions and responses which human beings are capable of expressing. Purim rounds out the Jewish festival cycle, closing the circle of what it means to be human and to have faith.—1992

19. Daily Sinais We Climb

With the reading of the Ten Commandments on Shavuot, we arrive at the mountain peak of Jewish history: *matan torah,* or the giving of the Ten Commandments. Judaism refers to them as *aseret hadibrot,* "the ten utterances."

Sometimes, we are stimulated to ask, "Why the number ten?" Why were they expressed in this manner? Why not nine or eleven, eight or twelve? The answer, I think, can be found in the immediate historic setting of their pronouncement. They were given to a rabble of slaves. They were placed in the hands of a people that had been in labor and concentration camps for centuries and were almost entirely illiterate. As the slaves of the Pharaohs, the Hebrews were given no time for education. What better technique than to establish a set of rules for civilized living in a set of ten, so that they could be ticked off on the fingers? In a matter of minutes they could be committed to memory. The number ten is obviously a stroke of genius.

As we read the words, their power and the reason for their compelling force becomes clear. It is the use of the singular "you" and "yours." This is God speaking directly to every person. One cannot read these words and be indifferent. They are either accepted or rejected, loved or hated, obeyed or shattered. When even one of these laws is broken, someone must suffer. A human being cannot be indifferent to these resounding moral words of God.

Wilson Mizner, the celebrated wit, once asked an individual who was notoriously dishonest if he had made a New Year's resolution yet. "Yes," said the man. "From now on I'm going to follow the Ten Commandments." Whereupon Mizner retorted, "You've been following them all your life. Why don't you resolve this year to catch up with them?"

As with all works of perfection, the Ten Utterances are perfectly simple. There is no mystery about them. Their clarity is such that they can be understood by the child and the adult alike. They are equally appealing to the schoolchild and the philosopher. Even as they are said they can be comprehended.

What is the role of Moses in *matan torah,* the announcement of the word of God? What kind of man was this whom Providence chose to be the midwife of a great truth?

A famous exclamation by the German poet Heine expresses the role of Moses with keen insight: "How little does Sinai appear when Moses stands upon it!"

The power, the passion, and the pain of Moses is as fascinating a study in its own right as is the Ten Commandments. Moses is at once man and superman, lawgiver and benevolent despot, highly emotional and keenly shrewd. He is many things that are contradictory.

The finest study in literature of *Haish Moshe,* "that person, Moses," was done by Thomas Mann in a thin little book that is now, unfortunately, out of print. Outside of the Biblical narrative he alone has understood Moses. Mann drew a superb sketch of this divine genius in the climax of his life, standing on the volcanic ash of Mt. Sinai. With powerful arms he rips two huge, irregular pieces of stone from the mountainside. Then he seizes a sharp, pointed stone and begins the hard, tedious job of carving and chiseling the 172 Hebrew words on two stones. In a primitive setting this task takes thirty-nine days. On the fortieth day, as he is about to descend with the two tablets of law, he pauses to survey the commandments. He examines his work and notices, to his dismay, that the impressions and indentations of rock are hardly noticeable at a distance. But where in the dry, barren area will he find color to highlight the writing?

Without hesitation he takes a jagged rock and slashes his hand and smears his own blood on the writing. Having accomplished his task he descends from the mountain to give the tablets through his people to humanity.

This is the crux of the Ten Commandments. They are to be written with a person's lifeblood or they are of little value. A good Jew does not worship the Ten Commandments but lives them. A Jew does not pay them lip service but gives them the service of the heart.

There is an old Bedouin legend. The leader of a tribe that was encamped at the base of a mountain was dying. So he summoned his three sons and said, "I am dying and one of you must succeed me as the head of the tribe, but I do not know which one. I am asking you to climb the mountain and bring me back the most beautiful object you can find. The one who brings me the most precious gift will succeed me."

After several days the sons returned. The first son brought his father a flower which he explained grew at the very summit and was extremely beautiful. The father indicated it was nice but he was not very impressed. The second son brought his father a stone which was handsomely round, having been naturally polished by the rain and the sandy winds. The father appreciated it but was not deeply moved. The third son said, "Father, I have nothing to give. But, as I stood at the mountain top I saw that on the other side was a beautiful land filled with green pastures and plenty of water and I had a vision of where our tribe could move to have a better life." And the head of the tribe replied, "You shall be the leader for you have brought the most precious gift of all, the gift of vision."

A poet once wrote: "Daily Sinais we climb and we know it not." Every day presents its challenges. Every day requires vision, effort, and determination. Mountain climbing is not an easy sport, just as living is not always easy. Shavuot comes to teach us through the lesson of Mount Sinai that if we make the effort we can reach the summit.—1983

20. Have a Faith Lift

Shavuot celebrates Torah. The Exodus from Egypt occupies a major role in the Bible and subsequent Jewish thought. However, the Exodus was only the prelude to the main event which was *matan torah,* "the giving of the Torah." According to tradition this occurred when Moses received the Ten Commandments on Mount Sinai and then gave them to the Hebrew people.

The upper reaches of the mountain flash lightning and a loud roaring noise fills the air. As God descends to its top, the mountain seems consumed in flame and the terrifying voice of an unearthly shofar issues out of its depths. Moses alone is present when God speaks the words of the Ten Commandments.

The experience of Israel at Sinai as described in the Bible was extended even further by the rabbis into a potentially universal experience, properly available to all peoples everywhere. Noah, the father of mankind after the Flood, they taught, was given a code of seven laws basic to a person's very existence. These Noachied Laws forbid theft, blasphemy, murder, adultery and incest, and eating any part of a living animal; they forbid idol-worship with all its immoral celebrations and enjoin the establishment of just law courts. Inconceivable to the rabbis, apparently, was a world lacking at least these minimal requirements of morality.

Moreover, we are told, "All the peoples of the world" *(ummot ha'olam)* heard the Ten Commandments at Sinai, for the Decalogue was spoken simultaneously in all the seventy languages of humans.

In the same vein, the Midrash asks: "Why was the Torah given at Sinai, in a wilderness so far from human habitation?" And the answer given is: "Just because it is wilderness, belonging to no one, so that no people can say the Torah was given in its land; thus no people will be able to lay exclusive claim to the Torah." The Torah is really meant for all people, not just for Jews.

Sometimes individuals read the Bible for what is called "proof texts": to prove that God exists, to prove a miracle, to prove a point, to prove that if you say this prayer or believe that idea you will find instant healing, or redemption, or whatever. But this approach misses the whole point of Torah—that the verses of the Bible as well as rabbinic phrases are not mystical or magical utterances but distilled wisdom.

A verse from Scripture does not represent the Holy merely because Moses taught it but also because it expresses a fundamental insight into human behavior or a vision toward which we should strive. It is not just the source but the content as well that is important.

Two mule drivers, bitter enemies, were walking down the road. The mule of one broke down under its load. The other saw the incident but proceeded on his way. After a while he thought, "It is written in the Torah, 'If you see the animal of your enemy lying under its burden, you shall not pass him by; you must relieve the animal of the burden.'" Immediately, he turned back and helped the other mule driver with the burden.

The first mule driver thought to himself: "My companion is really a good friend, but I had no idea." They then both went to an inn and ate together in peace.

What caused them to be reconciled? The fact that one remembered a teaching of the Torah. Indeed, let us look into the Torah, for through it we will learn to reconcile ourselves with our community, with our environment, with our very own selves. For Torah is not just a word; it is a whole way of life.

Shavuot comes to remind us that "The Torah is our life and the length of our days." Shavuot is a renewal of that commitment. Shavuot is a faith lift.—1990

21. Shavuot Combines Nature and Nurture

Shavuot is an early summer Jewish holiday that successfully combines the world of nature and the sphere of morality. It began as an agricultural festival marking the beginning of the wheat harvest but evolved to include celebrating the Ten Commandments, the foundation of the Torah, and the cornerstones of Western civilization.

Literally, Shavuot means "weeks," but its real meanings and modes of celebration are varied and complex. The weeks refer to the counting of the *omer* (sheaves of barley) for a period of seven weeks following the first night of Pesach and continuing until the fiftieth day, which is Shavuot. Greek-speaking Jews called it Pentecost (fiftieth), and this term later became prominent in Christian writings.

When the Temple still stood, Jews brought their first fruits as well as sheaves of grain to the sanctuary as an expression of thanksgiving. Hence, Shavuot also acquired the name *Chag Habikurim,* "the festival of first ripe fruits." With baskets of barley, wheat, olives, dates, figs, honey, and pomegranates, the pilgrims flocked to Jerusalem to witness the festival. Accompanied by music of harp and flute, they formed long processions, waving fronds and boughs of greenery. As they entered the Temple, they chanted: "This is the day God has made; we will rejoice and be happy in it." Today in Israel many kibbutzim celebrate this event with dances and music programs. Children wear garlands of flowers in their hair.

In Italy the holiday has become known as the Feast of Roses or the Feast of Flowers. Milk dishes (closely associated with nature), especially cheese blintzes (crepes), are featured. It is customary to decorate the synagogue with flowers and greenery to mark the season.

When the early rabbis considered this festival, they added to it the concept of *matan torah,* the giving of the Torah. They added to the liturgy the reading of the Ten Commandments. In the eleventh century, Rabbi Meir ben Isaac Nehorai's famous hymn *Akdanmot,* with its haunting melody, was included in the service. It was written in Aramaic and is chanted today in many traditional synagogues.

Confirmations are celebrated on Shavuot because it is appropriate to affirm faith on a day that marks the giving of the Torah. The timing also coincides with the conclusion of the school year.

Since, according to the mystic tradition, all Jews stood at Sinai to receive the Torah, a unique and interesting custom has developed. Known as *tikkun leil shavuot* (the vigil of the night of Shavuot), the custom is to stay up the entire night to study and discuss Torah. A small section of each of the Five Books of Moses may be read and discussed. At dawn, the morning service is chanted.

What is particularly fascinating is that the Book of Ruth is chanted on Shavuot. No one knows the origin of this tradition. Some say the book is read because Ruth was the great-grandmother of David. Others contend that it is because of the story's pastoral setting at the time of the gleaning. Yet all agree that Ruth is the model of the righteous convert. Indeed, the story probably was written and included in the Hebrew Bible to encourage full acceptance of the concept of conversion.

In this there is found great contemporary meaning. Today, Judaism has to face squarely the fact of increasing conversion and intermarriage without conversion. Almost every conversion includes the phrase from Ruth (1:16), "Your people shall be my people." There are many outreach programs in the Jewish community and within synagogues for Jews and their non-Jewish spouses, as well as a desire to accept, understand, and help. Much of this is based on the story of Ruth.

Shavuot is also a festival filled with humor. Most of it centers on the idea of Torah and, of course, the Ten Commandments. However there is one joke that combines nature and nuture.

During the week preceding Shavuot, a rabbi visited a number of his prominent congregants to solicit flowers and plants to adorn the synagogue during the festival. One nouveau riche, seeking to vaunt his erudition and his generosity, boasted: "Instead of giving flowers in honor of Shavuot, I will present the synagogue with the tablets of the Ten Commandments." The rabbi retorted: "It would be better that you keep the commandments and give something else to the synagogue."

On a more serious level, the essence of the duality of Shavuot was expressed by Immanuel Kant:

"Two things fill my mind with ever increasing wonder and awe—the starry heavens above me and within me the moral law."—1995

22. Let There Be Light

Hanukah, recalling the rededication of the ancient Temple in Jerusalem following the victory of the Maccabees over the Syrians, is celebrated for eight days. According to the legend, this is because only one clean jar of oil was found for the Eternal Light, and it was sufficient for only one day. But by a miracle it lasted eight days. An old Yiddish jest, based upon this explanation, asks "For such a little bit of oil, such a big festival is celebrated?"

The reason that so much emphasis is placed upon the Hanukah festival is that it commemorates the first successful revolt in history on behalf of religious liberty. The abiding miracle of this festival as stamped in Jewish observance reminds us of the value of religious freedom in our lives.

The spirit of Hanukah animates the Magna Carta and the Declaration of the Rights of Man, and there is a parallel to the Maccabean revolt in the Declaration of Independence. For without the willingness of early Jews to fight for their religious rights and the inspiration of Hanukah, these great movements on behalf of human freedom might never have been born. Not only Jews, therefore, but all humankind must be grateful for the abiding miracle of Hanukah.

On Hanukah, the lights of the Menorah are kindled by the *shamas,* the lead or service light. Every Menorah has such a special light, whose sole purpose is to provide the spark for others.

The importance of the spark is illustrated in the following story: A young man who had become an apprentice to a blacksmith learned during the course of his training how to hold the tongs, how to lift the hammer, how to smite the anvil, and how to blow the fire with the bellows. Having finished his apprenticeship, he was chosen to be employed at the royal smithery. But the young man's delight at his appointment soon turned to despair when he discovered that he had failed to learn how to kindle a spark. All of his skill and knowledge in handling the tools were of no avail because he had not learned the most elementary principle—to light the fire.

We are currently commemorating the fiftieth anniversary of the saving of the Jews of Denmark by the Danish people. That great act of courage and the Danish resistance to the Nazis was sparked by King Christian X. In 1943 the Nazis decreed that every Jew had to wear a yellow Star of David. King Christian X heard this and immediately went on the radio and said, "The Jews are part of the Danish nation. We have no Jewish problem in our country because we never had an inferiority complex in relation to the Jews. If the Jews are forced to wear the yellow star, I and my whole family shall wear it as a badge of honor." Needless to say, the badge was never introduced in Denmark. In fact, when the Germans did press for the deportation of Jews, the Danes retaliated by scuttling the Danish fleet. Many Danish officers and soldiers lost their lives shielding their Jewish friends.

This is the spirit of Hanukah—that men and women will voluntarily expose their lives to danger for what they believe. It is the inspiring story of self-sacrifice that lies at the basis of every great humanitarian achievement. Indeed, the verse selected as the theme for Hanukah by tradition is "Not by power, nor by might, but by My spirit, says the God of Hosts" (Zechariah 4:6).

Why did the rabbis choose this verse to epitomize Hanukah? Judah Maccabee was a war hero. The Maccabees won by force. The history of the events seems to indicate just the opposite of this verse.

If we consider that period in history, however, we will find that spirit was the ultimate determining factor. Indeed, had not the Maccabees been infused with the spirit of freedom and devotion to Judaism, they would never have had the strength and the courage to keep fighting. When there is spirit, there is strength; when there is no spirit, a cause vanishes like smoke on a windy day.

Hanukah is often described as a commemoration of the struggle between light and darkness. Coming as it does during the shortest days of the year, the holiday affirms that, although darkness seems poised to overtake the light, the days will again lengthen and the Light will shine.

That image seems particularly appropriate this year—if at times unduly optimistic. The rise of ethnic intolerance in Europe and our own country make a mockery of the celebrations that greeted the fall of the Iron Curtain. That is the reason the celebration of Hanukah assumes such importance this particular year.

There is the tale of the elderly rabbi who was asked by his followers to leave them one last message. He said: *Ir zolt haben kovod far alle mentchen,* "Have a sense of respect for all people."

They asked: "Rebbe, not before God?!"

He replied: "If you feel respect before all people, you will also have respect for God."

Small in size yet prodigious in symbolic dimension, the Hanukah lights remind humankind to quest for the inner light our confused generation needs desperately. Only such a light can dissipate the night in the human soul. Only such a light will bring nearer the day when people will unite in the spirit of the words written by Rabbi A. Alan Steinbach:

Out of the shadows of night
The world rolls into light.
It is daybreak everywhere!—1981

23. A Hanukiah is a Menorah The Menorah Is Not a Hanukiah

A *hanukiah* is a menorah. Menorah is the basic Hebrew term for any kind of light fixture. It could contain one wick or candle, or many. When used as the menorah, it is taken as a reference to the seven-branched candelabrum that was mandated in the Bible for use in the Temple.

The classic passage describing the menorah for Temple use is found in Exodus 25:31. It reads as follows: "You shall make a lamp stand (menorah) of pure gold...Make it seven branches." In Talmudic texts (Menachot 28b), we are informed that the menorah was 72 inches high and spread 36 inches. Its central shaft and six branches were of the same height, so that all seven branches were in a straight line.

When the Babylonians destroyed the Temple in 586 B.C.E., the menorah was probably taken as a war trophy by the conquerors. Some contend it was hidden by the priests and never found. When the Temple was rebuilt, another menorah of gold was created. This was in use until the Temple was looted by Antiochus Epiphanes at the time of the Maccabees. The menorah was melted down together with other Temple vessels and confiscated by the Syrian Hellenists.

When the Maccabees concluded their successful rebellion and returned to purify and rededicate *(hanukah)* the Temple for worship, they were faced with the problem of creating new instruments for worship, especially the menorah. It is here that we find different explanations why a special menorah of eight branches (nine, if we include the *shamas,* "the servant" candle) was created. This became the basis for the celebration of Hanukah and in turn gave birth to the term *hanukiah,* the special menorah for the new festival.

The most common and popular explanation for the number eight is based upon rabbinic writings, which tell us that when the Greeks entered the Temple, they defiled all the oils that were there. When the House of Hasmoneans prevailed, they found only one cruse of oil with the seal of the high priest that was not defiled. It had only enough oil to burn for one day. A miracle happened and the oil lasted for eight days. In the following year, they established eight days as the amount of time to celebrate the festival to commemorate the miracle.

Another explanation found in the Talmud is based on the passage that informs us that when the Hasmoneans entered the Temple, they held eight iron spears in their hands. They then put an oil lamp on each spear and kindled lights. This was in fulfillment of Isaiah's vision, "and they shall beat their swords into plowshares."

Yet another explanation in the Second Book of the Maccabees is based on the passage in which the Hanukah is described as "the feast of Booths in Kislev," or simply, "the December version of Sukkot." The fact is that both the First and Second Temple had been dedicated during the festival of Sukkot. This holy day lasts for eight days. Judah Maccabee and his followers made a point of copying the traditional ritual of that festival when they cleansed and rededicated the sacred edifice after two years of interrupted Temple services.

Yet one suspects that the primary explanation can be found in *halachic* (Jewish legal) writings. After the destruction of the Second Temple in 70 C.E., the rabbis placed a ban on the exact reproduction of the Temple menorah, particularly proscribing its use in synagogues. It was probably to discourage messianic pretensions, as well as to preserve the unique, sacred character of that which symbolized the Temple. This rabbinic interdiction brought into general use the eight-branch candelabrum, which, during the Second Commonwealth, became important as a reminder of the Maccabean victory over the Syrian Greeks. It is this explanation of the *hanukiah* that is more seriously considered in scholarly circles.

The manner of lighting the wicks or candles was the subject of debate in the first centuries. The School of Hillel ruled that one wick or candle should be lit on the first night and one additional light added every subsequent night. The School of Shammai suggested starting with eight lights the first night and decreasing every night. The tradition of adding lights each night won out on the grounds that holiness and sanctity should be directed toward growth.

This undoubtedly was the reason that the *hanukiah* was traditionally placed in front of the door or in the window. This practice is known as *pirsum hanes,* "spreading the miracle."

An American couple touring Israel went to visit Modin, where the Maccabean revolt began and where the Maccabees are buried. As they approached the area, they came to a sign marked "The graves of the Maccabees." They searched for the exact location but could not find it. By chance, there was an encampment of Israeli soldiers across the road. A squad was resting under some trees near the sign.

The Americans asked, "Fellows, where are the graves of the Maccabees?" The soldiers shrugged and one said, "I don't know." They then asked with some exasperation, "How is it you don't know the exact spot when you are so close to Jewish history?" The sergeant replied, "Mister, why do you bother to look for dead Maccabees? We are the living Maccabees, and we are here."

Israel, with the help of Jews all over the world, is living in the spirit of that miracle. The in-gathering of Jews from Ethiopia, Russia, and Romania is truly "spreading the miracle." It is the miracle that spreads from the Maccabees to modern times, and it lights up our lives.—1979

24. It Is Better to Light a Candle

In a recent issue of a magazine entitled *The Biblical Archaeology Review* there was a survey of the digs in Israel. The article began by asking the reader to guess which object turned up most in the excavations.

Take a moment to ask yourself which object you think would be the most common in these digs. The answer is a menorah. The reason is obvious. There were no electric lights and, therefore, people needed at least one in each room to provide light during the evening hours.

A menorah is any instrument that provides light. It comes from the Hebrew *min orah,* something that brings out light. A Hanukah menorah is a special kind of lighting instrument that has eight candles and a ninth candle serving as a *shamas.* It is called a *hanukiah.*

Then consider how we Jews have taken light and formed a ritual out of it or, if you please, hallowed it. There are the Shabbat and holiday candles which include a minimum of two. There is the candle that we use on the eve of Passover for *bedikat chometz,* the ceremony of the search for leavened bread.There is the *yahrzeit* candle lighting the memory of the departed whose life continues to lighten our own. Then, of course, there is the *havdalah* candle whose twisted, joined wicks provide the guiding light for the new week. All of them have special meanings and give us an opportunity to express our feelings about one another, about the world, and about God.

Light is also the source for many wonderful stories in Jewish literature. One of the most inspirational is the following. A man was once wandering the streets of a *shtetl* deeply troubled by a problem. He had done something that was not quite proper and he was wondering how he could mend his soul. He happened to pass a tailor shop and through the window he saw a man bent over a flickering candle repairing a garment. The man went into the tailor shop and said to the owner, "It is late at night and the candle is almost out and you are obviously very weary. Why don't you stop?" And the tailor replied, "As long as the candle is burning, one can still mend." "Ah," the man thought, "that is really a spiritual message. As long as we live, we have the opportunity to mend our ways."

As long as we live, we have the opportunity for reconciliation, for changing our ways, for adopting better standards of behavior. As long as the fire of life burns in us there is hope.

It is very revealing that in Israel the term for Hanukah is *hag haurim,* the Festival of Lights. What this refers to is the ancient legend that Hanukah lasts eight days because of a miracle of light. After the Maccabees had defeated the Syrian Greeks, they came to rededicate the Temple. However, when they began to kindle the Eternal Light, they found they had only enough pure oil to last one day. They did not know what to do but they did have faith. So they lit the Eternal Light and, behold, a miracle occurred and it continued to burn for eight days.

Now modern scholars give other explanations for the eight-day celebration of Hanukah. But the miracle still contains basic truth, and that truth is the miracle of Jewish survival throughout the ages. Not only on Hanukah but on Purim and on Tisha B'av and the remembrance of the Spanish Inquisition and upon recalling the Crusades and upon remembering the Holocaust...the important fact to remember is that we survived. By all the laws of logic, of history, and of sociology, we should not be here, but we are! We are the real miracles, and each Jew is a candle whose light proclaims that Judaism survives and will continue to survive.

There is a relevant story not only to Hanukah but to what occurred this week in Poland. It is humorous but it makes the point.

Three Soviet citizens, a Pole, a Czech, and a Jew, were accused of spying and were sentenced to death. Each was granted a last wish.

"I want my ashes scattered over the grave of Pilsudski," said the Pole.

"I want my ashes scattered over the grave of Masaryk," said the Czech.

"And I," said the Jew, "want my ashes scattered over the grave of Comrade Chernenko."

"But that's impossible," he was told. "Chernenko isn't dead yet."

"Fine," said the Jew, "I can wait."

We Jews continue to wait and wait and wait, and we always outwait our adversaries. That is the real meaning of Hanukah. Remember what we say when we sing *"Maoz Tsur:"* "Yours the message cheering that the time is nearing which will see all people free, tyrants disappearing."

Hanukah occurs near the time when we mark the shortest day and the longest night of the year. This is the time when we are enveloped in darkness and cold, with all kinds of feelings about the blackness around us. But along come festivals whose celebration centers about lights. It is a way of saying: we do not give in to darkness; we create our own light. The light of understanding, the light of knowledge, the light of good will.

Once a rebbe was teaching and a wind came in and blew out the candle. The students were frightened by the darkness. One student said, "Let's get sticks and beat out the darkness." They did so but there was no light. Another student said, "Let's curse the darkness." And they all shouted but it was still dark. Finally, the candle was lighted and its warm glow brightened the whole room. And that is why it is written: "It is better to light a candle than to curse the darkness."—1984

25. Maccabees Play to Mixed Reviews

Almost all Jews know that Hanukah centers about the Maccabees—more correctly, the Hasmoneans—who saved Judaism during the Selucid Syrian Greek times. However, few are aware that the Maccabees had meaning for Christians, and even in Jewish circles they and their descendants engendered great controversy.

To the Christians, according to the great scholar Elias Bickerman's study entitled *The Maccabees,* the Maccabees "became the prototypes of holy warriors." St. Augustine wrote, "Let men learn from them how to die for the truth." In the Eastern church, August first is dedicated to "the Sainted Maccabees."

The *Encyclopedia Britannica* explains that the origin of the term macabre, meaning grisly, grim, concerned with death, comes from the concept of *Danse Macabre,* Dance of Death. This, in turn, is based on the Latin *Machabaeorum Chora,* a medieval morality play depicting the martyrdom of the Maccabees. C.F. Handel composed an oratorio entitled *Judas Maccabeus.* Israelis today think of "Maccabee" in conjunction with the Tel Aviv Maccabee football team, as they joyously clink glasses of Maccabee beer when their team wins.

The historical basis of Hanukah is that when the Syrian government led by Antiochus forbade the daily sacrifices in the Temple, the observance of Shabbat, and the rite of circumcision, many realized it was the death knell of Judaism. Mattathias the Hasmonean and his five sons, who were rural priests, put together a coalition that led a successful rebellion and restored Jewish life. Their rallying cry and goal was *kanoo latorah,* "Fight zealously for the Torah."

But all zealotry that is based on righteous feeling eventually runs to excess. The Maccabees compelled the observance of the Torah by force, circumcising as many newborn infants as could be found. While that did succeed in reestablishing the Temple observances, as the years passed the heroes surrounded themselves with mercenary troops and hired bodyguards. Their descendants assumed Greek names and assimilated to Hellenism, the very thing their ancestors fought against and died for. The Hasmonean dynasty became corrupt, arrogant, and repressive, making a mockery of the Maccabean victory.

This presented the early rabbis with a serious dilemma. How could one celebrate Hanukah without glorifying the Maccabees and thereby giving tacit acceptance and approval to their hated Hasmonean descendants? Since the rabbis were at the time pushing a nonviolent strategy for survival under Roman rule, knowing full well that irrational revolt would lead to national suicide, they did not want to stress the Maccabean example.

Therefore, the rabbis shifted the focus of the celebration from the flawed leaders of Judea to the God of the Jews, the author of all victories. Instead of the eight-day celebration marking the original delayed observance of the festival of Sukkot (Tabernacles), the legend of the small jar of oil that burned for eight days became the "miracle" (Shabbat 21b).

The Talmud does not mention Mattathias the Hasmonean or Judah Maccabee. The Books of the Maccabees were not included in the canon but were assigned to the Apocrypha *(sefarim genuzim),* "books to be put aside." The *haftorah,* prophetic reading, for the Shabbat that occurs during Hanukah is taken from the prophet Zechariah (4:6): "Not by might, not by power, but by My spirit says the God of Hosts."

Yet, there was a body of religious and moral values for which the Maccabees fought justifiably. In the centuries of struggle between Judaism and Hellenism, the Jews, almost alone in the world, had a sense of the dignity of the life of each human being. The essence of the Jewish tradition taught that men and women were created out of clay and contained a spark of the Divine; each person had infinite moral significance. Jews were able to extrapolate the best elements of Greek culture, reject its negative features, and form a religion whose very center was built on freedom and *tzedakah.*

In modern times the remembrance of the Maccabees was of tremendous inspiration to the Zionist movement, which resulted in the establishment of the State of Israel. Fiery Zionist speeches and literature complete with constant references to the Maccabees rekindled the fight to reestablish the ancient homeland where Jews could find refuge and rebuild their Jewish heritage. Zionism, like the original Maccabees, rescued the Jewish people from powerlessness.

Of course, it should be recalled that if the original Hasmoneans had failed and the Jews had been swallowed up by the forces of Hellenism, as other groups were, there would have been no Christian history and no Muslim history; there would have been no Christmas, no Easter, and no *Id ad-Fitr* and *Id al-Adha.*

The spirit of Hanukah can inspire contemporary Jews to a rebirth of Judaism. As Jews now enter a period of religious and cultural diversity, it is the Maccabean determination to struggle and fight for Jewish survival that can guide us. The open society is the great challenge of Judaism today. It is the task of all Jews to deal with new concepts, extrapolate the best, reject the worst, and combine it with the greatness of Jewish experience. As Rabbi Abraham Isaac Kook once said, "The old must be sanctified and the new must become sacred." Is this not the meaning of Hanukah—Rededication?—1992

26. The New Year of the Trees

A beautiful Jewish festival bears the lovely name, "New Year of the Trees." The reason for this is found in the opening Mishnah, the very first passage in the Talmud volume of Rosh Hashanah: There are four Rosh Hashanahs and the Rosh Hashanah for trees is on the fifteenth day of Shevat.

So it is that this day came to be celebrated on the Jewish calendar as a minor festival. Ashkenazic Jews commemorated it by eating fifteen kinds of fruit and reciting fifteen psalms. The Sephardic community recites a special set of hymns and poems dealing with trees, fruit, and the produce of the land. In Israel the celebration is more direct and practical. The children go out into the fields and plant trees.

Unique to the Jewish tradition is a sensitivity to trees as well as all of nature. The Bible in Deuteronomy (20:19) compares the life of a tree to the life of a person. The tree, like a human being, comes from a seed: it grows, it breathes, it lives, and it dies. Sometimes it lives out its allotted span and dies at a ripe old age and sometimes through accident or disease it dies prematurely. Sometimes it becomes ill and the doctor—botanist—has to treat it.

The subject of trees occupies significant portions of the Talmud. We are instructed how to deal with the fruits of the tree and the tree itself and also where trees should and should not be planted. There are passages that deal with ecology, the use of trees in preserving the aesthetics of a city, and with the question of the damages that tree roots cause when they penetrate a neighbor's land. Other passages raise the question of who owns the fruit when a tree overhangs a neighbor's area. It is very interesting that the series of benedictions includes the *brochah borey pri haetz,* "blessed be the fruit of the tree."

Jews had and continue to have a great deal of respect for the land and the tree. One of the most beautiful customs in our tradition is that when a boy was born a cedar tree was planted and when a girl was born a cypress tree was planted. Then when it came time for them to be married, they would take branches from both trees, weave them together, and create the *huppah* (the traditional marriage canopy). As the children grew, the trees grew, and they saw the trees enter their lives at the moment that they began the process of creating a family

There are, of course, many legends about trees in Jewish literature. The following is one of the most instructive.

In the order of creation, trees were created on the third day. Following that, metal and its many uses came into being. When the trees contemplated this, they suddenly became alarmed at the possibility of the creation of an ax. They then protested to God saying, "Why did you create an ax which will destroy us?" God replied, "In order for an ax to function it must have a handle of wood. If you do not permit yourselves to be used improperly, you will not be destroyed."

This is a very profound thought. Trees, like all forms of creation, have the potential for good or for ill, just as human beings do. It is precisely their use that will determine their outcome. Wood can be used as the handle of a knife, which in turn can be used to kill someone or to perform healing surgery. A match has a base of wood. It can be utilized to begin a fire to heat a building or to destroy a building. A large piece of wood can be used to make a club to beat someone or crutches to help support someone. All of these are the potential of a tree. That is really the wonder of the tree to which we pay tribute on Tu B'Shevat.

It was best expressed by Joyce Kilmer who wrote the famous words:

"Poems are made by fools like me,
But only God can make a tree."—1982

27. Tisha B'Av and the Rebirth of Judaism

Tisha B'Av, the ninth day of Av, is known as the Black Fast and has been observed with mourning rites by Jews for thousands of years. Rightfully so, for it commemorates not only the destruction of the two Temples but also other calamitous events in Jewish history.

There is another side to the story, however. Napoleon, who once asked about the meaning of Tisha B'Av, observed, "A nation that remembers its defeats will also never forget its victories." Indeed, this has been true of Jewish history.

Tisha B'Av basically recalls the destruction of the first Temple in 586 B.C.E. Yet the Jews who went to Babylon created the model for surviving and thriving in the Diaspora. It was in Babylon that they created the synagogue, for they needed a form of worship since there was no more Temple. Babylon provided the setting for later Jewish studies that culminated in the Babylonian Talmud which, incidentally, was written in Aramaic.

The destruction of the second Temple in the year 70 provides an even more striking outcome. During the final stages of the siege of Jerusalem, Rabbi Yochanan ben Zakkai was spirited out of Jerusalem in a coffin. He established a circle of scholarship in Yavneh that resulted in Rabbinic Judaism, setting the mold for future Jewish life and thought.

In the year 135, after severe persecutions by Hadrian, the revolt of Bar Kochba was crushed at Betar. But not before Rabbi Akiva and his colleagues organized Jewish law, which later became the foundation of the Mishna.

In 1096 the First Crusade began, bringing destruction and death to Jewish communities up and down the Rhine valley. But at the time the great Rashi and the school of commentators that followed him provided the means to expand understanding of the Bible and the Talmud.

In 1242, twenty-four cartloads of the Talmud were burned in Paris by church officials. Driven by this form of persecution, Maimonides organized the Talmud in his *Mishneh Torah,* which inspired 220 major commentaries. In so doing, Maimonides enabled the lay person to study this masterpiece.

One particularly black Tisha B'Av occurred in 1492, the day the decree was issued to expel the Jews from Spain. But those Jews revived Judaism in the Ottoman Empire and spread Sephardic Jewish culture all over the Mediterranean basin and eventually to the New World.

This expulsion helped to spread the Kabbalah, Jewish mysticism, as a serious subject. It also resulted in the organization and publication of the *Shulchan Aruch* in 1567, the first real classification of Jewish law and its particulars for easy study by the layperson.

In 1648 Chelmnitsky's hordes massacred thousands of Jews in Poland. The reaction to this was the rise of the Hassidic movement, which gave hope to desperate Jews and started a great revival of Judaism.

In 1882 government-instigated pogroms began in Russia, continuing through the first decade of the twentieth century. Millions of Jews came to the United States and built the most powerful Jewish community in the Diaspora, enriching American life in every phase,

In 1945, one-third of the Jewish people, 6 million Jews, were murdered by the Nazis. This was a major factor in the thrust to reestablish the State of Israel in 1948. Since then, more than 2 million Jews in distress have come to Israel. The growing strength of Israel joined with Jewish communities throughout the world has been instrumental in causing churches to acknowledge their responsibility for the Holocaust, declaring anti-Semitism a sin, and finally compelling the Vatican to recognize the State of Israel.

Fifty-two is a contemporary metaphor for Tisha B'Av. Fifty-two percent is the level of Jewish intermarriages since 1985. Certainly this figure is distressing, but it is also a challenge. Synagogues are constantly adding converts to Judaism and establishing outreach programs. Jewish day schools are springing up like wildflowers after a rain. Money is pouring into Jewish educational institutions from federations and huge Jewish foundations. Thousands of courses in Judaica are offered on the American campus.

Orthodox Judaism is strengthening, and *havurot* of every stripe—even Humanistic Judaism—are experimenting with new forms. Adult Jewish-education courses range from "Avot In A New Age" to "Yoga, Zen and the Torah." New Jewish periodicals of all persuasions are appearing regularly. Hardly a day passes that a Jewish book is not published, some of superb scholarly and enduring literary value.

Judaism is not terminating, it is just transforming itself in preparation for the twenty-first century.

While we remember all the painful episodes that occurred on Tisha B'Av, it is with good reason that the rabbis observed, "On the day the Temple was destroyed the Redeemer was born" (Genesis Rabbah 55). To which Rabbi Yisrael Baal Shem Tov commented, "Remembrance is the key to redemption."

Through the blackness of this year's Tisha B'Av the careful observer sees the first rays of the dawn of the rebirth of Judaism. —1995

28. Tu B'Av: A Festival of Love

When most of us think about the Hebrew month of Av, we usually focus on the ninth day. That is because Tisha B'Av (the ninth day of Av) marks the destruction of the First and Second Temples. However, six days later there is also an historic Jewish holiday known as Tu B'Av (the fifteenth of Av). It might well be called "The Festival of Love."

According to the Mishnah (Tannit 4:8), the daughters of Jerusalem clothed themselves in white dresses (which they had borrowed so that "none should be embarrassed who did not have them") and went forth in the vineyards, singing and dancing. They would chant, "Young man, look carefully before you pick. Don't be lured by beauty; rather look for good family background, for 'charm is deceitful and beauty is vain. It is the God revering-woman who will be praised'" (Proverbs 3:30).

This was a sort of Sadie Hawkins day that was created to lift the ban on the tribe of Benjamin. Because of a tragic act committed by that tribe, as recorded in Judges 21:19-21, the other tribes were forbidden to marry men from it. Tu B'Av lifted that ban so that the tribe of Benjamin could survive.

Later, more fortunate events were associated with Tu B'Av. It came to commemorate the removal of check posts by King Hosea, so that Jews in the Northern Kingdom could visit Jerusalem. It was the day when the Romans permitted the burial of the soldiers who fell in defense of Bar Kochba's last stronghold. It was also the day of the wood offering when all the people brought kindling for the Temple altar. The wood most preferred was from fig trees, nut trees, and oil trees. This event was celebrated with torches and bonfires.

The fifteenth of Av was also known as the Festival of the Vineyards *(chagigat hakeramim).* Several kibbutzim have tried to revive it with festivities combining music, dance, poetry, and love songs.

There are still some vestiges of Tu B'Av in some traditional Jewish communities. Certain penitential and semi-mourning prayers that are part of the daily service are not said. Bridegrooms do not observe the prewedding fast. There are no yeshivah classes, and after the morning synagogue services teachers are supposed to treat their students to a glass of brandy and a piece of cake.

Last year Tu B'Av was celebrated in two novel ways—one simply silly and the other somewhat serious.

In Tzemach (near Tiberias), Israel, a gathering took place on Tu B'Av that was advertised as "A Night of Love on the Kinneret." Fifteen thousand boys and girls assembled to listen to a sort of rock concert. They spent a weekend together, mostly crowding before the stage. Some couples were rolling and wriggling in their sleeping bags. Many spent the night simply sleeping on the beach. It was a neo-Canaanite revelry that had nothing in common with the origins of Tu B'Av, and the ancient festival was exploited for questionable purposes.

The other Tu B'Av, celebrated more nearly in the spirit of the fifteenth day of Av, took place in Manhattan. A group of one hundred unmarried men and women in their thirties and forties gathered at the Rotunda, which is at the foot of 79th Street and the Hudson River, overlooking the boat basin and the New Jersey Palisades. The occasion was sponsored by Congregation Kehilath Jacob.

Because it was an Orthodox event, there was no mixed dancing. A small band of eight played Hebrew and Hassidic melodies. Working to get people together was Pincus Freiberg, a professional *shadchen,* or matchmaker, whose stated philosophy is, "God makes the match, I just provide the spark."

Like their ancient predecessors, some women wore white. Those who attended were men and women of all walks of life, including an interior decorator, a psychotherapist, a violinist, and a Jewish educator. Arlene Agus, who decided to forgo the traditional white for a lively print dress, set the tone when she said, "Matchmaking is like head hunting, except it's really heart hunting."

Tu B'Av, the fifteenth day of Av, is truly a holiday of the heart. May the day be appropriately celebrated all over the Jewish world and enjoy fulfillment and great success. —1992

29. Genesis is Only the Beginning

On Simhat Torah (the rejoicing of the Torah) and Shabbat Bereshit (the Sabbath of Genesis), we begin again the cycle of scripture readings. The Chumash (Five Books), a.k.a. the Pentateuch, is divided into fifty-two readings *(sidrot),* forming a cycle encompassing the year. This arrangement results in sets of regular passages for reading in the synagogue and for private study, keeping the basic text of Judaism before our eyes, in our minds, and in our hearts.

This year is different. As we begin Genesis again, we are reminded that since this time last year twelve books have been published on Genesis alone. Perhaps this focus is a result of Bill Moyer's public television series on stories in Genesis, now made into the book *Genesis: A Living Conversation* (Doubleday). The book version includes thoughtful comments of four dozen writers, theologians, artists, and thinkers.

Its companion book, *Talking About Genesis: A Resource Guide* (Doubleday), includes excellent supplementary material ranging from Abraham Joshua Heschel to Henry David Thoreau, the Talmud to Phyllis Trible, and Isaac Bashevis Singer to Elizabeth Swados. These passages stimulate our minds and give new meaning to the ancient texts of Genesis.

It is Burton Visotzky, professor of Midrash at the Jewish Theological Seminary, who stimulated the current interest in Genesis. His view of Genesis in terms of family dynamics and moral development are recorded in his book, *The Genesis of Ethics* (Crown). His irreverent reading opens the door to moral development for all readers: Christians, Muslims, Jews, and secularists. He tries to recreate the loving engagements with the Bible that have been the hallmark of two millennia of concerned religious thinkers and commentators.

In The Beginning (Knopf) by Karen Armstrong is exciting and refreshing, and it deserves thoughtful reading. This book views Genesis through the prism of the author's strongly held views about God's unknowability and the folly of some current denominations in second-guessing the Nameless One. Genesis is one of the tools that men and women have used, a ready dimension that transcends their normal lives.

David Rosenberg's collection of essays by writers and poets, *Genesis: As It Is Written* (Harper), is decidedly post-modern. This is a work of cultural outreach that breaks barriers between the religious and the secular, barriers that didn't exist in the biblical writer's day. Though the book itself is a strong anthology of essays penned by some of the most creative minds of our time, Rosenberg properly warns us about "the rush to relevance."

A remarkable translation of Genesis by Robert Alter, professor of Hebrew and comparative literature at the University of California at Berkeley, is entitled *Genesis: Translation and Commentary* (Norton). This book includes commentaries that illuminate the many tensions in the first book of the Bible. Alter's literary feel is exceptional, and his introductions discuss the difficulty of rendering ancient Hebrew words in another language.

In *Genesis: A New Translation of the Classic Biblical Stories* (Harper Collins), Stephen Mitchell embodies in English the simplicity, dignity, and powerful earthiness of the original. He also gives the text a stunning new clarity by separating texts that had been combined by scribes centuries after they were written. This strengthens the original stories, for it is like removing coat after coat of lacquer that has obscured the vibrant colors of the original masterpiece.

The Harlot by the Side of the Road (Ballantine) is as striking as its title. Although not limited to Genesis, the book's originality and power give us new insight into the Biblical text. Jonathan Kirsch, the author, makes us pause and reflect: "How come I didn't think of that?" Reading this book is a provocative and productive experience.

Aviva Zornberg, a Ph.D. in English literature from Cambridge University and an avid student of the Hebrew Bible and its commentaries, has penned an awesome book in breadth and depth. *Residing in Jerusalem: The Begging of Desire* (Doubleday) is filled with thought from Rashi to Rainer Maria Rilke, Lionel Trilling to Targum Jonath, Kafka to the Kabbalah, and Shakespeare to Sefat Emet. One does not read this book but studies it with great intellectual and spiritual enrichment.

Originally published in German and now available for the first time in English, *Genesis* (Mercer University Press) by Herman Gunkel is a massive work. It is astonishing. His commentary commands the attention of scholars who are interested in the interrelationships among documentary sources, oral tradition, and editorial activity.

The Five Books of Miriam: A Woman's Commentary (Putnam) is 3,000 years overdue. Ellen Frankel, the author, is editor and chief of the Jewish Publication Society. She begins with Genesis and continues beyond it, summarizing the *sidra,* the weekly portion, and adding commentary that combines traditional sources and imaginary women's voices. Expanding on this, she has woven a rich tapestry that reveals great imagination and is endlessly informing. This book is a delight to read.

The latest work on Genesis is a coffee-table book: *Genesis: World of Myths and Patriarchs* (New York University Press). Done in grand style by Ada Feyerick with contributing authors Cyrus H. Gordon and Nahum M. Sarka, it is a treasure. With more than 250 superb illustrations, including 64 color plates, it is a visual panorama that shows us what the authors of Genesis saw. Drawing upon the great archaeological discoveries of the past century, the volume illuminates the everyday life of the people of Genesis as seen through politics, geography, commerce, religion, and moral values. This book is particularly helpful because it traces what was borrowed and what was rejected, delineating the process that created a new and unique ethic that has continued to shape the world. It belongs in everybody's home

Burton Visotzky recalls that as a student at the Jewish Theological Seminary, he joined other students in worshiping at a nearby synagogue in Harlem. As they came out into the bright daylight of Saturday, he saw little black girls sitting on the bottom steps. One looked up at him and asked, "Hey, mister, is this the place where they kiss books?"

The Jewish reverence for books starts with Genesis—but that is only the beginning.—1997

30. Should Jews Celebrate Halloween?

Although Halloween is really a children's festival of fun and games, thoughtful Jews wonder if they should join in the celebration.

Halloween had its beginnings in a pre-Christian festival of the dead celebrated by the Celtic peoples of England, Ireland, and Scotland in the fall of the year. At that time, the festival was called *Samhain* (pronounced Sahween) and was the most significant holiday of the Celtic year. Celts believed that *Samhain* was a time when the souls of those who died during the year traveled into the other world. People gathered at that time to sacrifice animals, make offerings of fruits and vegetables, and light bonfires to help the dead on their journey. Ghosts, fairies, and demons roamed the countryside.

In the year 601, Pope Gregory the Great transformed this pagan festival into the Christian feast of All Saints. It honored every Christian saint and was supposed to be a substitute for *Samhain.* All Saints Day was also known as All Hallows Day, for hallow is another word for saint. Later on, the day became a time to pray for the souls of all the dead. Since dead souls, fairies, witches, and demons were on the prowl that day, people left out food and drink to placate them. As the centuries wore on, people began dressing as these dreadful creatures to disguise themselves, and some performed antics in exchange for food. That is the origin of Halloween.

Witches are emphasized on that day because they are the most dreaded of all creatures, based on the Biblical verse (Exodus 22:18) "You shall not permit a witch to live." This belief took on a very ominous form in the Middle Ages when, in the sixteenth and seventeenth centuries, thousands of innocent people were condemned to death in Europe and Great Britain because they were supposed to be witches. Under the Inquisition, Jews, and especially Jewish chemists, doctors, and women were often condemned as witches. Here, in Salem, witch trials took place in 1692, and twenty people were tortured and hanged on the testimony of some hysterical girls who said the accused were witches.

Now, let us turn to the Jewish attitude about these matters. The verse taken from the Torah about witches had meaning for Jews. A soothsayer, a diviner, a sorcerer, and anyone who uses magic is to be condemned. The Hebrew word for magic is *kishuf* and from that we get the Hebrew word for witch, *machashafa.* There must have been many magic-makers around in biblical times because again and again in the Torah we find them condemned. The stated opposition of the rabbis was found in the saying: "He who whispers charms has no share in the world to come."

There is a tremendous history and lore on the subject of Jewish superstition. Most of it was collected by Rabbi Hoshua Trachtenberg and published under the title *Jewish Magic and Superstition.* In the book he tells the following story: Once a teacher of his at the rabbinical seminary was out for a stroll and was suddenly confronted with a black cat from which he shied away nervously. One of his students observed this and teased him with the remark, "You are not really afraid of a black cat, Rabbi?" "No," he replied indignantly, "Of course I don't believe in such nonsense, but there is no harm in being careful."

In Jewish lore one finds the belief that demons go about at night to harm us. Some are *mazzikin* (troublemakers); others are *shadim,* which have human forms and eat and drink, and *ruchim,* which are completely disembodied and formless. A *dybbuk* is a wandering soul that enters people and causes them to act in strange ways. Lillith is a female demon who is particularly powerful against women. Of specific interest to us is the belief found in the Middle Ages and even up to modern times that there are ghosts. They are to be found mainly at times of death and in cemeteries. It was the medieval belief that going to a cemetery and praying to the dead would help people with their problems. However, this was considered very risky because sometimes spirits invite the living to come along with them, and to consent is tantamount to sealing one's death warrant. Therefore, one must say aloud, "By the will of God and by my own will I do not intend to go along with you or any other deceased."

Most thoughtful and religious persons only regard all the lore about magic and superstition as pleasant nonsense. However, even among scientists, there is always nagging doubt. But the authoritative word on the subject belongs to the Talmud (Pesachim 110b): "Superstitions can only harm those who believe in them."

As to the question originally posed: Should Jews participate in Halloween? The answer was provided by Judah Minz, the great rabbi of Padua in the sixteenth century. He points out that since the origins of Halloween are so vague and it has become such a secular holiday, it is no longer a religious event but simply a neighborhood fun fest. He cites a whole string of authorities and says that he and his famous predecessors observed wearing masks, costumes, and merry-making on Halloween all their lives and nobody raised any objection. He concludes by saying: "What is wrong with having a little harmless fun?" He was right!—1984

31. What Happens to Them Happens to Me

On Friday, January 16, American Jews and many others will commemorate the twenty-fifth *yahrzeit* (anniversary of death) of Rabbi Abraham Joshua Heschel, arguably the most powerful Jewish spiritual thinker of the twentieth century. On Monday, January 19, Americans of all faiths will gather to celebrate the birthday of Reverend Martin Luther King Jr., whose moral stature towers above us and whose life's work has profoundly affected the conscience and behavior of our time. These two dates may be accidental but they are not incidental, for the lives and thoughts of these men have changed America and the world forever.

The confluence of these dates reunites men who were the closest of friends and whose religious moral passion stirred our minds and ignited our hearts in the search for justice. Both men stood at the spiritual summit and, as time passes, their visions enlarge us and continue to guide us.

When Rabbi Heschel was my teacher at the Jewish Theological Seminary, he told his students, "A person cannot be religious and indifferent to other human beings' plight and suffering." Therefore, when Dr. King led the garbage workers' strike, Professor Heschel asked us to go through garbage cans in both the affluent and the blighted parts of our communities. What we learned was a revelation about our society.

Dr. King and Professor Heschel once wrote companion articles entitled, "What Happens To Them Happens To Me." King noted in ringing terms, "I am deeply in accord with what Rabbi Heschel has said concerning the injustices, the indignities, and all the humiliating experiences that the Jews of Russia are facing today." Heschel pointed out, "To think of a person in terms of white, black or yellow is more than an error; it is an eye disease, a cancer of the soul."

King and Heschel shared the concept of prophecy as theology and politics intertwined. They viewed the prophets not as "foretellers" but "forth tellers." Heschel wrote in a letter to President John F. Kennedy in June 1963, "Please demand of religious leaders personal involvement, not just solemn declarations." And in the same year King said, "Human progress comes through the tireless and persistent work of dedicated human beings who are willing to be co-workers with God." Both spoke truth to power.

Heschel stressed that the efforts for social justice were deeply rooted in Judaism. He emphasized the phrase in the Hebrew Bible, *lo tahamod ahl dam rayahchaw,* "Thou shall not stand idly by." Therefore, when King asked him to join arm-in-arm in leading the march in Selma, Heschel immediately agreed. Later, when asked how he felt when he faced the snarling dogs and jeering mobs, Heschel replied, "I felt that my legs were praying."

The close relationship of these two extraordinary men was expressed by the great American artist Ben Shahn. In 1964 he created a lithograph that depicts a white hand reaching down, clasping a black hand and lifting it up. Written in Hebrew and English above them is the phrase "Thou Shalt Not Stand Idly By." This powerful work is profoundly moving, as it expresses a great moral purpose of our time.

In the early spring of 1969, while attending a Rabbinical Assembly convention, Heschel asked a few of us to meet with King at midnight. The security was so tight that Heschel had to stand at the door and identify each of us by name. King was exhausted, but his commitment drove him on. He told us that our support meant much to him because the volume of hate in America was reaching an ominous level. I remember his very words: "Before the victory is won some may even have to pass through the Valley of Death. But if death is the price that some must pay to free their children from a permanent death of the spirit, then nothing can be more redemptive, because the moral arc of the universe is long and it bends toward justice." Six days later, King was assassinated.

The "official" memorial to Martin Luther King Jr. is in the form of a wheel with water permanently flowing over it. On it is engraved King's favorite quotation, taken from the Book of Amos: "Let justice well up like water and righteousness like a mighty stream." It is interesting to note that this same motif is an integral part of Temple of Aaron in Saint Paul, built fourteen years before King's death. The front of the building, facing the waters of the Mississippi River, is marked by a large sculpture in the shape of a wheel and flowing waters with the same verse.

While Americans this past year have been especially generous, deeply caring, and ardent volunteers, we still have "miles to go and promises to keep." We are climbing the mountain of racism. At this point we can look up and say, "See how far we have to go!" Or, we can look down and note, "Look how far we have come!"As Rabbi Tarfon, who lived in the first century, taught, "You are not obliged to finish the task, neither are you free to neglect it."

The pain and scars of hate and racism are far too deep and too many to be healed in a few years. It will take decades. Indeed, there has been mass suffering in our time in Russia, China, Africa—and all over the world. There are no equivalences in pain, yet our personal suffering can sensitize us to the agony of others. As Heschel noted, "In a free society, some are guilty; all are responsible."

In a recent conference at the Oval Office called by President Clinton and Vice-President Gore, nine prominent Americans discussed racism, emphasizing the complex subject of affirmative action. Probably the keenest observation was made by Rev. Thaddeus Garret Jr., former chairman of the board of trustees at Howard University: "Affirmative action and mechanical programs will mean not a whit if we don't start changing attitudes. We don't know each other in this country. We don't know who lives next door to us in condominium buildings."

In the Spring of 1964 the University of Minnesota invited Rabbi Heschel to deliver a series of lectures for the well-known Danforth Fellowship. He lived a few blocks from our home and worshiped in our synagogue. We renewed our close friendship.

Once, when we were walking across the Ford Bridge he asked that we stop in the middle and watch the Mississippi River flow by. He placed his arms on the railing and stared at the water and a small island, then turned to me and said, "Bernie, no religion is an island." Later, he took that as the theme of a significant address. In a moving passage he said, "We meet as human beings who have much in common: a heart, a face, a voice, the presence of soul, fears, hopes, the ability to trust, a capacity for compassion and understanding, the kinship of being holy....Many things on earth are precious, some are holy. Humanity is the holy of holies."

We do not understand because we change, we change because we understand.—1998

32. Thanksgiving and Torah

Thanksgiving is a religious festival that Americans have created and the United States government has proclaimed. In that process, Judaism and Jews have played a significant role.

Although there are many myths about the origins of Thanksgiving, the fact is that it was first celebrated July 30, 1623, by the Pilgrims. Interestingly enough, the Pilgrims based a great deal of faith on what they termed "The Old Testament." They tried to fashion their community and culture after the Hebrew civilization. Celebration of the Sabbath began on the previous evening. Children's names originated from "The Old Testament." Puritans were convinced that the American Indians were the lost ten tribes of Israel. New England became the "promised land," flowing with "milk and honey." Among the theses offered in the first class of Harvard graduates in 1642 was one entitled *Hebraea Est Linguarum Mater* ("Hebrew Is the Mother Tongue"). *The Bay Psalm Book,* a favorite seventeenth-century Puritan prayer book, was a direct translation of the Hebrew Book of Psalms. The Puritans went so far as to have special type cut so that certain passages could be reproduced in Hebrew.

Small wonder, then, that in this kind of atmosphere a holiday would evolve to express gratitude through sharing and caring. The very verse for this day was found in the book of Leviticus (23:39): "When you have gathered in the bounties of the land, you shall observe a festival of God." Although Jews have termed this festival Sukkot, it is also most appropriate to call it Thanksgiving.

Look up the word "thanksgiving" in the *Jewish Encyclopedia.* On the page entitled "thanksgiving" no explanation for the term will be found, merely the statement: "Thanksgiving—*See Benedictions.*" This is a fundamental insight of Judaism on the method of teaching the concept of gratitude. Every time we enjoy a gift of God's wonderful world we say a *berakhah* (blessing) and offer thanksgiving. Thanksgiving doesn't come just one day of the year for the Jew; rather, every day is an occasion for thanksgiving.

It is an old Jewish tradition that a pious Jew recites one hundred *berakhot* (blessings) every single day. This means that a hundred times a day we might find the opportunity for giving thanks to the Great Giver of all good things in life.

Not until 240 years after the Pilgrims did Thanksgiving became a national holiday. Was this in a period of plenty? No, it was during the darkest moments of the Civil War. In 1863 Abraham Lincoln issued a proclamation appointing the last Thursday in November the day of observance. The proclamation began with the words, "In the midst of a civil war of unequaled and severe magnitude . . . ."

The lesson of Thanksgiving is that even in the midst of trouble, we can find reason to be thankful. Even when things look dark, we can find glimmerings of hope and light.

Similarly, we each have our personal pack of troubles, and each year it gets a little heavier. But each year we also get a little stronger, a little wiser, a little more philosophical. Each year there are also *simchas*—Bar or Bat Mitzvah, a wedding, a graduation to enjoy, a promotion to celebrate, friendships to share, birthdays and memories of good times gone by but never forgotten.

That is why Judaism teaches that though ultimately all the prayers may be abolished, prayers of thanksgiving will still be needed. Or, as an American sampler saying put it, "Count your blessings, and when you are done, count them all over again, one by one."

How beautiful is the word "Thanksgiving," with emphasis on the "giving." If one could change it somewhat, it might be called "Thanks*living*." A truly sensitive person will live a life of gratitude, not only on the fourth Thursday of November but every day of the year.

A person can attain notoriety, rise to a high position, acquire vast fortunes or power, and yet his or her life is not necessarily a blessing. Blessing occurs only when we use our substance for others. To keep whatever we have for ourselves alone is simply ingathering. If we use it for others, it becomes a blessing.

One Thanksgiving season an American army general decided to send greetings to every unit scattered across six continents. But cables were limited in length, so he was forced to confine his message to a single word. What would best express the spirit and challenge of Thanksgiving? Finally, after deep thought, he made his choice: "Others."

This affirms the conviction that what we do for others ultimately determines our true meaning in life and whether we will be a blessing.—1998

Section II — Issues

1. Rabbinic Reflections on Work

Work is sacred. When we read the Fourth Commandment in the Ten Commandments, we usually focus on the Sabbath as a day of rest. We tend to overlook the opening words, "Six days shall you labor." Work is just as obligatory as any other commandment in the Hebrew Bible.

We are informed at the beginning of Genesis that on the first six days of creation, God worked to form the universe. In Jewish thought, humans are co-creators *(shutafim)* in the work of the world. What God began, we must finish. Work is a primary area in which the human and the divine intersect.

The rabbis advised, "Love work" (Avot 1:10), and they practiced what they preached. Hillel was a porter, and Rabbi Yochanan was known as *hasandler* (the shoemaker). Rabbi Yehoshua was called *napach* (the blacksmith). Rabbi Judah and Rabbi Simeon came to the academy, one bearing a jug he had made with his own hands, the other a basket he had woven. The greatest Jewish commentator of all times, Rashi, was a vintner, and Maimonides, who wrote the classic *Guide to the Perplexed,* was a physician.

Jewish thinkers understood that all work must be honored. A tanner was as important as a teacher, a writer as valuable as a carpenter, a homemaker as vital as a harvester, a secretary as worthy as a scholar.

I am constantly amazed and inspired by the relevance of ancient Jewish writings to the issues of today. The following admonition is repeated thirty-six times in the Bible: "You shall have regard for the stranger, for remember you were strangers in the land of Egypt." This has immediate implications for Proposition 187 in California. "You shall pay fair remuneration to a worker" (Bava Metzia 76-77) speaks to the issue of a minimum wage. "You shall not pray during your working hours for you may do so on your own time" (Berachot 2:4). Can a teacher pray during working hours? "Idleness leads to degeneration" (Ketubot 5:5) teaches the very issue of providing organized recreation activities in high-crime areas. "When a person stops working, she or he dies" (Avot 11). How can we use the ability, the experiences, and the wisdom of retirees for the benefit of society? "Work is therapy" (Gittin 67). Providing jobs is the way to heal our social fabric.

All of this comes under the Jewish concept of *tzedakah. Tzedakah* is not charity or philanthropy but a moral responsibility to see every segment of society being properly served and given the opportunity to serve.

We speak of a woman in childbirth as "being in labor." It is hard work. When we say we will "work it out," we understand negotiations are strenuous. "A labor of love" implies that certain dedicated efforts yield days of satisfaction. "Working out a solution" implies a commitment to solving our problems. Our vocabulary defines us even as we determine our attitude toward work.

I treasure the story about Sir Christopher Wren, the noted architect of London's St. Paul's Cathedral. One day, in the midst of construction, he decided to walk incognito among his workers. He asked the first one he met, "What are you doing?" The reply was, "Piling bricks." To the same question a second workman answered, "I'm making five shillings a day." When the third worker was presented with the query, his eyes lit up and with reverence he said, "I'm helping erect a cathedral to God."

Whether volunteer or paid, the worth of our work is to be judged by the value of making a positive contribution to society and the work of the universe.

When I was a child in Hebrew school and started to study the Bible in the original Hebrew, the verses that left a deep impression on me were the following: "The wages of a laborer shall not remain with you until morning" (Leviticus 19:13); and "You must pay him his wages on the same day before the sun sets" (Deuteronomy 24:15). The teacher explained to us that in a primitive agrarian economy hired workers subsisted on a day-to-day basis. If the worker did not bring home money, his family might have to go without food until the next day. This sensitivity touched me profoundly.

About fifty years later, when my wife and I were in Bangkok, we were invited to spend an evening at the home of some acquaintances. We found that the residential section was like a rabbit warren, and the house-numbering system was idiosyncratic. As we wandered around in search of the address, we saw a door open to a fully lit room. It was filled with men bare to their waists, sweating profusely in the humid atmosphere. Each was working at a sewing machine. We were informed that they were making garments for the United States and Europe, and this was the third shift. We were horrified to learn that their wages were less than a dollar an hour.

The biblical verses I learned as a child flashed before my eyes. This system of labor was morally obscene. In American markets, almost all labels indicate that the garments were made in Asia and Central America. Are we living off the sweat of laborers' brows?

Early Zionism elevated the ideology of labor to a basic philosophy, rooted in the soil of the homeland. A. D. Gordon was instrumental in disseminating the concept that only with hard personal work on the land itself would the Land of Israel be rebuilt. This was part of the philosophy of the early kibbutz movement, which helped to establish a renewed Jewish people in their own land.

In preparing a course at Macalester College this past fall entitled "The Jewish Experience in America," I did some research on the American labor movement. I was impressed by the number of Jews who were involved in founding and shaping the concept of united labor. Interestingly enough, many of their main ideas came from immigrants who quoted the Jewish concept of the ethic of work, which they had learned in Yiddish from the early school days in the ghetto.

In going through the archives, I found a picture of Samuel Gompers, who helped establish the American Federation of Labor. It shows him, wearing a *kipah* (skull cap), addressing a large gathering in an overcrowded synagogue; the men listening are similarly attired. He is speaking in Yiddish, appealing to the group to form a labor union to protect, strengthen, and advance their cause. This picture is worth a thousand Yiddish words.

During 1995 there will be many commemorations of the fiftieth anniversary of the liberation of the concentration camps created during the Holocaust. It was a bitter irony that the people who taught the world about "work with decency" (Avot 2:2) should have been reduced to slaves. Moreover, it was cruelty beyond measure that those brought to Auschwitz passed under the famous sign with its mendacious promise, ARBEIT MACHT FREI (Work Makes One Free). Their wages were the crematoria.

There is an ancient concept of *tikkun olam,* meaning "mending the world." It implies a responsibility to help repair the world of those torn by poverty, heal the sick, provide homes for the homeless, care for children, feed the hungry, support the disabled, sustain the elderly, and respect and preserve the environment. Meeting the needs of the world is God's work that humans must do on earth. It is not merely "social consciousness," but rather a religious responsibility that helps to endow our lives with holiness.

In Hebrew, the word for work is *avodah.* It is a bipolar word, for it also means "worship." In fact, prayer is called *avoda shebelev,* "service of the heart." It is very much like the English word "service," which can be described as a form of labor or religious devotions.

A couple was in a hurry to reach the synagogue. They arrived breathless and inquired of the rabbi if there was time at least to attend the end of the service. The rabbi replied, "The prayers are over, but the service is just beginning."

Work is pleasant or unpleasant, rewarding or unrewarding, meaningful or meaningless, only in the context in which it is experienced. The work we do and our attitudes toward it, whether as a laborer or volunteer, businessperson or babysitter, rag picker or religious functionary, is as servile or sacred as we choose to make it. It is the challenge we daily face in keeping our lives in working order.

Let's go to work.—1993

2. Rabin Remembered

Yitzhak Rabin was first in war, first in peace, and first in the noblest values of his country. He was the essential Israeli.

It was General Yitzhak Rabin, as chief of staff during the Six Day War in June 1967, who led the Israeli troops to capture the Old City in Jerusalem, the Golan Heights, the West Bank, and the Sinai Peninsula. He was hailed all over Israel as a genuine hero and was elevated to highest honors, for he gave Israel its strength and sense of security. But this victory was bought at a terrible price, and Rabin knew it. One could feel it expressed in his own words.

After nineteen years of neglect, the amphitheater on Mount Scopus became the scene of a symbolic event. Chief of Staff, General Yitzhak Rabin received an honorary Ph.D. degree from the Hebrew University. In his acceptance speech he said, "The men on the front lines saw with their own lives not only the glory of victory, but also the price of victory—their comrades fallen beside them soaked in blood. I know, too, that the terrible price paid by our enemies also touched the heart of many of our men."

The seeds of peace had been planted.

All during his life, as warrior, diplomat, and world leader, Rabin remained essentially Israeli and spoke *dugri* —straight talk—like an Israeli. No circumlocutions, no fancy words, just tell it like it is. He expected those who disagreed with him to do the same. He was not for polite dinner talk but face-to-face, honest exchanges of words.

Rabin always made it clear that he was making peace with the Palestinians not because he liked them, but because he believed it was the best way to guarantee a secure and prosperous Israel. He believed Israelis would never be able to feel at home unless the Palestinians did.

His thinking evolved over the years until he so boldly helped to set the peace process into motion. Few knew what it took for Rabin to shake hands with Yasser Arafat at the White House on September 13, 1993. In that one silent act the whole course of history changed in the Middle East and perhaps the world.

In April 1994, after a sleepless night in which he wrestled with uncertainty, Rabin wrote a Memorial Day letter to the Israelis he most admired: the families of the nearly 18,000 soldiers who had been killed during forty years of war. "I believe that peace is possible, that the time has come to put an end to wars." He continued, "I believe we must try to give it a chance, especially now when we are strong enough. Perhaps I am mistaken, perhaps not."

My wife and I own a condominium in Jerusalem which is five minutes from the prime minister's office. We have gone there every summer for twenty-five years. This year we noted the especially slanderous slogans, the vitriolic language, the incivility and incitement against Rabin personally. It was most distressing.

We have annually attended Jewish Agency meetings (the democratic gathering of representatives of world Jewry), representing the St. Paul United Jewish Fund and Council. By chance, I found myself next to Prime Minister Rabin at a social gathering. He was interested in my views, as a midwestern rabbi, on the subject of peace. I told him my reading of the issue but then could not refrain from asking, "Mr. Prime Minister, how can you not take steps to tone down these extreme manifestations of hate?" He replied, "Rabbi, Israel is a democracy and everybody is free to express their feelings. I will live or die by that." He did.

Those who look upon this merely in terms of politics are mistaken. The crucial battle in the Middle East is no longer between Jew and Arab. It is between the violent zealots on both sides. The assassin said, "I acted on God's orders."

In *The Revenge of God (La Revanche de Dieu),* French author Gilles Kepel points out that extremists in Judaism, Catholicism, Protestantism, Islam, Hinduism, and Shintoism are all breeding fanatics who are planning and acting out obscene moral acts "on God's orders." We must be aware of this and speak and act against these forms of moral madness. If we are not part of the solution, we are part of the problem. As King Hussein of Jordan said at Rabin's funeral, "We must not be silent."

In the last few days, as millions of Israelis filed past the coffin and grave of Yitzhak Rabin and world leaders gathered to honor his memory, a new slogan has arisen in Israel: *moto tzvah lonu shalom.* "His death commands us to peace."

That is how to remember Yitzhak Rabin.—1995

3. Toward a New Jewish View of Homosexuality—Let's Take Prejudice Out of the Closet

On November 8, 1988, the voters of St. Paul will decide on a proposed amendment to the City Charter. This amendment is an attempt to protect the civil rights of minority peoples in such things as housing and jobs and to protect them from prejudice and misunderstanding. The most immediately affected groups will be gay men and lesbian women who lost some of their civil rights in St. Paul in the 1978 referendum. In the main, this referendum passed because irrational fears about homosexuals were exploited in a hysterical campaign. Homosexual people were potentially denied their rights simply because of prejudice.

It would be correct to say that the traditional Jewish view of homosexuality is negative. To leave it at that, however, would be to ignore the perspective of Jewish thought and law, recent advances in the scientific understanding of homosexuality, and the classic Jewish components of understanding and compassion. This calls for a new view of homosexuality.

To begin, there are two—and possibly three—Torah-text references to homosexuality (Leviticus 18:22, 20:13, Genesis 19). References in Talmudic and post-Talmudic writings are relatively few and tend to reflect the negative biblical attitude. All biblical statements lend themselves to wide discussion and interpretation; some have been reversed, ignored, consciously neglected, and vastly misinterpreted.

The law of prosbul (restructuring debt) was a basic change in response to economic conditions. The law of a rebellious son was ignored because of changing and enlightened understanding. *Lex talionis,* the law of retribution, was changed from its literal meaning because of a more thoughtful and practical grasp of the human condition.

In relatively modern times the Mishnaic law declaring a deaf-mute *(heresh)* incompetent was reversed because of new evidence. No less a person than Rabbi Isaac Herzog (a chief rabbi of Israel) concluded that new research demonstrated that a deaf-mute had normal intelligence and should be treated that way.

Rabbi David Novak in *Halacha in a Theological Dimension* has described the dynamic of change that is central to the *halachic* system. *Halacha* is not monolithic and immutable. It may be stable, but does not stand still. We owe much to the late Rabbi Herschel J. Matt and Rabbi Robert Kirschner for their pioneering work in the changing relationships between *halacha* and homosexuality.

A basic consideration in Jewish thinking about homosexuality is the principle that *ones* (one who is shaped by outside forces) is understood by the Merciful One (Nedarim 7a). It has been assumed until now that being gay or lesbian was a free and considered choice. Only in our generation has homosexual behavior been found to be not merely a single overt act but a reflection of a profound inner condition over which one has no choice.

The fact is that one's particular sexual orientation is fixed around age three and is deep-seated. Sexual orientation, like the color of the eyes, perfect pitch, attitudes, and personality is a matter of biological and psychological roulette.

The fact is that homosexuality has been documented since the beginning of recorded history in all cultures and societies, among peoples of all ethnic, age, occupational, and educational backgrounds.

The fact is that in 1973 the American Psychiatric Society officially acknowledged that homosexuality is not an illness.

The fact is that the study of sex and the process of sexual difference and individuation reveals an amazing complexity that we are just beginning to understand. New research in psychology and genetics is reshaping our view of homosexuality.

The fact is, according to the FBI and the National Center on Child Abuse and Neglect, more than 95% of sexual assaults against female children are committed by heterosexual men.

The belief that we can recognize gays and lesbians by voice, gait, or manner of dress is a myth and sheer prejudice. It is time that we take prejudice out of the closet and recognize it for what it is—inappropriate, ignorant, immoral, and un-Jewish.

The fact is that gay men and lesbian women have made and are making outstanding contributions to the business, artistic, scientific, religious, athletic, and educational sectors of society.

A Jew should know what prejudice can do to a people and a person through our historical suffering. A Jew should know to be careful in making judgments because we were taught, "Do not judge anyone until you have stood in his or her place" (Avot 8:5). A Jew should be compassionate, for Jews are termed in literature as "compassionate people who are the children of compassionate parents."

The Talmud long ago noted that the Torah was given not to angels but to human beings (Kiddushim 54a). The authority to interpret Jewish law was delegated to the human intellect (Baba Metzia 59b, 86a). Each generation of Jews was entrusted with the responsibility to apply it in terms of new conditions, new facts, and new understanding of human behavior (Sanhedrin 6b, Nidda 20b, et. al.).

One of the real tests of morality and Jewish ethics today is not how homosexuals act, but how we do. The judgment is on us, not them. We are being measured for our fairness, for our compassion, and, yes, for our love and respect for all people created in the image of God—and that is all of us. Rights are indivisible.

We all have them or none of us has them.

Were we not taught to love our neighbor (without specification) as ourselves? As always, we Jews will measure up to the task of being just and loving, by accepting homosexuals as full, equal, and respected members of the Jewish and the human community.

Taking literary privilege with a story about Pastor Martin Niemoller, who resisted Nazism in Germany, makes the point exactly. He is reported to have noted: "In Germany, they came for the homosexuals, and I didn't speak up because I wasn't a homosexual. Then they came for the Jews, and I didn't speak up because I wasn't a Jew. Then they came for the trade unionists, and I didn't speak up because I wasn't a trade unionist. And then they came for me, and by that time, no one was left to speak up."

On November 8, 1988, let's take the prejudice out of the closet and expose it for what it is—inappropriate, ignorant, and immoral. Let's not bow to panic and unwarranted fear. For was it not written: "You shall know the truth, and the truth shall make you free."

Now is the time to speak up for human rights. We, the people of St. Paul, should do what is right and vote YES for human rights.—1988

4. *Kristallnacht,* 1938–1988 Broken Glass, Broken Hearts

Kristallnacht (Night of Broken Glass) occurred in Germany fifty years ago on November ninth and tenth. It was named the "Night of Broken Glass" because many windows were smashed during widespread attacks on the Jews by Nazi soldiers and the incited German populace.

No complete tally of the destruction of Jewish property and the harm caused to persons exists, but even a conservative reckoning is horrifying. Thirty thousand Jews were arrested and sent to concentration camps, 815 Jewish shops were destroyed, 191 synagogues were set afire, with 76 completely destroyed. Jews were killed and injured, and the number of broken Jewish hearts is beyond belief, much less description.

The official explanation for this action was that it was a response to the assassination of Ernest von Rath, third secretary of the German embassy in Paris by a young Jew named Herschel Grynszpan. The boy was driven to desperation because he learned that his father was among thousands of Jews deported to Poland in sealed boxcars. When the seventeen-year-old Herschel heard of the terrible journey and the inhuman conditions, he broke down. The action was his way of expressing his rage and protesting the awful suffering visited upon his dear ones.

The Nazi actions were far from "spontaneous." The night before, Goebbels notified Nazi Party chiefs to prepare for a pogrom. Heydrich, the head of the Gestapo and the Criminal Police, telegraphed specific instructions as to how the outrage was to be organized. The following are the exact words of the Gestapo teleprinter message:

"At very short notice *Aktionen* will take place against Jews, especially their synagogues, throughout Germany. Preparations are to be made for the arrest of about 20,000 to 30,000 Jews in the Reich."

There was a rally of about 30,000 Nazis in Nuremberg on the eve of *Kristallnacht.* They handed out hatchets, and Germans were given permission to do whatever they wanted to Jews. They then forced their way into homes, beat, humiliated, and killed Jews, and stole and destroyed property.

One Jewish woman saw an architect smash the furniture of a home he had built for her twelve years earlier. In another Jewish apartment, a beautiful grand piano was smashed to pieces and every string cut. In one Jewish child's room the arms, legs, and head were torn off a doll.

To add outrageous insult to demonic personal injury, the German government imposed a fine of 1 million marks on Jews and confiscated all Jewish insurance claims. This marked the beginning point of what would become the "Final Solution."

Despite the incitement and ferocity of the mobs, a few Christian church leaders did speak out boldly. Ignoring the Gestapo spies in his church, Father Lichtenberg of St. Hedwig's Cathedral in Berlin said, "The synagogue outside is burning, and that, also, is a House of God. Do not let yourselves be deceived by unchristian thoughts. Love your neighbor as yourself."

In Munich, Cardinal Faulhaber warned, "History teaches us that God always punishes the tormentors of Jews." The Bishop of Wurttemberg wrote to the authorities, "What is happening weighs heavily on the conscience of all Christians. A day will come when we will pay for all this." He saw as "just retribution" the screaming Allied bombs that gutted homes and churches and put to flight thousands of Germans.

But it must be kept in mind that close to half the population of the Greater Reich was Catholic and, in the main, their leaders were silent. The other part of Germany was Protestant, long conditioned by Martin Luther's vehement and coarse anti-Semitism. In no other century, with the exception of czarist Russia, were the clergy and the population so servile to the authority of the state.

Kristallnacht and all the horror to follow did not occur in a vacuum. Earlier in

July, representatives of thirty-two nations met at the Evian Conference, called together to consider the plight of the Jews. All spoke and expressed their country's sympathy with the victims of German persecution. But all regretted that social and economic conditions in their countries precluded an increase in immigration quotas. This included the United States.

The *New York Herald Tribune,* in an article published July 8, 1938, summed up the conference in a headline: "Powers Slam Doors Against German Jews." The *Reichwart* announced in large type one week later: "JEWS FOR SALE—WHO WANTS THEM? NO ONE." The silence of the world was a clear signal to Hitler and his cohorts that they were free to do with the Jews as they wished.

Aside from polite noises, President Roosevelt did nothing. Churchill was asked if German legislation against Jews was an obstacle to Anglo-German relations and he replied in the negative. France and the South American countries displayed similar views. The world abandoned the Jews.

Thus, in October, Germany declared that all Jewish passports were to be revoked. They were to be replaced with a document which bore a capital "J" in red ink one inch high on the left side of the first page. All Jewish men were required to change their first name to Israel and all Jewish women to Sara. Policies to make Greater Germany *"Judenrein"* (purified of all Jews) were put into effect.

From that to *Kristallnacht* to the Holocaust was a natural progression of events. On *Kristallnacht* not only were glass and hearts broken, but also world responsibility and trust were smashed. Dreams of peace were shattered perhaps forever.

Eventually, almost 6 million Jews lost their lives in the most savage manner recorded in history. Millions of other Jews lost their entire families and were made refugees. In the end, those dead on all sides because of World War II numbered 40 million. It is impossible to tally the price paid by Germany for its inhumanity and the world for its indifference.

The lesson of *Kristallnacht* must never be forgotten. Indifference to suffering ends in self-destruction. When human life is shattered, its shards enter all of us.—1988

5. When You Wish Upon a Star: A Jewish View of Astrology

The recent revelation that Nancy Reagan consults astrologers and the First Couple reads the daily horoscope has opened up a whole new area of decision-making in politics. Interpretations will vary on what that may imply. However, it should be understood that Nancy and Ronald Reagan were merely expressing a significant aspect of American culture: a preoccupation, often serious, with astrology.

Usually, we are not aware of the part that astrology plays in the culture of America. When a person escapes a misfortune, we often say, "Thank your lucky star." If one has good fortune, we say, "He (she) was born under a lucky star." In literature, a love relationship that has gone awry is characterized as "star-crossed." Horoscopes and columns that predict the future based on celestial signs can be found in daily newspapers. In every bookstore and in the magazine rack at local drugstores and supermarkets one can find dozens of magazines and paperbacks with astrological interpretations and predictions.

Astronomy is a science that deals with celestial bodies, their magnitudes, motions, and composition—all based on verifiable data. Astrology is a pseudo-science that treats the influences of the stars upon human affairs and foretells terrestrial events by the stars' positions and aspects. It pretends that the stars, the positions of the planets, the movement of heavenly objects have an effect on human lives. It is interesting to note what Jewish tradition has to say about these matters.

The prophets were aware of the practices of "star-gazers" *(hoverei ha-shamayim)* among the Babylonians and other peoples, but they scoffed at them. In the Book of Daniel, the Babylonian astrologers are called *kasdim* (Chaldeans). There is no explicit mention of astrology in the Bible, but two passages deal with the diviner *(menahesh)* and soothsayer *(me 'onen):* "You shall not practice divination or soothsaying" (Leviticus 19:26), and "Let no one be found among you who is soothsayer, a diviner, a sorcerer" (Deuteronomy 18:10).

The Talmud and Midrash have a great deal to say about astrology. However, there is no clear-cut view but rather various opinions (often conflicting) on whether heavenly bodies influence human behavior. On the one hand, the patriarch Abraham and his descendants are spoken of as having been elevated beyond subjection to the stars (Genesis Rabbah 44:12). But, on the other hand, the blessing bestowed on him in Genesis (24:1) is interpreted as the gift of astrology.

A number of important Talmudic rabbis, such as Rabbi Akiva, were of the opinion that the power of the stars over ordinary mortals did not extend to the People of Israel. Rabbi Johanan said: "There is no star *(mazzal)* for Israel (Shabbat 156a). But, on the other hand, we find the statement: "Life, children and sustenance—these things depend not on merit but on the stars" (MK 28a). In fact, so strong was the zodiac in popular culture in Talmudic times that we find aspects of the zodiac in parts of excavated synagogues. A particularly fine example is the mosaics of Bet Alpha, located in Israel in the eastern Jezreel Valley, which contain a complete picture of the zodiac, each figure bearing the appropriate Hebrew inscription.

During the eighth to the tenth centuries several famous Jewish astrologers lived in Islamic lands and wrote books on astronomy and astrology. For example, Ibn Ezra left astrological manuscripts. A very famous Persian Jewish astrologer, Andruzgar ben Zadi Faruk, lived during the ninth century. Abu Daud, a Jewish astrologer, who lived in Baghdad at the beginning of the tenth century, wrote an astrological treatise entitled *Book of Prophecies* that appeared in many translations. Among medieval Jewish scholars and philosophers who were versed in astrology and considered it to be a true science were Saadia Gaon, Solomon ibn Gabirol, and Abraham ibn Daud.

Others like Joseph Albo and Judah Halevi were skeptical about astrology. Hasdai Crescas came to the conclusion that while there is no clear evidence rebutting the assumptions of the astrologers, in view of human free will and divine providence it is nevertheless impossible to attribute an absolutely decisive character to astrology. Among the Jewish philosophers of the Middle Ages, Maimonides alone rejected astrology completely, referring to the astrologers' beliefs as vain superstitions unworthy to be called a science.

Kabbalistic literature takes astrology very seriously, if not for granted. The Zohar states explicitly: "All the stars and constellations in the heavens were appointed to be rulers and commandants over the world...there is not a single blade of grass in the entire world over which a star or a planet does not preside, and over that star one (angel) is appointed who serves in the presence of the Holy One, blessed be He, each according to his merit" (Mishnat ha-Zohar 2:171d). Jewish astronomers and astrologers served in various royal capitals of Southern and Western Europe as court astrologers and as consultants in Castile, Aragon, and Portugal, and even to the Pope and the Borgias.

In the Jewish religious literature of modern times there remain only vestiges of earlier astrological beliefs. On joyful occasions in individual and family life, Jews everywhere congratulate each other by saying: *mazzal tov* (good luck). A successful person is popularly referred to as a *bar-mazzal* (one of luck), and a perennial failure is known as a *ra-mazzal* (poor luck—in Yiddish *shlimazle).*

On the whole, the Jewish attitude seems to oppose astrology. The Midrash tells us: "God lifted Abraham above the vault of heaven, and said to him, 'You are a prophet, not an astrologer!'" (Genesis Rabbah 41:12). Maimonides wrote: "Astrology is a disease, not a science . . . it is a tree under the shadow of which all sorts of superstitions thrive. Only fools and charlatans lend value to it" (Maimonides letter Marseilles 1195, Responsa ii 25b).

Perhaps, the final judgment of the rabbis was made in the following quotation: "The Holy One forbade astrology in Israel" (Genesis Rabbah 44:12).

This is reflected in the words that were written by William Shakespeare in his play *Julius Caesar:* "The fault, dear Brutus, is not in our stars, but in ourselves, that we are underlings."

In the last analysis, a significant attitude on the subject is reflected in a contemporary anecdote. A stock market operator wanted to deduct the cost of fees paid to an astrologer for market guidance. He was told by the Internal Revenue Service, "Astrology is not for finance, but for fools!"—1994

6. Armageddon: The Jewish View

This past week in the synagogue we read the story of Noah, the flood, the destruction of humankind, and the rainbow. This is extremely relevant because on the previous Tuesday, October 23, the front page of *The New York Times* and the local press discussed Armageddon, which is very prominent in the thinking of President Reagan. The theory of Armageddon, to which Mr. Reagan has referred publicly at least eleven times (and privately on many more instances) is that the end of the world is coming, and it might be very near. Leaving aside all political considerations, this is a worthy topic for discussion.

Armageddon is the name of the site in Christian theology where the final battle between the forces of Good and Evil occurs. The name refers either to *ir megiddo,* the city of Megiddo, or *har magiddo,* the mountains of Megiddo. There is a possible reference to it in the Book of Isaiah. The Prophet Joel mentions three times that there will be a final worldwide battle before God steps in and restructures the universe and history.

Beyond that, there is no reference in the Hebrew Bible to this type of thinking. However, it figures very prominently in the New Testament, in several passages in the Book of Revelations. In Christian theology throughout history this theory of the final battle before the destruction of humankind has had its ups and downs.

During the past few years, particularly since the rise of the so-called Moral Majority, it has become prominent again. It is believed that the Russians and the Americans will be dragged into a worldwide conflagration which will ultimately take place in Israel near Megiddo.

There is ample documentation on how powerful a belief this is in contemporary evangelical thought. One need not even bother reading Jerry Falwell's book. Simply turn on the television any Sunday morning from 7 until 10:30 and you will hear the Armageddon theme repeated *ad nauseam.*

Now, here is the way it really works. Anytime there is trouble in the world, and there is always some, the evangelical preacher stands up, scares the congregation half to death, and says that the only way one can be saved is to accept Jesus Christ. I remember many years ago going to hear the grandfather of all these evangelicals, Billy Graham, on the grounds of the Minnesota State Fair the day after Marilyn Monroe committed suicide. I recall his words vividly: "The world is coming to a terrible state because look at what Marilyn Monroe did. So you better accept Jesus as your savior." At that point I did not know if I should laugh or cry, so I walked out.

The point I really want to make, and it is the only point, is that Jews reject this kind of theology as idle speculation. There were times when Jews were severely oppressed, and so they looked for some sign of hope, some tiny miracle of relief. There arose a series of "false messiahs." But no matter what the masses believed, the rabbis were clear in their view, and they expressed it in one sentence: *arur mechashvey hakaitz,* "Cursed be those who dwell on the end of time."

Even during the Holocaust no Jew ever gave a thought to Armageddon. They had their theological problems, but this kind of thinking did not arise. Why do Jews feel this way? The answer in the first place is that no one knows what is going to happen, not only in the next decade or next year, but even tomorrow.

But, more important, if one believes in the Bible deeply and in the passages found in Noah as I do, God created the rainbow to prove that the world would never be destroyed again. The real essence of the biblical section entitled Noah is not Noah or the flood, but the *brit*, covenant, that God made with human beings that the world would never again be destroyed.

Therefore, as a believing Jew, I reject all the talk about Armageddon. As a Jew, I resent its intrusion into a political campaign in these United States where there is separation of church and state. And, finally, as a religious leader, I am against frightening anybody into believing anything so that they will be saved.

I join with the major Christian and Jewish leaders who condemn this type of talk. Enough of speaking of the end of days. Let us talk about the problems of today, and let us do something about it. That is within our power and that is our responsibility.—1985

7. Dissent in the American Jewish Community: How Do We Handle It? What Do We Do With It?

One of the most pressing issues before us today is dissent in the American Jewish community. How do we handle it? What do we do with it? Religious groups have brought the Jewish community in Israel to the brink of a civil war. The present dilemma facing Israel has reverberated among us, testing our limits of tolerance. Bewildering forces and life styles have brought us factionalism that threatens to fragment us. Where are we now? What do we do now? How do we make the center of Jewish life hold?

Perhaps we might begin in the traditional and unique methodology of the Talmud. That is weighing and sifting, a thoughtful analysis, considering various alternatives, give and take, arriving at a consensus, or at least agreeing to disagree agreeably. In this method can be found a significant and a productive way to begin. Let us consider difference, diversity, dissent, and duty.

All of life in general and Jewish life in particular is built on difference. That is because people are intellectually and emotionally different. And as Jews say, "Life is with people." Jews have developed this process of handling difference to a fine art. Indeed, the Talmud is a centuries-long record of Jewish debates on the most important issues in life.

There is, to be sure, a classic passage in the Talmud (Erubin 14b) in which the House of Hillel and the House of Shammai disagree on several matters. Then the Talmud utters these splendid words: *aylu vaylu divray elohim chavim,* "both are the words of the living God." This is not double talk but an expression of the fact that there can be different perceptions of the same issue. Both can be correct depending on one's point of view, one's experience, and one's set of attitudes and priorities. This is tolerance raised to its highest level, and it is thoroughly Jewish.

The Talmud further points out that the rulings usually followed the House of Hillel "because they were kindly and modest and they respected the other point of view." Even in their opposing differences they carried on pleasant social relationships and maintained friendships. Is this not a role model for us? Can we do less?

In another remarkable passage in the Talmud (Berachot 58a) Rabbi Hamnuna urged, "If one sees a gathering of Jews, it is appropriate to recite the blessing, 'Praised be God Who has created each one different.'" From here we learn that difference is a blessing.

Consider these historical developments in the Jewish experience. Would we consider these historical developments in the Jewish experience? Would we have the prophetic legacy if the prophets did not dare to be different? Would the works of Maimonides have been written if he did not have the courage of his convictions? Would the poetry of Emma Lazarus grace the Statue of Liberty if she did not leave her middle-class comforts and espouse the cause of the immigrants? In every age, it is precisely those Jews who were willing to stretch the foundations of Jewish thought and experience who are remembered in the annals of Jewish history. From Moses to Maimonides to Mordecai Kaplan it was the willingness to broaden as well as deepen the Jewish mind that raised Judaism to a higher level. The truth is that Jewish life was fueled by those willing to disagree, to strike out in new directions, to advance the frontiers of Jewish thought and experience in every age. Therefore, in our so-called turmoil today, we might pause to ask ourselves: Can Israel and the Jewish people survive without difference, debate, and dissent? For in the last analysis, if everybody is thinking alike, nobody is thinking at all.

Let us now stop a moment to consider diversity. Diversity can be said to exist when differing points of view occur and one must be right—but we cannot be sure which one. The Talmud in its wisdom has developed a mechanism to handle that. It is called *Tayku.*

When the Talmud comes to a complex issue and the debate is intense, it sometimes concludes with the statement *Tayku,* which stands for *tishbi yetahretz kushiot veahbiyot,* "the *Tishbite* (Messiah) will resolve all questions and dilemmas." It is a way of saying that at present there is no way to know who is right. Therefore, let us accept each other, work for the common good, and let time and history decide not merely who was right or wrong, but what was the right approach.

It is a myth to see Judaism as a monolith in any age. There was not a generation in Jewish history that did not have differing sects and diverse interpretations of Judaism. One example will suffice: According to one calculation, during the first century about 2.5 million Jews lived in Eretz Israel and more than 6 million in the Roman Empire, 1 million in Alexandria alone. In the Diaspora, their beliefs ranged from allegorical interpretations of Philo to the literalists, the rabbinic, and the Hellenists, to the indifferent, the intermarried, and those who were assimilated into the Roman pagan culture. In Eretz Israel at the same time there were the Hellenists, the Herodians, the Scribes, the Sadducees, the Essenes, the Zealots, the Siccari, the Priests, the Am-haaretz, the Sectarians, the Jews for Jesus, and of course, the Pharisees. Even the Pharisees were divided into the School of Shammai and the School of Hillel. In time it turned out that the Pharisaic philosophy was destined to shape the future of Judaism, but at that moment in history, who could possibly know for a certainty which philosophy would emerge as the guide for the centuries to follow?

Transposing this to the modern scene, we might ask, Who is right? The Orthodox, the Conservative, the Reform, the Reconstructionists? Each has a right to advance its view without imposing its will on others. Coercion or force does not prove truth. What if one is wrong? Each group has a right to draw up rules for those who voluntarily adhere to it, but none has the right to impose its will through political stratagems, psychological pressures, or other manipulative devices to compel others to adopt its practices. After all, humility is a virtue and triumphalism is arrogance.

In Jerusalem today, the *Eda Haredit* (the ultra-Orthodox), which rejects the concept of a Zionist state, claims to be the sole legitimate heir of Orthodox Judaism and is opposed by at least three other Orthodox groups. The Orthodox Hasidim in America are split in several ways, often coming to blows.

The Conservative movement now faces a strong internal challenge from the Union for Traditional Judaism. The recent official position of the Conservative movement as expressed in the pamphlet *Emet Ve-emunah* endeavors to be all things to all views.

The Reform movement is deeply divided on the issue of officiating at mixed marriages and other matters. Judaism today is a house divided against itself—or a many splendored thing—depending on one's view. Then, for the sake of peace and mutual benefit, we must understand that while there is no need to stifle one's conviction and commitment, there is every need to respect the conviction and commitment of others. For in the end history will work its purpose. God moves in wonderful ways beyond our comprehension, our wildest imaginings, and our most subtle scenarios.

This might be an appropriate point to comment on the recent, tenuous growth of secularism in the Jewish community. While a rabbinic interpretation would hold that only a religious orientation toward Judaism can survive—and this view could well be supported by history—yet a secular orientation toward Jewish life is also legitimate. The rabbinic concept of *Klal Yisrael,* the whole congregation of Israel, recognizes that sacredness resides in the entire Jewish community.

In his recent book, *Fear No Evil,* Natan Scharansky calls *klal yisrael* "a mystical interconnection of souls." Indeed, we must note that Judaism can never be approached without a religious vocabulary, albeit in its broadest interpretation. It should be kept in mind that the most articulate exponent of Naturalism in our generation was Mordecai Kaplan, who defined Judaism as "a religious civilization."

To the question of which religious interpretation is correct, the answer is *Tayku,* for at present no one knows the final answer. Therefore, live and let live, until history provides the resolution.

This now leads us to the heart of the matter—dissent. In a democracy the majority view prevails. This does not mean that the majority is necessarily right, only that most people have chosen this option. In order for a society to function, a given course of action must be clearly defined and taken. It is not possible when driving the vehicle of state to turn both left and right at the same time. As the Talmud wryly observes, *ayn shenay dahbronim ledor echad,* "there cannot be two leaders at one time."

However, here the analogy falters, because in dealing with opinions and human policies, there is usually a minority that has strong feelings. Democracy was made to protect the minority, for the majority needs no protection. Therefore, the minority must be given an avenue for expression. When the issue becomes morally intense and deeply ethical, the minority feels the need to press its case to the utmost.

In that instance minority members may choose to break a law they believe to be immoral. They wish to remain within the system, and so they accept the consequence of violating the law because they believe they are obeying a higher law. At times their view is ultimately accepted and becomes the majority view, whereby the law is changed through due process.

During the civil rights struggles in the 1960s, those in favor of equality were often jailed because they broke the law. Their actions brought the issue to the attention of the nation, and a new law was created. In the Seventies there was objection to government policies in Vietnam. Again, demonstrations and other forms of expression, often illegal, were carried out. Infractions of the law were dealt with, but eventually government policy was reversed and American forces were withdrawn from Vietnam. But in all these situations, minority members stayed within organized society and accepted the consequences of their behavior. They deeply believed that despite their minority status they were right. And indeed, history proved them so.

In a voluntaristic, non-legal society, the same principle of majority/minority relationship holds but there is no institutionalized method to enforce a majority view. Thus the majority seeks to empower itself through peer pressure, scorning, or ostracizing the minority, intimidating or otherwise tyrannizing it. But the minority must persist because it has rights or because it may be right. This process is called dissent.

Today this process is to be found in the torn and tangled issue in Israel on what to do with the occupied territories of Judea and Samaria, the West Bank and Gaza, or whatever one chooses to call these areas. The issue is most complex. It is a concern that involves the body and the soul of Israel. It involves world Jewry generally and the American Jewish community specifically. The fate of all of us will be shaped by what is going on in Israel now. We have a share in its outcome and resolution.

Israeli views on the future of Israel can be divided into four groups. One vociferous group believes Israel should give up no land for peace because of its belief in the Bible and the *halacha.* This group is convinced it is part of God's plan that all the land belongs to Israel forever. Another vocal segment (Greater Israel) shares the sentiment of retaining all the land at all costs. They are, in the main, secularists and derive their conviction from a nationalistic historical view of the Jewish experience. Although both groups come to the same conclusion, they are based on diametrically opposed premises. On the issue and implications of secularism and religion they continually clash, often violently.

The third view, held probably by the majority, would be willing to give up some land for peace, providing there are guarantees of security. How one guarantees security is in itself another difficult matter. Here is where one finds a variety of scenarios. To round out the scene, one must cite a group that feels land should be given up without any security provisions, which will bring peace in itself. Only a negligible group holds this position.

How Israel dealt with the *intifada,* the so-called uprising of the Palestinians, and continues to deal with it is yet another matter on which emotions run high. Some say it was handled correctly, and perhaps there even should have been stronger measures. They argue Israel's security and its very life are at stake. It is a matter of survival.

Others argue that it was dealt with unnecessarily harshly. Human rights were violated, Israel's moral integrity was damaged. Ultimately, they contend that even the phrase "a good occupation" is an oxymoron, a contradiction in terms. Practically, no nation can control such a large mass of people over a period of time.

There are many opinions, and American Jews would do no wrong in advocating any given view, because there would be Israelis who have a similar view. But because of the delicate situation today in terms of Israel's precarious existence and our responsibilities, we are caught in a dilemma. It is a fact that the *intifada* and Israel's response to it have damaged her moral stance in the world in general and the United States in particular. It is a fact that the American-Arab power is a growing threat. It is very clear that Arabs have entered American politics, created alliances, and solidified their political clout on the highest levels. On campuses, the support for the Arab cause is growing, and the number of Muslims in the United States is steadily increasing.

These are serious threats that the American-Jewish community must confront. At the very most we must present a solid Jewish front to deal with these serious challenges that could make a significant difference in Israel's struggle to survive.

At the very least we must endeavor not to fracture the united strength of the American-Jewish community and give no aid or comfort to the enemy. Yet at the same time, we must preserve freedom of speech in the Jewish community and be able to question the wisdom of the majority view and strategy, and we must preserve the right to dissent.

One of the ways this dilemma can be handled is to use a proper forum for debate and airing views. It can be done at Jewish board meetings, at specially convened gatherings, and in the Anglo-Jewish press. It can be done by talking to friends, relatives, and at private gatherings. Consensus is formed in many ways.

But in the last analysis the foreign policy of Israel is determined by Israel and Israel alone, since it must bear the full brunt of its decisions. One can contact Israeli leaders, write to Israeli newspapers, or go to Israel and discuss one's views with the Israelis. The latter is the most effective and responsible way. It is putting our body where our mouth is.

Then it comes down to this. There are adequate forums in the American-Jewish community to discuss Israeli policy, Using the general press for press releases, advertisements, and interviews can be counterproductive and can lead to misunderstanding. It can be termed "washing one's dirty linen in public."

American Jewry speaks with many voices on this matter. No one speaks for the American Jewish community. Therefore, there must be room for dissent in the Jewish community or else we will be living with a totalitarian state of mind. Hewing to one line is a form of idolatry in which we enshrine a particular view, make it absolute, and worship it

If the general press on its own seeks to report the views of American Jews, so be it. After all, we believe in a free press. If the press calls individuals for statements, let them speak freely, but they must accept the consequences of their statements. Let all beware that those who speak out bear a heavy responsibility, lest Jews be harmed. On the other hand, silence can be golden or yellow. Restraint and thoughtfulness, as well as honesty and conviction, should be the order of the day.

How should this be done? It is not easy, but our tradition, as usual, provides us with good guidance on the matter. The Bible in chapter nineteen of the Book of Leviticus instructs us: *hocheeach tocheeach et ahmitahchu,* "You shall confront your friend when in error." And the very next verse reads: *veahavtaw leraycha kamocha,* "And you shall love your friend as your self." A point of view and criticism must be spoken out of love and responsibility. Let each Jew interpret these verses as he or she wishes. But let it be with integrity, with humility, and with respect for the opinions of others.

Then, finally, as Jews we must pause to touch on the concept of duty. After all, was it not written in hallowed words that *kol yisrael ahrayvim zeh bahzeh,* "All Jews are responsible for one another." Jews have an obligation to listen and give serious consideration to difference and diversity expressed in all Jewish attitudes and lifestyles. We must address ourselves to changing times and changing, diverse needs. We must concern ourselves with the elderly, new methods of education for the young, issues of mental health, the struggles of the chemically dependent, the intermarried, and those who choose to live in the *havurah* setting, including gay and lesbian Jews, as full and respected members of the Jewish community. After all, reaching out means bringing together. We cannot do it all, but we must surely do what we can.

In every covenantal relationship there must be reciprocity, and in every social contract there must be consideration on both sides. If Jews expect to benefit from the Jewish community, then they must be prepared as individuals to be involved in decision making, participate in volunteer work, and contribute financially a fair share to maintain the activities of the Jewish infrastructure. While there cannot and should not be a legal way to enforce responsibility, yet there is a moral power that entitles the representatives of the Jewish community to present a strong case in soliciting a contribution to maintain Jewish life. The ultimate pressure on the individual contributor should be from conscience and the weight of Jewish history.

Perhaps in the end it all comes down to this: Isaac ben Judah Abravanel, who lived in the fifteenth century in Spain, wrote a classic commentary on the Bible. It was known to East European Jews simply as *the abravanel.* It was to be studied on Shabbat while reviewing the weekly Sabbath portion. The style was fascinating. The author began each section with a long series of questions and then proceeded to answer them.

One Jew faithfully studied this work every Friday night. However, the problem was that after a week of work and a full Shabbat meal, he would begin his studies. Naturally, he soon began to doze. He found that he fell asleep around the third or fourth introductory question. So he came to the conclusion that Judaism was full of questions and had no answers.

Not so. We survived the centuries as Jews because we found the answers to problems. We have to be patient, for the solutions will come. The answers are there in Jewish history, experience, literature, and in ourselves. Our problem is to ask the right questions. Was it not written in *Pirkay Avot,* "The Ethics of Our Ancestors," "It is not for you to finish the work, yet you are not free from doing all you possibly can."

Then let me conclude with this true and striking incident. Pablo Casals was probably the greatest cellist of our time. Once he was rehearsing the orchestra for a performance in one of his famous programs in Puerto Rico. He wanted the orchestra to play with deep feeling. So as he was conducting, he shouted, "Rainbow, Rainbow, play Jewish."

When Jews work together and preserve their individuality but still blend together in community, then that produces a harmony that is as beautiful and as moving as a rainbow. Let us blend together the various shades of Judaism, but let no color or hue be left out. In our time, let us create a rainbow of Jewish life so that future generations will say of what we did: "Beautiful." To this end let us pledge our lives, our fortunes, and our honor.—1988

8. A New Look at the Old Issue of Intermarriage

It was with a sense of trauma that the Jewish community reacted to the revelation that since 1985 more than 50% of the Jews who married chose non-Jews as spouses. Understandably, reactions have been fraught with panic and desperation. Perhaps it is time to take a second look at the situation and see it in a fuller perspective, not as a problem but a challenge.

There is no need to blame but, rather, share responsibility. Conservative Jews must deal with the fact that 42% of young people raised in Conservative synagogues intermarry. Reform Jews must ask themselves if more than 60% of Reform rabbis officiate at mixed marriages, have they not accelerated the phenomenon? For all of the publicity, visibility, and triumphal talk about *ba'alay teshuvah* (return to Orthodoxy), less than 1% of American Jews are influenced by extreme Orthodoxy, and more than 90% of them ultimately drift away.

The basic fact is that the high rate of intermarriage is a function of our open society. Our culture places great value on individual choice, as opposed to group responsibility. Jews could hardly wait to leave the ghetto in search of greater freedom; little did they realize that freedom included the ability to make choices that did not necessarily help perpetuate Judaism.

With this in mind, let us look at the issue in historical perspective. Intermarriage is hardly a new occurrence in the vast reaches of Jewish experience. All of Jacob's sons, who later became the founders of the twelve tribes, were married to Canaanite women. Moses was married to a Midianite and later also took as a wife a Cushite woman. Interestingly enough, Cushite means "black." When the Jews left Egypt, they were accompanied by an *erev rav,* which is usually translated as a "mixed multitude" but really means "mixed marriages." During the time of Ezra and Nehemiah, and from the era of Hellenism through the emancipation period in Berlin, Warsaw, Paris, and Rome, there have been numerous periods of widespread intermarriage.

Responses have varied. In the Bible, Phineas slays the Israelite man who lived with the Midianite woman. Later Jewish generations felt distaste and embarrassment at this act of zealotry. Ezra resolved the situation by forcing Jewish men to divorce non-Jewish wives. Again, this was seen as harsh, if not cruel. Throughout history the reaction has sometimes been anger, sometimes stoic and painful acceptance, and sometimes even a desire to make the best of a difficult situation.

I recall several decades ago a couple asked, "Rabbi, when do we start sitting *shiva?"* I was startled and asked who died. They explained, "No one. Our son is marrying a non-Jew." I quickly relieved their guilt and indicated that this was no way to handle the situation emotionally or practically.

But what's to be done individually and on a group basis today? If a family member intermarries, there should be no sense of guilt or personal failure. Over 50% of our children have intermarried, and they have come from Orthodox, Conservative, Reform, or other forms of very Jewish homes. We must see ourselves as part of a trend. No one is immune. We must reach out, difficult though it may be, to help, to understand, to be noncritical and positive. It is not merely the proper way, it is the only way.

As a group, there is much we can do. The first act is to intensify Jewishness in the Jewish community. Greater emphasis on all forms of Jewish education, observance, and programming is in order. This is no guarantee, but it is helpful.

There must be greater efforts at *kiruv,* new attitudes, strategies, and programs that will bring mixed marrieds and their children closer to the Jewish community. We should not be condemning or critical, but caring and compassionate. Our stance can be open without lessening our own Jewishness or negating *halacha,* Jewish law. This is not a time for despair, but digging down deeper and coming up more devoted.

In the early Greek period the Jewish community included people known as *phoboumenous* and *sebemenos,* which mean "revering one" or "worshiping one." In Hebrew, they were called *yiray hashem,* "God-fearer/reverer," and their names were posted on the synagogue walls with honor. They were not full Jews, but "sympathizers." In the Talmud, there is a group known as *ger toshav,* the term for a non-Jew who takes on the obligation of not worshiping idols. Historically, our people found ways to relate to non-Jewish spouses in a positive manner.

After all, let us also look at the positive side of the experience. The Hebrew language and some basic cultural Jewish practices come from the Canaanites. The Greek mind enriched Jewish culture, as thousands of Greek words in the Talmud testify. The "Golden Age" in Spain would not have occurred without Arabic stimulus. Italian Jewry was ennobled by Renaissance culture. Even the Hasidic movement was profoundly influenced by Russian sectarian mysticism, Russian peasant melodies and mores, and the Starets concept.

The historical reality is that, had the Jews remained within the boundaries of Israel, they would have become another tiny culture among the squabbling nations of the ever-changing Middle East. All the great classic books of Judaism were written or begun outside of Israel. Even the Bible, if we follow tradition, was written by Moses, who never entered the Promised Land.

This does not negate the centrality of Israel in Jewish thought and life, as well as Zionism; it merely provides a sense of thoughtful balance in understanding Judaism. Actually, one of the main forces in the birth and development of modern Zionism was the great fear engendered by the high rate of assimilation among European Jewry.

In our day the miracle of Jewish life is commonplace. Who would have dreamed that after some 2,000 years of exile thousands of Ethiopian Jews would be transported to Israel in less than twenty-four hours? Or that Russian Jewry, after seven decades of systematic repression and persecution, would come to Israel by the hundreds of thousands. It was unforeseeable that after the Holocaust, American Jewry would become such a great center of learning, with thousands of Jewish courses being taught on campuses; revitalized Yeshivot, seminaries, and day schools; C.A.J.E.; enormous endowments for Jewish programs; and the publication of Jewish books in unprecedented numbers and variety. The ultimate miracle, of course, was the establishment of the State of Israel, itself.

What of the Jewish future? The only thing we have to fear is fear itself. The challenge is enormous, but, as Jews, we have always had the capacity to renovate and regenerate. Jewish history is filled with many gravestones but also many great events.

Who would have ever believed that *kaddish* would be recited in Red Square by a Jew wearing a *tallit* over a Jew named Ilya Krichevski, who was proclaimed a "hero" of the Russian people? The martyr's father, Marat Yefim Krichevski, was born a Jew but raised his family in a determined cosmopolitan atmosphere. This man, who, with his wife, was a dedicated Communist Party member for thirty years, made a profound point when he said, "I agree with whoever said Ilya was a Russian hero who became a Jew after he died." This, too, is a form of Jewish immortality.

Jewish life is stronger than logic. Jewish survival is more powerful than destruction. Jewish determination is more overwhelming than despair. The last chapter of Jewish history in America has not been written, but a new chapter may have begun.

In 1962 *Look* magazine featured an article entitled "The Vanishing American Jew." Today, *Look* has vanished, but American Jews are still here.—1991

9. Time for a Third Jewish Temple? In One Era and Out the Other

Recently in Jerusalem members of the Faithful of the Temple Mount, led by a *Kohen* in priestly robes with special vessels for the Temple ritual, two rams' horns, a clarinet, and an accordion, marched from the Western Wall to the Pool of Siloam to consecrate what they have designated as the cornerstone of the Third Temple. Police had prevented these people from having the "cornerstone" in the Western Wall Plaza, as they had originally intended. Gershon Salomon, head of the FTM, led the group in reciting the *shehecheyanu* blessing, in which one gives thanks for having reached a special occasion. The FTM maintains that we have reached the "end of days."

"The End of History?" is the title of an article that was published in an issue of the *National Interest.* Written by Francis Fukuyama, deputy director of the State Department's policy-planning staff, it contends that recent events indicate that history has come to an end.

The topic of "End Time" is hardly new. Discussions surrounding post-history usually accompany periods of political and social transition. One should view the present pronouncements in the context of history with a theological base. Jews have much to say in the matter of the end of history, for they have encountered the issue time and time again. They were probably among the first to raise it. The Bible refers to *acharit hayamim,* "The end of days," i.e., the "end of time." In the Second Temple period, it was often referred to as *kaytz hayamim,* literally, "the term of days."

Most of the discussion on this subject comes under the rubric of "eschatology," which designates doctrine concerning "last things." The word "last" can be understood either absolutely—as referring to the ultimate destiny of humankind—or relatively, as to an individual or a period of history.

Essentially, the origin of eschatology in Judaism can be found in God's promise to establish a divine kingdom of Justice, in which Israel would play a central role. The prophet Amos expanded on this by elaborating on divine judgment and calling it the "Day of the Lord." Later prophets referred to it simply as *hayom hahu,* "that day."

It is Isaiah who emphasized eschatology and incorporated the idea of the Messiah into it. He spoke of a Messianic Age, which would be brought about by the will of God. As the prophetic movement evolved, new ideas such as "Judgment Day," the rebuilding of the temple in Jerusalem, and an era of eternal peace were introduced. All were said to be part of the divine plan in which history was prearranged from beginning to end.

This thinking reached a high point in the Book of Daniel. The term "apocalypse" is appropriate. Often, this word is translated as revelation, which means literally "uncovering" the future, the final destiny of the world.

In the rabbinic period, we begin to come across the concept of *yemot hamashiach,* "the times of the Messiah." This gives birth to attempts to calculate the time remaining until this supernatural event will occur. It is generally accepted that there will be suffering before this happens, commonly known as *chevlo shel mashiach,* "the pangs of the Messiah."

Rabbinic times produced the concept of *olam habah,* "the time to come," in contrast to *olam hazeh,* "the present time." In *olam habah,* also translated as "the world to come," God will mete out full retribution for good and evil.

The Dead Sea Scrolls speak of the imminence of the "End of Days." This particular form of eschatology was developed and fully emphasized by Christianity as a central pillar of faith. It received its fullest development in the Book of Revelations and has become a subject for vast literature in Christianity that is popularly known as End Time.

The rabbis concentrated on *halacha,* the systematic development of Jewish law as it was applied to daily life, yet messianic speculation continued. It especially flourished in mystic circles and among those interested in the Kabbalah, Jewish mysticism. It is written in one edition of the Zohar, the classic text of Jewish mysticism, that "In the year 5408 of the Creation of the World the Rebirth will occur" (Zohar I 1396b). Passage after passage in Jewish mystic literature attempts to predict the exact date of "the end of days." Calculating the exact end of time was a favorite pastime of the Jewish community in the Middle Ages.

"False" messiahs mark great epochs in Jewish history. Shabbetai Zvi, David Ruveni, and Jacob Frank induced thousands of Jews to leave their homes and their possessions as they became "convinced" that the Messiah had come and it was the end of history. The fact that these beliefs brought disasters to the community and individual families among Jews is as sad as it is well known.

Small wonder that the outraged mayor of Jerusalem, Teddy Kollek, described the Faithful of the Temple Mount as "dwarfs walking in the steps of Shabbetai

Zvi." Rabbi Shlomo Goren described the ceremony in Jerusalem as "foolishness." *The Jerusalem Post* in an editorial pointed out that the ceremony of the would-be messiahs is a serious provocation to the Muslims, since the site of the Temple is underneath the mosque which is known as the Dome of the Rock. *The Jerusalem Post* went on to say: "Unless it puts these unfunny oddballs in their places, the government will have to bear responsibility for their words and deeds." Many leading Orthodox rabbis in Israel went to great pains to point out that the Third Temple would not be rebuilt by mortals, and the end of time could only be proclaimed by the Messiah.

Speculation and belief in the end of history have always coincided with periods of great suffering, great upheaval, and great change. People search for certainty in an uncertain world, yearn for stability in the midst of terrifying instability. Often the phenomenon appears as humankind approaches the end of one era and the beginning of another. Facing the unknown moves people to see the end of something as a final end. At the end of a period in history there is a tendency to feel that it is the end of history, period.

We are now living through such a time. In front of our eyes Communist countries are abandoning their political orthodoxy, and their influence is rapidly declining. We are looking to the twenty-first century. Vast technological advances such as computers, fax machines, lasers, and genetic manipulation are changing our lives at an unprecedented pace. Jewish life shifts from one moment to the next. We are now in the year 5750, and that number alone tempts us to contemplate its mystical meaning.

Messianic visions are dancing in the heads of some Jews in Israel and thereby causing political and social confrontations, adding to the problems of that state. In the United States, one interpretation of Judaism is actually giving voice to the thought that a specific rabbi is the Messiah. Bumper stickers on cars proclaim the demand, "We want the *Mushiach* now."

Small wonder that talk is surfacing about the end of history. But is history coming to an end or merely changing? Should we not consider that it may be just the beginning of better things?

The Talmud cautions us about talk of the end of history in these strong but wise words: "Cursed be those who calculate the days of the end of history." (Sanhedrin 97b). Thinking about end days as idle speculation is one thing, but misery has come to those who acted on these speculations.

A view of history generally and Jewish history specifically teaches us to be thoughtful, cautious, and patient when faced with a turn of historical events fraught with great challenge. It was all well stated in a classic rabbinic command: "If you are planting a sapling and someone tells you the Messiah has come, first finish planting the sapling and then go out to greet him."

The talk of the end of history and the building of the Third Temple should go into one era and out the other.—1990

10. Shavuot—The Issue of Revelation

Revelation is an issue that dominated medieval Jewish and non-Jewish thinking. How is God revealed to human beings? Is it through the intellect or the emotions?

In rabbinic terms is the concept *torah min hashamaiyim,* "The entire Torah has been revealed from heaven." Even more, every law that a scholar is destined to create has already been given on Sinai. The exact words are to be found in Leviticus Rabbah 22:1, "Even what a faithful disciple would in the future say in the presence of his master, was all communicated on Sinai. Even things which appear to you additions of the actual Revelation (for example, laws of fringes, *tefillin,* and of *mazzuzot)* are also included in the Revelation."

On the other hand is the concept of *torah lo bashaymaiyim hee,* "The Torah is not in the heavens." The full statement can be found in Deuteronomy (30:12-14), "It is not in the heavens . . . no the thing is very close to you, in your mouth and in your heart."

There is a tradition that sustains this view as well, and it is expressed in the following passage in the Talmud (Hullin 49b): "Tradition has it that on that day Rabbi Eliezer advanced every conceivable argument without persuading his fellows. Whereupon he said to them, 'If the law be according to my opinion, then let yon carob tree prove it.' And a carob tree moved one hundred cubits from its place!

"To which they responded, 'What sort of demonstration does a tree afford?' (Just one)

"Whereupon he said to them a second time, 'If the law be according to my opinion, let yon stream prove it.' And the stream flowed backward!

"To which they responded, 'What sort of demonstration does a stream afford?'

"Whereupon he said to them, 'If the law be according to my opinion, let the walls of this academy prove it.' And the walls bent to the point of falling until Rabbi Joshua rebuked them saying, 'When scholars contend with one another, what business have you among them?' And so they did not fall out of respect for Rabbi Joshua, and they did not straighten out of respect for Rabbi Eliezer, but remain slanting to this day.

"Whereupon Rabbi Eliezer persisted and said to them, 'If the law be according to my opinion, let them prove it from on high.' And a heavenly voice sounded forth and said, 'What have you against Rabbi Eliezer after whose opinion the law is always to be framed?'

"At which, Rabbi Joshua arose and said, 'The Torah declares concerning itself, "It is not up in heaven," that is to say, once the Torah was given on Mount Sinai, we pay no heed to heavenly voices, but, as the Torah ordains further, we follow the opinion of the majority.'"

The real issue is, does one have to be a great scholar, intellect, and thinker to know the will of God? Or, can God's presence be found through the emotions, simplicity, devotion and feeling? Is God to be found in the intellect as Maimonides claimed? Or is God to be found in the most ignorant, naive, but sincere shepherd, as the Baal Shem Tov indicated? Is God to be experienced in the mind or is The Holy One's presence to be discovered through the secrets of mysticism? Is the God experience to be found in the head or in the heart? Is the vehicle study or prayer?

Thousands of books have been written on the subject. Endless debates have been held. And one can still find heated discussions not only in theological circles but also in congregational meetings, university symposia, and synagogue gatherings.

The issue of revelation is very much on the agenda today everywhere. Perhaps it is not meant to be resolved. But, from the history of Moses on Mt. Sinai we can learn something about the matter. The lesson is to be found in two separate experiences on that magic mountain.

The most obvious one is the actual giving of the Ten Commandments, a strong, logical, and intellectual statement of morality. We don't know exactly how the process of revelation occurred, but we do know that it has held up intelligently for well over 3,000 years. Thereafter, Jews have devoted their lives to studying and interpreting these words. Clearly, then, one finds God's words revealed and interpreted by the mind.

But Moses had another experience on Mt. Sinai, at the burning bush. This was the first time he experienced the presence of God. The midrash asks why God chose to be revealed to Moses, when such a lowly thing as a wild bush was selected as the means. The answer is that God is to be found in the most humble person and experience on earth. God is everywhere.

Now, we have our answer. It is not an either/or situation. God can be found in the head and in the heart. God is with the intellectual and the ignorant. God is not only in the stars, the sun, and the moon, but also on earth in the grass, the flowers, and the bubbling brook. God is not only in the Bible and books but also in babies and butterflies.

Someone once said to a child, "I will give you an apple if you tell me where God is." The child replied, "And I will give you two apples if you tell me where God isn't."

Or in the words of a famous Hassidic rabbi: "Where is the presence of God? Wherever you choose to admit it!" To which we may add a passage from the Talmud (Hullin 7a): "But our ancestors left a place to enlarge (create new forms). So we were left a place by our ancestors to enlarge (create new forms)."—1991

11. Wrestling with God

The First Dissident: The Book of Job in Today's Politics, by William Safire. New York, Random House.

William Safire in his recent book described Job as the first dissident. Wrong. The first dissident was Abraham ("Shall the judge of all the earth do justly?" Genesis 18:25.) Indeed, in all of Jewish literature Abraham is viewed as the iconoclast and the metaphor for discontent with the divine.

Arguing with God is a Jewish tradition. The name Israel means "wrestling with God." We see this tradition in rabbinic texts, liturgy, Hasidic tales, and Holocaust writings—especially Elie Wiesel, where one finds pronounced dissent, protest, and personal argument with God.

Rabbi Levi Yitzhak of Berdichev, a noted defender of his people, once urged the town's tailor to make his confession publicly in front of the whole congregation. This is what he said: "I, Yankel, am a poor tailor who, to tell the truth, has not been too honest in my work. I have occasionally kept remnants of cloth and I have occasionally missed *mincha* (the afternoon service). But You have taken away children from their parents and parents from their children. So let us settle our accounts and come to terms. If you forgive me, then I will forgive you."

At this point the rabbi benevolently sighed, "O Yankel, Yankel, why did you let God off so lightly?"

Safire takes this human right to challenge God as a right to confront authority. He suggests that Job has attracted artists and thinkers because his story demonstrates the power of dissent to wear down the resistance of authority.

As an added bonus, Safire's book contains reproductions of sixteen plates of William Blake's remarkable illustrations of the Book of Job. They must be studied carefully for they are a stunning commentary of their own.

The Book of Job has been on Safire's mind for a long time, and he did his homework. He studied the major commentaries diligently, ranging from reading the 159 sermons of John Calvin on Job to consulting an aide to the Lubavitcher Rebbe. He has considered the English translation of the Rashi commentary and the works of Robert Gordis, Edwin M. Good, and Matitiahu Tsevat. *The First Dissident* is a brilliant verbal pyrotechnic display of threading the Book of Job through today's politics. It is a thoughtful, provoking, stimulating, and remarkable reworking of Job in terms of daily headlines. It should be read seriously.

Crucial events in the career of Richard Nixon, William Casey, Henry Kissinger, John F. Kennedy, Nelson Mandela, Norman Schwarzkopf, and Malcolm X serve to make ancient work contemporary. The most Joban president was Abraham Lincoln. Lincoln read Job regularly, particularly when he was "wrung by the bitterest anguish and was ready to hang himself."

Once, a free Negro seamstress, Elizabeth Keckly, who made dresses for Mrs. Lincoln, observed Lincoln in a dark mood reach forth his long arms, take a small Bible in his hands, and become absorbed in reading it. After a while, the president seemed more cheerful. The seamstress walked around the sofa and noted that he was reading the Book of Job.

William Safire, a master wordsmith, turns some interesting phrases. God is described as a "celestial cop" who has "other Leviathans to fry." The Book of Job "stands like a Mt. Everest in range of Scripture," and Safire's work is a result of "mental marination." The upper floor of the Hotel Rassiya is the "top of the Marx." Look Ma, I'm writing.

The book has universal appeal because it speaks to anyone who has been blindsided by life (and who hasn't?). Why me? A popular bumper sticker proclaims that a four-letter expletive happens. Life is a five-letter word that rhymes with "rich."

Insufferable outrage eventually ropes us all in. *When Bad Things Happen to Good People* is a popular rewrite of the Book of Job. But why doesn't someone write the companion volume, *When Good Things Happen to Bad People?*

A key verse is 13:15, which the 1611 King James version renders as, "Though he slay me, yet will I trust in him" (sic!), but quickly adds the subordinate phrase, "but I will maintain my own ways before him."

The 1985 Jewish Publication Society translation reads, "He may slay me; I may have no hope; yet I will argue my case before him." Safire phrases it, "If he would slay me, I should not hesitate; I should still argue my case to his face" (In Your Face). Dissident Natan Scharansky unconsciously gave the verse its best interpretation when he said, "I never compromised my soul, even under the threat of death."

Even though the Book of Job is included in the Hebrew Bible, Job, a man of blameless integrity, was not a Jew. He was probably a semi-nomadic chieftain of the tribe of Edom, about whom was constructed the story questioning how an innocent person could be visited with terrible and undeserved suffering. Many times in rabbinic literature spanning hundreds of years we find the statement: "Job never really existed; it was only a parable." Job is a remarkable statement of a universal problem put into the context of particularity.

In essence, the Book of Job comes down to the classic issue of theodicy—justifying God's ways to humans. One side contends (Chapter 38 - Out of the Whirlwind) that the finite mind cannot pass judgment on the infinite or even begin to grasp it. The universe and life are ultimately unknowable. You don't even get the big picture.

The other side argues that it is simply unthinkable that the source of justice should act unjustly. The terrifying question may very well be: "Is God not the ultimate terrorist?" Namely, "If you do not obey me and do not observe all these commandments . . . I will visit terror on you" (Leviticus 26:14ff). What else is left to the human being except self-defense by any means necessary?

The Book of Job crackles between these two poles. Who won? Both sides. It is not easy to be a human. It is not easy to be God.

In the Talmud, unanswered questions are called *tayku,* "in time we will find out." In the meantime, the Book of Job legitimizes dissent.

At the end of his opus, Safire concludes: "I started my journey into this book with doubt in faith and have come out with faith in my doubt."

Theologically speaking, nobody ever promised you a rose garden.—1978

12. Earth Day the Jewish Way

On April 22, 1990, we will mark the twentieth anniversary of Earth Day. However, Jews celebrate Earth Day every year on Rosh Hashanah, the first day of the Jewish year, which marks the first day of creation. Using Jewish tradition as a guide, we might say that the first Earth Day occurred 5,750 years ago.

The concept of Earth Day, expressing our appreciation of nature and our responsibility to the environment, was reinforced in Judaism through ceremonies commemorating Tu B' Shevat, the fifteenth day of the month of Shevat. According to the Mishna this day is the new year of the trees. On this day specific fruits are eaten, psalms are recited, hymns and poems extolling nature are read, and Jewish children plant trees.

The Jewish attitude toward the earth is immediately stated in the first chapter of the Bible in the Creation story. We are told after each of the six days of creation, "God saw that it was good" (Genesis 1:1-2:4). Jews have always understood that it is a Good Earth.

Furthermore, it has always been obvious to Jewish readers that the statement that Adam and Eve were placed in the garden "to till and care for it" (Genesis 2:15) implied responsibility. They singularly understood the phrase "And have stewardship over it" (Genesis 1:28) as meaning never to exploit and destroy it. In light of the entire biblical structure it was clear that humans are only caretakers and guardians of the earth, responsible for its proper maintenance and enhancement.

The Sabbath, as part of its proper celebration, forbids one to interfere in any way with nature for twenty-four hours. Even animals are to be left at rest. Shabbat is a truce with nature. The observance of *schmitta* was introduced to give the land a full year of rest, and it is forbidden to sow fields or prune vineyards every seventh year. On the Jubilee year (fiftieth) this land must not be exploited, and slaves must also be freed. "Sabbath" of the land is simply an expression of letting go and letting God.

The pilgrimage festivals of Pesach, Shavuot, and Sukkot reflect the change of seasons and celebrate the bounties of the earth. Natural resources are not to be taken for granted, but are to be used with reverence and a sense of the holy. Our response and responsibility are clearly delineated in the classic words of Psalm 24, "The earth is the Lord's and all that it holds, the world and its inhabitants."

The irresponsible destruction of the environment, the poisoning of rivers and streams is not only a physical threat but a sacrilege. The stockpiles of highly destructive weapons are not only a threat to our survival but a sin. The frightening changes brought about in the climate are not merely disturbing, they are demonic. In the face of all this, Judaism summons us out of our apathy and our indifference and demands that we act and make a difference.

The classic warning against destruction and wastefulness of our natural resources is to be found in Deuteronomy: "When you are at war and lay siege to a city . . . do not destroy its trees by taking the axe to them, for they provide you with food" (20:14). Based on this verse the early rabbis developed the concept of *baal tashchit,* "Do not destroy." It is forbidden according to *halacha,* Jewish law, to destroy or waste things even that are not needed.

Two more rabbinic concepts sound the call to action for the sake of the earth and its existence. The first is *sakanot nifashot,* "danger to life"; when there is direct or indirect peril to life, one must respond immediately. The second concept is the emphatic charge to save life. Rabbi Ezekiel Landau in the eighteenth century extended this thought to include every living thing. According to the Talmud

(Sanhedrin 74 a-b) all commandments (except the prohibitions against idolatry, murder, and unchastity) may be set aside to save life. This is based on Leviticus 18:5, in which we were told that commandments were given to enable one to live, not die.

When the first *chalutzim* (pioneers) came to Israel, they devoted themselves with a religious-like fervor to restore a neglected and devastated land. Motivated by the moral and ethical imperatives of the Bible, they renewed the desert, cultivated the soil, and cleared the swamps of malaria. With the help of world Jewry and through the Jewish National Fund, over 200 million trees were planted in Israel. In the Jewish state, the highest tribute and a living memorial is a tree. That symbol says more about the Jewish people than an encyclopedia.

The Talmud contains tractates and whole passages dealing specifically with environmental laws: grazing rights, waste disposal, aesthetics and preserving natural beauty, atmospheric and water pollution. Even noise is seriously considered.

Reverence for nature is also built into the ritual of Judaism and its system of blessings. The blessings to be recited over the "four species" on Sukkot, the spices at Havdalah, the appearance of the new moon, and at certain phases of the sun are part and parcel of the Jewish way of life. The *berchot hanhenin,* "the blessings upon enjoying nature," cover almost every conceivable wonder of the natural order: smelling fragrant woods or barks, witnessing lightning, hearing thunder, seeing falling stars, beholding lofty mountains or vast deserts, sighting a rainbow or the ocean, and so forth. This is reinforced by a particularly sensitive passage in the Jerusalem Talmud: "In the future a person will have to give account for everything that his or her eye saw and did not take time to appreciate" (J. Kiddushen 4:12).

Animals are viewed with a special sense of concern and consideration in Jewish tradition, for they, too, partake of creation. The Noachide laws, which are enjoined on all humankind, forbid cruelty to animals. Specific laws in the Bible express concern for animals. They must be given rest on the Sabbath. It is not permitted to muzzle an ox while the animal threshes corn (Deuteronomy 25:4). The eating of animals is severely limited by Jewish dietary laws, and great care is exercised in preparing the food. Only a *schochet,* a person trained in ritual and ethics, is permitted to take the animal's life and, then, in the way least painful. A blessing is to be recited, which is a combined expression of divine permission and something of an atonement. Indeed, according to tradition, when the Messiah comes, society will return to the ideal vegetarian state.

Jews have evolved the concept of *tzar baalay chayim,* "kindness to animals" or literally feeling "that which pains any living thing." Therefore, hunting for sport is scorned. This has direct application to abuse of animal rights. The Jewish attitude toward animals can be found in the biblical verse, "A religious person senses the feelings of an animal" (Proverbs 12:10).

It is particularly disturbing as an American Jew to note that the United States has 5% of the earth's population but uses 25% of the earth's oil, releases 26% of the world's nitrogen oxides, and disposes of 290 million tons of toxic wastes. The typical American discards 1,300 pounds of garbage a year. This is not a mere statistic, it is a moral scandal. For as Leopold Kompert, a Jewish-Austrian novelist of the nineteenth century noted, "Whatever is contrary to nature is contrary to God."

Today, the planet contains 5 billion people. During the next century this figure will double, with 90% of that growth occurring in poorer, developing countries. That means that swarms of people will be running out of space and food. Population may well be the cancer of the earth.

In light of this, it should be noted that Judaism has dealt with birth control. In the Talmud (Taanit Ila), Resh Lakish ruled that it is forbidden to have intercourse in years of famine. His ruling was adopted by the codes. To have only two children is considered sufficient to fulfill the commandment for procreation (Yavamot 6:6). All Jewish authorities agree that under certain circumstances abortion is permitted. David Feldman, a conservative rabbinic scholar, states explicitly: "It would be just as reckless to overbreed as to refrain from procreation." In this matter Jewish scholars based their views on Isaiah: "The Creator ... formed the world not for waste but for habitation" (45:18).

The nagging worry about nuclear accidents is ever present. Hiroshima, Three Mile Island, and Chernobyl are names that touch our deepest fears. Storing enormous amounts of nuclear weapons that might actually be deployed—when the use of a small part of the arsenal would cause irreversible damage to the planet and render impossible the survival of humankind, many species, and vegetation—is a moral scandal. Placing nuclear weapons in space most surely would be the ultimate blasphemy. Was it not written, "The heavens belong to the Lord" (Psalms 115:16). Star Wars is not merely human folly, it is human hubris. Its consequences are almost too horrible to contemplate.

We are given fair warning in the following Midrash (rabbinic comment) (Ecclesiastes Rabbah 7:28):

"When the Holy One created the first person, God took the first human before all the trees of the Garden of Eden, and said, 'See how lovely and how excellent My works are. All that I have created I have created for you. Consider this carefully. Do not corrupt or desolate my world. For if you corrupt or desolate it, there is no one to set it right after you.'"

It is clear from biblical, classic rabbinic, medieval, Hasidic, and contemporary Jewish sources that a strong bond exists between the creator and the created and that all species are bound together in the web of life. Although conservation is now obvious as a matter of self-preservation, it is also a supreme spiritual responsibility.

There is yet hope for the cosmos and humankind. According to Jewish theology there is always time to repent and repair. The very mind that disturbs the order of things may yet change its basic attitude and restore the order of the universe. A renowned nuclear physicist and a Nobel Prize winner was once walking with a companion along the seashore when he saw a beautiful crustacean. The scientist picked it up, examined it cautiously, and then carefully put it back precisely where he found it. His companion asked him why he replaced it so exactly. The scientist replied, "Perhaps I have already tampered too much with the universe."

Perhaps we all have tampered too much with the universe. Now is the time to reform our attitude, rearrange our priorities, and regenerate our planet. It is time for *tikkun olam,* "repairing the damage done to our world." Now is the time for all human beings to come to the aid of their Earth.

A traditional Jew is obligated to say the following prayer before partaking of bread: "Praised are You Adonoy our God, Sovereign of the universe who brings forth bread from the earth."

EVERY DAY IS EARTH DAY.—1980

13. Should a Jew Sell Guns?

Should a Jew sell guns? This is a question that must be faced by Jews who own gun stores. On a larger scale, it must now be considered by the Jewish people. Should the State of Israel continue to be involved in huge arms sales? Weapons kill and killing is contrary to one of the Ten Commandments; it violates the essence of all Jewish teachings—the preservation of life.

Judaism is not a pacifist religion, but a pacific one. It recognizes that weakness invites aggression. It does not advocate turning the other cheek, for this only encourages being struck on that cheek, as well. The Bible makes provisions for an army, and Jewish tradition fully backs a "justified war."

To the question of whether a Jew should sell guns, the answer is clear as stated by Maimonides (Hilchot Rotzeah 12:12, based on Avodah Zotah 15b), "It is forbidden to sell heathens weapons of war. Nor is it permitted to sharpen their spears, or to sell them knives, manacles, iron chains, bears, lions or any object which can endanger the public; but it is permitted to sell them shields which are only for self-defense."

The statement is direct. Now, to the argument that is advanced in the slogan, "Guns don't kill people, people kill people." Maimonides goes on to point out the following: He tells us that in selling arms to a heathen "one strengthens the hands of the evil-doer and causes him to transgress." If there are no guns, then people who have the urge to kill will have a difficult time finding a means.

The issue of the Israeli sale of arms for revenue is more complicated. Israel, with only four million people, is the third largest exporter of arms next to the Soviet Union and the United States.

Some Jewish background: In the face of implacable Arab hatred, Ben-Gurion knew Israel needed an army to defend itself and ensure its survival. Indeed, in the Talmud it is written: "If someone comes to kill you, stand up and kill him first" (Sanhedrin 72b). Of course, what constitutes self-defense is surely debatable.

Israeli businessmen are among the world's leading arms merchants. Israel competes head-to-head with such major industrial powers as Britain, France, and West Germany. The rebel forces in Nicaragua have Israeli-made weapons, as do the regular armies of Honduras, Argentina, South Africa, Chile, Belgium, Holland, Kenya, Singapore, Malaysia, Taiwan, and Thailand—to name but a few. According to widely used estimates, as many as 140,000 Israelis—ten percent of the workforce—are involved in manufacturing or selling military hardware.

If it be argued that the arms industry provides employment and balances trade, we may legitimately ask: Does a moral end justify immoral means? Moreover, what happens to the ideal that Ben-Gurion proclaimed in which Israel was to be "a light unto the nations"? Does this business impair the striving for ethical nationhood?

Shipments of arms to other nations as an instrument of foreign policy is another matter. The Israeli arms sales to Iran are only the latest example of how Israel can use military exports to establish contacts with regimes that would otherwise shun the Jewish state. Like it or not, say Israeli military experts, arms sales are now an integral tool of Israeli foreign policy.

"Were Israeli defense marketing strategies to fail, it would have a profound impact on Israeli security, economic viability and diplomacy," noted Professor Klieman. "Arms sales in the 1980s are a strategic national commitment for Israel."

The use of arms as an instrument of foreign policy is fraught with innumerable dangers. Once a nation embraces a Machiavellian policy, by definition it becomes involved in intrigue and deceit. The use of arms in Lebanon would hardly be called successful and has lessened Israel's moral credibility. Being used as a middleman to ship arms to free hostages is a slippery-slope moral stance. The life of one hostage may be saved, but the arms shipped in exchange will kill dozens of other human beings. Whose blood is redder? Moreover, once nations see that a hostage brings in arms, where will it end? Will ten hostages bring in a squadron of planes? Indeed, are we not all potential hostages? Or, to put it another way, are we not hostage to an unethical and impractical policy as Jews and as Americans as well?

During a recent Knesset debate about arms sales to Iran, these two schools clashed head on. Rabbi Menachem Hacohen of the Labor Party put the moral argument succinctly when he declared on the parliament floor: "Israel should revert to its normal size and avoid involvement in the sale of arms to corrupt regimes. Can the Jewish state afford to supply weapons for dark and deadly purposes?"

There are no easy answers to these issues. They trouble us, and they should. We should discuss them, examine them, and debate them. Whatever we decide, we should be clear about their implications in terms of conscience and consequence. Perhaps, the dilemma was best stated in a remark attributed to Golda Meir. During the end of the sixties she was reported to have directed these words to Nasser: "For killing our sons we can forgive you, but for forcing us to kill your sons we can never forgive you."—1978

14. A Jewish View of the Death Penalty

The movies *Dead Man Walking* and *The Last Dance* and the perception of increasing murders and violence have once more raised the issue of the death penalty. Law enforcement officers, whose lives are on the line and who see the results of violence, as well as approximately half the population, favor it. Those who oppose it include Cardinal O'Connor of New York and retired Supreme Court Justice William J. Brennan, Jr.

It might be interesting and instructive to consider a Jewish view of this recurrent and now intense dilemma. Several Biblical references center on such verses as "If anyone kills any human being, that person shall be put to death" (Leviticus 24:17); and "Fracture for fracture, eye for eye, tooth for tooth" (Leviticus 24:20). Professor Moshe Greenberg of the Hebrew University suggests that such retribution was a moral step forward. Not two eyes for an eye or a whole family for a murder, as the Babylonian and Assyrian codes of that era dictated. Greenberg points out that the instruction "You shall love your neighbor as yourself" is preceded by "You shall not take vengeance" (Leviticus 19:18). These laws were intended to regulate a chaotic and tribal society.

In the next few generations, Jewish law continued to grow and be refined. The early rabbis eventually ruled out physical punishment and substituted monetary retribution. The Talmud clearly said, "The worth of an eye for an eye." "The value of a tooth for a tooth" (Bava Kamma 83b–84a). A person had to be compensated not only for the loss in earning power but for loss in appearance as well.

The death penalty itself was severely restricted. According to ancient Jewish law, many steps had to be taken to condemn a person to death. These were highly complicated and intricate, and if they were not fulfilled, then the death penalty was automatically abrogated. The issue became moot with the destruction of the Temple, for all cases involving capital crimes could only be judged in the confines of the Temple mount (Sanhedrin 37b).

In our own time, when the modern State of Israel was presented with its first murder trial, the two chief rabbis cabled the minister of justice, calling for the immediate abolition of the death penalty. They warned that a capital sentence would be incompatible with and a sin against Jewish law (Elon, *The Principle of Jewish Law,* p. 530). The death penalty is imposed only in the rare case of genocide. Under those rules, only Adolph Eichmann has been sentenced to death. His execution made the statement that his crime and history demanded action of the most extreme kind.

This raises the issue of the victims. It is almost impossible to begin to comprehend the horror, lifelong pain, and extreme suffering of the families and friends of a murdered innocent person. The Biblical words in Genesis resound in our ears: "The blood cries out from the earth."

Over decades, I have counseled families who have had to deal with the loss of a dear one. This is no mere intellectual exercise, but something I have had to struggle with on the deepest emotional level, always remembering the lesser known "You shall not take vengeance."

Genesis teaches that *every* person was created in the image of God. If one person kills another, society has the right—indeed, an obligation—to restrain the killer but not to destroy a person who was also created in the image of God. The ultimate judgment belongs to God alone. Painful though it may be, one must take into account factors such as genetics, mental and emotional illness, family environment, chemical imbalance, peer pressure, and culture. This is not to excuse the perpetrator of a crime but to understand the criminal act. For it was also written in the Talmud, "A person is responsible, whether the action is intentional or inadvertent, whether asleep or awake" (Baba Kamma 2:6).

The Bible is clear: *midah keneged midah,* measure should be met with like measure. A lifetime sentence without probation, which is appropriate for murder in the first degree, provides a punishment that can be equated with the death penalty. After all, money can never replace an eye, yet for the sake of justice, thoughtful leaders were willing, with great effort, to make moral equivalences.

Lest we become smug and self-righteous, let us hold the moral mirror up to ourselves. We live in a culture that caters to killing. We use phrases without a moment's thought about their impact on the impressionable minds of children. "If I catch you doing that again, I'll murder you." Or go to the corner store, flip the pages of the comic books, and what you will see will not be so funny: murders to suit every taste and fancy. We cannot watch two hours of T.V. without seeing some aspect of killing in which the corpse is all but dropped into our laps. And let us hasten to add that the networks, movies, and newspapers give us exactly what we want—murder, mayhem, and crime. Child and spouse abuse open every newscast.

Is this a new phenomenon or simply an old pattern that constantly recurs? How many times have we read in the Bible that the earth was "corrupt and filled with violence"? What period in history was free of heinous crimes? Did the death penalty serve as a deterrent?

We cannot feel guiltless of society's crimes, for we, too, are part of society. Until we exert every moral pressure to change our way of life, we cannot condemn any person to death for any reason. When we do this, we condemn our own selves as well.

Human nature is never a fixed pattern, unalterable for all time. A human being can grow, learning *teshuvah*—sincere repentance in life. We must take a realistic approach to human behavior and not be naive enough to think that a person is without a flame of evil and hate that can burst into a raging, destructive fire at any given provocation. Yet it is not impossible for a person to learn to love, to redeem his or her soul.

For this reason, I am convinced that every person who murders or who commits a serious crime is sick, morally and emotionally. To be sure, a person who offends society should be confined where he or she can receive psychiatric treatment and religious counseling. If after many years, a person can be returned safely to society, well and good. If not, let that person be confined for life. But let us make every reasonable and honest effort to help.

This proposal is not so radical, for it is being done today in Sweden. Every major offender in Sweden is sent to a psychiatric clinic before sentence is passed. Then it is determined where he or she will go—to prison, an asylum, or a hospital. This makes sense.

A person placed in prison and forcibly confined to his or her own thoughts can experience tremendous spiritual growth and ultimately be beneficial to society. The change that is possible is illustrated by the following moving story. Years ago the world was shocked by the Leopold and Loeb thrill-slaying of their cousin. The supreme punishment was demanded, but it was not granted. Loeb, during his imprisonment, became more deranged and was killed in a prison incident. Nathan Leopold, on the other hand, worked, studied, and thought. He learned languages, taught fellow inmates to read, and even let his body be used for experiments. Later, he was paroled to go to Puerto Rico to participate in a health project in an exceedingly poor area. On the day of his release, a reporter asked him what had occupied his mind during his long confinement. He stood there thoughtfully for a moment, blinking in the strong sunlight, and then said, "I spent such time as I had to think, wondering whether I would be worthy of freedom when I received it."

And to think, we might have killed him.—1996

15. One Small Step at Hebron

On Wednesday at 2:45 a.m., January 15, 1997, Shevat 7, 5757, Ramadan 6, 1417, the Israeli Prime Minister, Benjamin Netanyahu, and the Palestinian leader, Yasser Arafat, announced that they had reached an agreement on Hebron. This was documented and witnessed by Dennis Ross, an American mediator, who played a key role in the negotiations. Perhaps lost in this was the fact that this date is also the birthday of Dr. Martin Luther King, Jr.—a rather significant and meaningful day.

Hebron has been in the headlines throughout the centuries. The first headline can be found in a very poignant scene in Genesis 23, when Abraham comes to the Hittites to purchase a burial plot for his wife, Sarah. One can only imagine his sons Isaac, the begetter of the Jewish people, and Ishmael, the founder of the Arab people, standing side-by-side at the Cave of Machpelah, mourning her death.

The term "Hebron" comes from the Hebrew term *haver,* which means "friend." In Arabic it is known as *Al-Khalil,* which also means "friend." At times it is called *Kiryat Arba,* "the place of the four," referring not only to the tomb of Abraham and Sarah, but also Isaac and Rebecca, Jacob and Laeh, and Adam and Eve, all said to be buried in the cave.

King David chose Hebron as his royal city. The first period of Arab conquest (638–1100) was a relief after a time of cruel Byzantine rule. Later, the city was occupied successively by the Crusaders, the Mamelukes, and the Ottomans.

Hebron became a center of Jewish mysticism. Arabs venerated it and called the cave Al-Haram al-Ibrahami (Abraham's shrine). It is clear that both Jews and Muslims throughout the centuries revered this area as the resting place of a common ancestor.

In Isaiah (41:8), Abraham is referred to as *Avraham ohavi,* "Abraham, my friend." The Koran states *Wa-ahaza Allah Ibrahim Khalilah,* "And God took Abraham as a friend." (Sura 4:125). There is a saying in the Middle East: "My friend's friend is my friend." Would that it were so.

Most of the best stone used in building the houses of Jerusalem actually comes from the Hebron area. The stones are harder there and less likely to break under pressure. So are the people—both Arab and Jew.

Arabs often talk about Hebronites as a stubborn lot, referring to the typical town dweller as *ras khalili*—a "Hebron head." This is meant to convey that Hebronites have heads as hard as stones. The sign at the gate of Kiryat Arba, the city's Jewish neighborhood, says, "Kiryat Arba—Zionist Political Settlement. And even as it is tortured it will thrive." The Jewish residents in the heart of Hebron are certainly like the Arabs.

The Arabs of Hebron have a lot in common with the Jews—more than they are willing to admit. Both are deeply committed in their religious beliefs and practices. Indeed, if Hebron's history is anything to go by, bloodshed has always been accompanied by bloodshed.

There was a massacre of the Jewish settlement of Hebron in 1929. This was impressed as deeply on the minds of modern Jews as the recent massacre has been on contemporary Arabs. Violent incidents have included the slaying of twenty-nine Arabs in 1994 by Dr. Baruch Goldstein, a settler who opened fire in the Ibrahimi Mosque, killing and wounding Arabs at prayer. At least six Arabs were wounded January 1, 1997, when Israeli Pvt. Noam Friedman fired into the marketplace. However, vengeance is not only forbidden, it is impractical, for it is a never-ending cycle. The line between martyrs and murderers becomes blurred. In the final analysis, we all suffer.

In truth, neither side in Hebron commands universal strength among its own people. Many Israelis revile the settlers as fanatics who distort Jewish and Zionist values and whose intransigence, they warn, may lead to a cataclysm of incalculable dimensions. And many Palestinians dismiss the Hebron Arabs as little more than inflexible hardheads. Indeed, Palestinians tell Hebron jokes the way some Minnesotans tell Ole and Lena jokes.

The time for acrimony is over. The Hebron agreement, Dennis Ross said, "is indeed a fair and balanced approach to dealing with the concerns each side had."

It is " a very important building block in terms of developing relations between the two sides and in terms of laying out a pathway of greater hope and the possibility of peace in the Middle East as a whole."

Certainly, there will be a great deal of political noise in the aftermath. Many protests, shrill editorials, and expressions of outrage will occur. That will eventually, and hopefully, quickly pass. What must be remembered is that Hebron in Hebrew or Arabic is rooted in the word "friend." Friends don't fight, they share.

In Hebron it was a small step for agreement and a giant step for peace in the Middle East.—1997

16. The Holocaust and American Slavery

I read *Vessels of Evil: American Slavery and the Holocaust* by Laurence Mordekai Thomas and shudders ran through my soul. This parallel study of the real and metaphoric implications of two of the most profound institutionalized evils of our time, American slavery and the Holocaust, was a shattering experience. This kind of study was waiting to be written, and its author is uniquely qualified. An African-American and a Jew, he is professor of philosophy and political science and a member of the Judaic Studies program at Syracuse University.

The reality is that people of ordinary moral decency can be swept up in social tides and do what, heretofore, would have been unimaginable even in their own eyes. To account for this dilemma, Thomas turns away from the theology of innate evil and fashions a model of "fragility-goodness" in which human beings are not generally disposed to perform great self-sacrifices on behalf of strangers. People are influenced by the "moral drift" of their times. Moreover, the author writes, individuals can choose not to choose. Human beings are capable of compartmentalizing their lives.

The Holocaust and American slavery were profoundly evil in radically different ways. Whereas the murdering of Jews in the camps was shrouded in secrecy, nothing of the sort was true of slavery. The Nazi ideology toward Jewish children and adults was the same: both were to be exterminated. By contrast, although slave owners devastated families, their purpose was to preserve blacks and exploit them for economic benefit.

The objective of the Holocaust was the extermination of the Jewish people. Judaism, in Western thought, gave birth to the concept of salvation and then rejected it. Indeed, the belief went, Jews killed Christ, the very bearer of world salvation. Christ reportedly accuses the Jews of having the devil as their father (John 8:42-47). Satan not only is evil but is irredeemably evil. The implications are obvious.

In a reasonable manner, Thomas describes "common sense" morality, beginning with the decent person who does not harm others. Then there are those of deeper conscience, such as the abolitionists, the "underground railroad," John Brown, William Lloyd Garrison, and Wendell Phillips. There are more than 10,000 "righteous gentiles," cities like Le Chambon and Delft, and remarkable individuals, such as Oscar Shindler, who saved thousands of Jews.

An ultimate evil, as Thomas' telling points out, is that of natal alienation, which renders a people without a narrative. This is a form of extinction. Aside from the death of slaves in the Middle Passage, the historical memories of Africa were wiped out. Thus a whole people was formed without historical moorings. This was different for Jews who, no matter what, were held together by tradition that was thousands of years old.

In light of this, one can only applaud the rise of African-American studies, the heroic efforts of members of the black community and other forces to create a tradition that will empower and sustain them.

Casting aside cliches, Thomas concludes with the relationship between blacks and Jews today in a most balanced manner. Admittedly there is some anti-Semitism among blacks and a measure of racism among Jews; the challenge is to understand those feelings. Jews and blacks have a history of alliance and argument, but each group must internalize the knowledge that it is useless, if not degrading, to hate back widely and ignorantly.

When groups are deeply motivated to wrestle with the suffering of the other, when there is a commitment to a common good and a narrative to give a group identity, there is hope for the future. It is either chaos or community.—1995

17. Who Needs Angels?

Who needs angels? God or humans?

To the human mind it is virtually inconceivable that the Creator administers the innumerable and infinitesimal tasks of the universe without a large celestial bureaucracy. Indeed, there are *tzvaot hashamayim* (the Heavenly Hosts), *famalia* (family or consultants), *mahlawchay hasharet* (angels of service), *chayot hakodesh* (holy beings), *serafim* (fiery entities), and *ofanim* (wheels) to accomplish this purpose. Sometimes they serve as consultants, other times as choirs singing praise to God, and on other occasions they are put to specific tasks.

The basic Hebrew term for angel, *malach,* "messenger," is inexact and often refers to a human agent. The term is rendered in the Greek as *angelos,* which has the same meaning. Some scholars believe the concept is derived from the Akkadian term *kerub* (cherub), which was depicted as a figure with the head of a human, the wings of a bird, and the body of an animal.

The Bible is filled with angels. The angels that visit Abraham, the angels on Jacob's ladder, the angel at the burning bush, the angels who appear to Hagar, Balom, Joshua, Gideon, and Daniel. The verse in Psalms (91:11-12) sums up the personal feeling about angels: "For God will order angels to guard you wherever you go. They will carry you in their hands lest you stumble on a rock."

In some views, it is impossible in a pure, monotheistic view of God for angels (other beings) to exist. No one has truly seen an angel; contemporary sightings are subject to vast speculation. Feeling the presence or the effects of angels is a highly personal experience. That is why there is vast debate in the Talmud and Midrash as to the existence, origin, and nature of angels. Some rabbis contend that there are at any given time 100 million angels. They are given names: Azriel, "Helper of God"; Raphael, "Healer of God"; Uriel, "Light of God."

Maimonides came down firmly against the veneration of angels. He observed on the practice of appealing to angels: "True penitence does not stand in need of intervention by the saints; feigned penitence will not be helped by either the saints, by man or angel."

With the rise of mysticism (Kabbalah), angelology took off with renewed vigor. The appearance of the Zohar in the thirteenth century gave belief in angels new life. Pages are devoted to specific details as to the names and functions of angels.

Of course, there are evil angels. How else in the popular mind can one account for evil in a world created by a compassionate God? The Angel of Death *(Malach Hamavet)* is the source of feared death. Satan comes from *sitna* (hatred or adversary), for how else can one account for evil in society? (The Devil made me do it). Also, one must not forget the fallen angels (half divine and half human); Lillith, the she-demon; and the dybbuk, who possesses souls and causes them to be demented, hysterical, or violent.

But, then again, can these not be projections of our own feelings and emotions, as well as our own lack of understanding of mental illness? As Adin Steinsaltz says, "Destructive angels created by human evil-doing is the objectification of malevolence."

The prayer book is ambivalent on angels. There are constant references to them in subtle ways, particularly through the soaring hymns of the mystics. Yet, when the Ark is opened, before the Torah is read, a prayer has been inserted which contains the line, "Not in humans do we put our trust, nor upon any angel do we rely, but only upon the God of heaven."

Angels can be rebuked. The classic instance in early rabbinic literature is found when the Hebrews are fleeing Egypt and the Egyptians are drowning in the sea. The angels in Heaven begin to sing hymns of praises. God silences them with, "The creations of My hands are drowning in the sea and you dare sing praises!"

Then there is the tale of Rabbi Moishe of Kobin who once lifted his head heavenward and exclaimed: "O angel on high, it takes no special effort to be an angel in heaven. You need neither food nor drink. You do not need to bring children into the world and then struggle to see them reared properly. Just come down to earth and let us see if in obligation to all these things you will remain an angel. If you succeed in that, you may well boast of your angelic character. But not until then."

There is a Hasidic doctrine *(chavruta)* that teaches that we create our own angels. The Rabbi of Kobrin interpreted the famous dream of Jacob's ladder to mean that man is the ladder standing on earth, with the top rung reaching heaven. Whether angels are going up or down depends entirely on what a human being does.

This echoes a Talmudic legend that tells that every Friday night when a person leaves a synagogue, he or she is accompanied by a good angel and a bad angel. If one is in a kind, warm, and loving mood, the bad angel is forced to say, "Amen." On the other hand, if one is in a bitter, angry, or hateful mood, the good angel is forced to say, "Amen."As Rabbi Morris B. Margolis noted, "The Hebrew word for angel, *malach,* does mean 'messenger.' But the message is one of our own making."

If we choose to eliminate kindness, justice, and peace from our lives, we create a vacuum that will soon be filled by the demonic. If we seek harmony, understanding and compassion, angels are at hand.

The choice is ours.—1995

18. Why the Jews?

Purim is the metaphor for anti-Semitism. Haman, the symbol of *seenat chinam,* "causeless hatred," represents all anti-Semitism from Hitler and Stalin to Father Coughlin and the elder Henry Ford to Torquemada and Chmelnitzky. But what Jews, as well as thoughtful non-Jews, have often wondered is, "Why the Jews?"

There is no intelligent, rational answer to this question because anti-Semitism is irrational. A simple illustration of this irrationality can be found in anti-Zionism. Why are 120 million Arabs afraid of a little more than 3 million Jews? Why did the whole United Nations vote that Zionism is racism? Israel just took in thousands of black Jews. If it weren't so tragic, it would be comic.

There are times when we can find specific causes for anti-Semitism, such as when Hitler used the Jews as a scapegoat for Germany's problems, or several years ago, when Jews were on the wrong side of the civil war in Morocco. In addition, there is fanatical religious hatred, such as the philosophy of the Ayatollah Khomeini in Iran. Sometimes there is a severely disturbed individual who is paranoid, and his or her paranoia fixes on a Jew or all Jews. These reasons are simple and clear. But what causes anti-Semitism in general is very complex. I would like to offer just three of the most prominent explanations.

The first is that Jews are different, and in a society people tend to distrust those who are different. This is a well-known psychological truism. For example, most nations read from left to right. Jews read from right to left. Men worship without head-coverings and Jews wear a *kipah.* Christians have Sunday as a day of rest, Moslems have Friday, but Jews have Saturday. And so on back to ancient times.

When Jews in the times of the Greeks refused to run naked in athletic contests and would not eat pig meat, the Greeks laughed at them for being stupid. In Roman times, when Jews would not worship the Emperor Caligula as a deity, he was enraged and made fun of them because they worshiped a God that no one could see, and, therefore, did not exist. The Romans laughed at the Jews because they took a day of rest, and they thought Jews were even more stupid because they gave their employees a day of rest.

So it has been all down the ages. We are a people with a unique set of rules, principles, and customs. We are almost always a minority and yet we rarely deviate from our rules, so the majority tends to look down on us. Whether we are right or wrong—or if there even is a right or wrong—does not matter. The fact is that we are different. In a sense, we are alien, and people fear those who are different.

Another reason for anti-Semitism is built into Christianity, the dominant religion in the world. The Torah, the Jewish Bible, is religious literature based on peoplehood. By interesting contrast, the New Testament is a series of religious theological tracts justifying Christianity. They are polemics written in heat and controversy trying to explain why Christianity broke off from Judaism. Everybody knows that pamphlets and articles written in controversy to justify a position tend to be extreme, and sometimes even distorted, to prove the point. This is the basis of the New Testament, as all Christian scholars will agree.

Unfortunately for the Jews, it has been raised to the level of Scripture and becomes the Holy Bible, the literal word of God: namely, the Gospel. Do we not use the phrase "the gospel truth"? Christians constitute one-fourth of all the people in the world; in the western hemisphere where we live, their percentage is closer to two-thirds.

Now, I do not wish to argue, but I want to point out that the New Testament is the most anti-Semitic book in history, particularly the Book of John. In the synoptic Gospels, the Jews cry out: "Crucify him! Crucify him!" So we become the Christ-killers. The fact of the matter is that Jews have never practiced crucifixion. The fact of the matter is that Jews never laid a finger on Jesus. The fact that there are many discrepancies in the four accounts of the crucifixion makes no difference whatsoever. The Bible says in Matthew (27:25): "And all the people answered [meaning the Jews], 'His blood be on us and on our children." This has been read every Easter for generations. Small wonder, then, that pogroms began on this day, and Jews approached this season with great terror in their hearts.

We could even go from the sublime to the ridiculous. The Last Supper was the Pesach meal. The fact that Jesus was a Jew, his mother was a Jew, all the disciples were Jews, even Paul was a Jew, makes very little difference to the anti-Semite. The fact that the New Testament is based on the Old Testament completely makes no difference to the Jew-hater. The existence of the centuries-old charge of deicide, of killing God, against the Jews, is absurd. If God is God, how can one kill the Eternal One?

This observation made no difference whatsoever in the church until just a few years ago. Now in many contemporary churches and theological schools these stories are set in the proper context. But most Christians consider these passages to be literal truths. With every generation, Christians have to be taught the historical context of the New Testament all over again. I do not cite this as reason to despair but simply to point out some facts that go into the making of anti-Semitism.

A third reason was suggested by Sigmund Freud and is worth considering. He said that in all societies when a father figure, whether it be a person or a group, presents an ethical code, there is a tendency to backlash because of an unconscious resistance to morality. Consider for a moment. Jesus, Gandhi, and Martin Luther King Jr. were all murdered. Now, the Jews were the first people to present a systematic ethical code to civilization. Freud argues that anti-Semitism is an expression of the unconscious desire to get even for the restraints placed on people by civilization. Moses and the prophets proclaimed a strong ethical code. On the conscious level people adopted and integrated these concepts into their system, but on an unconscious level they resented it, as often expressed through anti-Semitism.

One might consider: why it is that Hebrew was the language for the Ten Commandments and the Moral Code? Why was it that two Jews, Avraham Einstein and Shlomo Freud, shaped our thinking about our outer world and our inner world? Why was it that President Roosevelt used to refer to Justice Brandeis as "my Isaiah"? Why did the Jews, being .001% of the world's population, produce 15% of the Nobel Prize winners? Why did Jews like Sabin and Salk and hundreds like them, who have saved the lives of millions of children, have their origins disparaged? Why keep hating us? We didn't do anything to you. We only helped you.

Having said all this, what is to be done about it? As far as I am concerned, the answer is twofold, with a simple conclusion. Jews have to continue educating people about what Judaism really is. The possible anti-Semite says things that just are not true. Take, for example, the blood libel belief, namely that we kill non-Jewish children and put their blood in the matzah. That is absurd. We are forbidden to taste blood. That is why we even soak our meat in salt to remove the blood. As Meyer Levine, the American novelist, once said: "Anti-Semitism is not to be overcome by getting people to forget us but to know us."

The second thing, I think, is that we have to determine in our own hearts that nothing is going to get us down and nothing is going to knock us out. It never has and it never will. And so, as Israel Abrahams, the British scholar, said: "For the Jews the moral is to answer anti-Semitism with more Semitism, if by Semitism we mean greater devotion to the great ideals which Judaism proclaimed to the world."—1983

19. America is Choice

America is choice. Our ancestors chose to come here to escape persecution of the body and repression of the mind. They chose to fight for their freedoms. They chose to create a constitution and a democracy to guarantee the right of choice.

I believe in the sanctity of life. But I also believe in the sacred right of each person to define life—its meaning, its quality, and its style. When those rights come into conflict, it is the individual's right to choose the approach in keeping with his or her convictions.

It is contrary to the principles of a democratic America and conscience for anyone to control our bodies, dominate our brains, or designate our beliefs. Terms like "person" and "viability" are highly subjective. It stands to reason that in these matters, as in so many others, nobody has a lock on the truth. Everyone's interpretation and definition deserves equal respect.

Furthermore, our ancestors came here from their homelands because one group of people decided that their particular form of religion should be imposed on everyone. Our ancestors found this entirely unacceptable—and rightly so. Were we to permit one religious way of thought to dominate our society and deny choice, then we would breach the wall of separation between church and state that was so carefully erected by those who came before us. It would establish a precedent that could come back to haunt every religious denomination and each one of us.

Therefore, let us abort efforts to restrict our freedom of choice. Let us terminate all threats to the form of democracy that has benefited all of us. Let us be pro-life for the right of each American to pursue liberty free of legislation, intimidation, and a single religious view. For unless all are free in body, mind, and spirit, none are free.

Now is the time for all good people to come to the aid of freedom of choice—a basic historic American principle.—1979

20. America is a Salad

Success has a thousand parents; failure is an orphan. The fires of Los Angeles cast harsh new light on the reality of America. Emerging from the orgy of blame is the common acknowledgement that some are guilty, but all are responsible. There is an urgent need to change.

We all now know that we must restructure the priorities, purpose, and vision of America. Indeed, the definition of "America" has never been set; it has always been a process and a dynamic.

In the middle of the eighteenth century, a French immigrant named J. Hector St. John de Creve-coeur posed the question, "What then is the American?" He saw America as a transforming nation melting away ethnic differences.

This concept has generally dominated the history of the United States. As Arthur Schlesinger Jr. has pointed out, however, during these past few decades a new conception of America began to form. The dominance of male Anglo-Saxons is giving way to enriching diversity.

Women, Americans of South and East European ancestry, African Americans, Native Americans, Hispanics, Asians, Jews, Muslims, and homosexuals are raising their voices to highlight the indispensable contributions they have made to American civilization. The melting pot model is obsolete. In its place is the new and refreshing view of America as a salad.

A salad is made up of many ingredients. Each preserves its own integrity, yet only together do they make a tasty dish. Putting these ingredients through a blender only creates a bland, homogenized, tasteless pulp. America is multicultural, a many-splendored thing, each component with its own uniqueness. Masking the components into a monolith renders them meaningless, if not volatile.

The challenge we face is stated in the classic phrase *e pluribus unum,* "out of many, one." How can we preserve our individuality and yet remain in concord? Or how can we retain unity yet foster diversity? The answer to these questions is our great challenge and outlines the making of the new American. What is ultimately at stake is the American future.

The new American must learn to cherish and nurture the uniqueness of each ethnic group and yet not give in to "romantic" ethnicity. The new American must encourage spirituality, not triumphalism. The new American must see race as a biological phenomenon, not as an excuse for prejudice.

The new American must understand the dual purpose of democracy: to give expression to the will of the majority and to protect the rights of the minority. One-issue politics, "identity politics," personality politics—all are a distortion of the meaning of America and contain the seeds of their own disintegration. We must learn to live with difference or we will destroy ourselves. We must develop the art of compromise or our society will decompose.

The *unum* of America informs us that the poor, sick, and homeless who roam city streets are not the citizens or the products of Los Angeles or Detroit or Chicago or Washington, D.C. They are the poor, sick, and homeless of America. The looting of stores in Los Angeles is simply the reverse of the scandals of the savings-and-loan debacle. They are both part of the crime called "the greeding of America." The abuse of drugs is in the suburbs as well as the inner city.

If there were enough jobs, there would not be a need for affirmative action or welfare reform. If there was hope and opportunity, there would not be despair and anger, rage and riots. If there were more educational opportunities, more health care, more concern for children, there would be less despair, less self-abasement, and less societal destruction. If there was true justice and compassion in the land, there would be no need to act out pain, humiliation, and deep hurt.

America still has the potential to be the land of the free and the home of the brave. With all our faults, we are still basically committed to political democracy, the rule of law, human rights, and cultural freedom. When the Chinese students protested and died for democracy in Tiananmen Square, they brought with them a large cast of the Statue of Liberty. When *Vista,* a monthly publication for Hispanics, asked its readers which historical figures they most admired, Washington and Lincoln led the list, with Eleanor Roosevelt and Martin Luther King Jr. close behind. When the Soviet Union and Eastern Europe began to break up, it was the American economic system that they used as a model to rebuild their economies.

The American identity will never be fixed and final; it is always in the making. The late Gunnar Myrdal in his classic work on racism wrote, "America is continually struggling for its soul." America is always on a quest and defining responsibility. The word "questioning" contains the word "quest" and the word "responsibility" is based on the word "response."

If this sounds like a sermon, then so be it. In the end it always comes down to values. The text comes from the Talmud in the words of Rabbi Hillel, who lived in the first century: "If I am not for myself, who will be? If I am for myself alone, what good am I? If not now, when?"

The commentary is from the American Scriptures as written by Abraham Lincoln in his Second Inaugural Address: "With malice toward none; with charity for all; with firmness in right, as God gives us to see the right, let us strive to finish the work we are in; to bind up the nation's wounds . . . to do all that which may achieve and cherish a lasting peace among ourselves."

America is a nourishing salad. Second helping, anyone?—1992

21. A Jewish View of the Messiah

Most contemporary Jews view the messiah idea as a Christian concept. Yet its origin is Jewish and it is worth examining its place in Jewish tradition.

The word messiah is an anglicized version of the Latin *messias.* This, in turn, is an adaptation of the Aramaic *meshicha,* which is a translation of the fuller Hebrew term *hamelech hameshiach,* the "anointed king." This refers to a descendant of David who was endowed with special powers to bring the Jews from exile and rule over Israel. According to the Hebrew Bible, the kings of Israel, like David, were chosen by God. As a sign of consecration to the Lord, oil was poured on top of the head of the king when he was crowned, anointing him. The term was particularly strong during the Roman period when the Jews believed that a descendant of David would be raised up by God to break the yoke of the heathen, restore the kingdom of Israel, and gather all Jews back to the homeland.

Very little of this is to be found in the Bible itself. In the Book of Isaiah we find a small shift of thought from the emphasis on the Davidic dynasty that would last forever to the fact that the Divine King would also be distinguished by his passion for justice. Here we see the addition of an ethical and universal characteristic. Very little further is said about a messiah king in the Hebrew Bible. All references ascribed to the messiah in the Torah (Hebrew Scripture) are simply misinterpretations from the Jewish point of view.

The messiah idea, fully developed as someone who will save all mankind and come at the climax of history to establish the Kingdom of God, is a rabbinic concept. In the Talmud we find that the purpose of the messiah is to restore the people of Israel to the land, to bring in the blessings of the prophets, to introduce a period of spiritual and physical bliss. He was to be a prophet, warrior, judge, king, and teacher of Torah—a sort of spiritual superman.

There were a variety of beliefs about him. He was born in Bethlehem or in Jerusalem on the day of the Temple's destruction. He is hiding in Rome or in heaven, waiting for the time of redemption. He will come riding on a donkey or triumphantly flying on the clouds.

At the beginning of the first century a new Jewish sect began using the name Christians. It centered about a Davidic messiah who came once and will come again. The word Christian comes from the word *christos,* the Greek word for messiah. Christos, too, means "the anointed one." Later this concept became the center of a new and powerful worldwide religion known as Christianity. While the belief in the messiah is at its core, its ethical ideas are basically Jewish.

In the Middle Ages there were many messianic movements among Jews. There were many false messiahs; that is, Jews who claimed to be the messiah. Interestingly enough, these movements occurred when Jews were under extreme pressure of persecution. At those times, quite naturally, Jews needed a source of comfort and inspiration. But these movements always ended in tragedy.

In modern times classic Reform Judaism rejected the messiah idea and removed this term from the prayer book. Extreme Orthodox Jews, on the other hand, insisted that no great event in Jewish life could be achieved without the messiah. That is why they opposed the formation of the State of Israel. As a matter of fact, some extreme Orthodox Jews still will not acknowledge the state even when they live in Israel. Most Jews appear to be in between. They speak of *y'mot hameshiach,* "a messianic age." This means a vague time of world peace, justice, and good will. It is something that we all hope for, yearn for, and towards which we work. It is a direction and a destination rather than a goal.

The main body of contemporary Jews would undoubtedly agree with the rabbi who wrote about eighteen centuries ago: "If you had a sapling in your hand and were told that the Messiah had come, first plant the sapling, then go out and greet him."

Every age creates its own legends and stories about the messiah, reflecting its own needs and aspirations. There is a modern *midrash* about the messiah, and it happens to be true.

A young woman who has an excellent Jewish education and is interested in the feminist movement lives in New York and summers in Jerusalem. In downtown Manhattan the members of the Lubavitch group gather and, as men come out of the subway, they ask them to put on *tifillin* and ask the women to light the Sabbath candles. One day, this young woman was coming out of the subway in Manhattan and a Lubavitcher came up to her and asked, “Are you Jewish?” She said, “Yes.” He further asked, “Do you light *Shabbos* candles?” She replied, “Yes.” And then she added, “In fact, every day I put on *tifillin.*”

The Lubavitcher was shocked and said, “Why do you do that?” She replied, “There is an old teaching that when all Jews will put on *tifillin* the *meshiach*, the messiah, will come.” And the Lubavitcher said, “And when will that be?” And the woman replied, “Whenever she decides.”

When will the messiah come? The answer, from a Jewish point of view, is, “Whenever he, she, or it decides.”—1983

22. Boxed In

Recently, a Korean boxer, Duk Koo Kim, died as a result of injuries received in a boxing match in the world capital of boxing: Las Vegas, Nevada. One newspaper account said he was literally “beaten to death” by his opponent, Ray Mancini, the World Boxing Association lightweight champion.

In Miami, Alexis Arguello was endangered in a boxing match when he was hit in the head twelve times by Aaron Pryor. After the fight was stopped, Arguello was stretched out on the floor with an oxygen mask held to his face.

Sugar Ray Leonard just retired from the ring after he had surgery for a detached retina. At the age of twenty-six, he did not want to face any more beatings and injuries.

Events like these force us to pause and take a second look at professional boxing. Millions of people pay millions upon millions of dollars to see these matches. What brings them there? Entertainment, fascination, horror, sport, blood lust? Whatever the attraction, the fundamental question remains: is it right to derive amusement from watching men fight one another, knowing that there is a risk that one might be killed? Exactly what is the moral question involved when two men climb into a ring and, at the sound of a bell, begin to fight each other?

The prime aim of boxing is to render an opponent unconscious. This is done by repeated blows to the head. The strikes on the body generally are only a diversionary measure, to free the real target—the head—in order to secure a technical or a real knockout.

Scientists indicate that the human brain weighs about three pounds. It is fluid-packed, but not secured, within the skull. A blow to the head causes the fluid to wobble, slide, and bounce back and forth inside its cranial container. A strong blow can cause the brain to slam against a bony ridge and result in bruising and bleeding. When nerve cells are repeatedly destroyed, the damage becomes permanent.

The professional fighter is trained to such a degree that his right hand has the force of a baseball bat. Ben Skelton, a sparring partner of the heavyweight champion Sonny Liston, reported that Liston's left jab was so hard "that for a week after being hit with it I was taking pain pills." It is estimated that 85% of the blows land on the head or the face. Is it then any wonder that 60% of all professional fighters end up with mild to severe emotional and mental changes, which we laymen call being "punch-drunk?" The only surprise is that more fighters are not killed in the process.

Professional boxing is unique among the sports. It is the only sport whose primary objective is to batter and render an opponent helpless and unable to continue. In other sports, the object is to put a ball across a goal line, through a basket, or into a net. In these other sports, injury is incidental, and unnecessary roughness is penalized. Special head protection is worn to prevent permanent damage. But in boxing the infliction of bodily damage is rewarded.

This is exactly what brings the attendance—the lust to maim and kill. It is nonsense to talk about prize fighting as a test of boxing skill. No crowd was ever brought to its feet screaming and cheering at the sight of two men skillfully dodging and weaving out of each other's jabs. When this occurs the referee steps in and tells them "to mix it up." The crowd comes alive the moment a man is hit hard over the heart or the head, when his mouth sags, when blood squirts out of his nose or eyes, when he wobbles under the attack and his pursuer continues to beat him senseless with blow after blow.

Mike Jacobs, who was generally agreed to be the most knowledgeable person in boxing, was once asked by Norman Cousins if people really came out to see the killer. Mr. Jacobs said evenly, "They don't come out to see a tea party. They come out to see the knockout. They come out to see a man hurt. If they think anything else they're kidding themselves."

In view of these truths, which clearly present us with a moral problem, what should the religious attitude—specifically, the Jewish attitude—be toward professional boxing?

Let it first be noted that Jews have generally been interested in sports that were natural, that promoted the well being of the body, involved muscular coordination, and gave the spectator harmless pleasure. The Bible records sixteen kinds of sports that were most common. They include archery, swimming, running, and weight lifting, activities that are products of the exuberance of a hardy people.

In Talmudic times the rabbis held a view midway between the Pauline extreme of "bodily exercise profiteth little" (1 Timothy 4:8) and the Hellenistic devotion to physical culture. They cited Isaiah (58:11) to prove that "strong bones," i.e. a healthy body, was the best of blessings.

Later on, in the Middle Ages, Maimonides wrote that it is a mitzvah, a positive commandment, to find some form of exercise to promote good health (Hilkhot Deot 4:14-15). A responsum of Rabbi Moses Provencal, given at Mantua in the year 1560, even permitted the playing of hand tennis on the Sabbath!

All of this indicates the rabbis' encouragement of healthy forms of sport. But when it came to the worship of the body per se, or bodily harm, they drew the line emphatically. They first set this general principle of conduct: "He who lifts his hand against another, even though he did not smite him, is called wicked" (Sanhedrin 58b).

There are even specific references to boxing in the Talmud. This is not a modern form of entertainment, for it can be traced directly to the brutal Roman gladiator contests. The rabbis warned against attendance at the Roman circus, the theater, and other institutions where men were pitted in violence against each other or beasts for the pleasure of the mobs. In fact, one rabbi of the first century went so far as to say, "He who sits in the stadium and observes these bouts (gladiatorial matches) is guilty of shedding blood" (Yeramot Avodah Zarah 1:7). Even though this is an extreme statement, it gives vent to the feeling that any sport that involves violence and the shedding of blood, such as boxing or hunting, turns the stomach of the Jew.

Rahmanut (compassion), the rabbis maintained, was one of the three distinguishing marks of the Jew. In the Jewish pyramid of values, compassion stood at the highest point. The Talmud, as well as the Bible, contains passage after passage dwelling on this theme. Conversely, cruelty is considered as the worst of all the vices. The prophet Jeremiah condemns those who "lay hold on bow and spear. They are cruel and have no compassion."

Jewish sensitivity can be told in many ways. The following is a delightful but not uncommon story. An elderly Jewish grandmother on a hot summer's day was annoyed by a fly. She summoned one of her grandchildren and asked him to get rid of it. The child became particularly vigorous in pursuit of the fly. The elderly woman said quietly but firmly, "Chase it out, but be careful not to kill it for it is also a creature of God."

This is an expression of the Jewish reverence for life. Judaism is founded on the ideal of preserving and enhancing life. Anything that reduces pain and suffering, channels our anger in harmless avenues, and raises our level of feeling for others and for life itself is to be encouraged. On the other hand, anything that is harmful to others, that stirs our hate unnecessarily, or that destroys life is to be condemned and rejected.

William James, the father of American psychology, wrote an important essay at the beginning of this century, *The Moral Equivalent of War,* in which he pointed out that every society contains aggressions, competitiveness, and the urge to conquer. The only real issue is how these emotions are to be directed and channeled. The energy is there; how shall it be expressed and released?

Other societies have already demonstrated the way. In Japan a great national competitive event is the Tanbata Matsuri Festival. The entire Japanese population watches intensely as poets submit a special form of poetry and the winner is chosen. In Israel the *Hidon Ha-Tanakh* is an annual event in which Israelis compete in a national Bible contest. It is as exciting as anything one could imagine. In Holland the annual tulip festival is a tremendous event as the Dutch bring forth a variety of strains of the magnificent tulip plant.

Americans, as well, have many forms of good, healthy, national pastimes. Baseball and basketball are American creations. They help build physical fitness, and there is nothing more exciting than to watch the World Series or the annual state high school basketball tournament. The point is, there are many ways other than through blood and gore in which we can express our competitive feelings.

And while there are injuries in football and hockey, the primary purpose of these games is to score points and not purposefully harm an opponent. Injuries in these sports are by-products of physical exertion. Indeed, conscious harm ("roughing") is penalized.

It should be remembered that what we consider manly has a profound effect on our children. There was a direct connection between the Roman gladiator and the fine Roman art of crucifixion. There was a real relationship between the German dueling societies and the Nazi cruelty and barbarism. What we define as "manliness" is the goal of our society. What do our children see in our amusements? War or peace? Creation or destruction? Horror or hope? In our nation, dog fighting, cock fighting and bear baiting have been banned, but man fighting is still a permissible "sport."

It is never easy to question the moral character of our pleasure and entertainment. However, moral issues are not defined by the convenient or the inconvenient, the pleasant or the annoying. They reach to the division between good and evil, and this is the balance in which we must weigh all human conduct and activity. So long as we openly sanction brutality, we cannot expect to resolve the terrifying conflicts of the nuclear age in a peaceful and orderly way. We must look first to modifying our own individual appetites for savagery.

When one man, created in the image of God, beats senseless another man, created in the image of God, and this is applauded and cheered by other men, created in the image of God, it is offensive, brutish, and destructive, and, therefore, should be shunned by civilized human beings.—1982

23. Jesus in Contemporary Jewish Thought

Jesus in contemporary Jewish thought is seen as a Jewish teacher and miracle maker. He is part of the theological and social scene of the first century in Judea where such personalities abounded. Against a background rife with messianic speculation, it would be understandable that among his followers were some who deemed him a redeemer of mankind.

Jesus was a Jew named Joshua; his mother was named Miriam, and all his disciples were Jewish. The Synoptic Gospels (Matthew, Mark, and Luke) provide sufficient evidence that Jesus did not oppose any prescription of the written or oral Mosaic law. His beliefs, especially his moral teachings, are similar to the Pharisaic school of Hillel, which stresses the love of God and neighbor. However, he also accepted part of the Essene social outlook.

Although Jesus taught essentially in the mainstream of Judaism, he was unique in the great beauty of his language and the powerful simplicity of his illustrative stories or parables, in his humility and his obvious love for the poor and miserable. Maimonides, the authoritative Jewish philosopher of the Middle Ages, attributed his mission to the divine plan to bring the essentials of Judaism to a pagan world. Where Judaism parts with Christianity is not on the religion of Jesus, but the religion about Jesus.

Basically, Jews could not accept certain ideas that Paul introduced and were associated with Jesus. The ideas of a "god" dying and being reborn, of a child being born to a divine father and a human mother, or of joining one's god through eating sacred food were inimical to the Jewish way of life. Moreover, Jews did not need a new avenue to salvation because they already had the Torah and the Commandments. However, it was felt that the teachings of Jesus and the later interpretation of his theological role by Paul and others—the basis of Christianity—was a valid faith for others and a worthy route for salvation.

Statements in rabbinic literature that mention Jesus by name or that allude to him and to his actions are few. Nothing negative has been transmitted in the names of the rabbis from the early half of the first century. Polemics against the Christian dogmas that Jesus was the Messiah, the son of God, and God, are found in homilies and sayings of the rabbis of the third and fourth centuries. These homilies are merely a reply to the Christological interpretations of the Church Fathers who sought to find proof and supports for their teachings in the Jewish scriptures.

Jewish writings about Jesus in the Middle Ages are surprisingly gentle when seen in the light of Christendom's anti-Jewish edicts, inquisitions, forced conversions and disputations, the burning of the Talmud, blood libels, and expulsions. Despite the savage attacks in the name of Jesus on the Jews during the crusades, Jewish texts do not condemn the historical Jesus, and they avoid blanket condemnation of the entire Church and all Christians. In modern times Jewish attitudes must be viewed against the murder of 6 million Jews in the Holocaust by a nation whose population was 90% Catholic and Evangelical (E.K.D.). In a recent study entitled *Jewish Textbooks On Jesus and Christianity,* Judith Herschlog Muffs notes that Jewish books today express the view "that the best way to strengthen Judaism is not being critical of the next person's religion, but by better living our own."

In sum, Judaism recognized the fact that Jesus spread to the heathen and pagan world basic and Jewish values hitherto unknown. Jesus introduced to the non-Jewish world the possibility of human self-improvement, a monotheistic concept of God, the idea of a messiah, the moral instruction of Moses and the prophets, and the essence of Jewish ethical teaching. Indeed, the most important teaching of Jesus is his quotation from Leviticus (19:18), "Love your neighbor as yourself." Thus, we see an honest paradox wherein the historical Jesus has served as a bridge between Judaism and Christianity, as well as one of the causes of their separation.—1982

24. A Personal View of Black-Jewish Relations

I was born, as was my father, in St. Louis, which could be called the edge of the South. The Mason-Dixon Line, created to separate the North from the South, was drawn right through the heart of St. Louis, six blocks from the home in which I was raised.

By chance, my side of the block was the edge of a self-imposed white ghetto. Across the street was the beginning of the black ghetto. Every morning when I got up and looked out the window, I saw Blacks looking back. I wondered what they thought, and, no doubt, they wondered what I thought.

Of course, we went to segregated schools. Even so, the opening times were staggered by fifteen minutes. Heaven forbid, we should cross lines. I supposed the authorities believed we would clash, but underneath, perhaps, was the deeper fear that we might like each other and even become friends.

We were poor, but we didn't know it because nobody told us. I had three childhood friends. One friend was Jewish and, as a teenager, he drowned in the treacherous currents of the Merrimac River. Another white boy came from the deep South, and people called his family "white trash." The third friend was black, and in that day blacks were politely called "colored" or Negro, or impolitely "niggers" or "jigaboos."

When my black friend, Russell, was sixteen, he fudged on his age. Saying he was eighteen, he joined the Marine Corps. He was killed on Iwo Jima. I still grieve for him.

Because my parents often worked long hours at their Ma and Pa grocery store, I had many babysitters. Most were black. I still remember fondly how they mothered and nourished me.

I graduated high school at age sixteen and went to Chicago to further my Jewish education. I also entered a public junior college. It was there that I was shocked by my first encounter with racism.

In a required survey course, the books were loaned to us, and we had to return them. At one point one of the lecturers roared out, "Do you know why there are separate warehouses for books for white students and Negro students?" One student raised his hand and answered, "Because niggers have syphilis." The teacher yelled, "Right!"

I felt as if a hammer had hit me on the head. I knew syphilis germs were not transferred by books. I knew some Blacks had syphilis, but so did some whites. That such blatant prejudice was taught in a classroom of several hundred students in the great city of Chicago and no one said a word was the final blow. I quit at the end of the semester and entered the University of Chicago. Of course, I attended all the right political gatherings.

Then, I learned the second fact of racial prejudice. We were required to take a swimming course to graduate. Among other things, we had to demonstrate that we could swim two laps, presumably a survival skill. On the first day of class—all boys naturally, as that's the way it was done in those days—we lined up naked and were told to dive in.

But there was one problem. There were black students in the class. At the instruction, "Dive in," I thought, "Who, me? With them?" Here I was, this big liberal suddenly confronted with personal reality. All the myths of my culture ran through my head. I had no choice, so I jumped in. And you know what happened? Nothing. We played water polo, and it was fun. From that I learned that no matter how many intellectual decisions we make, we also carry around a lot of unconscious emotional and cultural baggage. I never forgot that lesson. We have much to unlearn.

About this time, on Shabbat in the synagogue, I was following the reading of Chapter 12 in the book of Numbers when a thought suddenly struck me. This Torah portion contains an account of Miriam and Aaron, who are admonished for speaking against their brother, Moses, because of his wife; God punishes Miriam with scales (leprosy?), and Aaron repents as he witnesses this.

Classic rabbinic interpretations cite this as a warning against gossip. Precisely what is the gossip? If this is Moses's first wife, is this because she was a Midianite? The Patriarchs had non-Jews as wives. Was it because she was a second wife? The Patriarchs also practiced polygamy.

The answer appears in the text that says, "because she was a Cushite." Emphatically so, because it is repeated again. Cush in the Bible usually refers to South Egypt, or Ethiopia, and means "black." The gossip was racial and God condemned it, particularly among the leaders. The message is simple and clear: it denounces racial prejudice and threatens dire punishment for it.

Centuries later the great prophet of social justice admonished in one of his orations (Amos 9:7): "To Me, O Israelites, you are just like the Cushim, declares Adonoy." Here there is explicit warning about prejudice against blacks and the affirmation of Chapter 2 in Genesis—that all human beings are created in the image of God.

This classic ambivalence is repeated in the history of Black-Jewish relationships during the past 300 years in America. We find the prejudices of some Jews against Blacks. We can also learn of great Jewish efforts, even martyrdom, to help free Blacks from slavery and advance their cause in our own time. Blacks and Jews have united in their quests for social acceptance as well as blamed each other for what appears to be the ills of our society. What is most interesting, however, is that for almost 300 years Blacks and Jews have struggled, both independently and collectively, with this relationship and its definition.

It is helpful to remember that in the 1700s international slavery was a very ecumenical business. It was invented by Arab Muslims; instituted legally and financially in the West by Christians; enthusiastically adopted by the Africans, who sold their brethren; and bankrolled in part by Sephardic Jews, who were involved in the sugar-processing industry. Some were guilty; all are responsible.

Black anti-Semitism, to the extent that it exists, is mostly an expression of desperation gone sour and the misdirected anger of some individuals. Jewish anti-Black feelings, to the extent that they exist, are an expression of the white ethos and resentment at the insensitive statements of some Black leaders. Sometimes, Black-Jewish tensions arise from a legitimate conflict of self-interest.

Sadly enough, Jews have not seen through this situation and used it as a reason to back off. Sadly enough, the important quest for Black self-esteem is reduced by empty yet cathartic phrases, gestures, and posturing. How terribly sad when Jews and Blacks, who are both victims, play the oppressor's game and turn on each other.

The time has come to rethink strategies. It will not be easy, and we must recognize different interests, but we have to work together. That which unites us is greater than that which divides us. We must recognize the common enemy: the attitude that denies individuality, grants no recognition to cultural diversity, denies free choice, and restricts religious freedom. The common enemy is prejudice, bigotry, injustice, greed, oppression, indifference, domination, xenophobia, and an unwillingness to share power. The enemy is a product of a cold-hearted and mean-spirited America.

As Thomas Jefferson once noted, "Indeed, I tremble for my country when I reflect that God is just."

Yet, there is every reason to hope, to repair, and to build constructively. I believe in America and its potential. We have had troubles before, but together we have worked them out. To do this now requires two basic approaches.

The first is to create an overarching alliance. The common enemy is too strong for any one group to go it alone. In the words of the title of Martin Luther King Jr.'s book, *Chaos or Community*, we need a coalition of Jews, Blacks, Hispanics, Asians, gays and lesbians, women, Native Americans, concerned citizens, compassionate people—Americans who truly believe in democracy. We can and we must work out our minor differences. We can disagree, but we must speak out in a loud, clear voice and vote with a common concern. We need each other.

The second part is a conscious effort to rediscover the purposes of America. We all know what they are. They were expressed in the Declaration of Independence, the writings of Abraham Lincoln, the arts reaching for the highest levels, and compassion digging down to the deepest. The America that created Social Security and Medicare and furthered education and research. The America that had a profound commitment to jobs and justice. The America that exhibited genuine care and concern for others.

In a border-state city desegregating on a grade-a-year basis, the opening of the fall semester was the fateful day for the second grade. The parents of one seven-year-old had prepared her for this traumatic experience. With her new notebook, pencils, and lunch box she bounced out of the family car in the crispness of the morning. On the ride home, in the warming sun, the mother chatted about trivial things. Finally, she asked the important question: "How did it go in school?"

The answer came sharply, "There was a little Black girl sitting next to me."

The constriction in the mother's throat was like a paralysis. She forced out the next question: "What happened?"

"We were both so scared that we held hands all day."

It is time to hold hands, join hearts, and share thoughts.—1992

25. The Banality of Justice

It is the beginning of a typical summer day in Jerusalem. The sun is bright, the sky is blue, the weather is warming yet still pleasant. The buses and cars are filled with passengers on their way to work. The children hop, skip, and jump on their way to school. Everything is as it always is.

I enter a typical courtroom in Federal Court. The three judges are dignified in their black robes. The prosecutor and his staff are on one side and the defender and his staff are on the other. The court reporter is recording the events; the bailiff is officious as usual.

But the accused is not the usual defendant. He is John (Ivan) Demjanjuk, and he is accused of being the man known as "Ivan the Terrible," the sadistic guard of the Treblinka death camp. In 1942-43, Ivan the Terrible helped to brutally herd the Jews into gas chambers and pulled the lever that put to death nearly 870,000 of them. If convicted, the penalty is death by hanging. Genocide is the only crime punishable by death in the State of Israel.

As if to underscore the drama, a woman stands up, with tears streaming down her face and shouts, "Murderer! I saw you kill my mother, father, brothers, and sister, and I am the only one left in my family!" The police quickly, firmly, but politely and with compassion, escort her out of the courtroom.

The international press and a stream of visitors gather every day to watch the proceedings. It is high drama, for a generation has passed since the Eichmann trial. Eichmann was a lofty official, but here is a man accused of being directly and physically involved in the killing process. He ran the death machine.

And if that were not enough, cruelty beyond belief is added to the charge. One of the few survivors of a revolt at Treblinka, Eliyahu Rosenberg, gave an account of being forced by Ivan the Terrible to have sex with the gassed corpse of a little girl. Josef Czarny remembers the vicious guard dog called Mensch (person) that was trained to snap at the genitals of helpless Jews when its S.S. master ordered, "Person, bite this dog!"

By choice, I am seated in the first row about twenty-five feet from John (Ivan) Demjanjuk. I study his face and his manner carefully. He is quite polite and listens intently with no reaction, as if this has nothing to do with him, and he is only sitting in a history class.

I wonder: How can all this be? Is this a human being? Am I watching some kind of surrealistic scene in an avant garde theatre?

The man in the dock is a middle-aged auto worker of Ukrainian extraction. Since 1952 he has lived a quiet existence in Cleveland, Ohio, as a devoted husband and the loving father of three children. Demjanjuk was first brought to trial in Cleveland in 1981 and was convicted of lying on his application for a visa. He admitted lying and was stripped of his American citizenship. After his appeals in the United States failed, he was extradited to Israel in February 1986.

As I observe him closely and listen to the parade of credible witnesses and qualified experts, questions flood my mind. How can a person present a face of utter morality to the world and yet have committed such atrocities? Why did it take so long to bring him to trial? How could such a monstrous event be judged in such a polite legal atmosphere, with lawyers being so courteous to each other, the judge impassive, and the procedure so legally proper?

The last question is easiest to answer. The only way to correct injustice is through a system of justice. To do otherwise would invite vigilantism, adopt the values, if not the techniques, of the perpetrator, and generally destroy civilization and a responsible society. Justice demands investigation, evidence, proof, and a verdict that is appropriate, insofar as it is humanly possible.

Why did it take so long to bring him to trial? There are multiple answers. Until the Eichmann trial, the world tried to cover up, deny, and pass over the horrors of the Holocaust. Perhaps it was preoccupation with other matters, perhaps it was a denial of guilt, or perhaps just indifference to suffering—or a combination of these. In the chaos following the war, records were lost, deeds suppressed, deals made. War criminals disappeared, went underground, and scattered all over the world. The process to set the record straight and the usual legal means to redress grievances takes time, effort, money, and commitment. The process is now reaching its peak in America, Israel, and all over the world.

It should be understood that the Holocaust, possibly the greatest evil of our time, was too much for the mind to grasp or believe. The survivors themselves suppressed much of the memory of what happened to them. The experiences were much too painful to relive, much less talk about. Many are just now coming forward to tell their heart-rending stories.

Because I was a daily visitor, I became friendly with the police assigned to guarding the prisoner. Once during a recess they called me into the control room to show me a closed-circuit television screen that was monitoring Demjanjuk while he was in a holding cell.

There was a different Demjanjuk. He paced back and forth like a caged animal. He gesticulated to the guards in anger and frustration. He shouted. I then perceived there were two Demjanjuks. One was the bored, indifferent defendant and the other was the hostile, staring prisoner.

This sheds light on the last question: the capabilities of a person for evil (as well as good). This question is one that continues to baffle the human mind. Certainly the human capacity for evil was expressed by the Treblinka guard known as Ivan the Terrible. His official job was helping to operate the pumps for the gas chambers, but he also missed no opportunity for individual acts of sadism. One witness at the trial said, "I cannot even describe him as an animal, for even an animal would not torture his own kind like that."

On the other hand, about ten minutes away from the courtroom is the Avenue of the Righteous. It is a long, shady area several streets long. Trees are planted in the names and memories of righteous non-Jews—Christians and Muslims—who risked and often gave their lives to save Jews. These, too, must not be forgotten. Indeed, they should be remembered with honor.

To be sure, as it has always been known by philosophers, theologians, psychologists, and all thoughtful persons, human beings are conflicted by opposing forces and emotions: good and evil. The best symbol of these opposing forces is the Roman god called Janus, who is always depicted with two faces. Every human being chooses the face that he or she wishes to show the world. But, in the end, as the trial in Jerusalem now going on evidences, the mills of the gods grind slowly, but they grind exceedingly fine.—1987

26. A Statement on the Minnesota Fetal Viability Bill

A very close look at the Minnesota bill on fetal viability renders it almost meaningless. Using 1986 statistics on abortion in Minnesota, it will affect less than 1% of those involved in this procedure. However, the rhetoric surrounding this bill is dangerously imprecise. The bill seems to be an effort to create another public debate in the legislature on a religious issue that has been ruled by the Supreme Court to be a violation of the time-honored principle of the separation of church and state.

The bill professes to limit late-term abortions. In pursuit of this aim, however, new definitions for terms like "abortion" and "viability" are slipped in. They are neither scientific nor accurate, but highly charged with emotion. Suddenly a new phrase appears: "born alive." This is not synonymous with the term "viable fetus." "Born alive" is an issue that has been debated in Western society since the Greek philosophers. It will hardly be resolved by a state legislature.

The proposed law puts great strain on physicians to determine the viability of a fetus that may be twenty weeks or more. Medicine, although today highly sophisticated, is not an exact science. More often than not, diagnosis is the most difficult area. Obstetricians have enough problems and do not need another set of legal eyes peering at them at critical moments.

The bill itself is a bit of statistical trivia, but its implication and its symbolism are not to be mistaken. We are dealing here with the slippery slope of personal freedom and the erosion of human rights. Abortion is a personal choice guaranteed by the Constitution. Efforts to undermine that concept should be resisted mightily by the citizens of the United States.

America was created as a haven for those whose freedoms were being denied or restricted. The Constitution of the United States set the principles of freedom and human rights on solid legal base. But this cannot be taken for granted. As Thomas Jefferson noted, "The price of freedom is eternal vigilance."

That is why in 1989, here and now, in the State of Minnesota, the effort to preserve human rights must not slacken. This bill is a subtle, probing attack on those rights and is contrary to the whole thrust of the concept at freedom. We do not need—indeed we resent—any government effort to monitor our bedrooms, designate our beliefs, control our bodies, or regulate our brains. This bill attempts to do just that.

We are all well aware that issues surrounding abortion evoke deep and conflicting feelings and opinions. A significant portion of citizens of this country who hold profound religious convictions believe that any form of abortion is morally wrong. We should support their right to hold that view. We can understand their concerns and even share some of them. However, we must not, we dare not, accept the premise that through legislation the state has the right to foist the religious or philosophical conviction of any one group upon all citizens. This is a matter of personal and private morality.

Conservatives should resist this effort as an invasion of privacy. Liberals should resist it in protection of freedom.

This past year I taught a class in contemporary ethics at a local college. In the section dealing with medical ethics, we discussed terms such as "life," "fetus," and "person." We could not come to a common definition. There was much discussion and even debate, and we did not ever agree. But we did agree unanimously that it was each person's right to decide what should be done with his or her body. Nobody, no society, no one group has a right to impose its views, standards, or philosophy on a person or a segment of society in these matters.

As a rabbi in St. Paul for thirty-eight years, I have walked the corridors of the maternity ward and of the children's ward in hospitals day and night. I have spent countless hours counseling in matters of conception, abortion, birth, and death, in almost all of their ramifications. I did not find any two instances that were exactly alike. I further discovered that the best way to be helpful is to listen to clarify the issues, make no judgment, and respect the individual's decision. No more, no less.

In first-century Jewish thought as recorded in the Talmud, there were two schools of thinking. One was called the House of Hillel, the other the House of Shammai. One tended to be a little more liberal in the interpretation of Scriptures and the other somewhat more conservative. The Talmud has preserved their debates and in the end concludes, "Both are the words of the Living God."

Life is often a matter of interpretation and just as often depends on perspective. It is important to understand and respect this. It is not mere tolerance, but understanding someone else's mindset and background. In complete honesty and in all humility, is it not possible for my view to be right for me and someone else's view to be right for them?

We have reached a point of choice in these United States with reference to matters of abortion. Let each view be expressed in the church, mosque, or synagogue, debated in the press, advocated by any peaceful means—all within the law. But, in the end, let each person's choice be respected and upheld.

On behalf of human rights, in defense of freedom, seeking to respect a person's right to choice, I respectfully ask you to consider the possibility that this small bill is a big mistake. Extinguish this spark of legislative controversy, lest it become a raging fire that threatens to destroy the fragile fabric of our freedom.—1989

27. Arabs and Jews Can Live Together

War has many parents but peace is an orphan. That is because conflict is exciting and dramatic but cooperation is a peaceful and slow process. Hatred creates headlines and draws the media, but harmony is on the back page and does not particularly attract the T.V. camera. But oh, what a difference war and peace make in our personal lives!

For the past six months, the painful confrontation between the Israelis and the Palestinians, and by implication, Arabs and Jews, has dominated the news. The differences in attitudes, needs, strategies, and goals are real. However, the shared history, the enlightened self-interests, and the recognition of each other's aspirations, as well as other commonalities and instances of cooperation are just as real.

From the tenth to the twelfth centuries, Jewish and Arab cultural relations were such that the era is known in Jewish history as "The Golden Age." Hebrew linguistics, philosophy, and biblical studies were enriched by Arab contacts. The Arab communities benefited greatly from Jewish contributions in political leadership, medicine, and translations that bridged the Greek and Arab cultures.

Admittedly, Jews experienced discrimination and distress while living among the Arabs, particularly in later centuries. But students of Jewish history agree that Jews suffered more in Christian lands than in Arab lands.

In recent times, especially the last twenty years, there have been great confrontations between Arabs and Jews in the Middle East, yet quietly and steadfastly fruitful contacts have been made, neighbors have lived in peace and mutual helpfulness, and many dialogues have been held. One especially fine example of this is documented in Dr. Jack Cohen's newly published book, *The Reunion of Isaac and Ishmael.*

In 1962 Dr. Cohen, the head of Hillel House at the Hebrew University in Jerusalem, began to bring together Jewish and Arab students. Eventually these meetings broadened, and now teams of students jointly visit and stay in Arab villages and Jewish settlements. In thoughtful but honest ways, they confront the differences, cultural backgrounds, and perceptions that Jews and Christians, Muslim and Druse Arabs have about each other.

They have learned how to listen to each others' needs and aspirations. Ultimately, they have discovered that so-called national interests need not be treated as an unchangeable law of nature. Arabs and Jews are capable of empathy for each other. What they finally came to understand can be expressed in the words of the eminent scientist, Anatol Rapaport: "To resolve controversies, there must be a desire to resolve the controversy and this desire must be stronger than the desire to win the controversy."

This kind of experience has been mirrored many times over, and a few more examples might prove enlightening. To begin, all one has to do is read the Israeli or Arab press. Buried within are reports of these events. Books like *The Yellow Wind* by David Grossman, *The Black Box* by Amos Oz, and *Bullets of Palestine,* by Howard Kaplan air the relationships with sensitivity, skill, and literary grace.

The most popular television show in Israel today is "Neighbors." It is similar to the Archie Bunker theme, where a family of Arabs and a family of Israelis are neighbors. Misconceptions are dispelled, prejudices are examined, and perceptions are thoughtfully conceded. It is done with a great deal of self-recognition and self-humor.

A more telling experience occurred last week in Nazareth. An estimated 3,000 Arabs gathered with 300 Israelis for several days of meetings and camping. This year's gathering was somewhat unusual, because it was the first real contact since the *intifada* (Uprising) between Israeli and Arab families in the West Bank and Gaza. Yet the attendance this year was greater than ever—a tenfold increase. For five days, these Arabs and Jews cooperated in 65 projects in the vicinity of Nazareth. They paved streets and patched water pipelines, and in the evenings they held discussions. For many Arabs it was the first time they met Jews who were not soldiers or settlers. For some Jews it was the first time they could sit quietly and over a cup of coffee listen to Arabs express their feelings without argument or defensiveness.

Thirty-three-year-old Nabila Yispanoli of Nazareth probably summed up the experience when she observed, "This proves that we have a lot in common. We may have different political positions, we can all be different. But we all want the same—peace."

This summer we arrived at our condominium in Jerusalem with mixed feelings. We had seen the pictures on T.V., we had followed the press reports, and we had been carefully monitoring articles and interpretations of events. But now we realized we could be directly involved.

Our building complex is maintained by a service organization that is made up of Arabs and Jews. On the first day there, I was in the elevator which, by American standards, is rather small and narrow. The elevator stopped at a floor and one of the Arab workers stepped in.

We knew each other from the past years. We did not greet each other because we both were obviously a little anxious, so we just exchanged glances and used peripheral vision. I happened to be wearing my Twins cap, which is excellent protection from the summer sun in Israel.

Ahmed and I had had serious discussions the previous summer on the standings in the American League. Seeing my cap, he suddenly said, *"Shalom,* Rabbi Minnesota." I quickly responded with, *"Salaam, Ahmed habibi* (friend)." We both had a good laugh and a good summer.

There will be peace in the Holy Land when Arabs and Jews look in each other's eyes and see the promise and the pain. Arabs must recognize the Jewish need for security. After centuries of persecution and particularly during the last half-century, with a Holocaust and five wars in Israel, it will not be easy. Jews must try to understand the Palestinian needs for dignity and self-determination. After a period of neglect, manipulation, and abuse, it will be difficult. But if an "evil empire" can become an enthusiastic equal in the search for co-existence, then anything is possible.

One must never lose hope.—1988

28. The Tie that Binds

Human beings are unique among all the species, in part, because it takes almost a decade and a half for their offspring to become independent. Implicit in this long-term nurturing is the idea that children should return the compliment of caring, commitment, and concern for parents as they age.

In so-called primitive societies and cultures that have a sense of kinship, the issue of generational obligation rarely arises. When Moses confronted Pharaoh to free the Hebrew slaves, Pharaoh began to negotiate and Moses immediately responded, "We will all go, young and old." One may find similar incidents in the writings of Christianity, Islam, the Eastern religions, and other sacred literature.

Now, why in an age when we know about things like atoms, space travel, and genes do we have to ask questions about the generation gap? It appears to me that in human relations today, particularly in the family, feelings and emotions are extremely complicated and extraordinarily uncertain.

There comes a time when a child must struggle to become an individual, and this is usually accompanied by degrees of tension. Generational values differ, sometimes intensely in our exceedingly complex and increasingly mobile society. There is a well-known generational principle: *autres temps, autres mores*—other times, other fashions. Religion can serve as the bridge for generations to understand each other. The principles of religion, while remaining fixed like the stars, can guide us through stormy waters or when the currents run against us. Religion, with its long history of negotiating between the shoals to the shores, is the ballast that steadies us.

Although the times and circumstances change, one constant in religious literature through the ages is emphasis on responsibility for the young and respect for the elders. Religious literature is also filled with instances of conflict between generations, but these are regarded with extreme pain and a desire for resolution. It is helpful for those on opposite sides of the generation gap to remember that each person is created in the image of God and is, therefore, unique, to be respected for his or her feelings, needs, and opinions. This basic religious value contains seeds for a functional and responsible family as well as a culture or a nation.

Religion helps tremendously during rites of passage as we move up the ladder of years and new generations follow us. Birth, adolescence, marriage, and death are times of transition, filled with ambivalences. At each step, religion provides the known passageway. Perhaps its most basic function is encouraging maturity and mandating responsibility. Its moral and ethical admonitions are demands on the conscience.

Religion insists on justice to all—young and old alike. It knows that where there is no justice there will be no peace. This applies to generations and to societies as a whole.

The only religious holiday that America has created is Thanksgiving. It should be a day not of overeating but of opening our hearts, a time not for football but for celebrating family. Indeed, all religious holidays are times for generational gathering and healing. Grandparents should be integrated into families, not merely as passive keepers of a heritage, but, as in Russia and China, as active helpers, educating and watching over grandchildren.

Competing needs, not competing values, shape yet another unfortunate generational conflict. Society in general is struggling with ways to balance the financial obligations to the elderly and the young. Save taxes, at whose expense? Mothers and fathers in the sandwich generation, torn between the need to help aging parents and care for growing children, are often in a terrible financial and emotional bind. Religion must articulate that there is enough in our society for everybody's need but not everybody's greed.

Religion has taken the lead in many instances of helping the young and the elderly. Day care centers can be found in religious institutions all over the country. Religions have literally opened their doors to the elderly homeless. Food shelves can be found in almost all religious structures. Compassion, not exclusivity, is the hallmark of religion.

Religion comes from the Latin word *religare,* which means to bind together. Religions bind our lives to the great moral truths they enunciate. Religion binds our lives with all humankind. Religion binds the generations together so they will be more understanding, caring, and above all, responsive to each other's needs in a changing world.

Perhaps that is why we were told at the end of the Hebrew book of the prophet Malachi that Elijah will be sent before the coming of the great day of God, and

God shall turn the heart of the parents to the children and the hearts of the children to their parents.

This is a vision that we must hold steadily before us.—1996

29. A Glimmer of Humanity in the Holocaust

***The Book of the Just: The Unsung Heroes Who Rescued Jews from Hitler,* by Eric Silver. New York, Grove Press, 1992.**

Forty moving and courageous stories about the Holocaust are to be found in this new and remarkable book, published in London in June. A Hebrew edition, *Hatzadikim Baseter,* followed in July. The book will receive its American debut September 14.

The author, Eric Silver, lives in Jerusalem and is a regular contributor to several British newspapers and a senior writer on the *Jerusalem Report* staff. He has written simply the best book on the subject. With great warmth and sensitivity, the author, through personal testimony, enables the reader to feel the constant fear of betrayal and execution that the rescuers all lived with. The book belongs in every caring home, every seminary, and every course on the Holocaust. It is also an excellent text for teenagers in terms of values orientation.

The reason Eric Silver's book is so timely is that the State of Israel, through the Yad Vashem Holocaust Memorial Commission in Jerusalem, has just honored its ten thousandth "righteous among the nations," a Ukrainian librarian. Ludmilla Bondarenko took in a Jewish colleague, Revka Kogut, who had crawled, sick and wounded, from under the corpses of Babi Yar, where the Nazis killed 30,000 Jews on September 29, 1941. Bondarenko's family sheltered Kogut for two years before the Red Army drove the German Army out of the Ukraine.

"Righteous among the nations" *(Chasiday Umot Haolam)* is an honorary term applied to those non-Jews who saved Jews during the Holocaust, often by endangering their own lives. Dr. Mordecai Paldiel, director of the award program, estimates that at least 300,000 Jews owed their lives to gentiles. Yad Vashem, after proper testimony, honors the righteous among the nations by inviting them to Israel and planting a tree on the Avenue of the Just, which leads to the Holocaust Memorial. They are also given a medal bearing the Talmud saying, "To save one life is considered as having saved the whole universe."

The obverse side of the medal shows emaciated hands clutching at barbed wire, the strands intertwined to form a lifeline around the world. On the reverse is a picture of the memorial hall of Yad Vashem. If the honoree is dead, then members of the family are invited to Israel to receive the tribute in memory of the hero, often in the presence of the very Jews who were saved.

The range of those who performed these righteous deeds is stunning. They come from a score of centuries and had varying motives, but all risked their lives and liberty when it was open season to kill Jews. They include Christians, Muslims, diplomats, and illiterate peasants. They are the ones who testified to a common humanity when most people looked the other way.

Some fascinating and inspiring examples found in *The Book of the Just* are the following:

In 1989 Israel honored 120 Calvinist peasants from a cluster of Delft pottery villages in Holland. They were linked by canals and plank bridges. By skillfully removing the bridges at the right time, they sheltered 300-400 Dutch Jews from deportation. They constituted "a conspiracy of goodness."

On Christmas Eve in Andonno, 6,000 feet above the Italian Riviera, Father Borsotto told the story of the way Jesus was born alone in a manger. He pointed out that there were two Jewish families alone "and hunted for no reason except being Jews." The next day villagers brought the Jews gifts of food, clothing, and wood. Poor people shared their meager resources with the Jews because "it was the Christian thing to do."

Sempo Sugihara was officially the Japanese Consul in Kovno, but in reality was a spy for the Japanese. Moved by the plight of the Jews, he saved 4,500 of them by issuing fictitious visas. He was also responsible for saving all 300 staff and students of the famous Mir yeshivah.

Although the International Committee of the Red Cross was properly neutral, many of its workers were not. Henry Slawik issued thousands of documents certifying that Polish refugees were Christians. He was apprehended and executed at Mauthausen. Friedrich Born, an official of the Swiss Red Cross, looked after 7,000 Jewish children in sixty institutions.

Dr. Adelaide Hautval was a French psychiatrist who intervened on behalf of Jews so that the local Gestapo officer said, "Since you wish to defend them, you will share their fate." She was sent to Auschwitz. While there she was asked to participate in the medical experiments on Jewish women and she refused. One Nazi doctor in charge told her, "These people are different than you." She replied, "And so are you." When she was given the Medal of the Righteous she noted, "What I did was perfectly natural, logical and derived from a moral obligation."

Eric Mygren, a pastor of the Swedish Church in Berlin, a Greek archbishop, an Italian monk, a Hungarian pastor, a Belgian pastor, and others risked their lives to save Jews. Anna Borkowska was a Polish Mother Superior who was called *Imma*

(Hebrew for mother) by Jewish resisters. She dressed Jews as nuns and taught them how to use hand grenades. Father André not only hid Jews but helped them keep their customs. Father Niacci enabled Jews to keep their own kosher kitchen.

Mustafa Hardaga, a Muslim merchant in Sarajevo, told his Jewish friends, Yosef and Rivka Kabilio, "Yosef, you are our brother, and Rivka, you are our sister, and the children are our children. Everything we have is yours, this is your home." Ahmed Sadik, Zayneba Hardaga's father, a devout Muslim, hid the family of Jews. Sadik was later denounced for helping Jews and was killed.

What goes around comes around. In July, when Tova Kabilio Greenberg, the daughter of Kabilios, heard in Jerusalem about the plight of the Muslims in Sarajevo, she immediately thought of Mustafa and quickly got in touch with his family. Greenberg then went to the Interior Ministry to get them a visa and then sent them tickets on an El Al flight to Israel. Igor Berjan and Tanja Berjan, the grandchildren of Mustafa, now live safely in Israel.

There is general knowledge that Monsignor Roncalli, later Pope John XXIII, issued false baptismal certificates to Jews when he was Vatican nuncio in Istanbul, thus saving thousands of lives. Last month in Istanbul, Nedim Yahya, a prominent leader in the Turkish Jewish community for more than fifty years, told me that he once waited with Roncalli on a cold, misty night at the docks for a ship to come in. Yahya several times urged Roncalli to return to his home because it was so uncomfortable. Roncalli replied, "No. I will stay here until the boat docks and I will see with my own eyes that the Jews are safe."

In an important epilogue in this book, Silver raises the issue as to why some people indulged in cruelty or looked away, while others went out of their way and risked their lives to help Jews. To be sure, for many self-protection was reinforced by a tendency to conform. The Nazis and their allies and collaborators created a climate in which it was legitimate to slaughter Jews. There is also a tendency in a society that perceives Jews as outsiders to dehumanize them.

Most who helped echoed the words of one Righteous Gentile: "Please don't paint me as a hero, it was the natural humane thing to do." In the end, however, a decision to act was taken individually, on the spur of the moment. One had to say "yes" or "no." But altruism is not born in the flick of an eyelash. The instincts of empathy and compassion were already rooted in personal history.

Nechama Tec, in an in-depth study of Polish rescuers, tries to identify six common traits. Eva Fogelman argued in a paper in 1990 that child-rearing was the most significant factor. Samuel and Pearl Oliner in *The Altruistic Personality* seem to agree. They wrote, "Care was not a spectator sport. It compelled action."

As Silver notes: "Family upbringing? Yes, but what about Countess Maria von Maltzan, whose mother, brother and sister were Nazis? Liberal politics? Yes, but what about Giorgio Perlasca, who was a dedicated Fascist? Christian charity? Yes, but what about all those God-fearing Christians who stoked the furnaces? A high moral code? Yes, but what about Oskar Schindler, who was a gambler and a womanizer?" There are no easy answers.

Abraham Joshua Heschel, the great American Jewish theologian, once noted that the world may be destroyed by *sinat chinam,* "unmerited hate," but saved by *ahavat chinam,* "unmerited love." Or, simply put: What will prevail in all of humanity and in our own humanness? The human tendency to hate or the human urge to love?—1992

30. Should a Jew Listen to the Music of an Anti-Semite?

Should a Jew listen to the music of an anti-Semite? This painful question recently came to the fore again when the Israel Philharmonic Orchestra, under the direction of conductor Daniel Barenboim, sought to play works of the nineteenth-century composer Richard Wagner, an avowed anti-Semite whose music was idolized by Adolph Hitler.

Those who argued for playing the music, such as Barenboim, contended that even though Wagner was a notorious anti-Semite and a Nazi icon, his music is a critical element in the repertory of any major orchestra. In addition, proponents appealed to the concept of artistic freedom.

Those who opposed it included many concentration camp survivors, who pointed out that Wagner stands as an enduring symbol and cultural hero of the Nazi mentality. Wagner wrote in 1881, "The Jews are the born enemy of peace, humanity, and every thing that is noble in it." Hitler himself is said to have told Wagner's wife, Cosima, that when he attended the Wagnerian opera, Riczi, "It was there that it all began."

Wagner's music is an anguishing reminder of the horror of the Holocaust, reawakening old, painful memories among the more than 300,000 survivors now residing in Israel. The music would offend their sensibilities and harm them psychologically.

The dilemma of appreciating the art of an anti-Semite is a matter that confronts every thinking Jew. Chopin, Degas, Kant, Rodin, Joseph Campbell, and Roald Dahl, among others, displayed forms of anti-Semitism. Should the positive, creative concepts of their efforts be ignored? Were they expressing the popular sentiments of their time? Should they be understood as prisoners of history?

Yet, can a Jew remain silent to a hate that has hurt and killed so many fellow Jews? Who can forget and who shall forgive this great hatred?

In 1985 Leonard Bernstein conducted an all-Wagner program at the Vienna State Opera. At that time he wrote an article entitled, "Wagner's Music Isn't Racist." His conclusion was: "Wagner is long dead and buried, as is the Third Reich, but we music lovers are alive and hungry for great music. And if Wagner wrote great music, as I think he did, why should we not embrace it fully and be nourished by it?"

Avraham Melamed, a violinist with the Israel Philharmonic Orchestra who survived a concentration camp in the Ukraine, asked his colleagues not to play Wagner's music, and argued: "Wagner was a great symbol for Hitler. He was not just another composer with anti-Semitic views. Hitler copied a lot of his ideas and books. The skin on which the numbers were tattooed is getting wrinkled and old. Let them wait a little. Time does move along."

There are several interesting historical aspects to this issue. German Levi, conductor of the Royal Munich Opera Orchestra, directed the musical program at Wagner's funeral in 1883. Levi, a rabbi's son, was a conductor and a leading interpreter of Wagner's music-dramas. Wagner was prepared to forgive Levi his Jewishness if he would submit to baptism; and despite Levi's refusal, he recognized him as a great conductor.

Wagner, like Verdi and Dvorak, Bartok, and Mussorgsky, was a romantic nationalist imbued with the belief that music was the forge of ethnicity. Theodor Herzl, the founder of political Zionism and author of *The Jewish State,* was inspired by Wagner. Even though Herzl heard crowds chant *A mort les Juifs*—"Kill the Jews"—Wagner's nationalism struck a chord in Herzl. Amos Elan writes in his biography of Herzl: "For inspiration and to dispel occasional doubts, Herzl turned to Wagnerian music. He was enraptured by the music of the great anti-Semite." Indeed, Herzl wrote, "Only on those nights when no Wagner was performed did I have any doubts about the correctness of my idea."

This puts the dilemma squarely. Has art any relationship to moral behavior? Is there a universality about art? When we hear a musical interpretation, do we hear the inner character of the musician, the fruit of a life's experience and ideas? Should we play and listen to the works of Mendelssohn and Mahler, both of whom converted to Christianity? Should Jews conduct and play Handel's *Messiah?* Should Shakespeare not be read because Shylock has entered the English vocabulary as an anti-Semitic word? Should Israelis stop using Mercedes cars as taxis and American Jews refrain from driving Volkswagens? Ambiguities abound.

Then there is the matter of freedom of expression. Here the field becomes wide open. What pleases one offends another. What insults one inspires another. As in the controversy over Mapplethorpe's work, who is to judge what is obscenity and what is art? How can one decide what is of redeeming social value and what is identity politics? These are thorny questions, and the answers come mostly in shades of gray.

Yet, some clarification may be found. If there is to be a public performance or exhibit, the matter may be simple. One need not purchase a ticket. Again, even if admission is not charged, one may choose not to attend. To the credit of the Israel Philharmonic Orchestra, those musicians who cannot in good conscience play at a Wagner concert are excused with understanding, and there is no penalty. People do vote with their pocketbooks and their feet.

If art is used blatantly in a hateful, prejudicial, and biased manner, it can be dealt with in several ways. In a free society it can be exposed, opposed, ridiculed, and protested. If it is defaming or harmful, if it inflames, prejudices, or incites violence, it is subject to libel suits, police intervention, and other legal remedies. Civic, governmental, and religious leaders have a moral obligation to speak out and to be held accountable.

In the main, it becomes a matter of individual taste and decision. My wife and I once attended a concert of Mozart's *Requiem* in the Jerusalem Theater in Jerusalem. The text was entirely in Hebrew. This classic, sacred work was performed by the Jerusalem Symphony Orchestra and an Israeli chorus. Some of the musicians and singers wore *kipot.* It took place a little later in the evening because it was Saturday night. The performance was sold out and at least one-quarter of those who attended also wore *kipot.* No one seemed uncomfortable.

An episode that occurred in early rabbinic times might be helpful. Elisha ben Abuyah, who lived in the first half of the second century and was one of the great Jewish sages of his day, renounced Judaism. As a result, his former colleagues disassociated themselves from him, with the exception of his pupil, Rabbi Meir. In fact, in rabbinic literature Elisha ben Abuyah is cited only as *acher,* "another person."

Many wondered how the great Rabbi Meir could continue his relationship with an apostate, even though he was learned in Judaism. The answer to their query is in this phrase: *rimon matzah tocho ahchal klipato zahrak*—"He (Rabbi Meir) found a pomegranate. He ate the inside and threw away the rind" (Haggigah 15b).

Should a Jew listen to the music of an anti-Semite? Well, that depends. The meaning of music is in the ear of the listener.—1992

31. The Eleventh Plague: A Jewish View of Mental and Emotional Illness

Physical illness is, in the main, something we can see and identify. It is organic and we can, to a large degree, deal with it through medical procedures and without a great deal of guilt, blame, and shame. Regarding mental and emotional illness, on the other hand, we are still in the Dark Ages. Although we have made great strides in these areas in the past half century, in the popular mind mental illness is still surrounded by myths, prejudices, and feelings of shame.

This is particularly true of Jews, who traditionally prized the life of the mind and extolled intellectual achievements. Consequently, illnesses of the mind or the emotions were seen in terms of embarrassment and failure, and with these judgments inevitably came shame, blame, and guilt. This reaction is rather ironic, since some of the greatest advances in understanding these problems have been made by Jews. Now the time has come again to speak openly in the Jewish community about mental and emotional illness, the eleventh plague.

Psychiatry and religion have different purposes. Psychiatry looks at human beings analytically. Religion looks at men and women synthetically. The first removes conflicts and disturbances; the second offers a guide for living and identity, reverence for life, and purpose.

Almost all types of mental disorders and emotional ailments are described in the Bible and subsequent Jewish religious literature. There are at least thirteen Hebrew terms in classic Jewish literature to describe inappropriate behavior. Rabbis and Jewish leaders deal with the incidents with great compassion and efforts to understand. For example, the Talmud records, "A person does not sin except that the spirit of *shtus* enters him" (Sotah 3a). *Shtus* can mean disorder, conflict, depression, or mental illness, among other ailments. This passage clearly rejects blame and seeks understanding.

In another passage (Niddah 13b) we are told, "That is, a *shoteh* (a disturbed person) whose mind has become weakened as a result of illness." Here the causal relationship between mental illness and physical illness is clearly stated.

Dr. Moshe Halevi Spero, an Israeli psychiatrist and devout Jew, recently published a superb book entitled *Handbook of Psychotherapy and Jewish Ethics*. It is must reading for those who deal with and care about mental and emotional illness. In it he writes: "All emotional states, including so-called functional disorders, have physiochemical correlates even though such correlations have not all been demonstrated or are not yet manageable."

Compulsion in rabbinic literature is termed *oness*. With extraordinary compassion the Talmud records *oness rachmana patreh,* "The Merciful One exempts from punishment one who is compelled" (Baba Kama 28b). There is a vast reservoir of writings on the conflict between *yetzer hatov* (conscious thoughts and values) and *yetzer hara* (unconscious drives and instincts). The roots and propellants of human behavior have been thoroughly discussed in rabbinic literature. Perhaps the best summary of Jewish religious thinking can be expressed in the words of Maimonides (Hilchot Deot 9:10): "It is not possible to give exact assessment of the mind in writing."

There are numerous types of mental illnesses that range in severity from mild to disabling. Three examples of the more prominent are schizophrenia, depression, and organic brain disorders. Schizophrenia is a term for a group of diseases characterized by disturbed or bizarre behavior and thinking, extreme withdrawal, and hallucinations. Depression is persistent unhappiness characterized by listlessness, sleep disorders, and thoughts of suicide. Organic brain disorders are caused by brain tumors, injuries, and hardening of the arteries.

In the United States alone more than 20 million people will have a major affective disorder. There are as many schizophrenics in America as there are people in Oregon, Mississippi, Kansas, Wyoming, Vermont, Delaware, and Hawaii combined. Schizophrenia is as real as diabetes, multiple sclerosis, and cancer. It is no one's fault. Or as one authority put it, "People do not cause schizophrenia; they merely blame each other for doing so." More than 75% of individuals with the illness respond well to medical treatment; nearly all patients respond at least partially. Most individuals who seek treatment and follow the recommendations of their doctor can lead productive, useful, and reasonably stable and satisfied lives.

Brain disorders are now being understood for the first time. New studies are increasing our knowledge with dazzling speed. For example, very recent findings seem to point to chromosomal causes of Alzheimer's disease. In this area new techniques of diagnosis and cure offer much hope.

Depression is probably the most common emotional ailment known. In its milder forms, depression is a natural reaction to everyday stress and frustration. Each of us goes through times when our lives are marked by sadness. Normally, the intensity and duration of our response relates to a life event, a loss of some kind. And even though the loss may be severe, we expect in time to recover from our setback and resume a normal life.

For victims of depressive illness, there is no immediate recovery. Instead, these individuals become overwhelmed by their feelings and find it difficult to function. Their depression drags on and on. Studies by the National Institute of

Mental Health have indicated that more than nine million people in the U.S. are suffering from depression serious enough to require treatment.

But keep in mind that the success rate for treating people with depression is 90%. A new study points out that certain forms of depression have a genetic link. This finding will help us understand and treat a wide range of mental illness.

There is no shame in calling upon a psychotherapist for professional help when we or members of our family are feeling depressed. It is only a shame not to get help and suffer needlessly.

Psychotherapy is a process in which one develops a relationship with another person for the purpose of self-exploration and self-discovery. By understanding thoughts and feelings, we can gain a deeper understanding of both our self and our situation. Whether we are considering help for a life crisis (divorce, death of a loved one, loss of a job) or for ongoing personal problems (loneliness, low self-esteem, difficulty with relationships), the thing to keep in mind is that most people can use help when they are troubled and are not adapting well to the stress in their lives.

Winston Churchill struggled with depression all of his life. Moses Maimonides was so depressed after his brother David died that he took to bed for a year, yet he emerged from it to write the greatest book of all time in Jewish philosophy, the most masterful classification of the Talmud, and significant medical works. Depression can be handled and overcome, and the individual can not only continue in positive and productive living but also can make significant contributions to the community.

In the treatment of mental illness a quiet revolution has been taking place all over the country. Twenty-five years ago most of those needing care for serious mental illness were sent away to huge institutions. For hundreds of years before that, they were quite literally "put away" in asylums isolated from the community, often far from their homes and families. In the 1960s, the picture began to improve at a rapid pace. We are now in a promising new era in the treatment of mental illness.

Those patients with serious mental illness (psychosis) who go to the better hospitals today are receiving intensive treatment. Most are back with their families in a matter of a few months; many continue to receive treatment while living at home. In addition, new mental health services have made treatment available in the community. These innovations will have far-reaching effects—not just on patients but on all of us. There will be a growing number of patients in the community who are either completely restored or who are still in need of continued treatment while living and working.

In light of this, the Minnesota Rabbinical Association has joined a group of concerned members of the Jewish community to assess the needs of those who are mentally or emotionally ill. There is a general feeling that we can do more in service delivery as a caring and responsive Jewish community, whether in the form of aftercare, clinic services, homemaker services, or a Jewish community home.

But, above all, we must endeavor to educate people about the facts and dispel the myths and stigma of mental or emotional illness. Mental or emotional illness affects nearly 20 people in 100. This means that we and our families—all of us—are involved. We need to relieve those who are anxious, fearful, angry, and guilt-laden. We have to remove the words "shame" and "blame" from our vocabulary. We have to bring help to the helpless and hope to the hopeless.

The distance that once separated us from the mentally ill is fast vanishing. We are all living and working with people who are patients or former patients. Our attitude toward them, what we say and do when we are with them, is all-important to their well-being.

There is hope for the mentally and emotionally ill. Most who receive good care and treatment can be restored so that they function better than they did before the signs of illness appeared. To maintain this functioning they may require controlled use of drugs, much as diabetics must depend on insulin. They may also need to avoid certain kinds of social and emotional pressures that can bring on a return of their illness, much as those who have had a heart attack may need to avoid certain kinds of physical exertion. But the important thing is that with new treatment and services their functioning can be restored. They can carry out their part in family life—as parent, spouse, sibling—as they once did; they can return to jobs or school and do their work as well as ever; and they can participate once again as members of the community.

To paraphrase the words of a part of the classic Amidah: *baruch rofeh cholim,* "Blessed are those who cure the ill."—1987

Section III — Identity

1. The Greatest Mitzvah of Our Time: Operation Exodus

1990 will be recorded as one of the momentous years in history. The fall of the Berlin Wall, the emerging independence of the Soviet-dominated countries, and the collapse of Communism is indelibly impressed on the human mind. Similarly, 1990 in Jewish history will stand next to the years 70 and 1492. Some historians believe that the current Jewish migration from Russia may turn out to be even greater than migrations in those years. In scope, method, and meaning, it will mark a turn in the Jewish experience.

In sheer numbers, rapidity, processing, and resettling, Operation Exodus is unprecedented and staggering. Jetliners from Europe roar into Israel's Ben Gurion Airport almost every day delivering thousands of Jews to their homeland. This year the government of Israel expects more than 100,000—perhaps even 200,000—Soviet Jews coming in *aliyah.* It is estimated that 750,000 Jews might return to their "ancient" homeland in the next three years. Zvi Gittelman, author of *A Century of Ambivalence: The Jews of Russia and the Soviet Union,* estimates that almost ¾ million Jews requested visas during the past twelve months.

During the same year some 50,000 Soviet Jews will come to the United States. The American Jewish community is now actively involved in welcoming, housing, educating (both in language and Judaism), finding employment for, and helping their fellow Jews. The commitment is deep and the responsibility is enthusiastically and widely shared.

This response is typical of world Jewry today. Nor is it unprecedented. Following a wave of persecution in Russia in 1881 the then tiny Jewish community in St. Paul welcomed so many Jews so quickly on the eve of Passover that they had to house them in tents on the flats of the Mississippi River. In Baltimore the Hebrew Benevolent Society and the Hebrew Hospital offered their real estate assets of $200,000 for the release of detained Jewish refugees in Russia.

At that time (August 1881) Julius Loeb of New York, whose city welcomed 54,000 Jewish refugees, wrote to Adolf Loeb, chairman of the Russian Aid Society in Chicago: "We look upon the reception of these people as the first and highest duty, a duty that one human being owes to another, and by that law that one Jews owes another."

This comes out of the heart of Jewish tradition. The commandment of *pidyan shevuyim,* "saving and redeeming captive fellow Jews," was set as one of the highest priorities by the Talmud (Baba Batra 8a, 8b). Even money set aside for charity purposes or building a synagogue may be used to ransom captives (op. cit. 8b). Maimonides further explains, "That the duty of ransoming captives supersedes the duty of giving to the poor" (Yad. Matanat Aniyim 8:10).

This tradition continued with increasing force in the Middle Ages when many Jews were held prisoners under Roman, Christian, and Islamic rule. In the seventeenth century the Council of the Four Lands, the supreme Jewish authority, noted: "The quicker one acts in this matter, the more praiseworthy will he be deemed and his reward will be paid by the One who dwells in abundance."

The Talmud (Hullin 7a) records this remarkable event: "When Rabbi Joshua ben Hananiah was in Rome he learned that a young Jewish man was imprisoned. He went and sat in front of that prison everyday and said, 'I swear not to move from here until I ransom him no matter what the price.' The Jewish community raised the ransom for the young man and he was freed. In time the young man became Rabbi Ismail ben Elisha, one of the great rabbis of the Talmud."

Who knows how many Freuds, Einsteins, Chagalls, Salks, Bellowses, Agnons, and Singers are beating their fists against the prison doors in desperation? The keys for their freedom are partly in our hands. How much greater would we be and how much humanity would be enriched if we would free them.

Although the highest government in Russia and the K.G.B. assure us that they will not permit anti-Semitism, the smell is in the air. Pamyat and other native anti-Semitic organizations are beginning to spout their venom. There have been a few incidents and, few though they may be, the fear among Russian Jews is real and palpable. Jews have inborn barometers for bigotry. They are well aware how the scapegoat principle operates, particularly in Russia.

Bloody and cruel persecutions and pogroms against Jews fill pages of Russian history books and Jewish memory. From the times of the landowners, the boyars, the czars, and the peasants to the era of Stalinism, bureaucrats, intellectuals, and nationalists, anti-Semitism has worked its deadly purpose. It should be recalled that the most vicious and effective anti-Semitic document in modern history, *The Protocols of the Elders of Zion,* was commissioned by the Russian *Okrina* (Secret Police) under the czar. The overwhelming majority of American Jews have at least one parent or grandparent who came to America because of Russian anti-Semitism. The fact is that anti-Semitism is a deep part of the Russian national character and could flare into open hatred at a moment's notice.

David Wyman in *The Abandonment of the Jews* points out that in the 30s and 40s American Jewry's efforts to save Jews before the Holocaust was hampered by lack of unity, preoccupation with other matters, and a weakness in resolve. Indeed, prominent American Jews were painfully silent. The parallel between those days and these days is obvious. We must learn from history that a lack of commitment and resolve will lose lives and dishonor names.

The rescuing of Jews now through Operation Exodus is a moral imperative, and no one can be neutral. We have done well in demonstrations, protests, political action, and modest giving. The core meaning of our collective and personal Jewishness is now being put to the test.

The Zionist dream will be fully tested. Israel will be strained to the limit to accept the massive Jewish influx. The economy, social structure, the idealism, the people, the very purpose of Israel as a home for Jews will be the foremost item on the new state's agenda for the next few years.

World Jewry will now be the center of the eyes of the world. Our very concept of Jewish mutuality and responsibility will become an open book. World Jewry is asked to give $600 million, of which $420 million is assigned to American Jewry as the cost of *pidyan shevuyin,* rescuing our fellow Jews. This is exactly the meaning of Operation Exodus.

Arab leaders are heartless, but they are not stupid. The prospect of a million or more Jews in Israel changes all demographic assumptions. Israel will be more Jewish than Arab. Moreover, this particular Jewish immigration is filled with doctors, engineers, computer experts, artists...highly motivated and intelligent Jews. This is why Arab leadership will leave no stone unturned to stop the migration.

But they will not stop it. We will not let them, and the force of history is against them. Operation Exodus takes its name rightly from the first Exodus, and as it succeeded and became a symbol in history for liberation, so will the 1990 Exodus.

To be sure, some Russian Jews will choose to remain in Russia. Jews have been in Russia for 800 years and their roots are deep. They are determined to regenerate Jewish culture and, to a measure, they are succeeding. The Soviet Ministry of Culture has set up the Mikhoels Center to provide Hebrew classes and encourage Jewish culture. In 1989 Adin Steinsaltz of Jerusalem set up the Moscow Yeshivah with government support. The first Talmud in history published with Russian translation and full Russian commentary was just issued with a government subvention. Jewish schools, concerts, and lectures (with audiences in Leningrad, Vilnius, and Kiev totaling 56,000) are occurring everywhere. The Joint Distribution Committee plans to create 150 Jewish libraries in more than 30 cities. The first national Jewish organization of Russia (the *Vaad)* has just been created through a representative congress.

Perhaps this will all bear fruit...who knows? Let there be a flourishing of Jewish life in Russia, and let Russian Jews who seek a freer Jewish life elsewhere do so. Whether it be redeeming Jewish culture or redeeming Jewish lives, our duty is clear.

When it comes to Jewish lives, we take no chances. The Chief Rabbinate on Israel has ruled that planes carrying Russian Jewish refugees may land on Shabbat. There was not one dissenting voice, because everyone knows *pikuach nefesh dochay et hakol,* "The saving of human life takes precedence over all."

Operation Exodus is the greatest mitzvah of our time, *Lekach notzartah:* It is for this we were created. We must waste no time fulfilling our Jewish responsibilities and be Jewish in every sense of that term. For were we not taught: "A person who delays the fulfillment of the duty (redemption of captives) and causes undue prolongation of his fellow Jew's imprisonment is regarded as if he spilled his blood" (Yad 8:12).

Let there be no blood on our hands but instead let there be honor in our hearts and satisfaction in our souls. No hesitation, no delays, no pettiness, no turf fights, no theological wrangles, nothing but saving Jewish lives. Let's get them out as fast as we can. Let's save them now. Now! Now! Now!—1990

2. The Israeli-American Jewish Dialogue: Duet or Duel?

With the founding of the State of Israel, its increasing strength, and the perceived weakening of the Jewish community of the Diaspora through intermarriage, it has been conceded that Israel was the center of Jewish life. However, since 1984 new events have caused many in the American Jewish community to question Israel's centrality. Some have boldly declared, "America is the promised land." This has come about because of the deterioration of Israel's moral case after invading Lebanon, the embarrassing quarrels between the ultra-Orthodox and the ultra-secular, the deep division over the occupation of the West Bank, the high rise of *yerida* (exodus from Israel), the numerous scandals, the decline of the kibbutz movement, and the general feeling that the Zionist dream has been spent or, at least, is undergoing unhealthy change.

The emergence of the power of the American Jewish community has encouraged some to state that the United States is on a par with Israel and can claim central importance in contemporary Judaism. After all, the American Jewish community numbers twice the size of Israel. The Day School movement, the geometric increase in teaching chairs in Judaism in American universities, the strengthening of traditional Judaism, the publication of so many Jewish scholarly books, the sheer economic power and political strength of Jews in America, certainly challenge, in one form or another, Israel's centrality today.

But before judgments are made, or indeed if they can be, this whole issue should be placed in historical context—not merely the past ten years or ten centuries, but through the whole arc of Jewish history. Realize at the very outset that no other people has had such a curious ambivalence as the Jews toward the possession and the occupation of land. No people has maintained over so long a period so emotional an attachment to a particular corner of the earth's surface.

But neither has any shown so strong and persistent an instinct to migrate, such courage and skill in pulling up and replanting its roots. For more than three-quarters of their existence as a people, a majority of Jews have always lived outside of the land they call their own.

Abraham was a migrant from Ur Chaldes to Canaan, and at the call of God was the first to receive the Divine promise: "I give you all the land that you can see to you and your offspring forever" (Genesis 13:15). Yet he wandered to Egypt for a while. His nephew, Lot, wandered away from him. His grandson, Jacob, took his whole family to Egypt.

When the First Temple was destroyed in 587/6 B.C.E. and the Jews were exiled to Babylon, some refused to sing and pledged in sorrow, "If I forget you, O Jerusalem, let my right hand wither, let my tongue stick to my palate if I do not keep Jerusalem in memory even at my happiest hour" (Psalms 137:5). Yet, at the very same time, Jeremiah counseled the exiles, "Build houses and live in them, plant gardens and enjoy their fruit" (Jeremiah 29:28).

A more telling statistic (*Encyclopedia Judaica* VIII, 871) can be found in the Herodian period just prior to the destruction of the Second Temple. The total Jewish population at that time was eight million. Of this number, approximately six million lived outside of Palestine. There were almost a million Jews in Alexandria, Egypt, alone. Whether by choice or by chance or by force, Jews have always been a migrating (nomadic) people, and to a considerable degree were shaped by the forces surrounding them.

But wherever they roamed, the centrality of Israel was before them and the yearning to return to Zion was within them. The liturgical calendar was based on the seasons of *Eretz Yisrael.* When the Jews built a home, they left part of it unfinished to remind themselves that there was a perpetual obligation to finish the task of rebuilding their ancient homeland. At a marriage, a glass was broken to remind them of Israel, and at death pious Jews were buried with some earth from the Holy Land. At the end of Yom Kippur and the Seder, two of the most sacred events in Jewish observances, they shouted, "Next Year in Jerusalem!"

However, even as they remembered Zion, they lived in their environment, interacted with it, and were influenced by it. At times they were assimilated into it, and in other instances they rejected it, but generally they learned to absorb its best elements and make them Jewish. The Jewish genius was in recognizing elements that were hostile to it. But in the end, the challenge of a foreign environment contributed to the continued growth of Judaism. Almost every major Jewish book except the Bible was written outside of Eretz Yisrael.

Jewish history and direction have been strung between the poles of loyalty to Zion with a yearning to return to the homeland and living in a foreign environment with all of its benefits as well as impediments. The connection was made when a Jewish state was declared in 1948. Then Jews had to face the choice between living as a minority or being part of the majority.

The contemporary challenge began to take shape in the nineteenth century. When Theodor Herzl converted Zionism (the centrality of Eretz Yisrael) into a political movement whose ultimate aim was to solve "the Jewish problem," he was articulating a basic premise of Judaism. But then he clashed directly with another basic Jewish view that maintained that Judaism was a religion that thrived on challenges of the non-Jewish environment. This approach was advocated by the newly born forces of emancipation, which argued that the integration of the Jew into the non-Jewish majority was the proper course for Jewish salvation.

Of course, there were fundamentalist Jews who did not wish to be integrated into the general society but believed that only through Divine intervention (the Messiah) could Jews return to Israel. Woven among these basic approaches was a whole variety of movements and combinations of movements, essentially all variations on the bipolar nature of the Jewish struggle: nationalism and autonomy versus universalism and religion. At no time were they purist or mutually exclusive; there was much overlapping. It all boiled down to the question: Was there one national home known as "the State" or were Jews at home and fully Jewish wherever they lived? Were Jews outside of Eretz Yisrael in *galut* (exile) or merely *golah* (dispersion)?

The Holocaust seemed to put an end to the conviction that Jews could live safely anywhere outside of Israel. Even among American Jews there lurks the spectre of anti-Semitism. A democracy is ultimately based on public opinion, and public opinion can be a fickle matter. It can happen here.

On the other hand, Jews are beginning to question whether Israel has not turned out to be a form of false messianism. In the wake of so many scandals—all the way from the army to the business world—and with the decline of the kibbutz, is the Zionist dream fading? Did the creation of Israel end Jewish powerlessness, or is there more anti-Semitism in the world than ever before? Did Israel unify Jews or did it exacerbate the conflict between political extremes—the cultural Jews, and the territorial Jews? Why is *aliyah* (the imperative to settle in Israel) giving way to *yerida* (leaving Israel)?

Where, then, shall we proclaim the center of Jewish life in our time? Is Israel still the "Promised Land," or is "Israel" the Jewish people wherever they choose to reside (in this case America)? Proponents are lining up on both sides and the duel is beginning.

But, then, is it not possible to offer a third alternative? Does one need to quarrel over a real or mythical center of Judaism? Could we not dip into history and observe that there have always been two foci around which Jewish life has revolved? Can there not be a partnership? Cannot Israel and the American Jewish community (as well as all Jewish communities) live as a duet?

The key words here are to be found in the classic phrase *klal yisrael,* "the whole community of Israel." This is suitably expressed in Mordecai Kaplan's use of the term "peoplehood" and emphasis on *kehilla,* "the *whole* community."

Was the creation and maintenance of Israel without American (and world) Jewry possible? Equally so, the failure of Israel (Heaven forbid) would shatter every Jew living today and would affect generations to come. Is it not ingrained in the Jewish psyche that "all Jews are responsible for one another?"

Perhaps our generation should consider itself most fortunate. After 1,900 years, American Jews have a choice. They can live in America with its advantages and twin threats of intermarriage and assimilation. Or they can live a full Jewish life in Israel, with all of its attendant social, religious, political, and economic problems.Today with so many means available, it is possible to experiment with living in both cultures. There should be discussion. There should be friendly debate. There should be constructive criticism, and honest difference should be expressed. But there is no need for acrimony or confrontation. There is no need for a duel and every reason for a duet. We all need each other, and we all need to help each other fulfill the purpose of Judaism. Perhaps we are only expressing the ancient creative tension in Judaism between the universal and the particular, and we are simply reenacting the previous forms of Jewish history.

In the end, should not Jews heed the admonition of Kohelet: "It is best that you grasp the one without letting go of the other" (7:18)? Or, in the words of Dr. Alice Shalvi, professor of English literature at the Hebrew University, "Two people may not agree on everything, but they should work together in those areas where they do agree, on that which binds and unites us."—1987

3. Jewish Unity: Myths and Realities

Jewish unity is now being discussed in America, in Israel, in the media, in books and magazines, in the pulpit, in public forums, in the living room, and in the bedroom. It has become the "in" topic among Jews. There is even a book on it entitled *The Coming Cataclysm.*

It is now time to step back and consider this issue historically and thoughtfully. We ought to ask ourselves even more fundamental questions. Was there ever one Jewish people? Is there one Jewish people now? Do we really want one Jewish people?

There was never one Jewish people. Abraham parted from his nephew Lot because they could not get along. Abraham hardly fared better with his sons, the second generation of Jews. After Moses led the Jews out of Egypt and gave them the Ten Commandments, the Jews paid him back by trying to stone him, and Korach led a rebellion against him.

After King Solomon's death, the Davidic kingdom immediately divided into the northern and southern kingdoms (Israel and Judah). The Talmud is a long record of the debates of Jews. Pharisees and Sadducees and lesser sects had monumental quarrels. Even the simplest student of history is aware that the Talmud declares that Jerusalem fell because Jews were internally divided.

Generations of Jewish history follow that pattern, whether it is the Rabbinites and the Karaites, the Maimonideans and the anti-Rationalists, or the Hasidim and the Mitnagdim. Pick any age in Jewish history and you will find quarrels, excommunications, informers, and even fist fights among sects.

So the real question is *ma nishtana,* why is this generation different from all other generations? There are many explanations, and one could hardly be simplistic. But there are some considerations to heed if we are to help ourselves and keep from further damaging or, *lo ahleynu,* destroying ourselves. Difference will not be solved by pious pleas for unity, sincere though they may be. It will not be mitigated by convening conferences or love-ins. It will only be helped by hard-thinking, historical analysis, mutually beneficial attitudes, and realistic programs that will lead us to change.

As far as the Jewish masses are concerned, the contemporary concern can be expressed in the slogan "We are one." That has been exhorted in appeals, T-shirts, celebrated in song, and chanted at rallies. While this slogan implies that we are one in supporting Israel's security and one in our concern for Jews throughout the world, it also had another effect. It has created a myth that Jews were united in everything. If a Jew raised a question, even tentatively, questioning whether this was the proper approach, he or she was immediately swamped in a tidal wave, which was tantamount to accusing one of the final heresy: "You are un-Jewish!" What started out as a strong positive commitment, as is often the case, turned into the beginning of a nightmare.

Until the eighteenth century, Western European Jews had a sort of unity. The words "sort of" are appropriate, for out of this time comes the old saw, "Where there are two Jews, there are three opinions." Forced to live in the same ghetto, they studied the same holy books, they used the same language (a form of Yiddish), they worshiped in the same type of synagogue, with but minor variations they wore the same clothes, and they shared the same universe of discourse. But under the impact of the Emancipation, the Enlightenment, and nationalism any chances for Jewish unity were shattered forever.

When the movement for Emancipation gathered force, Jews were free to mix with Christians. Once they were given this freedom, they soon saw the ways of their neighbors, were influenced by them, and then eventually intermarried with them. The process continues today.

Under the impact of the Enlightenment, Jewish authority was undermined forever. All was called into doubt. The Torah and Halacha lost their binding force. Jews began to study a whole variety of subjects with a vengeance, being no longer limited to the Talmud. Preaching in the synagogue was not only in the vernacular, but even worship forms were profoundly affected.

Some Jews reacted by completely assimilating to the dominant culture. For example, one-half of the children of the first Jew to walk out of the ghetto, Moses Mendelssohn, became Christian. Some Jews created their own physical, intellectual, and spiritual ghetto. They refused to read other than authorized books, they refused to change their language, they refused to change their garb, and they even said, "Everything outside the Torah is forbidden." Some Jews tried to bridge the gap with the synthesis of the "best" of both cultures. Whether they have succeeded is still open to question. At any rate, all approaches are still in process, and this is part of the problem.

Nationalism was the third force to have its impact upon Jews. Now that feudal estates, ducal sovereignties, and church lands were being forged into a nation, what were the Jews? Were they a "nation within a nation"? Were they just another religion? Were they German Jews or were they Jewish Germans? Or were they a nation without a land but, given a land, would they become a true nation (Zionism) where all of their problems would be solved?

Now that Zionism has turned into the reality of the State of Israel, are more Jews united than ever in that land? Is anti-Semitism lessened in the world? Are Jews safer elsewhere? Or, did we expect too much from Zionism, and has it become another form of false messianism, from which we Jews have suffered all these years?

What's to be done?

The answer is to learn the reality of Jewish history. Accept disagreement and difference among Jews as not only part of the Jewish condition but also the human condition and work with it. Work together for the common good when and where we can. Accept the right to be different as a Jewish right and glory in it.

The reality of Jewish history is that from our birth we were (and are) a stubborn, "stiff necked people." Difference isn't bad; it is only the way we use it that can be bad. If everybody is thinking alike, no one is thinking at all. We can disagree without being disagreeable. If we do not agree on halachic or philosophic issues, let us say so, but always with respect for others. Let there be an open market of Jewish ideas and let each Jew pick the rabbi and/or movement or interpretation he or she wishes. Let there be variations on the grand theme of Judaism. Ultimately, history will pass final judgment (if there is ever a right or wrong in these matters).

On those issues where there is a common cause, let us work together. All Jews should be concerned for the freedom of our Russian brothers and sisters. All Jews should join in the fight against anti-Semitism. All Jews should be concerned about the security of Israel and the welfare of Jews all over the world. There is such a crying need for Jewish unity that diversity should be a small part of our agenda.

Let us recognize that the State of Israel has its problems for historic reasons. Ben-Gurion, to keep a fragile unity, granted fundamentalist Jewry sovereignty over religious issues. He ignored the well-known, tragic consequences when the powers of church and state are not separated. He did not foresee that the lack of a concept of pluralism would lead to a *Kulturkampf,* a culture war. To be sure, ironically enough, many of the Jews in America who fight vigorously in the United States for the separation of church and state battle just as hard for the union of synagogue and state in Israel. It is sheer intellectual dishonesty.

As an American Jew committed to Israel (my wife and I own a condominium and grave plots there), I support Israel, but I have chosen to live in the United

States. When Israel is right and needs me, I will support it with all my heart, my soul, and my might. When Israel is wrong, I will express my opinion in appropriate ways and with tact, for I will offer no comfort to Israel's enemies.

In the last analysis, let us accept the reality of Jewish history, life, and experience. Why should we all agree on everything? Why shouldn't we be proud to be able to be different? Why shouldn't we be responsible and reasonable in stating and accepting our differences? Why shouldn't we work together as Jews when we have a common cause? Let us reject all extremism as extremely distasteful yet realize that between the poles is a whole world of difference.

We are all part of Jewish peoplehood. We can all create a unity within our diversity. We can all respect each other, accept each other, and help each other. In the end, the words of an old Yiddish song ring true:

"Vas meir zeinen, zeinen mir, ober yidden zeinen mir.
Vas mir tuen, tuen mir, ober miyzvas tuin mir."
What we are, we are, but one thing is certain.
We are Jews. What we do, we do, but we do mitzvot.

As we all should agree, it is not what a Jew says that counts, but what a Jew does that matters. That is why Jewish unity is a myth and Jewish mutuality is a reality.—1988

4. My Shtetl, Radun

A Lament

The main street is only four blocks long, but it is my shtetl, Radun. It was where my mother was born and my parents were married by the illustrious Chafitz Chayim.

As we were making arrangements this year for our annual visit to our home in Jerusalem, I suddenly said to my wife, Laeh, "I would like to visit Radun—or what's left of it." I don't know whether my urge was prompted by desiring to find my roots or wondering about the origins of my immediate family or sensing that the shtetl would be soon consigned to history. My wife readily and enthusiastically agreed to the visit.

It was not so easy. We had to fly to Amsterdam, change for a flight to Vilnius (Vilna), and then pick up our minivan and guide. Then two more hours to Radun. Radun is in Belarus, now under an autocratic and paranoid dictatorship, on the country's border with Lithuania. Our guides had a great deal of trouble getting visas, although we had arranged to have them in advance, and we had to go through four border checkpoints. With that out of the way, our excitement mounted as we saw the lush country and traveled the road as my family had for the past centuries. About an hour later, a road sign appeared announcing Vitsbk.

That is where Marc Chagall was born, named Moishe Segal. Upon further reflection, I wondered, "How many Chagalls, Einsteins, and Golda Meirs were lost in the Holocaust?"

As this was going through my mind we were suddenly in Radun. It looked like a scene from *Fiddler On the Roof* but without the music and romance. Some of the houses were redone, but most of them were 75 to 100 years old. The only way to travel was with carts and horses that looked like nags.

We stopped at the site where the synagogue had stood, now a cultural center. The women managers were very pleasant. When my wife had to use the facilities they led her into a small room and handed her a pail and some tissues.

We went to the cemetery where my grandparents are buried. All that remains are forty stones artfully placed—a token. It was almost impossible to read the names, and some were upside down. The only new addition was a large granite monument where the Chafitz Chayim is buried, listing all the books he wrote.

We walked back and stopped at a sort of tavern and lunch bar near where my grandfather had his small place of business. We had *shav,* a spinach-like cold soup, and smetana (sour cream) on tomatoes and cucumbers. All these years I thought I was eating Jewish home cooking, and it was really Lithuanian.

I say Lithuanian because, although the area constantly changed hands, the Radunites always considered themselves "Litvaks." My mother once told me that every little store had to have a large picture of the reigning king on the wall. In my grandfather's store they had a frame with kings in the front and back. When the Germans came in, they showed the picture of the Kaiser, and when the Russians took over they turned the picture over and there was the Czar.

The last Jew in Radun is ninety years old. That is why I went alone with a guide to Ponar, a death camp in nearby Vilna. Among the 60,000 Jews murdered there were my uncles, aunts, and cousins. They were shot, then thrown into pits. Gasoline was poured over them and then the bodies were burned. The choice of Ponar was obvious, for it is deep in the forest but near a railroad line.

Ponar is a long series of mounds covered by green forest plants. It is bisected by roads, and there are several moving monuments. Two pits were left open, filled with sand and ashes.

On an impulse, I put my hand in the sand and black ash. As I was gently rubbing off the mixture, I suddenly fainted and was caught by our guide and driver. It was a deeply painful experience but a necessary one.

In Vilnius, by diplomatic arrangement, we met with Dr. Regina Varniene, director of the Lithuanian National Library. In an old, abandoned Catholic church, St. George, is a collection of more than 100,000 Jewish books, newspapers, and other materials, including what remains of the world-famous Strashun Library. Most of the Jewish literary items that were left after the Nazi destruction were devastated in 1950 by the Russians. These remnants were saved because the chief librarian piled them behind the altar and threw old Lithuanian newspapers over them. These items are now being cataloged, and editions of the *Forward,* a Yiddish newspaper, are being microfilmed. Thirty-five boxes have been sent to YIVO in New York for further examination and documentation. The total collection includes rabbinic texts, a community ledger kept by *Chevra Tehillim* of Brisk (the Psalm Society), records of births, marriages, deaths, and business transactions. I even saw an invitation to a jazz concert.

I met with the Jewish leaders of Vilna-Vilnius, conversing in Yiddish. Out of a community once known as *Yerushalayim d'Lita* (Jerusalem of Lithuania) there are only 1,000 Jews left. Laeh (Larissa) Lampert, who teaches Hebrew and Hebrew literature at Vilna University, talked to me in Hebrew and told me there is some interest in Jewish culture but not much. Simon Aperovich, the president of the Jewish community, informed me there was a daily minyan of elderly Jews, but they had to be paid to attend services.

Dr. Chaskel Lemchenas, a philologist who is ninety-two years old, is working on his fifth edition of a Lithuanian-Russian dictionary. He showed me an article he wrote in Yiddish seventy years ago. As we were talking, he abruptly rose and went into the kitchen. I found him leaning on the refrigerator. He had turned his radio on to listen to the news coming from Kol Yisrael (the Voice of Israel), the daily broadcast from Jerusalem in Yiddish. Every word from Israel is precious to them.

Lithuanian Jewry, or what's left of it, is now preparing to commemorate the two-hundredth anniversary of the Vilna Gaon (Excellency), Elijah ben Solomon, one of the greatest Talmudists of all time. Planners invited me to consult with them. They had prepared a convocation of international scholars from institutions ranging from the University of Texas and Hebrew University in Jerusalem to New York University. It will take place in September.

Naturally, we visited the grave site of this man whose towering intellect changed the flow of Jewish scholarship and influenced Jewish history. It is a mausoleum with a blue-and-white tower on top. Inside one can see his grave and those of his family. They are covered with stones that visitors leave and with paper prayers and supplications.

There is one more fascinating bit of information. Originally, the Gaon's grave was in the old Vilna cemetery. When that was razed by the Russians to make room for an apartment complex, the Jewish community removed his remains and reburied them with the ashes of the Jewish convert, Count Potocki. Count Potocki was the gifted son of an aristocratic Polish family who, after studying in Paris and the Papal Academy in Rome, decided to go to Amsterdam to become a Jew. He eventually settled near Vilna, where he was arrested and put on trial. Despite the pleas of fellow aristocrats, he refused to recant. On the second day of Shavuot, he was burned at the stake at the front of the fortress of Vilna.

Potocki died with the Jewish martyr's prayer on his lips: "Blessed be to You God . . . Who sanctifies Your name in public." A local Jew, paying the requisite of fees, collected the ashes of the corpse. Astounding!

While at the Jewish collection at the Lithuanian National Library, I found a poem by Gittel Farkas of Bialystok which began with: "The shtetl is sleeping/ The farm is shut/ I come to you/ In the middle of the night."—1997

5. The Jewish Badge: Humiliation or Honor?

An elderly Jewish woman approached a blonde, blue-eyed man and said, "Excuse me, mister, are you Jewish?" He regarded her disdainfully for a moment and then replied, "No, madam, I am not!" Still uncertain, she repeated her question. Irritated, he replied icily, "I told you, I am not a Jew!"

But she was persistent and put the question to him for the third time: "You're sure you're not Jewish?" The old lady's determination finally broke down his defenses. "Yes," he confessed, "I'm Jewish." To which she replied, "That's funny—you don't look Jewish!"

The Jewish badge was a distinctive sign worn to designate Jews, to distinguish them as not belonging to the majority faith. The Jewish badge was usually considered a humiliation, but it could also be viewed as an honor.

The idea was first introduced by Caliph Omar II (717-20), who ordered that every non-Muslim *(dhimmi)* wear a garment *(giyar),* a different color for each minority group. The edict was unequally observed. In Sicily, the Muslim ruler compelled Christians to wear their garments and put on their doors a piece of cloth in the form of a swine. Jews were compelled to affix a sign in the form of a donkey. How strange it must have seemed for Jews, who for thousands of years have placed a mezuzah on their doorposts to emphasize love, learning, and the presence of one God. That Jewish badge is the symbol of holiness and hospitality. For instance, at the very beginning of the Passover Seder each Jew recites, "Let all who are hungry come and eat."

At the conclusion of the fourth century Christendom evolved the theological basis for a badge to degrade Jews. Augustine in Book XII of *Reply to Faustus* argued that Cain represents the Jews and wrote, "The Church admits and avows the Jewish people to be cursed." He counseled that, because of the mark of Cain which protected them, Jews should live in a degraded condition as witnesses to the Truth until their conversion to Christianity.

In reading the episode of Cain, however, the rabbis saw him as a repentant sinner and an expression of God's mercy. The passage in Genesis (4:13-15) reads as follows:

Cain said to God, "My punishment is too great to bear! Since You have banished me this day from the soil, and I must avoid Your presence and become a restless wanderer on earth—anyone who meets me may kill me!" God said to him, "I promise, if anyone kills Cain, sevenfold vengeance shall be taken on him." And God put a mark on Cain, lest anyone who met him should kill him.

This is a remarkable statement about forgiveness and, surely, a warning about capital punishment and its implications. This passage also speaks of compassion, understanding, and the protective mercy of God.

Although the mark of Cain was originally bestowed as a sign of God's protective mercy, over the course of time its meaning was inverted and it was interpreted as a curse. In 1215, under the leadership of Innocent III, the Fourth Latin Council promulgated legislation requiring Jews (and Saracens) to wear distinctive clothes or badges that would separate them from the Christian populace. The seeds had been sown, although the confusion was such that there were various expressions of this noxious canon. In some places it was totally ignored, and in others it raised resentment in the majority population.

In England in the *statutum de Judeismo,* Edward I stipulated that a piece of yellow taffeta, six fingers long and three broad, was to be worn over the heart by every Jew over the age of seven. The badge took the form of the Tablets of the Law. What irony that the symbol of the Ten Commandments, moral foundation of the Western civilization, be the mark of the Jews!

In Spain the badge was a red bullseye; in Sicily, it was of bluish color; in Rome, it was a yellow hat for men and a yellow kerchief for women; in Venice, a red hat. In Salzburg Jewish women had to attach bells to their dresses; in Austria Jews wore a yellow circle. Small wonder, then, that the Nazis picked up on the idea of a modern Jewish hate badge.

There were at least ten forms of yellow badges used in Germany and other countries to designate the Jew. Since 1933 most of them were yellow and shaped like the Shield of David with the word for Jew written on it. Sometimes it was simply a "J." In concentration camps, Jews were forced to wear a yellow badge, often a triangle to distinguish them from political prisoners, homosexuals, Romas, the mentally retarded, and other "sub-humans."

But there were some surprising reactions. Jews wore the mark with dignity, as a decoration. It was to commemorate the yellow badge that Theodor Herzl chose this color for the cover of the first Zionist periodical, *Die Welt.* During World War II in Holland, out of solidarity with Jewish citizens, 300,000 replicas were distributed inscribed "Jews and non-Jews stand united in their struggle!" In Denmark the badge was never introduced as a result of the courageous resistance of King Christian X, who was said to have threatened to wear it himself.

Perhaps the strongest statement on the subject was made on April 4, 1943, after the Nazis scrawled the word *Jude* on Jewish property. Robert Weltsch, editor of *Juedische Rundscham,* wrote a memorable editorial which contained the words, "Jews pick up their yellow badge (Shield of David) and wear it with pride."

Before and since the establishment of the State of Israel under the Jewish government, millions of Jews and others of all faiths in distress have been saved and helped by organizations bearing this symbol.

Today the *kippah* (skull cap), a sure Jewish symbol of identity, can be seen on men in investment houses and grocery stores and on women at the synagogue and study groups. Chunky *chais* (life symbols) and Stars of David abound, proudly displayed in materials and design from filigree to porcelain. Waterproof *mezzuzot* are worn on chains even in showers. Scotts are turning into Sholomos and Shirleys are becoming Shoshanas.

So it is that this badge of hate became a symbol of hope.—1997

6. What I Learned from Going Back to College

Five years ago, I went back to college. Two years before retirement, I began to plan for that event. So I started to teach one course in the religious studies department at Macalester College. Upon retirement, I became a professor in religious studies and later the first Jewish chaplain in the history of the college.

I teach one class in the fall, one in interim, about ten independents, and I am counselor to Hebrew House and all the Jewish students and adviser to all my students. I am a member of the Council for Religious Understanding, the Multi-Cultural Committee, the Service Committee, and adviser to the college on all Jewish matters.

My first class had five students, then it went on to eleven. The third year, it was seventeen. Then twenty-five. Last year I had thirty. In January interim I had forty and now use the audio-visual amphitheater.

I teach variations of Judaica but never the same course twice. For three of them I have written my own syllabus book. Here are some of the courses: Jewish Values as Reflected in Jewish Literature, A Rabbinic Commentary on the New Testament, Contemporary Ethical Issues from a Jewish View, the Living Jewish Community (which I taught on a bus), the Art of Judaism, which approached Judaism from the perspectives of music, dance, poetry, painting, and sculpture. I taught the Holocaust through film, guest lectures, and discussion, and enrollment rose to seventy-five. When I offered a course entitled the History of God, the number was near ninety.

I conduct services on Rosh Hashanah and Yom Kippur and arrange celebrations for Jewish festivals.

There are about 150 Jewish students on campus. With them, as with other students, I live in the twenty-first century. Although 90% of my students are non-Jews, they come to me with their intellectual, identity, and personal problems. The Jewish students do this, but more so. I deal with children of divorce and mixed marriages, with personal crises, intellectual doubts, ferment, and problems that do cross a rabbi's eyes.

I have learned a great deal about Jewish young people between eighteen and twenty-two. They are all in the midst of forming their Jewish identity. Jewish education helps, but when they get on campus they need mature, adult understanding of Judaism to make their choices. I believe this area, long neglected, is the real firing line of Judaism, overlooked, unattended, and misunderstood. I feel here I am doing some of the most important work of the rabbinate.

When I first came, the students in class did not know what to call me. I gave them the options of calling me Professor, Doctor, Rabbi, Mister, or Bernie. Guess what they chose 90% of the time? Rabbi.

During the first year, the faculty and staff eyed me cautiously. What was I? The Jewish faculty wasn't sure of my scholarly credentials. The administrative staff seemed to think I was probably a Jewish priest. Now the Jewish faculty yell, "Shalom," to me across campus and some are starting to teach Jewish subjects in their disciplines. To most of the faculty I am now "IN" because they tell me off-color jokes. The administrative staff call me Bernie and keep wanting to take me out for coffee.

Incidentally, in all the official college announcements they list me as "Rabbi."

That is a signal to attract Jewish students. Jews have increased from 7% to 9% of the population since I have been there, and the numbers are going up fast. We are now in the process of trying to create an endowed Judaic program.

Of course, the best part of teaching is learning from students. They have shlept me from protests to experimental dance, to avant-garde art, esoteric subjects, mystical experiences, veggie meals, parties, and all kinds of *mishugas.*

I dress like them—casual. But I draw the line at torn jeans.

I find their eagerness to learn about Jews and Judaism overwhelming. If approached properly, Jewishness can be the hottest item on campus.

Let me share a few brief personal experiences with you. One student named Johanna told me that her mother was a convert to Judaism from Episcopalianism but her maternal grandparents were converts from Judaism to Episcopalianism. I said, "Run that by me again." She explained that her grandparents fled Germany when Hitler came to power, and they were Jewish. When they arrived in America, because of emotional conflicts and fear, they decided to become Episcopalians and took their daughter to church every Sunday. Their daughter fell in love with a prominent composer who was Jewish and insisted that she become Jewish if they were to marry. She did, and Johanna was born of that union.

I asked Johanna what she was. She replied, "I don't know. That's why I am taking your course and talking to you." We left it at that. A few weeks later we were talking about contemporary approaches to Judaism. I invited Rabbi Feller (Lubavitch) and Rabbi Offner (Reform) to present their interpretations at separate sessions. Feller has a clever *shtick* to open his presentation. He begins by asking, "When I say the word 'Jew,' what do you think? Tell me in one word." We get varied answers, most of them positive. He turned to Johanna and asked, "When I say 'Jew,' what do you think?" She replied quickly and firmly, "Me." I got the message.

Johanna is now doing an independent with me next semester. She is an art student who works in plastic and acrylic. She is researching and creating an original art object made out of plastic, acrylic, and parts of the Torah. Her title is, "Homage to the Torah."

Kevin Olson is a bright, fair-haired boy from the farm belt. I encourage the students to write papers out of personal experience in reaction to class topics. One day in class we were discussing the crucial passage in Genesis where God creates a human in the Divine image. Then I pointed out that this well-known phrase is followed by words that most people overlook. They are, "male and female were they created," which clearly states that man and woman were created equally and at the same time. This powerful statement has been overlooked or at least suppressed over the centuries.

The next day I got a paper from Kevin. That night he told me he attended a Timberwolves basketball game. A trio of women opened the game with "America the Beautiful." They came to a well known stanza and changed it in this manner: "And crown Thy good with brotherhood and sisterhood."

He noticed the applause afterward was deafening, as if someone had hit a slam dunk. He said he thought about class and tears were streaming down his face. At the bottom of the page I wrote, "Only when knowledge and experience intersect does true learning occur."

Another student is named Inoshita. He is Japanese and his father, as a child with his family, was interned in camps during the Second World War.

Inoshita is into judo. He practices two hours every day. I kept getting these papers comparing Judaism to Japanese culture, particularly judo. One day he wrote a paper explaining that the essence of judo is *chi,* meaning "the life force." It started me thinking. *Chi,* or more correctly *Xhi,* is the Greek letter *X.* It is usually mispronounced by fraternities as *Kai.* At any rate, *Xhi* is only one step from *chai,* which is Hebrew for "life."

Following that, we had a long conversation on the meaning of life in the Jewish and the judo cultures.

On the last day of class, a student named Jasna Jasnic, who is on a study program from Yugoslavia (Serbia), came up to me after the session to say goodbye. She informed me that she was going to Sarajevo for the winter holidays. I said, "Are you out of your mind? Your family sent you here to get out of that hell." She replied, "You know, Rabbi, we talked about the Holocaust. If, in 1939, your mother was in Warsaw, wouldn't you want to see her on Rosh Hashanah?" Then she added with a smile, "It's a mitzvah."

I was very moved and in a choked voice I said, "Jasna, when you return, write up your experience for me and I will give you an 'independent' worth three credits. Shalom."

I am going to conclude with an illustration of what it means to be a practicing Jew on campus today. If you recall, during the Los Angeles riots following the King beating, the Black community was deeply angered. At Macalester the Black students called for a rally the day after the L.A. happening. They wanted only Black students to speak—no whites, no faculty. When the administration pointed out that they should have at least one representative of the college, they said, "O.K., let the rabbi come, but only as the rabbi—no other titles."

I came the next day. When I was called upon to say something, I began by saying, "I came as a Jew." Then I explained, "When a Jew experiences death, he or she is supposed to put on a black ribbon, cut it, and recite a prayer, indicating that there is loss and suffering."

Then I put on my *kippah,* put a black ribbon on my coat, cut it and recited the prayer in Hebrew and English. Then I said, "I mourn the death of justice in America. I am part of the suffering community." I sat down and there was total silence for thirty seconds, and then the program went on.

The next day, I was invited to four Black rallies. Now every time there is a gathering of this sort, I get invited as a friend.

It's exciting being a Jew on campus today, where the real battle for Jewishness is going on. I love every minute of it because it is alive, vital, challenging, and I hear the bugles calling me to battle for what I have believed in all my life.—1993

7. That's a Lot of Chutzpah

Chutzpah by Alan M. Dershowitz. Boston: Little, Brown and Company.

How does one define chutzpah? Pushiness, assertiveness, verve, cheek? Louis Armstrong was once asked to define jazz. His reply was, "Man, if you don't know, I can't tell you." Alan Dershowitz *is* chutzpah.

His central thesis is that American Jews need to be more assertive. He argues (after all, he is a lawyer) that they do not value themselves even though they have contributed so much to the greatness of this country, and they have rights. It is time to drop the defensive posture of *shanda fur de goyim* (an embarrassment for the gentiles) and speak out on a first-class basis with our peers.

Dershowitz's career has been marked by chutzpah. While being Orthodox and strictly observant, he graduated from Yale Law School and clerked for a Supreme Court Justice for whom he refused to travel on the Sabbath. He became a professor in the Harvard Law School. It was only later, particularly upon the questioning of his sons, that he abandoned some of his ritual observance. However, his loyalty to the Jewish people, Israel, and social justice does not waver in the slightest. Indeed, it intensifies.

What is interesting is that though Dershowitz has a classic Jewish education, he never refers to the prophets who, after all, laid the foundation for the commitment to social justice. Perhaps even the Talmud, with its questioning style, unconsciously left its mark on him, enhancing his expertise as a defense lawyer.

The book is an excellent primer on anti-Semitism, Israel, world Jewry, the various forms of Jewish commitment, and some fascinating insights on the condition of being a Jew in "Christian America." His views are challenging, well thought out, but not definitive. Nor are they meant to be.

Chutzpah is a sort of autobiography which narrates his fascinating life, both personal and public. He displays intellectual honesty in both areas, and we can identify with his struggles. Many charming anecdotes are also included. He records a conversation with his mother involving her strong views. She tells him with finality, "The difference between a Jewish mother and a terrorist is that with the terrorist you can negotiate."

Dershowitz passes severe judgment on some of the Jewish leaders of the past generations, especially during the Holocaust. They are characterized as "house Jews" who unconsciously (or consciously) tried to be a part of the establishment. True enough, but this is hindsight, and they were prisoners of history. Passing judgment, as Dershowitz knows, must be balanced.

There are some powerful phrases in the book that blend Jewishness and Americanism to make a striking recombinant. Thus, Judge Bazelon orders the writer to issue a "writ of *rachmones*" (compassion). Judge I. Leo Glaser tells a defendant who purports to be a religious Jew to be careful of *chilul hashem* (a disgrace to the name of God or dishonesty that a Jew commits and therefore brings unnecessary embarassment to the Jewish people).

One is a bit perturbed by some of Dershowitz's shady clients, such as Claus von Bulow, Leona Helmsley, and Jim Baker. But after all, every person is entitled to his or her day in court. And Dershowitz is among the very best in his field. His fees enable him to battle for Jewish and civil rights with great effectiveness. His efforts on behalf of Natan Scharansky are a brilliant sun illuminating the bleak horizon of injustice as well as indifference.

The book has enormous value for all Americans. Dershowitz points out that America has changed from a homogeneous nation of white Protestants into the most heterogeneous, religiously diverse society in the world. The benefits of this in terms of human rights, civil rights, and freedom of conscience for each American are not to be taken lightly. Indeed, he speaks to the "right to be outraged."

For Jews, particularly of this generation, the book provides an important corrective as well as a good perspective. American Jews must speak up for their rights or be silent forevermore. Certainly, there will always be some form of anti-Semitism, but we do not have to put up with it whether it be small slights or huge hate. Also, we are not alone, and we have responsibility to world Jewry and Israel, as well as a concern for the rights of all human beings. There is no conflict between being Jewish and being American; indeed, they go hand in glove.

Chutzpah warns us to recognize the risks of being too thin-skinned, and we know the dangers of being too lethargic when it comes to Jewish interests and survival. In the author's own words: "As a people who came close to having no future, we guard our future as if it were the present."

In sum, Dershowitz tells it like it is (chutzpah). So have a little cheek, make out a check, buy a copy of *Chutzpah,* and send it to your favorite college student or graduate.—1991

8. Glasnost, Perestroika, and a New Era in Jewish Scholarship

The new Russian policies of *glasnost* (openness) and *perestroika* (restructuring) have already started a process that indicates a bright new day is dawning in the history of Jewish scholarship. Jewish scholars have been aware for years that great treasures of Jewish manuscripts, collections, and other data were stored in Russian institutions, including material of enormous value that exists nowhere else.

The key figure in this new beginning is the Talmudic scholar Adin Steinsaltz, one of the foremost Jewish scholars in Israel. Steinsaltz is the head of the Israeli Institute For Talmudic Publications in Jerusalem, which produced his renowned commentaries and translations of the Talmud. He recently announced in Jerusalem that the USSR Academy of Sciences has agreed to join forces with western scholars under his direction to examine the vast treasures of Judaica in the Soviet Union that have been closed to outsiders for some seven decades.

The institutions taking part in this historic project read like a *Who's Who* of world scholarship. They include the Bibliotheque de l'Alliance Israelite Francaise, the Bodleian Library at Oxford, the British Library, the Geneva University Library, the Israel National Library, the Royal Library of Copenhagen, the New York Public Library, the U.S. Library of Congress, and the YIVO Institute.

According to a survey done twenty-five years ago, there are more than 18,000 known Jewish manuscripts in Russia. Twelve thousand are in Leningrad Public Library alone. There are almost 2,000 manuscripts in the Lenin Library in Moscow. Others are to be found in Odessa, Crimea, and in many villages and monasteries. An unusual biblical codex of the tenth century is preserved in Tiflis. Undoubtedly, several hundred thousand Jewish books and ethnographical data—such as stories, local histories, and music—are yet to be discovered in libraries throughout Russia. The writings are in Hebrew, Russian, Yiddish, Polish, Arabic, Aramaic, Judeo-Arabic, Judeo-Persian, and several Slavic languages. Also included are fifty mathematical, astronomical, and astrological works. It will take scholars generations to study and interpret this data.

An interesting example of what awaits examination is to be found in the two Firkovitch collections in the Leningrad Public Library. Abraham Firkovitch was a Karaite leader who was born in Poland. He was zealous in trying to establish Karaite independence from the Rabbanites. In his travels through Crimea, Turkey, and Palestine, he collected manuscripts in Hebrew and Samaritan as well as tombstone inscriptions. His collections are among the largest single holdings of Hebrew manuscripts in existence today.

According to *The Jerusalem Post,* this project took shape over the past several months, with the help of U.S. Secretary of State George Schultz. The first major advance occurred last month when Steinsaltz had preliminary talks with the vice-chairman of the USSR Academy of Sciences, Evgeny Velikhove, while they were attending a conference at Oxford University. Since then he has traveled to libraries and institutes in Europe and the U.S. to put together the international team of scholars.

Some members of the team, Steinsaltz said, will stay on in Russia "to form the basis of an institution to train a new generation of Soviet Jewish scholars and religious leaders. We can't overestimate the importance of this development for the renewal of Jewish cultural and religious life there." However, a well researched article by Charles Hoffman noted that rabbinical academies have not operated openly in Russia since the 1920s. The Soviets may find it easier to connect this institution to the University of Moscow than to establish it as an independent body.

The team of scholars is to organize and record these materials using advanced computer technology so that the data will be available for researchers all over the world. The project could start within the next year, although there is still much red tape to cut through in the Soviet Union.

This is the third great Jewish scholarly find in the past one hundred years. The first was the discovery of the famous *Geniza* in a Cairo synagogue by Solomon Schechter in 1896. More than 100,000 pages were found and sent to Cambridge University in England. That filled a large gap of knowledge of Jews in Arab lands, liturgical works of Jews in Palestine, Spain, and Babylonia, and the discovery of the Hebrew text of Ben Sira.

The second find was the Dead Sea Scrolls in the Judean wilderness in Qumran near Jericho. This discovery included books, scrolls, and fragments. It broadened our knowledge of the Jewish sectarians of the first century. The scrolls helped to authenticate the traditional Hebrew text of the Bible and are also invaluable to the study of the roots of Christianity.

The latest "find," through access to the vast material legacy of Russian Jews, may turn out to be the most significant of them all. It will give us a better understanding of how Jewish life began and developed in Russia. We will learn how Russian and Jewish life interacted. Many new spiritual gems (including Hasidic works) will be discovered that will enrich our lives. Records will turn up revealing untold information about the Jewish experience in the Crimea, Ukraine, and small villages all over Russia.

Finally, there is the excitement of a new scholarly venture. Will a by-product of this process be a revival of Russian Jewry? What will we learn about Jewish history that will yield proven solutions to our contemporary problems? Since the greater portion of the American Jewish community has its roots in Russia of one, two, or three generations ago, what will we discover about ourselves?

It is a bright new beginning for Judaism, and only the future will tell us what great intellectual, spiritual, and historical treasures await us.—1990

9. A Fringe Benefit from the Bible

An evolution in fashion is a by-product of the renewed study of the Bible in Israel. Bypassing the dress of the eighteenth-century Polish and Russian nobility adopted by some Orthodox Jews and Hasidim, an Israeli is creating a fashion that follows Jewish tradition. It takes the form of a long, fluid, tunic-style shirt with ritual fringes on the corners.

All this began one Sunday at dawn when Reuven Prager, a 29-year-old Jerusalemite who immigrated from Miami, looked over the Temple Mount from the Tel Arza section in Jerusalem. He was reflecting on the early history of the Jews and tried to draw a mental picture of them coming up to Jerusalem to pray in biblical times.

He began to study those passages in the Bible that pertained to dress. Then he researched the Mishna and Josephus for additional material. Following that, he began to cut up bed sheets and clothes and started to restitch the material. What emerged was fascinating.

What distinguished Jewish dress from the garb of other people of that era were the *tzitzit* worn on the edges of the garment. This is based on the verse in Deuteronomy (22:12), "You shall make fringes on the four corners of the garment with which you cover yourself." Later, the threads and knots were fashioned to equal the Hebrew numerical value of 613, the exact number of biblical commandments.

However, when the Jews went into exile, they began to wear garments with rounded ends, particularly in Europe. A person not wearing a four-cornered garment is exempt from wearing *tzitzit.* There were times during persecutions when it was not prudent to wear them. However, pious Jews, in order to fulfill this biblical commandment, wore a *tallit katan* (a small four-cornered garment) under their shirts.

In the classic passage (Numbers 15:37-40) on wearing the *tzitzit,* Jews are required to include a cord or thread of blue *(techaylet).* The precise color of blue is no longer known. But some feel it is closer to purple, and others contend it is a shade near to crimson. Still others claim it resembles indigo. The Talmud informs us that the color was extracted from the chillazon, a snail found in the sea between Tyre and Haifa. However, the exact formula for the dye has passed into history. Apparently, it was discontinued in the early centuries. Some scholars contend simply that the formula for the dye was lost in the exile. A modern investigator extracted 1.4 grams of purple dye from 12,000 snails. He concluded that it was simply too expensive. Mordecai Kaplan theorized that it was forbidden during the Roman era because it resembled the purple that only emperors and other members of the royal family and nobles were entitled to wear.

It probably can be safely said that it is a color between green and blue. The explanation is found in the Jerusalem Talmud (Bereshit 1:5,3a): "*Techaylet* resembles the sea, the sea resembles grass, and grass resembles the heavens." This follows the reason given in the Bible to wear *tzitzit,* namely, to remind one to keep God's commandments.

In 1888, Rabbi Gershon Leiner, the Hasidic rebbe of Radzin, proposed that the precept of *techaylet* be reintroduced. He concluded that the dye could be extracted from the cuttlefish, which secretes a blue-black substance. Based on this, Reuven Prager began to create garments of square corners with fringes, including the blue cord. He has produced more than 500 garments in many designs and materials.

At first, when he began to wear these garments, he was considered a hippie. Often children would walk after him and shout: "*Avraham Avinu!*" (Our father Abraham) or "*Moshe Rabenu!* (Moses our teacher). When he was in the Israeli Army, he almost landed in jail after transforming his standard-issue olive-green shirt into a four-cornered garment and attaching fringe to it. Prager's commander was not swayed by the contention that instead of desecrating the uniform, he was actually honoring it by saying a blessing over it.

Prager's line of clothing is called *Begged Ivri* (Hebrew dress). He sells it on Friday morning in a small mall on Ben Yehuda Street in Jerusalem or by appointment in his home. It includes everything from the standard "Joseph's Coat of Many Colors" shirt to hand-woven, floor-length caftans for special occasions. He has even designed children's clothes in the biblical style.

The clothes, however, are only one of several projects Prager has planned. He is interested in recreating the *apirion* (a palaquin or tent-like litter) used at Jewish weddings until it was abolished by the rabbis after the destruction of the Temple in the year 70.

The *apirion* as described in the Mishna (Sotah 9:14) was a hand-borne carriage made of golden hangings. It was used to carry the bride from the house of her father to the house of her husband where the wedding ceremony was performed. As the *apirion* with the bride was carried through the streets, crowds gathered and sang happy songs, applauded, and paid her honor. Reintroducing it is an attempt to recreate a Jewish custom marking Israel's return to its ancient homeland.

Reuven Prager is also working on a translation into English of the exhaustive three-volume work of the Radziner Rebbe on the *techaylet* blue dye. By this, he hopes to convince even the most observant to include a blue cord into the ritual fringes on the *tallit* (prayer shawl).

Prager's purpose is to provide another way for Jews to identify with Jewish history. He has spent years studying the matter and has drawn on Jewish classic texts, including the Kabbalah (Jewish mystic literature) and other sources. His belief in the importance of Jewish attire is based on a Talmudic quote (Shabbat 23b) of Rav Huna, "The one who is careful with the observance of *tzitzit* will be blessed with beautiful garments."

This research into "authentic" Jewish attire in Israel is another stimulating expression of the contemporary search among Jews for Jewish roots. It should be encouraged.—1984

10. Minnesota Jewry Looks Forward

In the Bible Amos proclaimed, "I am not a prophet, nor the son of a prophet." A Yiddish proverb has it nor a *naar zogt nevius,* "Only a fool predicts the future." Mordecai Kaplan used to warn his students, "Don't be Ifistic." With these caveats in mind, I would like to cautiously stimulate our thoughts about the Jewish future of Minnesota. Jews tend to be students of history, and from Jewish history we can learn that Judaism and Jewish experience are shaped by economic conditions, the zeitgeist (spirit of the times), and inner visions.

Economic conditions will surely help determine Minnesota Jewish history in coming times. If the state economy is strong there will be more dollars for Jewish activities. More people—and this includes Jews—will enhance our population. Contrariwise, a diminishing economy will mean less Jews. The Duluth Jewish community is an example of that.

It is estimated that 20% of all Americans will eventually settle in a community other than the one in which they were born. Although Jewish institutions in Minnesota are now linked by highways, young Jews will purchase homes in areas with desirable housing and good schools, not necessarily near established Jewish communities.

There will continue to be large synagogues and small synagogues. Large synagogues are able to provide a diversity of services for events that range from the womb to the tomb. Small synagogues, on the other hand, provide intimacy and more opportunities for leadership. It is good to have both, and the community will naturally respond to these needs.

There is a saying today that Jews tend to divide themselves into four sects: Orthodox, Reform, Conservative, and Federation. In a narrower definition of religion, I don't think these terms will have any meaning, except to the historian, a hundred years from now. Even today there are but two types of Jewish religious approaches: fundamentalist and non-fundamentalist.

If one accepts the principle that Judaism is a divinely revealed religion, then all else is commentary. All other expressions of Judaism range from nostalgia and ethnicity to reinterpretation and cultural evolution. Secularists will be hard put to convince young Jews to remain Jewish, for they will be "a generation without memory."

Of course, Judaism always responds to the spirit of the times. Will people tire of the current trend toward conservatism and moral absolutes? Or will they, indeed, intensify these factors? Will they become innovative and liberal? History has a habit of acting like a pendulum swinging between extremes and excesses. Following the history of Jewish life in post-emancipation countries, one can say that the rate of intermarriage will remain the same, while conversion to Judaism will steadily rise for a variety of reasons.

Of course, there will be differences among Jews. Hasn't there always been? Those who prefer a more structured approach or a more fixed system will choose a course to satisfy those needs. Those who prefer a more open approach will select a system and a view that makes them comfortable. One should not be concerned here, because all of life changes and, besides, variety is the spice of life. Jews facing the future must learn to live and let live.

Relationships with Israel will continue to be firm but in a different manner. When Israel is in clear and present danger, when a Jewish community anywhere is being oppressed, Jews will respond in appropriate ways. But now that Zionism is rapidly losing its messianic fervor, now that we realize that our expectations of

Israel were too high, we will begin to settle for reality. Israelis are not super-humans nor are they without their faults. They are people—but our people. We will criticize them as loving relatives and will continue to support them.

On an intellectual level, Jews in Minnesota will advance. Almost every institution of higher learning in the Twin Cities and other parts of the state now offers courses in some phase of Judaism. Many young Jews who missed the opportunity to study Judaism during adolescent years will now do so on a more mature level. Eventually this process, which is occurring all over the United States, will produce some great Jewish intellectual works in this land. Unlike Israel, which is plagued with extremism, religion in politics, and intracultural differences among Jews, American Jewish scholars will concentrate on developing a philosophy of Judaism to face the realities of the times.

The Federation has and will continue to face changing needs. Challenges include a graying population, the movement of larger contributors to the sunbelt, the need to find new rationales for giving, changing styles of campaigns, and a more intense concern with the quality of Jewish education. This latter does not always mean raising allocations, because merely throwing dollars at educational problems does not solve them. The issue is quality. How do we produce better teachers? How do we create a better environment for learning? How do we preserve democracy in the Jewish community?

Judaism has always been driven by its own inner vision and fueled by the dynamism of Jewish experience. The Bible and prophets will continue to provide ethical goals, the Talmud and Jewish literature will continue to offer wisdom and comfort. Jewish culture will continue to provide inspiration and entertainment, and Jewish history will continue to be written. In the end, the Jewish people generally, and the Jews of Minnesota specifically, will decide the direction they should take. And so it should be. But no matter what, there will be Jews and Judaism in Minnesota because "the Keeper of Israel does neither slumber nor sleep."—1992

11. Is the Magen David Really Jewish?

Is the Magen David really Jewish? Now, that's an interesting question. If we asked, "Was the Magen David a universal Jewish symbol prior to the twentieth century?" the answer would be definitely in the negative.

W. Gunther Plaut, in a well-written booklet entitled "The Magen David," cites three interesting historical facts. In 1879 when it was proposed that the new synagogue in St. Petersburg be decorated with the Magen David, the poet and journalist Judah Leib Gordon strongly protested and called it a "heathenish symbol."

In 1917 the French War Department considered burying the Jewish dead under the emblem of the Magen David. French rabbis objected and instead insisted that the emblem be the Ten Commandments.

The harshest pronouncement on the Magen David as a symbol was delivered in the same year by the Viennese scholar and Orthodox rabbi Moritz Gudeman when he wrote these strong words: "Men of learning cannot accept the fact that the Jewish people would dig out of their attic of superstition a symbol or emblem that it shares with the stables."

The Magen David is a geometric figure known as a hexagram. It consists of two equilateral triangles, one placed upon the other. Its sides are also equal so that the six points are part of a circle. It has been used in many cultures, particularly in the Near East, for decoration as well as magic and religious purposes.

The greatest student of this subject was Professor Erwin H. Goodenough, who published seven volumes filled with many variations of this symbol. He points out that its perfect shape and many variations carry with them a special mystique. Also, the Magen David reflects the stars of heaven, thus endowing it with special meaning.

Astrologers used the Magen David. It decorated Christian shrines and for centuries was the emblem of the Order of Franciscan Friars of the Atonement. It was widely used in Islamic culture, which relies heavily on geometric designs. It may also be found on the back of the United States one dollar bill and is the basic shape of an American sheriff's badge.

In most mystical writings the hexagram was known as the Seal of Solomon, no doubt because of his reputation for wisdom and magical powers. According to Gershon Scholem, the late professor of mysticism at the Hebrew University and the greatest authority on the subject, the first authenticated Jewish usage of the Magen David dates from the beginning of the fourteenth century.

A Spanish Kabbalist (mystic) named David ben Yehudah in his work *Sefer Hagevid* pictured the hexagram twice and called it Magen David. No doubt David, from whom, according to tradition, the Messiah would spring, had profound meaning for the mystics of that time. Moreover, the founders of the Davidic dynasty, which made Jerusalem the center of Jewish life, thought that the hexagram was the preeminent symbol of redemption. One of the blessings after the reading of the Haftarah (prophet portion) actually ends with the words "magen david", referring to God.

During the following centuries the hexagram was used on Jewish amulets. It became popular to display the hexagram designed with verses from Psalm 121 to protect women during childbirth. Belief in the magical powers was further enhanced in the pseudo-messianic movements of David Reubeni and Shabbtai Tzvi.

The Jewish community of the city of Prague in 1716 displayed as its flag a yellow Magen David on a red background. The Magen David can be found on tombstones in cemeteries in Prague as well as on the official seal of the community. A synagogue key from Prague in the late nineteenth century contains a design with the Magen David repeated three times. It was also incorporated into logos of Jewish printers in Italy. In a boundary marker for the ghetto of Vienna there is a cross to mark the Christian side and a Magen David to designate the Jewish area.

However, the movement toward the Magen David as a universally accepted Jewish symbol began with the Zionists. There are many versions of how it occurred, but it is accepted by all scholars that the Magen David appeared in the flag of the first Zionist congress. It was used on the masthead of Theodor Herzl's journal, *Die Welt.* It was the official emblem of the B'nai Zion society in Boston, and Dora Askowitz, the daughter of the maker of the flag, Jacob Baruch Askowitz, describes the flag as "two horizontal blue stripes, enclosing a *Shield of David* (italics mine).

The official designation of the Zionist flag did not occur until 1933 when the 18th Zionist Congress adopted it by resolution. It became the banner of Britain's Jewish Brigade in World War II. The State of Israel adopted the blue and white flag with the Magen David in the center as its national ensign on October 28, 1948.

On April 1, 1933, the Nazis struck the first blow against the Jewish community and scrawled the Star of David and the word Jude on Jewish property. Of course, we are all painfully aware of the many forms of the Magen David that Jews were forced to wear during the Holocaust.

Since the establishment of the State of Israel, we have watched the Magen David raised to new heights as it graced the Israeli flag. Under its banner thousands of Jews were saved and millions of others attained new strength and dignity.

Then, is the Magen David really Jewish? As a well-known aphorism puts it, "If it walks like a duck, has a bill like a duck, and quacks like a duck, then I call it a duck." If millions of Jews wear the Magen David, synagogues and other Jewish institutions employ it, and the State of Israel uses it as its emblem, then I call it Jewish. —1995

12. The Color Blue

When visiting an Arab village in Israel, one quickly notices that the doors are painted blue. Men saunter the streets fingering strings of blue beads (the so-called worry beads), Women decorate their faces with blue dots on their foreheads, around their lips, and on their chins. The Bedouins, both men and women, paint a blue frame around their eyes with kohl (eye shadow).

If one inquires about the use of the color blue, the answer invariably is that it is a protection against the evil eye. The evil eye is feared by people all over the world, but particularly in the Middle East.

By the same token, if one walks the streets of Jerusalem in the Jewish Quarter of the old city, or in the other quarters inhabited by Jews who have lived in Arab lands, one notices that the doors and windows of many houses are surrounded by a light blue frame. One Yemenite rabbi in Jerusalem explained the practice this way: "We paint our houses blue against the evil eye because the Holy One, blessed be He, also painted his dwelling place, heaven, with the sky-blue color. If we want to protect ourselves from the evil eye, we do as God did and paint our houses blue."

Blue color and blue dye played an important role in biblical and talmudic times. The two primary colors in decorating the first tabernacle were blue and white. The ark, which contained the Ten Commandments, was covered with "a cloth of blue." The garments of the priests were predominantly blue.

One of the most important commandments, the wearing of the *tzitzit* (fringes) required that a cord of blue be appended to the four corners of every garment worn by a man. The function of these fringes was to remind the wearer of "all the commandments of the Lord" (Numbers 15:39). According to Maimonides, "Our rabbis explained that the blue is like the sea, all the sea is like the heavens, and the heaven is like God's Throne of Glory."

Blue, in the early Jewish tradition, was known as *tehelet.* The process of making this color dye for the fringes has been lost, so the fringes are no longer dyed blue. However, Talmudic law still holds that one cannot recite the morning *shema* prayer until it is light enough to distinguish between *tehelet* and white (Brachot 9b).

Blue has an important function in many cultures. It was the symbol of serenity and the abode of the gods. Egyptian gods were painted blue, and so were mummies. Zeus and Jupiter in Greek and Roman pantheons were represented by blue. The Assyrian moon god, Sin, was always portrayed with a blue beard. Today it is the Buddhist color of religious devotion; it is sacred to the moon and the dispeller of evil thoughts.

Turquoise was the national color of Persia, the source of some of the oldest turquoise gemstones, which were called *perusah,* meaning "joy." Ancient Persians trusted this lively blue to ward off the evil eye, protecting their animals as well as themselves with turquoise charms. Perhaps this is the reason that in so many Persian synagogues the ark covers and the Torah mantles were colored blue.

It is of interest to note that for 200 years Wedgewood blue was the best seller in china and decorative pieces in England. Josiah Wedgewood performed more than 16,000 recorded experiments to find the right mixture of blue and white to achieve this color combination. To commemorate the two-hundredth anniversary of Josiah Wedgewood's success, the Jewish community produced a special Wedgewood mezzuzah made in white on pale blue jasper.

Coming to modern times, beginning with the 1950s and escalating madly in the succeeding decades, the jeans revolution began. Jeans are made of cloth woven with a blue warp and a white weft. As it wears, the white shows through. The original brand of jeans was Levis. They were made by Levi Strauss, who was Jewish. The family today is still extremely active in the United Jewish Appeal.

Of course one could go on and on about the color blue. The uniform for the Union Army in the Civil War, as well as the police today, is blue. There are blue-chip stocks, and in surgery it is the blue beam that guides the healing ray of the laser. But there are two specific uses of blue that are most meaningful to contemporary Jews.

One is the flag of Israel. Blue and white are first mentioned as the colors of the Jewish flag in the latter third of the nineteenth century. In his poem *Zievei Eretz Yehudah,* the poet Ludwig August Frankl writes:

All that is sacred will appear in these colors:
White—as the radiance of great faith
Blue—like the appearance of the heavens.

The Zionist flag in its present form—two blue stripes on white with a Star of David (Magen David) in the center was, interestingly enough, displayed in Boston by the B'nai Zion Society in 1891. However, this was not known to the delegates of the First Zionist Congress, and it was David Wolfson who created the flag on the model of the *tallit* (prayer shawl), which, he pointed out, was the traditional flag of the Jewish people.

In this past decade a Hebrew song has arisen. It has become very popular in Israel, and it is the theme song of the Jews in Russia, like Natan Shcharansky, who are determined to be Jewish and to be free. The refrain of the song is:

"Kachol velavan, kachol velavan
Zeh tzeveh sheli—Kol Yamai l'olam."

"Blue and white, these are my colors
These shall be my colors all the days of my life—forever."—1977

13. As a Brand Plucked from the Fire

Every Jew living today whose family originated in Europe has a relationship with the Holocaust. Permit me to tell you mine.

My first awareness of what has often been termed "The War Against the Jews" occurred when I was nine years old. I learned that all of the Jews of Germany were forced to wear a yellow Star of David. I had a set of small figures made in Germany that I loved to play with. But I was so angered by this attempt to humiliate my fellow Jews that I snatched the figures, rushed outside, and flung them into the street.

When I attended the Jewish Theological Seminary in New York in 1945, the first exhibit of Holocaust artifacts was shown at YIVO, an institution dedicated to the preservation of Yiddish language and culture. Among the items displayed was a bar of soap made of the remains of Jews murdered in a concentration camp. I stared at it in horror. On an impulse, I touched it. I did not wash my hand for a week.

In the course of events I became a rabbi in St. Paul, where I have been affiliated with the Temple of Aaron for more than forty years. In 1978, President Carter appointed me to the United States Holocaust Memorial Commission. As co-chairman of the museum committee, I toured concentration camp sites in Europe and repeatedly visited Yad Vashem, the Holocaust memorial in Jerusalem, as well as other remembrances, structures, and archives in other parts of Israel. I also became friends with the great scholars of the Holocaust who came to the commission meetings in Washington, D.C.

Now the story takes an intense personal turn. My father was born in St. Louis in 1888. When he was a young man he went to Kovno, Lithuania, a famous, centuries-old center of Jewish studies. When he was about to complete his program, he decided to spend a year studying with the outstanding Jewish ethicist of that time who lived in a nearby town of Radun.

It was there that he met and married my mother. My sister and brother were born of that union. In order to support them, my father became a pharmacist. In the early part of 1914, my father received a letter from his father informing him of his desire to settle in Jerusalem. Because my father had not seen his parents since he left for Europe, he wanted to see them before they left for Palestine.

My father arrived in St. Louis in the late spring of 1914. Before he could return, the First World War broke out. Because my mother and her family lived in an area that was controlled by constantly changing armies of occupation, she and my father could not contact each other for more than four years. It was not until 1918, after the war, that they were in communication again.

But my father could not leave St. Louis because he was maintaining his father's dairy business, which was jokingly referred to as "a cow, a dipper, and a pail." This left my mother in a terrible dilemma. She did not want to leave her parents, her family, and her roots to come to a foreign land. On the other hand, she loved my father and wanted to join him. It was suggested to her that she see her uncle, the rabbi of the neighboring village of Aisheshuk (Lithuania—Eiszyszki), who was known for his scholarship, his wisdom, and his good judgment.

My mother went to see him. After a lengthy conversation he told her, "You must now make a decision. Either stay here and get a divorce from your husband or join him." She decided to come to America to unite the family. Her uncle supported her decision. Had she remained, she and her family would have been destroyed in the Holocaust, for there were no survivors of the Radun Massacre.

The story is not over.

My mother settled in St. Louis, and after several miscarriages, I was born. My parents decided to name me after the Rabbi of Aisheshuk, for if not for his counseling my mother would not have come to America and I would not have been born.

In May of this year I went to see the completed United States Holocaust Memorial Museum in Washington, D.C. The core of this extraordinary museum is a three-story collection of photographs of the Jews of Aisheshuk. These photographs were gathered over a period of twelve years by Professor Yaffe Eliach, a child survivor of that town, and the families from three continents. At one of the Holocaust council meetings we had a lengthy discussion about it. She told me she did this so that people would see faces and names and not just numerous corpses.

There had been Jews in Aisheshuk for 900 years; at the time of the Holocaust they numbered about 3,000 souls. When the Nazis arrived, the rabbi tried to organize resistance but could do little because of the massive power of the German army. In September 1941, on the eve of Rosh Hashanah (the Jewish New Year), the Jews were assembled in the main synagogue and two study houses.

Then they were systematically killed over a period of forty-eight hours. As a punishment for resisting, the rabbi was forced to watch the slaughter of his people. He was the last to die. These pictures are all that remain of that horrendous event.

In my recent visit to the Holocaust Museum, when I looked at the Aisheshuk pictures, I was stunned to see how much I resembled the rabbi for whom I had been named. As I viewed these pictures intensely, I saw features of my sister and brother, as well as my own children. I walked out of the museum thoroughly shaken. But for a quirk of fate, I would never have been born. Or, again, I might have been murdered in the Holocaust. For the first time I felt I was a survivor.

I have reflected on this profound experience over these past few months. I feel, in the words of Isaiah, "as a brand plucked from the fire." I often wake up in the middle of the night thinking, or at odd times in the middle of the day I wonder, "Was my purpose on earth to become a rabbi and take the place of my great-uncle, the Rabbi of Aisheshuk?"

This coming Rosh Hashanah, I shall reflect deeply on this as I recite the Kaddish (the Jewish memorial prayer) for my namesake, the martyred, hero-rabbi.—1994

14. The Jewish Component of the Statue of Liberty Centenary

Beginning on July 3, there will be four days of celebration throughout the United States, commemorating the one-hundreth anniversary of the dedication of the Statue of Liberty. The refurbished statue, gracing New York's harbor, will pay tribute to the millions of immigrants that passed by this symbol of freedom to enter the United States. However, not all are aware that the words on the base of "the lady with the lamp" were by a Jewish poet, Emma Lazarus. Her story is a fascinating one.

Emma Lazarus was born on July 22, 1849, in New York City, into a Jewish family that traced its ancestry back to Portugal. Family members considered themselves "Jewish nobility," superior to the Jews of eastern Europe. Although the Sabbath and the Jewish holidays were observed, the Lazaruses viewed themselves as thoroughly American and were more interested in the Civil War and American politics than persecuted Jews.

Emma Lazarus was educated at home by private tutors, as was typical among affluent families during that era. She was a sensitive spirit and tended to be introverted. She showed interest in music, the German poems of Heine, and English literature. Her earliest poems dealt with sorrow and longing and were dedicated to a young man whose name we do not know.

In 1867 her first book, *Poems and Translations,* was published. She met the foremost poet of the time, Ralph Waldo Emerson, and he asked her for a copy of the book. They became friends, and he served as her adviser. Her next work, *Admetus,* a mythological story, was dedicated to him. Emerson's correspondence with Emma Lazarus is treasured in the manuscript room of the library of Columbia University.

The esteemed Berlin rabbi, Gustav Gottheil, was called to the prestigious pulpit of Temple Emanu-El, on Fifth Avenue in New York, in 1873. As he began his rabbinic career there, he decided to create a new prayer book that would draw upon the richness of the English language. He read Emma Lazarus' poem, "In the Jewish Synagogue at Newport," and invited her to join him in his beloved project. She was evasive and seemed to balk at becoming a "Jewish writer."

But in the early 1880s a wave of persecutions occurred in Russia that traumatized Emma Lazarus and turned her into a "Jewish writer." As a member of the Jewish Welfare Committee, she went to Ward's Island to welcome persecuted Jews, There she saw all occupations represented: the peddler who spoke Yiddish, the big merchant, the engineer, the tavern keeper, the university professor, the doctor, the lawyer—all Jews, and all carrying their possessions wrapped in a small bundle.

When she returned home, she could not sleep. She was haunted by people who had nothing material left except what they could gather in a scarf or a kerchief. She responded with a poem, *Songs of a Semite,* which was destined to stir thousands. What she saw on Ward's Island, the pitiful mass of humanity brought low, the innocent misery of Jewish refugees, made a new person and poet out of her.

Emma Lazarus' voice rose like a trumpet, and her accusations were powerful and direct:

When the long roll of Christian guilt
Against his sires and kin is known,
The flood of tears, the life-blood spilt,
The agony of ages shown,
What oceans can the stain remove,
From Christian law and Christian love?

But she did not merely accuse, she inspired her fellow Jews to stand up for their brothers and sisters. She appealed to the memories of Jewish heroics and Jewish courage. Her moving words were best expressed in a work entitled *The Banner of the Jew.* Let her words speak for her:

Wake, Israel, wake! Recall to-day
The glorious Maccabean rage,
Say not the mystic flame is spent!
Your ancient strength remains unbent,
Let but an Ezra rise anew,
To life the Banner of the Jew!

Dipping into Jewish history, her poems became polemical and forceful. Emma Lazarus did not merely play the intellectual but agonized and attended mass meetings on behalf of persecuted Russian Jews. To her the Jewish question became the issue of humanity itself. When Jews were defamed in an article in the popular magazine *Century,* Emma Lazarus answered it point by point with fire and brimstone. She countered the old nonsense that there were "two kinds of Jews"—good and bad. For her all Jews were one. She thoroughly demolished the anti-Semitism of the original article.

Emma Lazarus now emerged from being a shy young lady and learned to write with speed, vigor, and assurance. She grew closer to her Jewish roots, even espousing an early form of Zionism. She wrote about the persecution of Jews in medieval Germany.

In May 1883, at the age of 34, her strength began to fail. She tried a trip to Europe, but it became clear that her days were limited by cancer. When Emma returned to New York, she found a strange request.

She received an appeal from a committee that was planning to set up, on Bedloe Island in New York harbor, a colossal statue, "Liberty Enlightening the World." Some decades earlier two Frenchman—Laboulaye, the statesman, and Auguste Bartholdi, the sculptor—had conceived the idea of this statue—a gift to symbolize France's true friendship for America.

The request that she write a sonnet to be placed at the base of this statue came from the chairman of the committee, her old friend William M. Evarts. In the last week of November 1883, Emma Lazarus wrote fourteen lines that have become immortal.

The New Colossus

Not like the brazen giant of Greek fame,
With conquering limbs astride from land to land;
Here at our sea-washed, sunset gates shall stand
A mighty woman with a torch, whose flame
Is the imprisoned lightning, and her name
Mother of Exiles. From her beacon-hand
Glows world-wide welcome; her mild eyes command
The air-bridged harbor that twin cities frame.
"Keep, ancient lands, your storied pomp!" cries she
With silent lips. "Give me your tired, your poor,
Your huddled masses yearning to breathe free,
The wretched refuse of your teeming shores.
Send these, the homeless, tempest-tost to me.
I lift my lamp beside the golden door!"

Emma Lazarus lived to read that President Cleveland unveiled the Statue of Liberty containing her words on October 28, 1886. Nine months later, she died. During the interim, she wrote her last Jewish poem citing Maimonides, Judah Halevi, Ibn Ezra, and Ibn Gabriol. She was drawn to her people for faith and comfort.

This July the Statue of Liberty, bearing her immortal words expressing the soul of America, will celebrate its centenary. After that, around Bedloe Island the winds will sing, the waves slap, and the sea gulls scream. But for the millions of immigrants who passed by the lady holding the torch of freedom, the lady who wrote the words welcoming the "tired," the "poor," the "huddled" and the "tempest-tost" will not be forgotten. They will remain as a tribute to the land of freedom and the memory of Emma Lazarus—a Jewish woman.—1986

15. Makuya: The Japanese-Christian-Zionist Connection

When I was recently in Tokyo, the first conversation I had was in Hebrew. It was with Dr. Akiva Jindo, the head of the Makuya Bible Institute. I first met Dr. Jindo when he was studying in Jerusalem several years ago. Now I wanted to arrange a meeting with the Makuya group.

Makuya is a Japanese-Christian sect that is theologically and actively pro-Zionist. It now has 50,000 members throughout Japan, mostly in Tokyo. Makuya in Japanese is a translation of the Hebrew phrase *ohel moeid,* "tabernacle."

The founder of the sect was Professor Abraham Ikuro Teshima. In 1948 he had a religious experience at Mount Aso, and his philosophy—that history is directed by God, as shown mostly in the Torah and somewhat in the New Testament—began to evolve. According to him, its purpose is to restore Israel to its land. In 1967, when Jerusalem was reunited, he took this as a divine sign that God's word was being confirmed.

Professor Teshima's words were backed by action. He established a relationship with Kibbutz Heftsibah, where hundreds of members of Makuya have lived to learn Hebrew and the ulpan. When the Lod Massacre occurred, the Makuya donated an ambulance to Magen David Ada. In November 1975 when the United Nations, to its discredit, declared that "Zionism is racism," 3,000 Makuya marched in downtown Tokyo, proclaiming that Japan had dishonored itself with its affirmative vote. Then they collected a petition of protest with 37,000 signatures and presented it to the Secretary General of the United Nations. The Makuya have sponsored countless group visits to Israel, sometimes numbering 400 people.

Even so, when my wife and I visited one of the assemblies in Tokyo we were hardly prepared for the experience. We entered a room overflowing with people sitting with their legs folded under them, barefoot. In a side room a teacher was instructing teenagers in a lesson based on Isaiah's verse: "Nation shall not lift up sword against nation." In yet another room the activities in the main room were being shown on closed-circuit T.V. for the benefit of mothers with infants.

We returned to the prayer meeting and were formally escorted to the front platform. As we walked down the aisle, hundreds of Japanese were singing with wild enthusiasm *Heveinu Shalom Aleichem.* Imagine being in downtown Tokyo and hearing Japanese people singing as loud as they could in Hebrew.

When we sat down I saw large Japanese signs. I asked Dr. Jindo what they meant. He told me one sign contains the words of God's promise to Abraham as recorded in the Book of Genesis: "I will give this land to you and your offspring forever." On the other side of the room there was a quotation from Abraham Joshua Heschel, "Just to be is a blessing. Just to live is holy."

They asked me to speak. First I spoke in Hebrew with no translation. I was amazed at the number of people who understood me. Then I spoke in English with a Japanese translator. Afterwards my wife offered greetings. When we concluded, the Makuya sang in perfect Hebrew with wild clapping: "May God bless you from Zion and may you see the good of Jerusalem." We were deeply touched.

We were then introduced to individuals that we selected at random. They came from all walks of life.

After we left the assembly, we agreed that it had been an unforgettable experience.—1985

16. Halacha k'Hitler

The Russians have come! It is estimated that more than 600,000 Russian *olim* have emigrated to Israel during 1990. While this is very exciting and a great redemptive force in our time, it is a mixed blessing. There are severe problems of absorption, housing, education, and employment. Another hidden challenge will soon surface.

There is the possibility that 30% of the Soviet Jews are not Jewish according to the classic interpretation of Jewish law. Even if this figure is not entirely accurate, the number is significant. It is abundantly clear that a large majority of Soviet Jews are involved with non-Jews and have been for decades. Now they are coming to Israel as family units. Since Judaism has been effectively destroyed in the Soviet Union for the past 70 years, it is hardly surprising that there are so many mixed marriages. But what should be done about them—if anything?

The non-Jews (but they surely are not Christian) along with their families will absorb Judaism as a natural process. In Israel they will learn Hebrew and Jewish traditions and will serve in the army as well as participate in daily Israeli living.

The issue here is not "Who is a Jew?" That can be left to the Halachists and other interpreters of Jewish law. The real issue is "What is a Jew?" or, more nearly, "What should a Jew do?" How shall this category of immigrants be treated?

There is ample tradition and history relating to sympathetic non-Jews living in the total Jewish community. When Moses left Egypt, he was accompanied by *erev rav,* which is often translated as "a mixed multitude," a euphemism for mixed marriage.

Using this and many other instances as guides, we should welcome wholeheartedly the Soviet non-Jews who are coming with Jewish families. They should be given equal treatment, and there should be no rush to judgment about their legal status as Jews. In the natural process of events, by accepting and becoming full participants in Jewish life, they will most naturally wish to take the last appropriate step.

Several rabbinic guidelines have already been established. For Soviet Jews this is *shahat hadachak,* "a time of oppression." Judaism understands how important it is to be understanding and compassionate when there is suffering. We Jews who have suffered so much can surely reach out to others who are now experiencing so much pain and disruption in their lives.

There is also in Judaism the principle of *metoch shlo lishma bah lishma,* "those who learn or do things without commitment, eventually come to commitment" (Pesachim 50b). By learning about Jewish traditions and customs, by becoming aware of the Hebrew culture, by participating in Jewish ceremonies and events, will not Russian non-Jews, who are an integral part of Jewish families in Israel, come to look upon Judaism with great favor?

There is a time when there should be an attitude of *kiruv,* "drawing closer," and welcoming without judgment. To turn now to raucous arguments about the Jewish status of immigrants would be a *chillul hashem,* a profanation of the essence of Judaism. While Judaism does not necessarily seek converts, it is not averse to converting those who intend to join their destiny with the Jewish people. The emigrating non-Jews to Israel will do so willingly, sooner or later. Most will do it sooner if received with warmth, understanding and, yes, love.

In this sense, we must praise Rabbi Menachem Porush of Agudat Yisrael and Shevach Weiss, a Labor member of the Knesset, who publicly declared our obligation to absorb every Russian immigrant from the Soviet Union "without classification, reservation or selection." They are acting in the spirit of Isaiah who praised those "strangers who willingly associate with the Jewish people" (Isaiah 14:1, 56:13).

In the end, acceptance and love for the stranger in our midst is a deed of Jewishness. To be sure, it is more than simply a deed; it is the very foundation of our faith. It is written: "And you shall love the stranger for you were strangers in the Land of Egypt" (Leviticus 19:34). This concept was emphasized thirty-six times in the Bible. For were we not taught to love our neighbors as ourselves? If we do, we walk in the tradition of our people who were called "the compassionate ones, the children of the compassionate ones."

Shortly after the State of Israel was established, many Jewish refugees came to Israel from Europe under the Law of Return. There was the anecdote about one refugee who wanted to enter Israel under the Law of Return. He was asked if he was Jewish and to tell of his background. He replied that only his grandfather was Jewish. The immigration officer then told him that this did not sufficiently qualify him as a Jew for the purpose of immigration to Israel.

The immigrant then said: "I lost immediate members of my family because Hitler considered me Jewish. I was forced into slave labor and placed in a concentration camp because Hitler considered me Jewish. And now, after paying this price, you do not want to consider me Jewish?"

The Israeli immigration officer replied: "Halacha k'Hitler" (the judgment according to Hitler) and passed him through immediately.

After all is said and done with reference to Russian immigrants, this should be the last word.—1991

17. Karaite Jews are Back in the News

The Karaites are a sect of Jews who have almost been forgotten by history. Suddenly, several events have propelled them back into the news.

In San Francisco, Karaite Jews have purchased a house to establish their first synagogue in America. In Israel a Karaite wedding took place in the presence of 500 guests, with 10 rabbis clustered under the chuppah (wedding canopy). In Russia the St. Petersburg (Leningrad) Library opened to scholars the Firkovitch collection, which contains the greatest number of Karaite works and, altogether, is a true mother lode for Jewish history.

The Karaites came into being at the beginning of the eighth century. The name of the sect, *Karaim,* means "people of the Scriptures" and implies the main characteristic of the movement: the recognition of the Hebrew Bible as the sole and direct source of Jewish religious law. This, of course, is a rejection of the

Oral Law, which is based on the talmudic-rabbinic tradition.

The founder was Anan ben David, an ascetic sage, who lived in Babylonia. He was influenced by the writers of the Dead Sea Scrolls, the Sadducees, and contemporary Muslim thought. His main thrust, however, was the assertion of the Bible as the literal source of Jewish practice and thought. He expressed his basic philosophy in this teaching: "Search thoroughly in the Torah and do not rely on my opinion."

In the centuries that followed there was much controversy between the Karaites and the Rabbinites. *Beliefs and Opinions,* the first systematic theological work in Judaism, was written by the eminent rabbi Saadiah Gaon (882-942) in response to the challenge of the Karaites. The Karaites produced many scholars, but the greatest was Abu Yosef Yacov al-Kirkasani, who lived in the tenth century.

The Karaite sect spread all over the world, including Egypt, North Africa, Babylonia, Persia, and as far as the Crimea. Jerusalem became a very strong center of activity and thought.

Today, the majority of Karaites, some 25,000, live in Israel—primarily Ramalah, but also in Ashdod, Ofakim, Beersheba, and Bat Yam. Several thousand reside in the United States, mostly in San Francisco. Another 2,500 more are in the Soviet Union, mainly in the Crimea.

Although they are recognized as Jews in Israel according to the Law of Return (a large number were airlifted from Egypt by the Israeli government in 1948-49), the chief rabbinate calls them a "cult" of "non-Jews." Shlomo Ovadiah, a Karaite leader, responded, "They call us 'goyim' because we don't put on *tefillin*. But the Bible doesn't mention *tefillin.* Is it better to put a verse in a box on your forehead, or give it to your son and say, 'Read it and remember it?'"

Other people define identity in different ways. At the beginning of the Holocaust the German Ministry of the Interior expressly stipulated that the Karaites did not belong to the religious Jewish community because "social psychology" was considered non-Jewish. On the other hand, in the Arab lands following the establishment of the State of Israel, the persecution of the Jews caused the Karaites to flee to Israel, where they were welcomed and allowed to carry on their particular form of Judaism under the protection of the state.

It was a Karaite Jew named Abraham Firkovitch who established the best collection of Hebrew manuscripts in the St. Petersburg Library. Now known as the Firkovitch Collection, it numbers 15,000 Hebrew manuscripts and is the largest such private collection amassed in the last two centuries.

In 1830 Firkovitch accompanied the chief *chacham* (spiritual leader) of the

Karaites in Crimea to Palestine. There in the Karaite synagogue in Jerusalem he retrieved old manuscripts from the *geniza,* a synagogue storeroom where worn-out holy books are kept until they are buried. Later, as a Karaite rabbi in Turkey, he continued his collecting. At the age of 76, Firkovitch visited Jerusalem again, as well as Nablus and Cairo, where he obtained many rare manuscripts and books.

In 1859 Firkovitch sold the bulk of his collection to the Imperial Public Library, as it was then called. The sum for the purchase was the substantial amount of 25,000 rubles. This year the library was visited by Prof. Malachi Beit-Arie, director of the National Library of the Hebrew University in Jerusalem. He arranged for a team of four to photograph and record all of the dated items. It will be a harvest for Hebrew scholarship.

In 1980, during a visit to Cairo, I had the extraordinary opportunity to become acquainted with the few remaining Jews of the once large Karaite community. I attended services, but there were only six or seven people present. The synagogue resembles a mosque with no seats, but rugs. The service is Muslim-style during which men remove their shoes and prostrate themselves. The *tallit* they wear contains a blue thread.

I was presented with a Karaite prayer book which was published in 1900 in Cairo. It is entirely in Hebrew with an Arabic index. The prayers are mainly taken from the Psalms; others were written by Karaite leaders. What is most striking is that there are no *berachot* (blessings), which most of us associate with Judaism, since these were created by the rabbis.

By great good fortune I was privileged to see the famed Ben Asher manuscript which is owned by the Karaite community of Cairo. It is so precious that it is kept in an iron box with two locks. Two different persons have keys so that it can never be removed independently. The codex was written by Moses Ben Asher, probably a Karaite scholar and scribe in the second half of the ninth century in Tiberias. The manuscript is important because it carefully preserves the *massoretic* (official) text of the Torah. It contains the former and latter prophets with points, accents, notes, and decorative art. As one looks at the manuscript closely, one feels the presence of history and the hand of the writer.

Karaite Jews in the news today seem to be saying to us, "Remember, Karaites, too, are part of the Jewish experience."—1993

18. What is a Jew? The Fight for the Children of Israel

The designation of Shulamit Aloni as minister of education and culture has fanned the embers of the religious-secular fire-fight in Israel into a flaming conflagration. Aloni, anti-religious agitator or an inspiring fighter for human rights, depending on one's point of view, is a symbol that goes to the heart of the Jewish experience. Is Judaism solely a religion with strict interpretations or is Jewishness something to be seen from many points of view?

Shulamit Aloni is an avowed Jewish secularist but a firm believer in pluralism. She was a schoolteacher when she was first elected to the Knesset 27 years ago. Aloni served on the culture and education committee and is the author of *The Rights of the Child.* She has fought the religious establishment on behalf of civil marriages, abortion, and other such issues for more than two decades.

The *haredim* (ultra-Orthodox) have reacted to her appointment with unprecedented fury. *Yated Neeman,* the daily Orthodox newspaper, compared what she will allegedly do to Israeli youth to what Hitler did to one million Jewish children fifty years earlier. One respected Zionist rabbi questions whether the prayer for the welfare of the state, recited in many synagogues, should continue. One *haredi* coalition is considering a no-confidence vote in the Knesset because of her.

Aloni appears unruffled as she says, "First of all, I recognize the right to be different; secondly, they are legitimate citizens of the State of Israel and are entitled to rights and representation." However, she adds, "Today the entire battle is over the education of secular children. The religious say what's mine is mine and what's yours is mine."

In fairness, it should be noted that when National Religious Party member Zevulun Hammer was minister of education, eleven senior positions were awarded to the members of the national religious movement. Many classroom hours were cut, and the only way school principals could get some of them back was by accepting religious programs.

Shulamit Aloni envisions a school system open to all Jews. She would send children to museums and theaters and have them meet face-to-face with artists. More science hours would be added to the curriculum and Jewish life would be taught in the context of world developments. She adds, "You cannot teach Jewish history in isolation from world history."

Dr. Barry Chazen, professor of education and Jewish education at the Hebrew University, in a brilliant and seminal study entitled *The Language of Jewish Education,* makes some important observations on the issue. His studies on indoctrination point out that religious values can be taught in such a way as to permit the pupil to make up his or her own mind. Religious values can be imparted without prejudice and in the atmosphere of choice.

A crucial element in the whole controversy is the "peculiarity" of Judaism. A Jew may be non-observant and anti-religious and still be a member of the Jewish people. Yet all the roots and the foundation of the Hebrew language and Judaism itself are "religious"—the Bible, Mishna, and Talmud. Can one really separate the ethical components of Judaism from its ritual customs and ceremonies? Some Israelis reject the haredim on the basis of "religious coercion," but their love for Jewish traditions and religious practices is deep.

The struggle is not unlike the one occurring in America. The issue of prayer in the public schools, the view of evolution, attitudes toward abortion and tax credits for private religious education are high priorities on the political agenda of American politics, no less than in Israel. They lie at the heart of the American psyche.

Indeed, an American principal was asked, "When do you teach religious values?" The reply was: "All day. We teach it in arithmetic: accuracy. We teach it in language: learning to say what we mean. We teach it in history: humanity. We teach it in breadth of mind. We teach it in handicraft: thoroughness. We teach it in astronomy: reverence. We teach it on the playground: fair play. We teach it by kindness to animals, by courtesy to workers, by good manners and by helpfulness in all things."

The Hebrew prophets struggled with the issue of the definition of religion. Micah summed up the general expression of their attitude (6:6-8): "With what shall I worship God? Shall I come before God with burnt-offerings? . . . Does God need thousands of rams and rivers of oil? You have been told, human being, what is good and what God asks of you—only to do justly, to practice compassion and conduct yourself with humility."

Students of Judaica such as Moshe Kohn continually point out that this was not a rejection of ritual but rather an attempt to see its place in the totality of religion. The seder service begins with inviting the poor to the table; on Purim gifts are given to the needy. On High Holy days the central call is for "Repentance, Prayer, and Charity." The Holiness Code in Leviticus (the priestly book of ritual) is a sublime statement that combines ritual and ethics.

While Israelis who attend secular schools need more understanding of ritual practices, traditions, and observances, they resent "religious coercion" and the use of public funds for private Orthodox enterprises. There is today a real need for a broader Jewish education in the context of choice. At the same time, those who are Orthodox must realize they cannot force their views on others through the political system.

The religious issues that divide Israelis are real. But in a democracy one must learn to live with difference and, indeed, to respect the right of each person to choose his or her philosophy of life. The Jewish character of Israel is indisputable, but the details are variations on this theme. Jewish history is filled with too many divisive doctrinal disputes that have been horrendously destructive, and the lesson is clear.

For the sake of the children of Israel, it is time for compromise in educational policies and programs, as well as in other areas. One hopes that all sides are capable of rising to the opportunity of dealing with cultural attitudes in a manner acceptable to reasonable and responsible secularists and religionists.

Let us pray so.—1992

19. Ladino is Still Alive

Ladino is the spoken and written language created by the Jews of Spanish origin. It had its beginnings in Spain around the time of the Spanish persecutions and was spread by the Jews fleeing expulsion in 1492. Most scholars agree that the term Ladino comes from *enladinar*, which refers to Latin or the language of cultured people. It is also referred to as Judeo-Spanish, Judismo, Nuestro Espaniol (our Spanish) and Espanolit. It should be noted that the last term already incorporates a Hebrew ending.

Ladino is based on classic Castillian Spanish combined with Hebrew. Since the Jews who left Spain were scattered all over the world, the language later absorbed terms from Arabic, Aramaic, Greek, English, Italian, French, Turkish, and Portuguese.

This beautiful and melodious language was first written in cursive Hebrew script derived from Rashi characters. Later, rabbinic square characters were used. Since the beginning of the twentieth century, it has been expressed in Latin letters.

At first it was the language of the Jewish ghetto in Spain and often that of the Marranos, the Jews who were forcibly converted to Catholicism but secretly maintained their Jewishness. Surrounded by danger and intolerable pressures, Jews needed a secret language to communicate with each other, preserve their distinctive culture, and celebrate festivals and life-cycle events. They had to have a way to bond in the home and unite in the synagogue.

As a Jewish language, it was a powerful carrier of Jewish culture. Spanish Jews and their descendants put their prayers, legends, poems, ballads, translations of the Bible, and correspondence into Ladino. Of extraordinary importance is the encyclopedic work, *Me'am Lo'ez,* begun by Jacob Culi in 1730 and continued by other writers after his death. This thesaurus draws its inspiration from such sources as the Talmud, Mishnah, Midrash, and Kabbalah.

A particularly rich literature of proverbs exists in Ladino. They are compact and pithy, and no part of human life is untouched by them. There are no fewer than 145 collections of Ladino proverbs. Aryeh Kaplan has collected more than 6,000 *refanes* (Judeo-Spanish proverbs) in one volume alone.

Between 1901 and 1938, more than 150 novels were translated into Ladino. Many original novels and biographies have been published in this remarkable language. The musical tradition of the *romancero* (ballad) in Ladino is especially rich. Through the singing of wedding songs, lullabies, and dirges to celebrate life-cycle events and the singing of liturgical hymns at circumcision rites, Bar Mitzvot and holiday gatherings, the Sephardim perpetuated their splendid heritage.

There are some remarkable combinations of word forms to be found in Ladino. After a coughing spell one says *Malachin que te acompanen* (May angels accompany you). Malachim is Hebrew for angels and the rest is Spanish. *Havia mabul de gente* means, "There are many people." *Mabul* is the Hebrew for flood (i.e., many) and the rest is Spanish. *Afilu el chazan se yierra* teaches, "Even the cantor makes mistakes," i.e., no one is perfect.

Immediately recognizable Hebrew and Arabic words have become central to Ladino, but many words are fascinating combinations. *Alchad* is Ladino-Hebrew designating Sunday. *Cumpliar minyan* means "one who reaches the age to be counted in a minyan." *Darshar* is Hebrew-Ladino for "to deliver a sermon"; *sedakero* is a person who collects charity.

Other words are also fascinating. *Rubissa* is Ladino for a rabbi's wife. *Akadosh baruch hu* is "The Holy One Blessed be He." *Anos* is the Ladino term for yahrzeit. *Esnoga* is shul. *Chacham* or *ribbi* is rabbi. *Razal* is the abbreviation for *Rabotenu Zihronom Livracha*, "Our Rabbis of Blessed Memory." *Metsia* has the universal meaning, "a bargain."

Many combination words reflect the international character of the country in which those who speak Ladino have lived. *Bagaja* is Ladino-Italian for suitcases. *Achilear* is Turkish-Ladino for "to illuminate." *Gazeta* is French-Ladino for newspaper. *Ala Moda* is French-Ladino meaning "according to modern style." *Barbunua* is Ladino-Greek-Turkish for a red-scaled fish. *Depot* is English-Ladino for railroad station.

Today, Ladino is spoken in Turkey, Greece, and Bulgaria and by 100,000 Israeli citizens. Kol Israel presents a fifteen-minute Ladino nightly program that is made up of news, folklore, music, and history. There are two remaining Ladino publications.

Prior to World War II, more than a million people spoke Ladino. The Nazis cruelly decimated their numbers. Yet there remains a ten-volume *Anthology of Judeo-Spanish Liturgy.* Over 3,000 *romanceros*—traditional Ladino folk songs—have been recorded at the Jerusalem Music Centre in the Hebrew National Library in Jerusalem.

Recently, there has been a revival of interest in written and spoken Ladino and an intense desire to preserve the precious heritage of Sephardic Jewry. This comes as no surprise to an elderly Jewish grandmother living in Turkey who commented, "*Se lo dishe,*" meaning, "I told you so!"—1992

SECTION IV— NOW AND THEN

1. Judaisms

A well-known Jewish aphorism states "Wherever there are two Jews there are three opinions—at least." Of course, when it comes to helping Jews in distress, factions quickly unite. This has been a dominant theme of Jewish history from tzedakah in the Torah to the American Jewish Joint Distribution Committee. Nevertheless, in every era of history, Jews have disagreed among themselves on subjects ranging from atheism to Zionism. Judaism comprises a world view and a way of life that, together, are expressed in action. While all Jews hold some traits in common, different groups have developed different systems and thought patterns that more often than not have clashed with the beliefs of other groups. Perhaps it is time to rethink Jewish history and use the more accurate word "Judaisms" in discussing the Jewish experience.

Judaism has always demonstrated internal tensions. Moses came down from Mt. Sinai the first time and what did he see but the people worshiping a golden calf, to which they contributed eagerly and generously. Moses was angry and shattered the tablets. The worship of Baal, Asherah, Astarte, and other Canaanite deities was a source of common struggle throughout subsequent Biblical literature. There were also Nazarites and Rechabites. The prophets struggled to present their ideas.

When Cyrus of Persia allowed the Jews to return to Zion some forty years after the destruction of the First Temple in 586 B.C.E., some went back but some preferred to stay in Babylonia. Thus the Diaspora was created. Jeremiah himself expressed this ambivalence. In one passage he counseled, "Thus said God to the whole community which I exiled from Jerusalem to Babylon: Build houses and live in them . . . seek the welfare of the city to which I have exiled you" (Jeremiah 29:4-7). Yet later he wrote, "For lo, the days will come, says Adonoy, that I will turn the captivity of My people Israel and Judah, and I will cause them to return to the land that I gave to their forefathers and they shall possess it" (Jeremiah 30:1-3).

During the Maccabean period there was a struggle between the Hasmoneans, who believed in the letter of the Law, the Maccabees, who felt the need to extend the Law, and the Hellenizers, who were drawn to the Hellenistic culture. Even as the Hasmonean dynasty triumphed, they were opposed vigorously by the rabbis who felt they corrupted and distorted the basic meaning of Judaic values.

Near the end of the Second Temple period there were the Pharisees, Sadducees, Essenes, Zealots (Sicari), Hellenists, the Dead Sea sects, and Therapeutae. Dr. Adolpho Roitman, curator of the Shrine of the Book, estimates there may have been at least twenty-four streams of Jewish thought during this period. Within the

Pharisaic movement itself were the opposing schools of Shammai and Hillel.

The mid-second century uprising of the Jews against the persecutions of Hadrian was led by Simon bar Kochba (star). Often termed Kosiba (liar), he was recognized by some as the messiah. Akiva ben Joseph, the greatest rabbinic scholar of the age, said of him, "This is the King Messiah." To which Rabbi Yochanan ben Torta replied, "O Akiva, grass will sprout between your jaws and the Son of David will still not come" (Yerushalayim 47.69d, Lamentations R.2.2). Clearly a difference of opinion there.

The Karaites, a sect still in existence, came into being at the beginning of the eighth century. The name *Karaim* ("the people of the Scriptures") implies the main characteristic of the movement, which recognizes the Hebrew Bible as the sole and direct source of Jewish law. This view was opposed by the Rabbinites, whose support of the oral law led to the first theological work in Judaism, *Beliefs and Opinions,* authored by Saadia Gaon.

Moses Maimonides is considered the greatest Jewish mind since Moses. His *Mishne Torah,* the summary of the Talmud, and his *Guide to the Perplexed* are the basis of Jewish thought from the Middle Ages even until this day. Yet few are aware that his works were banned by the rabbis of northern France and burned in the synagogue in Barcelona in September 1304. The battle between the so-called rationalists and anti-rationalists in Judaism raged for years.

Judaism underwent other traumas due to the Jewish pseudo-messiahs. Men like Shabbtai Zvi, David Ruveni, and Jacob Frank induced thousands of Jews to leave their homes and their possessions, convinced that the Messiah had come and it was the end of history. "Shabbatarianism" was denounced as heresy, but the immersion in mystic calculation was so pervasive that the rabbis quoted the Talmud (Sanhedrin 97b), "Cursed be those who calculate the days of the end of history."

In response to disillusionment, persecution, and intellectual arrogance there arose the Hasidic movement. Founded by the Baal Shem Tov (Besht), it introduced joy, enthusiasm, spirituality, and many other features into Judaism. In time, opposition began in the form of the *Mitnagdim* (opposers). The enmity between the two Jewish sects included public burning of writings and, again, excommunication.

In the second half of the eighteenth century, the Emancipation and Enlightenment profoundly affected Judaism. These developments spelled both triumph and tragedy. Increasingly, Jews moved into a more open society and a wider culture. But at the same time, Judaism was influenced by the larger world and in some ways became more fragmented, never to be made whole again.

Words like orthodoxy, reform, conservative, secular, humanistic, and reconstructionist are now part of our vocabulary. Zionists, influenced by anti-Semitism and nationalism, and their opponents began to duel intellectually. The battle for the soul of Israel today and the future of world Jewry and Judaism is at the top of the agenda.

Perhaps this is the final word in the matter. It was Rabbi Zvi Yehudah Kook who proclaimed on June 6, 1967, "We are living in the middle of redemption. The kingdom of Israel is being rebuilt." Thus began the strong current concept of the land being holy. However, few realized that Rabbi Kook also warned, "No one should decide . . . that he has the complete justice and the complete truth."

Enough said.—1995

2. Challah: Slice It or Tear It?

There are two traditions for eating challah on Shabbat. One is to slice it and the other is to tear it. While these customs may seem nothing more than a bit of folklore, they contain elements of a Jewish legal, if not ethical, nature.

Those who tear and share challah after the prescribed blessing on Shabbat maintain that it is contrary to Jewish law to use a knife to cut anything on the Sabbath. When faced with the fact that tearing is also forbidden on the Sabbath, they respond that they are simply pulling apart bread. When asked if they use a knife and fork to eat meat or fish on this day, they point out that a table knife is simply a utensil, unlike a bread knife, which has to be sharpened or is serrated, much like a weapon.

Those who slice challah simply maintain that it is the common way to serve bread. To tear it with one's hands and pass it can spread germs. They point out that all food, including fruit, is passed in plates or bowls. After reciting the *motzi* prayer, the natural way is to cut and pass the bread on a challah tray made of wood, metal, or simply a plate.

Whatever one's preference may be, the history of challah is interesting in itself. The word challah suggests a perforated or rounded loaf, It is close to the Akkadian *ellu* (pure), referring to the sacred use of bread. Indeed, the first time that challah is mentioned in the Bible is in Leviticus (24:59): "You shall take choice flour and bake of it twelve loaves. Place them on the pure table of the Lord in two rows, six to a row, as an offering." Later the verse instructs that it is to be arranged "every Sabbath day for all time."

A treatise in the Talmud entitled Challah contains four chapters. The commandment to present a portion of challah as an offering continued long after the Temple was destroyed. I remember in my childhood that whenever my mother baked challah for Shabbat, she always cut off a small piece of the dough and threw it into the fire, saying, "This is in remembrance of the Temple."

By the eighteenth century when challahs in the form of twisted breads came into vogue in Europe, the twelve round loaves became two, usually containing six humps each. There are two explanations offered for this. One is that in the Ten Commandments, which are printed twice in the Bible, one version reads, "Keep *(shamor)* the Sabbath" and the other says "Remember *(zachor)* the Sabbath." Thus, two loaves help to commemorate the fourth commandment in both versions.

Another interpretation for the use of two challahs on Shabbat is to recall the miracle of the manna given to the Israelites in the desert during their forty years of wandering before they entered the Promised Land. On Friday they were given a double portion of manna so that they would not have to work on the Sabbath.

No one is quite sure what the substance of manna really was, but according to Deborah Wigoder in her *Garden of Eden Cookbook,* it is like coriander seed, which is second in importance to salt. It is probably the oldest recorded herb, going back to 5000 B.C.E. She thinks the first Sabbath loaves were sprinkled with cumin or fennel flower seeds. This is similar to present-day pitas in Israel, which are sprinkled with *zataar,* a combination of indigenous herbs.

The *Encyclopedia Judaica* editor, Dr. Geoffrey Wigoder, created an illustration of twelve different challahs for pages 1419-1420 of volume six. The challah for Shavuot, which commemorates the giving of the Torah, has a ladder to symbolize the ascent to heaven. The challah on Rosh Hashanah is round to symbolize the cycle of the year. Challah from Volynia has a key to release one from sins. A challah with a hand from the same area was used before the Yom Kippur fast to show we are in the hands of God. A challah was baked there in the shape of a bird's head to express the verse in Isaiah (31:5) that God will hover over Jerusalem like a bird to protect it.

Since the eighteenth century, most European Jews have eaten what Joan Nathan, author of four cookbooks, calls "Challah with a twist," or braided challah. No one really knows the source of this, but some say it is the interlocking of the aims of Jews everywhere on the Sabbath. Whatever the explanation may be, impoverished Jews with an everyday diet of buckwheat groats, black bread, potatoes, and herring looked forward to the Sabbath and holy days for a break in the monotony of meals. White-flour challah with a little bit of sweetness on the Sabbath was a treat to be savored.

When Isaac Bashevis Singer and his brother were little boys in Poland, their mother prepared challah each Thursday evening and Friday morning for Shabbat. With the scrapings of leftover white-flour dough she made a turnover filled with jam to hold the boys' hunger. They waited all week for that cherished delight.

Today there is a resurgence of interest in homemade challah. Many American women attend classes in challah baking at synagogues and Jewish centers. They also experiment by making it out of whole wheat and adding other tasty ingredients. It is increasingly popular at a Bar or Bat Mitzvah celebration to serve loaves spelling out the youngster's name. Huge challahs adorn many a Jewish festive event.

Challah: whether you slice it or tear it apart, it is an important part of Jewish life. Besides, it makes excellent French toast.—1993

3. Jewish End Time? Or in One Era and Out the Other

"The End of History?" is the title of an article that was published in the summer issue of the *National Interest.* Written by Francis Fukuyama, deputy director of the State Department's policy-planning staff, it contends that recent events indicate that history has come to an end.

With the decline of Fascism and Communism, he argues, Western liberal democracy has triumphed and mankind has reached its peak. Therefore, we are entering "Post History."

Aside from the fact that the pronouncement of the death of the "-isms" is slightly premature, aside from the fact that liberal democracy has hardly solved all of its problems (racism, poverty, drugs, crime, disunity, etc., etc., etc.), the topic "End Time" is hardly anything new. Discussions surrounding post-history usually accompany periods of political and social transition.

One should view the present discussion on this matter precisely in the context of history with a theological base. Jews have much to say in the matter of the end of history, for they have encountered the issue time and time again. They were probably among the first to raise it.

Most of the discussion in history on this subject comes under the rubric of "eschatology," which designates the doctrine concerning "last things." The word "last" can be understood either absolutely as referring to the ultimate destiny of humankind, or relatively, referring to an individual or a period of history. In the Bible, this is known as *acharit hayamim,* "the end of days," i.e., the "end of time." In the Second Temple period, it was often referred to as *kaytz hayamim,* literally, "the term of days."

Essentially, the origin of eschatology in Judaism can be found in God's promise of the establishment of a divine kingdom of justice, in which Israel would play a central role. The prophet Amos expanded on this by elaborating on divine judgment and calling it the "Day of the Lord." Later prophets referred to it simply as *hayom hahu,* "that day."

It was Isaiah who emphasized and incorporated the idea of the Messiah in it. It became a Messianic Age, which would be brought about by the will of God. As the prophetic movement evolved, new ideas such as "Judgment Day," the rebuilding of the temple in Jerusalem, and an era of eternal peace occurred. It was all a part of the divine plan in which history was prearranged from beginning to end.

This reasoning reached a high point in the Book of Daniel. The term "apocalypse" is appropriate. Often, the word is translated as revelation, which means literally "uncovering" the future, the final destiny of the world. The literature of this period is usually called "apocrypha," which means left "hidden" or excluded from the canon, the regular Bible (Tanach).

In the rabbinic period, we begin to come across the concept of *yemot hamashiach,* "the times of the Messiah." This gave birth to attempts to calculate the time remaining until this supernatural event would occur. It is generally accepted that there will be suffering before this happens. This was commonly referred to as *chevlo shel mashiach,* "the pangs of the Messiah."

Rabbinic times produced the concept of *olam habah,* "the time to come," in contrast to *olam hazeh,* "the present time." In *olam habah,* often translated as "the world to come," there will be full retribution for good and evil meted out by God.

The Dead Sea Scrolls speak of the imminence of the "End of Days." This particular form of eschatology was developed and fully emphasized by Christianity as a central pillar of faith. It received its fullest development in the Book of Revelations. It has become a subject for vast literature in Christianity that is popularly known as End Time.

Although the rabbis concentrated on *halacha,* systematic development of Jewish law as it was applied to daily life, yet messianic speculation continued. It especially flourished in mystic circles and those interested in the Kabbalah, Jewish mysticism. It is actually written in one edition of the Zohar, the classic text of Jewish mysticism, that "In the year 5408 of the Creation of the World the Rebirth will occur" (Zohar I 1396b). Passage after passage in Jewish mystic literature attempts to predict the exact date of "the end of days." Calculating the exact end of time was a favorite pastime of the Jewish community in the Middle Ages.

"False" messiahs marked great epochs in Jewish history. Men like Shabbtai Zvi, David Ruveni, Jacob Frank, etc. induced thousands of Jews to leave their homes and their possessions as they became "convinced" that the Messiah had come and it was the end of history. The fact that these beliefs brought disasters to the community and individual families among Jews is as sad as it is well known.

It is safe to generalize that speculation and belief in the end of history always coincides with periods of great suffering, great upheaval, and great change. It was a search for certainty in an uncertain world, a yearning for stability in the midst of terrifying instability. Often the phenomenon appeared as humankind was approaching the end of one era and the beginning of another. Facing the unknown moved people to see the end of something as a final end. Whenever there is a *fin de siecle,* the end of a period in history, there is a tendency to feel it is the end of history, period.

We are now living through such a time. In front of our very eyes Communist-oriented countries are abandoning their political orthodoxy, and the influence of the philosophy of Karl Marx is rapidly declining. It is nearing the end of the 1980s, and we are looking to the twenty-first century. Vast technological advances such as computers, fax machines, lasers, and genetic manipulation are changing our lives at an unprecedented pace. Jewish life shifts from one moment to the next. We are entering the year 5750, and that number alone tempts us to contemplate its mystical meaning.

Messianic visions are dancing in the heads of some Jews in Israel and thereby causing political and social confrontations. In the United States, one interpretation of Judaism is actually giving voice to the thought that a specific rabbi is the Messiah. Bumper stickers on cars proclaim the demand, "We want the *Maschiach* now."

Small wonder that talk is surfacing about the end of history. But is it? Is history coming to an end or merely changing? Should we not consider that it may be just the beginning of better things?

The Talmud cautions us about talk of the end of history in these strong but wise words: "Cursed be those who calculate the days of the end of history" (Sanhedrin 97b). Thinking about end days as idle speculation is one thing, but acting on these thoughts has only brought misery.

A view of history generally and Jewish history specifically teaches us to be thoughtful, cautious, and patient when faced with events fraught with great challenge. The talk of the end of history should go in one era and out the other.—1989

4. I Shall Not Die, But Live to Tell

The Fiftieth Anniversary of the Warsaw Ghetto Uprising

This year Holocaust Remembrance Day occurs at the same time that we commemorate the fiftieth anniversary of the Warsaw Ghetto Uprising, April 19. This was the first uprising in German-occupied Europe. It took Nazi troops longer to put down the ghetto revolt than it took them to conquer all of Poland.

In the main it was led by three Zionist groups that joined to create the *Zydowska Organizacja Bojowa* (Jewish Fighting Organization: ZOB). The total fighting force consisted of twenty-two platoons numbering 700 to 750 Jews. They were under the command of Mordecai Anielewicz.

The first encounter took place on January 18, 1943, when German police and S.S. planned an *Aktion,* a wave of deportation. A Jewish platoon, armed with pistols, deliberately broke into a column of Jews that was being marched to the *Umschagplatz* (assembly point). They confronted the German escorts in a face-to-face battle.

That fight was the first in which Germans were attacked in the ghetto. Most of the Jewish fighters fell in the battle, although Anielewicz was able to overcome the German soldier with whom he was struggling and was saved. The long column of Jews scattered in all directions. News of the battle soon reached the rest of the beleaguered Jews. There was a decisive change in their ghetto pattern of behavior. When the first column had dispersed, the Germans were no longer able to set up another one, since the Jews refused to respond to the shouts ordering them to get out of their houses and report to the assembly points. The majority of ghetto Jews were concealed in improvised hiding places. The Germans also acted in a different manner, desisting from their usual ear-splitting cries, moving quietly, and keeping away from places where Jews might be hiding. The Polish underground also learned that the Jewish resistance had compelled the Germans to interrupt the *Aktion.*

The civilian population of the ghetto underwent a transformation that was to have a decisive impact on the course of events during the uprising. The Jews in the ghetto believed that what had happened in January proved that offering resistance might force the Germans to desist from their plans. Many thought that the Germans would persist in unrestrained mass deportations only so long as the Jews were passive, but that in the face of resistance and armed confrontation they would think twice before embarking on yet another *Aktion.* The Germans would also have to take into account the possibility that the outbreak of fighting in the ghetto might spread the rebellion to the Polish population and might create a state of insecurity in all of occupied Poland.

These considerations led the civilian population of the ghetto, in the final phase of its existence, to approve of resistance and give its support to preparations for the uprising. The Jews used the interval to prepare and equip a network of subterranean refuges and hiding places, where they could hold out for an extended period even if they were cut off from one another. In the end, every Jew had a spot in one of the shelters set up in the central part of the ghetto.

The last *Aktion* and resistance campaign that came to be known as the Warsaw ghetto uprising began on April 19, 1943, the eve of Passover. The ghetto fighters had been warned and were on a permanent alert. That morning, when the German forces entered the ghetto, they did not find a soul in the central part, except for a group of policemen. The entire Jewish population had taken to the hiding places and bunkers, and by refusing to comply with the Germans' orders they became part of the uprising.

The face-to-face fighting lasted for several days. The Germans were not able to capture or hit the Jewish fighters, who after every clash managed to get away and retreat by way of the roofs; nor could the Germans lay hands on the Jews hiding in their bunkers. The Germans therefore decided to burn the ghetto systematically, building by building. This forced the fighters to take to the bunkers themselves and to resort to staging sporadic raids. The flames and the heat turned life in the bunkers into hell; the very air was afire, the food that had been stored up spoiled, and the water was no longer fit to drink. Despite everything, the bunker dwellers refused to leave their hideouts.

Twenty-seven days later, General Jurgen Stroop, commander of the heavily armed German force, announced, "The Jewish Quarter of Warsaw is no more."

Near the end, Mordecai Anielewicz wrote: "I cannot describe to you the conditions in which the Jews are living. Only the chosen few will hold out; all the others will perish, sooner or later. The die is cast. In the bunkers where our comrades are hiding out no candle can be lit at night because of the lack of air. The main thing is that my life's dream has been realized: I have lived to see Jewish defense in the ghetto in all its greatness and glory."

Kibbutz Yad Mordecai in Israel has been named after Anielewicz.

All the Jews in the Warsaw ghetto were heroes. But there is one that should be mentioned by name, Janusz Korczak. He was a physician, writer, and educator. He was born Henryk Goldszmit but assumed a pen name to write his popular books because of anti-Semitism. He became the Dr. Spock of Poland. His *How to Love Children* and *The Child's Right to Respect* and other works earned him enormous respect.

His basic work was with the Jewish orphanage, but he was also asked to take charge of two orphanages for Polish children in Warsaw and teach at boarding schools and summer camps. He was sought out as a lecturer in universities and seminaries.

When the Germans occupied Warsaw he refused to wear a yellow badge. Although elderly and tired, he took charge of the orphanage in the ghetto. He was tireless in counseling the staff and caring for the physical and emotional needs of the children. When the Germans rounded up two hundred of the orphaned Jewish children, Korczak held hands with the children in the front row and led them singing to their fate.

When I finished the research for this article, I was sad and pained. As I left the library in the synagogue, I heard children singing. The chapel was open and the children in the lower grades of the Jewish Day School were singing as the Torah was being returned to the ark. The phrase was *aitz chaim hee,* "It (the Torah) is a tree of life to all who take hold of it."

I felt reassured. It was as if the children of the Warsaw ghetto were living in the souls of these children. In Jewish children the world over, in the strength of the State of Israel, the uprising of the Warsaw Ghetto lives on. As the verse from Psalms (118:17) proclaims: "I shall not die, but live to tell."—1993

5. Jewish Women in Hebrew Printing

In the making of the Jewish book, women have played a role as publishers, printers, and writers. Indeed, even before the invention of printing, Jewish women served as copyists. There is a fourteenth-century Hebrew Bible with a note from a woman in Sana, Yemen, that says, "Please be understanding of my script, for I am a nursing woman. Miriam the daughter of Benyahu, the scribe."

The first woman involved in printing Hebrew books was Estellina, the wife of the physician Abraham Conat, who introduced Hebrew printing in Mantua and published six Hebrew books there in 1474-77. Her husband said, "She wrote the book with many pens without the aid of a miracle." He used these words because the term "printing" had not yet been coined.

Appropriately enough, most of the information on the role of Jewish women in Hebrew printing can be found in the scholarship of Jennifer Breger, who has been a serious collector of Judaica for many years, with particular emphasis on books by and about Jewish women and works printed by them. She holds a master's degree from St. Hilda College in Oxford and a master's degree from the Hebrew University in Jerusalem.

Printing in the beginning was a cottage industry. Living and printing areas were next to each other, so that the whole family joined to help with the many tasks involved. Often, when a husband died, the woman took over the printing press so that the business would continue and support the family. The earliest recorded woman who owned and operated a press was the widow Ann Rugerin of Augsburg, Germany. Her name was recorded in a book dated June 22, 1484.

The story of Hebrew printing is in many ways the story of the Jewish people. Hebrew books were censored, confiscated, and burned. Printing presses sometimes were moved across borders during the printing of a book. Always present was the risk of having the press closed down by the authorities. The romance of Hebrew printing must also be seen as the perils of Hebrew printing.

That is why it is so remarkable that there have been at least fifty-four Jewish women whose names were on colophons or title pages up to the twentieth century. Because so many Hebrew works were lost or destroyed over the centuries during different periods of persecution it is hard to estimate how many. There have been many more in the twentieth century,

For example, we know from the records of the Spanish Inquisition that a Marrano, Juan de Lucena, and four of his daughters who were accused of printing Hebrew books in Toledo before 1480. One of his daughters confessed before the Inquisitors that she had helped her father print Hebrew books as a young girl. Another daughter was condemned fifty years later to life imprisonment following a similar confession. Juan de Lucena is considered to have created the first Hebrew printing press in the Iberian peninsula.

Dona Reya Mendes is particularly interesting as a Jewish woman printer. She was the daughter of Dona Gracia Mendes, the famous Marrano businesswoman and philanthropist who came to Constantinople in 1553. Dona Reya established a press in this city and published at least fifteen Hebrew books, including prayer books, a tractate of the Talmud, and a scholarly book in Ladino, a Spanish dialect spoken by Jews and written in Hebrew characters. She was the first woman to establish a press herself. It is important to remember that the first Turkish book was not printed until 1729.

Famous in the annals of Jewish women printers were two sisters at the end of the seventeenth century, the daughters of a convert to Judaism named Moses, who first worked as a printer and then had his own printing houses in Amsterdam, Berlin, and Frankfurt. One daughter, Ella, set type in her father's house. In 1696 she included at the end in Yiddish rhyme: "These Yiddish letters I set with my own hand, Ella, daughter of Moses in Holland. My years are no more than nine, a girl among six children. If you find an error, please remember that it was set by a child."

Perhaps the most interesting phenomenon in the history of Jewish women printers is the preponderance of them in the city of Lemberg in the nineteenth century. This city, which at various times since the eighteenth century has been

Polish, Austrian, Soviet, is now part of the Ukraine. As such, Lemberg became an important printing center for Jewish books in the nineteenth century. Judith Rosanes established a printing press in that city and printed at least fifty books. She was the first woman to print Hebrew books on a commercial basis over a long period of time. She distributed widely the Yiddish book *Tzehneh Ureahnah,* a sixteenth-century paraphrase of Bible stories and commentaries that was popular among Jewish women.

Many other Jewish women printers also flourished in Lemberg. Chaya Taube ran a press for more than thirty-three years. Chave Grosman printed many rabbinic titles and liturgical texts. The title page contained the phrase, *"gedrukt bei Chave Grosman."* The well-known Balaban press was owned by Pesel Balaban. She produced high-quality editions of Halachic texts such as the *Shulchan Aruch,* the Code of Jewish Law.

One of the most famous printing presses at the end of the nineteenth century and one that was known all over Europe was that of the widow and brother Romm in Vilna. The Romm firm began in 1799 and continued printing until 1940, but it was under the management of Devorah Romm that it achieved its greatest success. The Romm edition of the Babylonian Talmud in the 1880s was a landmark in Hebrew printing. It took six years to produce—from 1880 to 1886—incorporating textual differences from rare manuscripts in different libraries. Twenty-two thousand copies of the first volume were sold by advance subscription.

This edition became the model for all later editions of the Babylonian Talmud. More than 100 printers and craftsmen did the typesetting, and fourteen proofreaders were employed. It is interesting that at a time when the very thought of a woman studying Talmud was an aberration, many of the editions of the codes and Talmudic literature were printed by presses controlled in part or in the main by women.

The outstanding memoir of women printers was the work of the famous Glückel of Hameln, a later seventeenth-century widow who took over her deceased husband's business. She describes both her personal life and the way she conducted business, traveling to fairs, establishing credit for herself, and so on. Her memoir is a treasure and a great insight to life in that era and to her life specifically.

The gender of the owner of a printing press was never a factor. The definitive role of Jewish women in printing is a book waiting to be written. More research and scholarship is needed. Suffice it to say that the contribution of Jewish women to Hebrew printing has been considerable and invaluable.—1993

6. A Rabbi is a Rabbi is a Rabbi

Nothing annoys a member of the younger generation more than to receive unsolicited advice from the older generation. With this caveat in mind and with some hesitation, I am responding to the request of Gene Borowitz to share some feelings about special problems that rabbis face today. I do so in the mood of Dr. Israel Davidson, who assembled the first anthology of medieval Hebrew poetry and said, "I throw out some ideas, and you can throw them out too."

I believe that articles about the special problems rabbis face today should be placed in a file and periodically removed, dusted off, and passed around. Conditions change, technology changes, forms of issues change, styles of leadership (both professional and lay) change, problems change, but the basic dynamics and function of the rabbinate have not changed since the first century. The same *sturm und drang* of Jewish life. The same drives, generosity, egos, humility—the same everything. A rabbi is a rabbi is a rabbi.

Looking back over nearly four decades with the same congregation, I feel fulfilled, gratified, and thankful that I could serve in such a noble profession of my choice. I admire my younger colleagues and honor them for choosing as their vocation not only a way of life but their entire life.

Our times mirrored the ups and downs of the Jewish people. The Holocaust, the establishment of the State of Israel, the Vietnam era, the fight for social equality, the fight to free Soviet Jewry. It was exciting. One is reminded of the words of Wordsworth: "Bliss was it in that dream to be alive . . . But to be young was the very heaven."

But fear not, my younger colleagues, all battles have not been fought and the causes are not exhausted. Can you not hear the call of the trumpets? The real battle for the survival of Russian Jewry is just beginning. The security and unity of Israel and the Jewish people is the highest priority of the 1990s. Bioethics, hunger, freedom for the oppressed, AIDS, new understanding of human behavior, and greater research in Jewish archaeology, linguistics, history, and other disciplines are yet to be explored. A new compelling Jewish philosophy and form have to be created. We leave you the whole world and yourself to conquer.

You have the opportunity to find a meaningful life through the rabbinate. You have the pulpit, the power to move others, to participate actively in the activities of your time. You can shape your responses and help shape the responses of others to the great issues of your time. *Carpe diem*!

But in the end, the rabbinate will still have to operate in its particular set of historic circumstances. The priest-prophet tension will continue. Rabbis will need to be mutually supportive. Nothing is more painful than for a rabbi (and his or her family) to be emotionally tortured, underpaid, and subjected to enormous pressures. While there must be professionalism to protect the rabbi, there is the danger of over-professionalism and institutionalism.

Act like a C.E.O., and you'll be treated like a C.E.O. Be a negotiator, then don't complain if you're out-negotiated. Be an ecclesiastical functionary, then you'll be treated like a hired hand. Have integrity, you'll be respected. Dare and you will be criticized and praised. Speak for justice and face unpopularity. You will be reviled, but you will also be remembered. The old axiom still holds: *lefum tzarah agrah,* "according to the pain so is the gain."

Remember, we bear the tradition of Moshe Rabbenu (Rabbi). He was the subject of gossip, and he experienced deep disappointment. Rabbi Akiba taught Torah with literally the last ounce of his tortured breath. Rabbi Leo Baeck endured a concentration camp and created a legendary name. Deborah rallied the Jewish people in the time of need and took the risk and strain of leading Jews in battle. Beruriah taught Torah whether the men liked it or not. Hannah Senesh gave up her life for the Jewish people and earned an immortal place in Jewish history.

You will forgive me for sounding like a preacher. After all, I am one by calling (and I use this word deliberately) and training. I have earned my battle stripes and have the right to speak with some degree of authority. I do not wish to indulge in self-serving piety or be holier than thou, *et chatawai ani mizkir hayom.* I have been tempted by fame, illusions of power, ego. I have been tested by *kinat sofrim.* At times I have fallen, but Yom Kippur is for rabbis too. I tried the best way I knew how with whatever means I had at my disposal.

Would I do it again if I could? You bet. It was (and is) an honor and a privilege to be a rabbi. If "we are small in our eyes, we are yet the heads of the children of Israel." If we become arrogant, overly ambitious, and amoral, we deserve to be chastised.

Teaching is the essence: after all, we're all all taught *talmud torah keneged kulam.* But preaching is essential. Take it seriously in all its forms—logic, delivery, learning, reaching people, integrity, sensitivity. *Hachamayim vehamovet beyad halashon.* We will probably never be charged with malpractice, but we will be accountable to malpreaching.

We must be aware of becoming mere prayer wheels when we should be ethical trailblazers. Participation in life-cycle events is crucial, but beware lest you become the magic man or woman. Folk religion is often at odds with rationality and intellectual honesty. Morals and manners are often in tension. We all know that ritual has preserved Judaism. But a rabbi obsessed with rituals can neglect the real meaning of religion.

Several years ago in Israel, my wife, Laeh, and I attended the burial of our lifetime friend, Rabbi Pinchus Goodblatt (Pinky). The only people that were there were the usual *Chevra Kadisha,* his wife Shirley, and his three children. There was no eulogy, but at one point Pinky's daughter came forward and read from his book entitled *No Policemen At My Mouth.*

Pinky had no big-time pulpits, his name never got in *The New York Times*; he served simply, honestly, and sincerely wherever he was. He spoke the truth as he saw it. In my view, Pinky was a success. *Kayn yirbu.*

A rabbi has a need to study, to read, to grow. A rabbi has a right to rest and recreation. A rabbi has a right to a degree of privacy. But a rabbi has to remember that he or she can be unreasonable. A rabbi is not God, merely works for God. A rabbi may need help, guidance, or therapy. A rabbi has personal or family problems. In short, a rabbi is a human being, but a special human being. Only God is omniscient; rabbis are ordinary people with an extraordinary heritage.

What really matters? Woody Allen has just produced a thoughtful movie entitled *Crimes and Misdemeanors.* Actually, it is a modern statement of *Kohelet.* It is the first time in modern film that I have seen a rabbi portrayed with understanding, sensitivity, and touching respect. In the final scene, the rabbi, blinded by a progressive illness, is dancing with his daughter at her wedding. It is very tender and touching. The music is the song "I'll be seeing you in all the old familiar places that this heart of mine embraces," as if to say that we cannot understand the whims of fate or the cause of the events; what really matters are the familiar things that we do—express our love for others, help others—and our general relationships that are so familiar but constitute the power that turns the wheels of the universe.

And, as rabbis, don't we all know this? As rabbis, don't we all know the passage from Shabbat 127a that we read every day and that spells out the familiar things that matter? They include, among others, deeds of loving kindness, attending the dead, providing hospitality, celebrating marriages, counseling, advancing peace, and, above all, studying and teaching.

We will all remember when we made a difference—when we were called out of bed in the middle of the night to help with a tragedy. We will recall when we were helpful in a conflict. We will reread the record when we spoke out for those who were hurt, shamed, treated unjustly, when we have given voice to the voiceless and power to the powerless. We will be recorded in the hearts of others through the Torah we taught when we were really so tired.

You will forgive me if I break off now. I have to look up some sources for a class in Jewish thought. You see, *torah hee velilmod ani tzarich.* I am a rabbi; I have no choice. I want nothing else. I was part of the past of my people, I am privileged to be part of the Jewish present, and I hope to be with Jewish destiny for an eternity. *Btoch ami ani yoshev!*

Just remember, what we do and everybody knows gets us in the headlines. But, what we do and nobody knows will get us into Heaven.—1989

7. The 200th Anniversary of the Death of Moses Mendelssohn—The First Modern Jew

This year, 1986, marks the 200th anniversary of the death of Moses Mendelssohn—the first modern Jew. He was the first Jew to be accepted in the European literary world because of his extraordinary facility with the German language. At the same time, he opened up Western thought to the Jewish community. His goal was to make Jews acceptable to Christians as equals and to bring about the inner liberation of Jews through cultural enlightenment and outer liberation through civil emancipation.

Moses Mendelssohn was born in Dessau in 1729. During early childhood he suffered from a disease that left him with curvature of the spine. It was remarkable that a small, homely, humpbacked man afflicted with a slight stammer managed to gain acclaim for the charm of his language, the elegance of his style, and the clarity of his thought.

The story is told that his father, anxious not to have his son miss a single lesson, wrapped the boy in an old coat on winter mornings and carried him through the darkness and cold to the *cheder.* Moses soon showed such brilliance that he attracted the attention of the rabbi of Dessau, David Frankel, the author of a well-known commentary on the Jerusalem Talmud.

In 1743 when Frankel accepted a call to become the rabbi of the Jewish community of Berlin, Mendelssohn, then fourteen years old, followed him and entered a different environment: an exotic, intoxicating, intellectual world. Mendelssohn's poverty was great and often he could not afford the books he wanted to read. At times, his only food for days was bread. But he did not allow hardships to deter him from his studies, and he made rapid progress. In addition to his fluent knowledge of German and Hebrew, he became familiar with Latin, Greek, English, French, and Italian.

In 1750 he became a teacher in the house of Isaac Bernhard, owner of a silk factory. Later he was entrusted with the bookkeeping of the factory and eventually he became a partner in the enterprise. During the day he was a businessman and in the evening he dwelt in the world of ideas. He married Frumet Guggenheim of Hamburg and began a family. Finally, in 1763 he was granted "right of residence" in Berlin by the king.

Mendelssohn's first impulse to write came from the brilliant German critic and dramatist, Gotthold Lessing. The two men became acquainted at the home of a friend. A few years earlier, Lessing had written a drama, *Die Juden (The Jews),* in which he exposed the bigotry and ignorance of the Christian world. He was delighted to find in Mendelssohn a brilliant intellect, moral integrity, a quest for truth, modesty, gentleness, and a love for people. Lessing's most important play, *Nathan the Wise,* was inspired by Mendelssohn and became a powerful plea for religious tolerance.

In 1755 Mendelssohn published *Letters on the Emotions in German,* which brought him instant recognition and fame as one of the leading minds of Germany. The work centered about a new understanding of the nature of beauty and aesthetics. His theory paved the way for ideas later expressed by Schiller, Goethe, and Kant.

Mendelssohn went on to publish important works on the proof of God's existence and the immortality of the soul. His books, based on the use of reason, stressed the dominant themes of the Enlightenment. Translated into several languages, they were widely read throughout Europe. Mendelssohn was often referred to as the "Jewish Plato," and his home was the magnet for many visitors to Berlin.

In 1769 an event occurred that challenged Mendelssohn's Jewishness. Johann Lasper Lavanter, a Swiss preacher, had visited Mendelssohn on several occasions to discuss religious questions. Lavanter translated a book into German entitled *An Examination of the Proofs for Christianity.* He dedicated the translation to Mendelssohn and challenged him either to refute it or convert to Christianity.

Mendelssohn hated controversy of any kind and was reluctant to be drawn into a public dispute about the merits of Judaism or Christianity. However, he had no choice and responded in a letter in which he defended his loyalty to Judaism tactfully but forcefully. Rebuking Lavanter for his ill-concealed zeal, Mendelssohn pointed out that Judaism was tolerant of the convictions of others; it never sent out missionaries to make converts, and, unlike Christianity, maintained that even the unbeliever was in God's care and could attain salvation if he or she was of moral stature. Lavanter then publicly apologized to Mendelssohn.

Thereafter, Mendelssohn became actively involved in the struggle for the protection and the civil rights of Jews all over Europe. Out of these struggles he evolved the philosophy of the separation of church and state that continues to guide our thinking. He reasoned that the church has the right and, in fact, the duty to seek to influence by instruction and persuasion. But this is where its power ends. It can neither control actions of private individuals nor impose its beliefs on all citizens, nor can it punish one who is not a member. The state governs the relationship between its citizens and has no right to regulate, to control, or to regulate the thought of its citizens. If the law is just and for the good of all, the state may compel its citizens to obey or punish them for infractions. But the state cannot pressure the convictions and consciences of its citizens and must not be allowed to hold particular beliefs as conditions of citizenship.

Mendelssohn then turned toward the revitalization of Judaism. He was deeply attached to Jewish life and observed all the mitzvot. He concentrated all his efforts on translating the Bible from Hebrew into German. The beautiful German prose was printed in Hebrew letters with which Jews were more familiar. Each volume contained not only the German text but also a commentary called a *Biur,* written in Hebrew and designed to provide a better understanding of the text.

This achieved several purposes. Mendelssohn's translation opened the door of the German language and the Enlightenment to Jews who heretofore had only used the Yiddish language. The graceful *Biur* was one of the forces that contributed to the renaissance of Hebrew, the language in which Jews of Eastern Europe pursued enlightenment and sought to acquire the culture of the world.

Mendelssohn, through his personal example and work, tried to bridge the two worlds. His final work caused a cultural revolution and provided the means to pass from the ghetto to greater Europe. Some outstanding spokesmen of traditional Judaism, however, objected to the translation precisely because they feared that Mendelssohn's plan would succeed and that a knowledge of German would tempt youth to neglect their Jewish studies for the pursuit of secular interests. Three leading rabbis issued a ban against the book and threatened to excommunicate those who read it. In some communities, the book was burned publicly as a gesture of protest and warning.

Mendelssohn, as the first modern Jew, raised questions that continue to confront us. He was the first to recognize and formulate the central problems that had begun to trouble his generation and to which each new Jewish generation has had to find a meaningful answer: how to live without surrendering either the values of Judaism to the modern world or the wisdom of the world to Judaism.

On the 200th yahrzeit of Moses Mendelssohn, we could best pay tribute to him by continuing what he began: a struggle with the challenge of harmonizing

Jewish tradition with contemporary thought. Like him, we modern Jews must always remember that in the Bible Jacob was blessed only after he struggled with the angel that symbolized the unknown.—1986

8. A Treasure Beyond Measure: Facsimile Edition of the Oldest Complete Hebrew Bible Now Available

Arguably the largest collection of Hebrew manuscripts in the world is to be found in the Russian (formerly Imperial) National Library in St. Petersburg (formerly Leningrad), Russia. In May 1990, armed with an official invitation, I visited the collection. My host was Victor V. Lebedev, former curator of Eastern Manuscripts in that great scholarly treasure trove.

While strolling through the stacks, I stumbled into Bruce and Kenneth Zuckerman, who were beginning the process of photographing the Leningrad Codex, catalogued as Firkovitch B 19 A, and dated 1009. This is the oldest complete Hebrew manuscript of the Hebrew Bible in the world. Dr. Zuckerman and his team of West Semitic Research, located in Claremont, California, planned to photograph the original and publish a facsimile edition. Realizing that this was a historic moment, I gave him a check and told him that I wanted to purchase the first copy.

In 1998 this great treasure arrived. Every page is a trove of information that will take decades to study. Captured in precise detail are also breathtaking full-color, illuminated pages representing the loveliest of medieval Jewish artwork. Included are five essays written by members of the production team.

Why is the Leningrad Codex so valuable?

Referred to as the *keter* (crown jewel) of the unpublished medieval manuscripts of Judaic texts, it is the single most important complete Hebrew manuscript of the Bible. In the colophon (a publisher's note appended to a text) we learn that the scribe was Shmuel ben Yaacov, and the manuscript was ordered by Meborak Ha-Kohen ben Netanel in Cairo (Medinat Mitzrayim). Completed in 1009, it is a product of the Ben Asher scribal dynasty, who faithfully followed the Masoretic scholars. There is a tradition that Maimonides (1135-1204) himself saw the codex and referred to it as the authoritative source for textual study.

Who were the Masoretes?

The *Baaleh Mesorah* (Masters of the Tradition) gathered in Tiberias from the eighth century through the tenth century to ensure a uniform reading of the Hebrew Bible. In early times, the books of the Bible were written in scroll form, using an alphabet of twenty-two letters, and the text in this form had been required for use in the liturgy. Vowels and cantillation signs had to be added for pronunciation, study, and meaning. The Masoretes dedicated themselves to producing a full, annotated copy with all the variants. The Leningrad Codex is based on the work of the most eminent Masorete, Aharon ben-Moshe ben-Asher, as its scribe testified.

What is a codex?

Early writing was done on a scroll that was made of parchment (the hide of an animal) or papyrus reeds and similar compounds, which the Chinese invented and we now call paper. The difficulty in studying a scroll is that one has to constantly roll it to refer to passages. Scrolls are written on one side only, in columns. In the ninth century, the codex evolved. It is simply pages bound together—a book. One can write on both sides of a page, it is easy to turn to any part of the book quickly, and when placed on a shelf, it is easily identifiable.

Why is it called the Leningrad Codex?

From the new book's colophon, introduction, and ending note, we learn that the codex was faithfully copied in Cairo from an authorized text during the years 1007-09. The next information we have is a bill of sale in Damascus in 1489. The trail vanishes then until 1838 when Abraham Firkovitch, a devout Karaite Jew and chazzan, appeared on the scene. Karaite Jews, as differentiated from Rabbinate Jews, believed in the literal meaning of biblical verse without interpretation. Therefore, they had an intense interest in old manuscripts, which they used to establish the exact text. The Karaites opposed the oral tradition of rabbis as recorded in the Mishnah and Talmud.

A number of Karaite scholars had settled in Jerusalem and Cairo in the ninth century, and many of the manuscripts they studied came from Egypt because the hot, dry climate preserved them.

Firkovitch, born in Poland and living in the Crimea, was both a Karaite and successful nineteenth-century businessman who traveled for years throughout the southwestern regions of Russia, Constantinople, Jerusalem, and Egypt. He was zealous about discovering the origin of his sect. He was an expert in evaluating ancient Hebrew texts. As he traveled, he collected the largest assemblage of Hebrew manuscripts in the world. He sold this collection to the Russian National Library in St. Petersburg in 1859 for 25,000 rubles in silver.

After another two-year-long trip he gathered an even larger collection of Hebrew manuscripts, which the library acquired in 1865. Hence, the codex was cataloged as Firkovitch B 19 A. Housed in St. Petersburg-Leningrad when it was discovered to be the most important manuscript for establishing the Hebrew text of the Bible, it became known in scholarly circles as the Leningrad Codex.

The codex itself clearly states that it was written in Old Cairo. Firkovitch brought it to Odessa in 1838, but the scholarly community does not have a clue how he managed to procure it. He was an expert at ransacking old synagogues and their *genizot,* which stored worn-out manuscripts in order to preserve them. Firkovitch probably found this one at the Ezra Synagogue in Fostat (Old Cairo), which was later to become famous because of Solomon Schechter's discovery and work.

We cannot overestimate the value of the *Mesorah* (traditional text) preserved in this manuscript, which is in mint condition. It is enough to say that the *Mesorah* to Genesis alone includes 2,570 notes, the *Mesorah* to the whole Bible about 60,000, and the *Mesorah Magna* at the end of the codex comprises 4,271 notes. In the reading of the Prophets and the Holy Writings there are about 250 variants. Serious study of all this material is now progressing with the help of computers and other technology.

Finally, the Leningrad Codex is an astonishing example of medieval Jewish art, one of the oldest illuminated Hebrew biblical manuscripts. It contains sixteen full-color carpet pages (letters in small print that form designs) decorated with painted gold, blue, and red ornaments. It is probable that the master of micrography (tiny, hand-painted letters) was the scribe himself. His name is printed in the center of the Star of David design.

The Leningrad Codex includes 966 black-and-white pages, each twelve inches high and ten inches wide, while the size of the text is nine inches high and eight inches wide. It is now available through Wm. B. Erdsmans Publishing Company in Grand Rapids, Michigan. This facsimile edition of the oldest complete Hebrew text of the Bible belongs in every Jewish school, synagogue, and university. It is a treasure beyond measure.—1998

9. People of the Body

Eros and the Jews: From Biblical Israel to Contemporary America. By David Biale. New York, Basic Books, 1992

Are Lenny Bruce, Erica Jong, Philip Roth, and Doctor Ruth in the Jewish tradition or are they aberrant? What parts do eros and sex play in the dramatic rise of intermarriage in the United States? Will Zionism and the new wave of feminism create a new sex ethic? Is there a classic Jewish view of sex?

David Biale, professor of Jewish History and director of the Center for Jewish Studies at the Graduate Theological Union in Berkeley, California, deals with these issues in a new work entitled *Eros and the Jews.* The book is steeped in scholarship, balanced in judgment, and always stimulating. It begins with biblical times, travels through the rabbinic period, examines Kabbalistic literature, probes Zionism, and considers the American scene in light of sexuality and eros. This is a serious study, containing some 870 scholarly citations and a bibliography of 273 books. Yet it is well written and its observations are cautious, if not often tentative, leaving the reader to weigh the evidence and come to his or her own conclusion.

If sex is the physical act that takes place between people, sexuality or eroticism is the way a culture imagines sex and assigns meanings to it. Jews are not only a people of the book, but also a people of the body. Jewish culture across the years has not been monolithic when considering eros but a dialectic of desire, always in flux. The challenge was not the body but the psychic state of the passions. Passions, in Jewish experience, were both necessary for the existence of the world and exalted thinking, and at the same time a potentially destructive, evil force. Contrary to conventional wisdom that Judaism always advocates sane married sex, the Jewish view of eros is fraught with ambivalence.

Procreation is the first commandment, yet is more than that required or desirable? There is a dispute in the Mishnah between Hillel and Shammai about the length of time a man may take a vow of celibacy without his wife's permission (Ketabot 5:6). There is a strong strain of asceticism in medieval Jewish philosophy; the *perushim* (abstinents) studied all week only to return to their homes on Friday evenings. The last monk in the 600-year-old Ethiopian Jewish heritage of celibacy and prayer is alive and well and living in Ashdod, Israel.

In the first edition of the early nineteenth-century biography, *In Praise of the Baal Shem Tov* (Shivchei ha-Besht, p. 258), the founder of Hasidism relates that when his wife died, his followers suggested that he remarry. The Baal Shem Tov replied, "Why do I need a wife? For the last fourteen years I refrained from sleeping with my wife and my son Herschelah was born by the word." No doubt scandalized by even the suggestion of the Christian notion of immaculate conception, the editors of the text omitted this story from later editions.

Although the central purpose of sexual relations, according to the rabbis, was to fulfill the commandment of procreation, they also recognized another commandment known as *onah,* fulfilling the sexual pleasure of their wives. Sex manuals tell how to do so. *Iggeret ha-Kodesh, (Letter of Holiness),* written in the thirteenth century, states clearly: "We who have the Torah believe that God in his wisdom did not create anything inherently ugly or unseemly. If we say that intercourse is repulsive, then we blaspheme God who made the genitals. Marital intercourse under proper circumstances is an exalted matter."

The Kabbalah raised eros to the level of theology. It stated that God had both male and female components. The female is given equal status in the *sefirot.* Men and women are unique, and only when they complement each other is the universe complete. This protofeminism has had implications for contemporary Jewish feminists such as Sylvia Plath and Susannah Heschel.

We might well ponder the sex life of the mystics and its effects on Jewish law and culture. When Solomon Alkabez in his popular Sabbath hymn *Lecha Dodi* wrote that the mystical love of God was like "the desire of a bridegroom for a bride," was he projecting his own sexual experience? Or was he expressing his frustration and transferring his eroticism to the divine realm? Joseph Karo, author of the monumental and influential *Shulchan Aruch* (Code of Jewish Law), codifies the extreme position on male sexuality, forbidding any male pleasure. Was his dour view a reflection of his own severe conflicts over sex and other matters that he describes in his autobiography?

Biale's book abounds in exotica about erotica. Shabbtai Zvi, the pseudo-messiah, married the Torah in a wedding ceremony in Salonica. A bizarre critique of Hasidism claimed that followers moved back and forth in prayer as in an act of intercourse. *Sefer Hasidim,* a thirteenth-century Ashkenazic pietist book, suggests that an adulterer who is prepared to repent should sit in an icy river for the time elapsed from the moment he first spoke to the woman until the consummation of the affair. If it is summer he should sit on an ant hill for that period of time.

Sexual experimentation, either permissiveness or sexual repression, often occurs during times of upheaval. During the Enlightenment, for example, Jewish literature expressed a variety of views. In Anski's play *The Dybbuk,* the hero Chanan, a mystic, gives voice to erotic modernism and calls it the "holiness of sin." Yiddish novellas became a source for romantic ideas, especially for female readers. Even in Orthodox circles young marriages were discouraged.

As for Zionism, some considered it an erotic revolution, if not erotic liberation. Creating a new image of the Jewish body became a symbol of creating a new nation. Max Nordau's Zionism reflected the concept of a Judaism with muscles "in which Jews must develop their bodies instead of remaining slaves to their nerves." Even Abraham Isaac Kook, the chief Ashkenazic rabbi of Palestine, wrote, "We have greatly occupied ourselves with the soul and forsaken the body . . . Our return [to Zion] will be marked, along with its spiritual glory, by a physical return which will create healthy flesh and blood, strong and well formed bodies, and a fiery spirit encased in powerful muscles."

The new Zionist who wrote more explicitly on the subject of sexual health did not demand libertarianism. Excessive sexual desire, no less than excessive abstinence, was a sign of degeneration. Stable and sober marriage was the cure. While the *halutzim* experimented with new techniques of communal living, the idea of "free love" was a myth. The Tenth Commandment of Hashamer ha-Tzair's secular decalogue read: "The Shomer is pure in his thoughts, words and deeds. He does not smoke or drink alcohol and he guards his sexual purity."

Eros and the Jews provides a perspective and a framework for considering the contemporary challenge of intermarriage. Intermarriage was a defining and controversial issue, even in biblical times. Moses, all the sons of Jacob, David, and Solomon married non-Jewish women. Esther intermarried, yet a book in the Bible was named after her. Ruth was sexually bold and a non-Jew (convert?), yet her story is part of the canon.

In the Middle Ages, both the church and the synagogue passed laws stringently opposing sex between their congregants. The intermarriage rate in pre-World War II France and Germany was exactly the same as today in the United States. Each generation of Jews thinks it is the last generation of Jews. Yet Jews always manage to survive and thrive.

Portnoy's complaint and his preoccupation with the *shiksa* is merely the reverse of the *bellejuive* (the beautiful Jewess), a concept that obsessed men in the Renaissance. It is the lure of the Other. Erotic desire operates in constant tension between the familiar and what is different, even forbidden.

As Biale notes, whether the larger culture was Canaanite, Roman, medieval European, or modern and national, the Jews and their sexuality reflected the issues of their times, while their vocabulary was often inherited from their ancestors. The history of Jewish society must therefore be the history of a cultural system in all its conflicts, varieties, and interactions with other cultures. Jewish culture throughout the ages is the story of actual people and not only values found in texts.

Eros and the Jews is an original and worthy study and represents the work of younger Jewish scholars who have now come to maturity. Men and women in the United States and Israel thoroughly grounded in Jewish studies, but also well trained in the disciplines of social anthropology, linguistics, archaeology, psychology, and textual analysis, are producing monographs and studies enriching Jewish scholarship and literature. They are also heeding the rabbinic counsel of raising many disciples. May their tribe increase.—1995

10. First Jewish Commodore in United States Navy Honored

Uriah Phillips Levy, the first Jewish naval officer to rise to Commodore, was recently inducted into the Jewish-American Hall of Fame located at the Judah L. Magnes Memorial Museum in Berkeley, California. His is the twentieth commemorative medal in the annual Hall of Fame series issued by the museum. Previous honorees have included Albert Einstein, George Gershwin, Herbert H. Lehman, Levi Strauss, Jonas Salk, and Isaac Bashevis Singer.

Levy was born in Philadelphia in 1792, the grandson of a *schochet.* He faithfully attended the Mikveh Israel Congregation on Cherry Street where his other grandfather was a *parnas,* or president. However, the lure of the sea was too much, and at the age of ten he made up his mind to ship out as a cabin boy on the *New Jerusalem.*

Two years later, Levy came home to prepare for his Bar Mitzvah. He studied with Amos Hart, a learned Jew recently arrived from Holland. Hart was also a ship's furnisher by trade and knew a great deal about the sea. Young Levy managed to acquire as much knowledge of winds and waves as he did of the Torah.

On the Shabbat following Uriah's thirteenth birthday the boy was called before the Torah. He read his haftorah well. Following the service, his parents gave a feast in their son's honor, and Uriah delivered an appropriate address to the guests.

But the pull of seafaring was strong and two months after his fourteenth birthday, Uriah went to sea again, this time as a common seaman. His parents discovered they could not dissuade him. Therefore, they sent him off with their blessings and a mezzuzah, which he nailed to the door of his cabin.

Levy adhered to his Jewish beliefs. He would not eat pork or shellfish. Because he was a Jew, he did receive some chaffing. Later on he was subjected to vicious anti-Semitism, but he held his ground. As he wrote in his famous *Memorial* to Congress, "I am an American, a sailor, and a Jew." And he never let anyone forget it.

On one occasion, Lieutenant William Potter, a big, red-faced man and a violent anti-Semite, called Levy "a damned Jew." Levy ignored him, but at a party later that night Potter pushed Levy, insulted him three times, and forced him into a duel.

Dueling was still in vogue in 1816. Before the duel the judge asked, "Have either of you anything to say?" Levy then recited the *sh'ma.* He added, "I also wish to state that, although I am a crack shot, I shall not fire at my opponent. I think it wiser if this ridiculous affair be abandoned."

Potter insisted that the duel continue. Potter fired four times at Levy, who did not lift his pistol. On the fourth shot, he nicked Levy's left ear. Potter still persisted and insisted on a fifth round. Finally Levy lifted his pistol intending to shoot Potter in the leg, but the ball struck Potter in the chest and he fell back dead.

Levy went to seaman's school and continued to sail. Six months short of his twentieth birthday he took command of his first vessel, the *George Washington.*

The so-called second American War of Independence was fought not for political freedom but for the right of American vessels to sail the high seas unmolested. When the White House declared war on June 18, 1812, Levy, ever the patriot, immediately decided to join the Navy. He made the United States Navy his career and rose from Captain to Commodore, the first Jew so designated when he was appointed flag officer of the Mediterranean fleet.

During his service in the Navy he could never reconcile himself with the use of the lash. When he saw his first flogging, he was filled with determination to end this brutal practice. He devoted much of his time and used every means possible to halt whipping as a form of discipline. Finally, due to his persistence, Congress outlawed this practice.

Levy venerated Thomas Jefferson. When he witnessed the famous home of the great president, Monticello, fall into ruins, he could not bear it. He purchased the estate for $2,700 and then, at his own expense, undertook a costly restoration program. Upon his death he bequeathed the house and 2,500 acres of surrounding property "to the people of the United States."

When Levy was ordered to bring his fleet home from the Mediterranean, he dispatched one ship, the *Macedonian,* to bring a wagonload of earth from the Holy Land. He then presented this earth to Congregation Shearith Israel, so that a small portion of holy earth could be used in the traditional Jewish burial service.

Throughout his life, Levy was active in Jewish life. He was the first president of the Washington Hebrew Congregation. In 1854 he sponsored the new Hebrew School of the B'nai Jeshurun Educational Institution in New York. His wife, Virginia (of the famed Sephardic Jewish Lopez family), once revealed in her diary: "Spent Yom Kippur with Baron and Baroness Rothschild who had a synagogue in their home."

Levy's funeral, as recorded in *The New York Herald* on March 26, 1862, was most remarkable. In addition to the United States Naval traditions and honors, a full Jewish service was conducted by Rabbi Lyons of Shearith Israel Congregation. Hebrew prayers were recited and three captains and three lieutenants carried his coffin. They stopped seven times as the Hebrew Psalms were chanted. The Kaddish was recited and dust was thrown on the coffin.

During World War II, the destroyer *U.S.S. Levy* was named in his honor. The first permanent Jewish chapel built by the United States Armed Forces is the Commodore Levy Chapel at the Norfolk, Virginia, Naval Station. At the dedication, Rear Admiral George H. Rosso, Chief of Chaplains, noted: "This ceremony today embodies a great tradition, freedom of religion for the individual and for the community in which he lives."

The Uriah P. Levy medal features on its obverse a front-facing portrait of him by nineteenth-century artist Thomas Sully. Behind him is a scroll bearing the inscription, "Abolished flogging in the U.S. Navy." The reverse carries a rendition of Monticello with Thomas Jefferson's signature.

It is a fitting tribute to Commodore Uriah Phillips Levy.—1986

11. Passages on Sacrifice in the Bible: Are They Still Relevant?

The third book of the Bible is known as Leviticus (in Hebrew, *Vayikra),* after its opening word. It is also known as *torat kohanim,* the "priestly code," because it deals, mainly, with the laws of sacrifice. It was traditional to begin a Jewish child's Hebrew education with this portion of the Bible.

Why begin Jewish education with the study of the sacrificial cult? After the destruction of the Second Temple in the year 70, the sacrificial system ceased for good, so what sense does it make to concern ourselves with that? If passages in the Bible on sacrifices are not relevant today, why should we read them at all?

We must understand that the sacrificial system was very complicated, and there are many types of sacrifices. One whole treatise in the Talmud (Zevachim) is devoted to it. The basic concept behind the sacrifice was the presentation of an offering (often substantial) either as an expression of atonement or thanksgiving in celebration of a festival, as a prayer, or as a set ritual enactment. This was not done only by the Hebrews but was common practice in the ancient world.

Cain and Abel brought each other sacrifices as did Abraham, Isaac, Moses, and all the Israelites of the Bible. Very early, however, there was an attempt to give it perspective. Thus, the prophet Samuel said: "Does the Lord delight in burnt offerings as much as in obedience to the Lord's command? Surely, obedience is far better than sacrifice, compliance than fat of lambs" (I Samuel 15:22).

The prophets of the First Temple period often spoke out against sacrificial rituals. Amos, Hosea, Isaiah, and Jeremiah contrasted righteous and just behavior along with obedience to God with rituals unaccompanied by proper ethical and moral attitudes. The prophets did not reject sacrifices or formal rituals; it was the offering of both without proper moral commitment that was being denounced. They opposed the empty, hypocritical formalism practiced by their contemporaries.

Micah best articulates this view. His sentences echo down the centuries with eternal validity: "With what shall I approach the Lord, do homage to God on high? Shall I approach Him with burnt offerings, with calves a year old? Would the Lord be pleased with thousands of rams, with myriads of oils? . . . He has told you, O man, what is good, and what the Lord requires of you: Only to do justice and to love goodness, and to walk humbly with your God" (Micah 6:6-8).

When the First Temple was destroyed in 586 B.C.E. and the Hebrews were exiled to Babylonia, the sacrificial cult ceased for a period of time. Faced with the challenge of living on foreign soil and the cessation of the cult, the Jews responded by creating the synagogue. Here portions of the Bible were read, including sections describing the sacrificial cult. Prayers were fashioned as a substitute form of worship. Interpretations of biblical passages were added to respond to immediate needs. This process ultimately developed into the sermon.

When the Second Temple was totally destroyed in the year 70, it brought the sacrificial system to a complete end. This posed a staggering problem to believing Jews. How should Jews worship God since there was very little hope that the Temple would be rebuilt? Fortunately, the answer is preserved for us in an ancient rabbinic text (Avot d'Rabbi Natan 11a):

"Rabban Yohanan ben Zakkai once was walking with his disciple Rabbi Joshua near Jerusalem after the destruction of the Temple. Rabbi Joshua looked at the Temple ruins and said: 'Alas for us! The place which atoned for the sins of the people Israel through the ritual of animal sacrifice lies in ruins!' Then Rabban Yohanan ben Zakkai spoke to him in these words of comfort: 'Be not grieved, my son. There is another way of gaining atonement even though the Temple is destroyed. We must now gain atonement through deeds of loving kindness.' For it is written, 'Loving kindness I desire, not sacrifice'" (Hosea 6:6).

From that period on, attempts have been made to find a spiritual meaning for the sacrificial system. They can be divided into three categories.

For the true believer, the answer is obvious. Sacrifice was commanded by God. It is the revealed word of the Almighty. Whether we understand it or not is really not relevant. It was spoken on high and must be followed.

Others found the explanation through symbolism. Philo, in the first century, devoted a treatise to the subject *(De Victimus)*. He contended that the law that a sacrifice had to be free of blemish meant that the offerers had to be wholesome in body and soul. Lions and tigers could not be offered because they preyed on other animals. Similarly, the sacrifices of a persecutor are not accepted. Later rabbis all the way to the twentieth century struggled to find the ethical meanings through the symbolism of the sacrifices.

Quite different is the historical view of sacrifice that Maimonides advocated in the twelfth century. Maimonides held that the sacrificial cult was not really of Jewish origin. It was the universal custom during the time of Moses, and he used it until Jews could be taught a higher form of worship. The sacrificial system was only a transitional phase that would be abandoned once a deeper perception of religion and worship was reached. What Maimonides wrote in *The Guide to the Perplexed* (3:26) has been the basis for a strong school of thought among Jewish theologians.

In contemporary times, the Reform movement abolished or modified liturgical references to sacrifices, believing that this service will never be restored. Some Conservative congregations have rephrased references to sacrifices making it clear that they belong solely to the past. Orthodox Jews, nevertheless, continue to pray for the restoration of sacrifices, which they believe will occur when the Messiah comes.

So, what should we do with the passages in Leviticus that contain the sacrificial system? Ignore them? Read them because they are in the Bible? Reshape our entire Torah reading system to conform to some contemporary thinking?

I would like to suggest that the readings be retained according to the ancient cycle for three reasons. The sacrificial system is part of the history of our people. Let the record stand. I do not believe in revisionist history. Let the sacrifices be studied each year, and let us learn how Judaism evolved. Only those who know the past can hope to know in what direction they should go in the future.

Secondly, the Jewish system of biblical interpretation is very complex. Many fine ethical and social customs have been developed that were based on passages dealing with sacrifices. Ritual and religion, morals and mores, ceremony and culture are so closely bound that at times it is impossible to separate one from the other. It is worth noting that the Holiness Code, which many contend is the highest ethical expression of religion, is found in the heart of the passages on sacrifice (Leviticus 19). The phrase "Love your neighbor as yourself" is set at the center of the most complicated section on sacrifices. We do not know exactly why, but they are somehow intertwined. That must be preserved.

Finally, I think the word "sacrifice" is a word that must be emphasized again and again. It is central to religion, a moral life, and an ethical society. The word itself is a benchmark to help us evaluate how we think and how we act.

Have we ever thought of the manner and meaning of the way in which we help people? It is noble to bring a can of food for the food shelf. But if we are bringing one can or one package from a well-stocked pantry, how much are we really offering? If we have plenty of time on our hands and we volunteer our services, it is a mitzvah. But then again, if we have a lot of free time, what are we really giving? If we are asked to contribute to an important cause and we give a quick check, that is valuable. But honestly, in most of our contributions to causes, how much are we really sacrificing? In other words, in today's society, what is casual giving, what is responsible giving, and what constitutes a sacrificial gift?

In today's society our lives seem to be dominated by consumerism, by materialism, by me-ism. We are concerned about how much we are going to get rather than what we can give. In this sense, it is important to keep the term "sacrifice" before us so that we can understand that making sacrifices for others and society in general is a religious concept. Sacrifice serves as a counter-balance for selfishness.

There is the story told of a woman who brought her small son to see the great man, General Robert E. Lee. She asked General Lee: "How can I educate my child properly, and what is the most important thing I can do for him?" Lee replied, "Teach him how to deny himself."

The essential problem of living life is not how to do with but how to do without; not how much we make but how much we give. In the end, it is not how much we take with us but how much we leave behind in helpfulness, in sharing, in loving that really matters in this world.

It is interesting to note that the Hebrew word for sacrifice, *karbon,* comes from the root *karov,* which means "to come near." This seems to indicate that we come nearer to God and the spiritual life when we learn to make sacrifices for others.

Yes, the passages on sacrifice in the Bible are still relevant today. Perhaps now more than ever.—1978

12. Our Hope is not Lost
The History of Hatikvah

As Jews in Israel and throughout the world prepare to celebrate the fiftieth anniversary of the birth of the third Jewish commonwealth, it is appropriate to learn the story of *Hatikvah* (The Hope). *Hatikvah* is the national anthem of Israel, expressing deep feeling among all Jews and moving them to identify with the Jewish past, present, and future.

The words were written as a poem, *Tikvatenu,* by Naphtali Hertz Imber in Jassy, Rumania, in 1874 and published in 1884 or 1886. (One cannot be entirely certain of events in his life because he was inebriated most of the time.) Imber was born in Galicia in 1856, where he was an *illui* (child prodigy) in Hebraic and Talmudic studies. His urge to write poetry began early. At the age of ten, on Yom Kippur in the middle of *shacharit* (morning) services, the boy persuaded his friend to leave the synagogue for a while. In a neighboring alley he asked his friend to record the poem that he had composed in his mind.

Later he left Galicia and traveled all over the world: Paris, Berlin, London, Bombay, Palestine, and finally, New York. He lived an extremly unconventional life of restless bohemianism. In Yiddish, Hebrew, English, and German, he constantly wrote poems, prose, and articles while in an alcoholic haze.

Imber met Sir Lawrence Oliphant in Constantinople in 1882 and became his secretary for Jewish affairs. He moved with Oliphant to Palestine and lived there for six years, roaming the land and falling in love with it. He was so excited by this experience that he devoted the rest of his life to dreaming of its restoration. In fact, he claimed he founded Zionism.

Under this influence he reworked his poem, *Tikvatenu.* While it shows the influence of Germanic and Polish nationalism, its dominant theme is rebuilding the land of Zion and the concept of hope.

Imber first read his poem in 1882 to the farmers of Rishon Lezion. Shortly thereafter Samuel Cohen, one of the farmers, set it to music derived from a Moldavian-Rumanian folk song. Some would trace the music to the Czech composer Smetana. Others base it on a Sephardic melody for Psalm 117 in the *Hallel* service. In 1884 or 1886 it was published in Jerusalem in his book of poetry, *Barkai* (Dawn).

Hatikvah has gone through nine versions but its basic text emphasizes the overwhelming desire to return to Zion, rebuild the land, and never lose hope—even after centuries. The anthem received a real boost in 1890 when Rehovot was established. Each new community in Eretz Yisrael chose a song or poem, and the people rebuilding Rehovot chose *Hatikvah (Tikvatenu).* That is how it came to pass that scores of workers would set out from Rishon Lezion each morning and sing *Hatikvah* all the way to Rehovot. When Herzl visited Rehovot in 1898, he was greeted by a crowd singing *Hatikvah,* which had caught on quickly in Palestine and throughout the Jewish world.

Just before the First Zionist Congress in Basle in 1897, Herzl and Max Nordau decided to hold a contest to select a hymn. They received forty-five entries: thirty-three in German, three in Italian, and just one in Hebrew. These songs were so bad that Herzl ordered them to be destroyed. Finally in 1933, the Zionist Congress formally adopted the blue and white flag and *Hatikvah* as the symbols of the movement.

Naphtali Hertz Imber died in New York on October 8, 1909, in abject poverty but well known for his writings, his alcoholism, and his unwavering devotion to Zion. The Attorney Street Synagogue was designated as the locale of the funeral services, but the officers of the synagogue objected, saying, "The poet was not orthodox." Finally, the Educational Alliance was substituted for the synagogue. Chopin's Funeral March was played and many eulogies were delivered. One was spoken by the rabbi of Temple Emmanu-El, Dr. Judah L. Magnes, who was to become the first president of the Hebrew University in Jerusalem.

The cortege of about 10,000 people, according to *The New York Times*, proceeded to the cemetery in Maspeth, Long Island. The immortal anthem *Hatikvah*, printed on a large tablet and draped in black, was borne behind the coffin. Imber himself had hoped that, when Palestine became a state, he would be reburied in Jerusalem. And he was.

Though physically ill, embattled, and penniless, he never lost the feeling of elation and the exuberance of hope, particularly in Zion. After his death, three suitcases full of poems and articles written in Hebrew, Yiddish, and English, as well as other unpublished items were found in his room. The entire treasure trove was deposited with the trustees of Har Moriah Hospital where he died. When it was decided to publish his manuscripts, they could not be found. One hopes that they will be discovered some day .

The fate of *Hatikvah*, like its author's life, was stormy. After 1933 *Hatikvah* swept the Yishuv (Jewish settlement in Palestine) and the Jewish world. During the Mandate, the British banned *Hatikvah* from the airwaves, so broadcasters played a section of Smetana's work instead. The British responded by banning the composer's music from Hebrew broadcasts.

Just before statehood was achieved in 1948 the director of Ohel Theater asked Ben-Gurion to find a new hymn. He did not, and so *Hatikvah* became the national anthem of Israel.

Numerous attempts have been made to replace it since then; however, none of them has succeeded. Zubin Mehta has called it the most beautiful anthem on earth. Those who have heard the Israel Philharmonic Orchestra play it accompanied by hundreds of voices would agree.

The first fifty years in the life of any state is filled with tensions and enormous problems. Add to this the searing memories of the Holocaust, the awesome humanitarian effort of reaching out and gathering in some 2 million Jews in distress from more than 100 cultures and diverse interpretations of Judaism, and the fighting of six defensive wars—the State of Israel is an enormous, unprecedented achievement.

That is why even amidst days of internal conflict and international tension Israel stands out in world history. Almost two millennia of Jewish life are proof of that.

Our hope is not lost.—1998

13. Jews and Books: A Love Affair

The alphabet was invented shortly after the time of Abraham and Sarah. According to Jewish legend, however, writing and its implements were among the ten special acts of creation that took place on the sixth day just before the Sabbath. Another legend has it that Moses invented the alphabet for the specific purpose of writing down the Torah he received on Mount Sinai.

The Torah scroll *(Sefer Torah)* itself, which is generally known as the *Pentateuch,* comprises the Five Books of Moses and is treated with special reverence. It is obligatory to stand in its presence. When the Torah becomes too worn for use, it is buried with a special ceremony. The ark, in which Torah scrolls are kept, is always the focal point of the synagogue.

The second most important book in Judaism is the Talmud. The Talmud is an attempt to harmonize the laws found in all twenty-four books of the Hebrew Bible with the realities of life in the post-biblical period. It evolved over seven centuries and is concerned with every conceivable subject that arose during those years. Winding through some thirty-five volumes (sixty-three tractates), the Talmud contains 5,800 folio pages and about 2,500,000 words. Almost 3,000 rabbis participated in it. The remarkable feature of the Talmud is that it is a book on faith filled with questions and skepticism. Common phrases in the Talmud include *dilma ipcha,* "perhaps the opposite is true"; *vedok,* "the matter requires further study"; *mah,* "what?"; and *lamah,* "why?"

Such is the Jewish love for books that one was traditionally placed in the crib of a child to familiarize the infant with the book. True wealth was books, and it was considered a good deed to loan them (Ketubot 50a).

Hebrew books were never thrown away or destroyed. When they became old and not usable, they were stored in a *geniza,* a hidden room or treasure house in the synagogue. One *geniza* attached to the old Ezra Synagogue near Cairo became famous when Solomon Schechter discovered it in 1897. More than 200,000 literary, biblical, talmudic, musical, legal, and personal records, written from the seventh century to the nineteenth, were found.

The great prince of medieval Jewish book-lovers was Judah ibn Tibbon, who lived in Provence in the thirteenth century. His will, in the form of last injunctions to his son, deals to a large degree with the treatment of his library. His exact words are: "My son, make books your companions, let your bookcases and shelves be the pleasure grounds and gardens."

Jewish people in every stratum of society shared this love for books. A Christian scholar who visited Warsaw during the First World War found a great many coaches parked but no drivers in sight. A Jewish boy standing nearby noticed his dilemma, so he showed the visitor the way to the drivers. In a courtyard on the second floor was the driver's synagogue, consisting of two rooms: one filled with volumes of books and the other for prayer. All the drivers were engaged in fervent study and discussion. On further investigation the scholar found that Jews in most of the professions—the bakers, the butchers, the shoemakers—had their own study houses. Every moment they could take off found them in their libraries. One book now in the Yivo Library in New York City bears this stamp: "The Jewish Society of Wood-Choppers for Study."

Women were important contributors to the Jewish love for books. The prophet Deborah's poem occupies an important place in early Hebrew poetry. Two books of the Bible chronicle the deeds of women—Ruth and Esther. Beruriah and Imma Shalom are quoted in the Talmud with authority. The popular *T'zenah U'renah* was written for women. Up to the twentieth century, at least fifty-four Jewish women have been listed on colophons or title pages of books.

Perhaps women's most important contribution to the Jewish love of books before this century was their creation of the ambience for study and reading in the home. This tradition has carried into our times. I recall that when I first began to read my mother encouraged me to read a series called the Big Little Books. I believe each cost a quarter. As I finished each one, she taught me how to place them on a shelf and start a library. I read and reread them. She told me, "Save them and some day give them to your children." I never forgot that.

The story of the Jewish book must also include burning and censoring. In 1294 in Paris, twenty-four wagonloads of copies of the Talmud were burned. The popes censored Jewish books over the centuries. The Nazis burned nearly 800,000 Jewish volumes. When people burn books they usually end up burning people.

The Jewish Theological Seminary of America owns the first printed Hebrew book—a code of Jewish law edited by Jacob Asher, printed in Italy in 1475. As was the practice at the time, the book had to be submitted to the censor, and he carefully inked out all the complimentary references to Judaism. Recently, when librarians at the seminary checked the holdings in the rare book section, they found that a remarkable thing had happened to this volume. The ink used by the censor had almost faded away, but the original Hebrew text of Jacob Asher was still clear as ever.

So great is the Jewish love for words that, in different times and places, people have created new languages. Using Hebrew characters, Jews have invented Yiddish (Hebrew German), Ladino (Hebrew Spanish), and Judeo-Arabic (Hebrew Arabic). Few are aware that there are also Judeo-French and Judeo-Italian. Altogether, Jews have fashioned sixteen variant languages.

The number of Hebrew writers through the ages staggers the imagination. From Abravanel to Shai Agnon, Isaac Babel to Saul Bellows, Ibn Ezra to Nora Ephron, Yehuda Halevi to Glückel von Hameln, from Solomon ibn Gabirol to Nadine Gordimer, Isaac Luria to Emma Lazarus and Nechama Leibowitz, Maimonides to Moses Mendelsohn, Amos Oz to Cynthia Ozick, Rashi to Anne Roiphe, Spinoza to Isaac Bashevis Singer and Maurice Sendak, Sefer Yetzira to Anzia Yezirska. Make up your own list and you will have written an encyclopedia. Of Jews, it is truly said, "Of making books there is no end" (Ecclesiastes 12).

To which one can add, "To the love affair between Jews and books, there is no end."—1995

14. Gossip from a Synagogue Attic: Jewish Daily Life Ten Centuries Ago

Aside from the amazing autographs of Yosef Caro, Yehuda Halevi, and Maimonides contained in the fifty fragments now on display, the exhibition at the Israel Museum also informs us about every facet of Jewish communal life in Egypt between the tenth and thirteenth centuries. This exhibition commemorates the one-hundredth anniversary of the discovery by Solomon Schechter, the second president of the Jewish Theological Seminary, of a treasure trove in the *geniza* (hiding place) in the attic of the Ben Ezra synagogue in Cairo. The sample of 150,000 fragments now stored mainly in the library of Cambridge University in England and the Jewish Theological Seminary in New York yields an astounding amount of information about this crossroads of the Jewish centers of Eretz Israel, Syria, Lebanon, Yemen, and Egypt.

There is a record of a heated dispute between Shlomo ben Yehuda, the Jerusalem sage and head of the Eretz Yisrael academy, and Yosef Ibn Al-Sijelmasi, representing the Jewish community in Fustat, outside of Cairo. At issue was the authority of the rabbinic courts in various cities, particularly in marriages and fund-raising. Because the sides would not compromise, the matter became so overheated that the caliph, Excellency Al-Mustansir, had to make the decision.

Other fragments show that, as the first millennium approached, the Jews of Sicily expected the imminent arrival of the Messiah. A pregnant woman became hysterical and shouted unusual Hebrew phrases, two travelers saw a fiery angel enter the synagogue, and a Jew named Leon said the "Hidden King" was on the way to lead the Jews back to the Holy Land. Branch Davidians, Heavens Gate, and some Jewish sects—move over.

Feminists might be interested in learning that one fragment contains the sole record of a medieval female poet writing in Hebrew. Dunash ibn Labrat, one of the greatest Spanish Hebrew poets of the tenth century, left on a long voyage. His wife wrote him poetry with meter and rhyme that, in the original Hebrew, is truly a gem:

Will her beloved remember the graceful doe
on the day of separation, her only son on her arm
He set the signet [ring] of his right hand on her left
while she placed her bracelet on his arm.

The controversy between the Karaites (who interpreted the Bible literally) and the Rabbinites (who followed Talmudic interpretations) is also well documented. We have the exact words of Aban, the founder of the Karaite sect, and Saadia Gaon, the rabbinic leader, who changed the face of Jewish literature. Yet we find a rabbinically approved marriage document from 1082, written in Aramaic, that permitted the Karaite bride of a rabbinic leader to follow her own strict customs.

There are also checks that Jewish merchants used. On the upper left-hand corner is the amount in Coptic numerals. The rest is written in Judeo-Arabic in Hebrew letters. Each contains the names of the bearer, the banker, and the signer. Some people added an *alef, mem,* and *tav,* which stands for the words *emet mayaretz titzmach,* "truth springs from the earth" (Psalms 8:12) as a warning against misuse of the check.

While most of the documents are written in Hebrew readable by today's 10-year-old schoolchild in Israel, many others are in Aramaic or dialects such as Judeo-Arabic and Judeo-Persian. There is a copy of the Koran in Hebrew characters and, amazingly, the oldest known epic poem in Yiddish.

Also discovered in the *geniza* trove were a few remarkable fragments of the work of Obadiah the Proselyte. A Norman priest born in Italy and named Johannes of Oppido, he was inspired by a dream to become Jewish in the year 1102. Warmly welcomed by the Jewish community, Obadiah recorded Hebrew prayers and used special marks called "neumes," which are notes. Thus, we have the first written documentation of Jewish music, thanks to a Jew by choice.

There is the notice of a book sale of the estate of Rabbi Abraham Hasid. The reconstructed advertisement reads as follows:

On Tuesday, 26 Adar, books on Jewish subjects will be sold. On the following Tuesday, 4 Nisan, books on general subjects will be sold. Sale supervised by Rabbi Abraham the son of Moses Maimonides. Works by Saadia Gaon, Shmuel Havagid and many famous authors. The following week: Medical books by ibn Rushd, Hippocrates, Galen, medical treatises, and more.

A rare find is the illustrated page of a child's primer on the Hebrew alphabet. It looks exactly like those used for teaching Hebrew to American children. There is also a child's Hebrew alphabet exercise book with doodles, both from the eleventh century.

Still other fragments document that a Jewish woman had an affair with a Christian doctor and the Muslims considered it a scandal. A Jewish mother complained that her son never came to see her or wrote to her. There are appeals in the Jewish community for the Jews of Kiev, Byzantium, Yemen, and Eretz Yisrael. And much, much more.

The more the Jewish world changes, the more it stays the same.—1997

15. The 90th Anniversary of the First Complete Hebrew Reference Book of the Bible

Complete reference books (concordances) to the Hebrew Bible or to major works of literature are now compiled with the aid of computers. Therefore, it is difficult to imagine how, in the past, lone scholars toiled on the compilation of vast word indexes without copying machines, typewriters, or ballpoint pens.

The enormity of the task of compiling a complete reference book of the Hebrew Bible is best illustrated by the following figures: The Hebrew Bible contains 23,203 verses, 304,901 words, and 1,512,207 letters. Therefore, each verse will appear in the reference book about 13 times—a total of 304,000 references. A staggering task.

Until the thirteenth century, neither Christians nor Jews felt any need to compile a reference book for the Bible. The Latin translation used by Christians, known as the Vulgate, was not always accurate. As for the Jews, since they studied the Bible day and night, almost everyone, from the humblest worker to the most learned rabbi, knew the Hebrew scriptures by heart.

Then in the fifteenth century, Jews were challenged by the church to public disputation on the meaning of the verses of the Scriptures. This motivated the beginning of Biblical reference books. A Dominican cardinal, Hugo de Sancto Caro, aided by 500 of his fellow Dominicans, tried his hand at such a work using the Latin text, but it only listed nouns and verbs and it was incomplete. A rabbi, Yitzchak Nathan, set himself to the task using the Hebrew text, but he encountered the same difficulty, and his work also did not fulfill the goal of a full reference work.

After that, many tried their hand at it in Hebrew, Latin, and other languages—even English—but they all failed in producing a full work.

Finally, in the nineteenth century, along came a strange Jew who set himself to the task with ferocious dedication. His name was Shelomoh ben Simcha Dov Mandelker. He was born in a little town near Dubnow between Russia and Poland in 1846. There he received a classic Jewish education. He decided to Europeanize his name so he formally changed it to Solomon Mandelkern.

One day, he felt compelled to write a little poem on the margin of a work by Maimonides. He was caught in the act by the synagogue *shammus* who gave him a dressing down: "Do you want to defile a sacred book with your own scribblings? Why don't you leave for a larger city? There you will find your kind, heretics who will welcome you!" So he left.

Mandelkern now steeped himself in secular studies ranging from biblical commentary to German and Russian. He went to St. Petersburg to study Oriental languages with the greatest scholars of that time. In 1868 he was ordained as a government authorized rabbi.

But, unfortunately, he was a difficult person. He quarreled with his wife, his congregants, and his colleagues. Like many another genius, a relentless urge drove him to self-destructive acts. Sad as this may be, his brilliance and single-mindedness pushed him in one creative direction.

His restlessness drove him to Leipzig, Germany, which was then a center of German book production. To sustain himself he worked for a publishing firm that specialized in cheap, paper-bound translations from foreign literature. He received 10 marks per printed sheet. That was less than the daily wage of a factory worker. But it was here that Mandelkern got his idea of editing a definitive and complete reference of the Hebrew Bible.

In 1884 he published a pamphlet in German in which he set forth the principles on which his work would be based. Then he got a printing firm to undertake the project. But his troubles were just beginning. The printers, not really knowing Hebrew, could not read his cursive script. He was then forced to hand copy each of the tens of thousands of lines in square letters.

In the introduction to his great book he wrote (and it was no exaggeration): "For now my soul is weary and my power has been broken by this work. But from the depth of my heart I can testify publicly that I did not shy away from hard work and drudgery, and all that I undertook I did faithfully." Indeed, it took him five years just to proofread the galleys.

The moment he had been looking forward to during two decades finally arrived in 1896 when the firm of Veit and Company published the two huge folio volumes under the Hebrew title *Hechal Hakodesh (The Temple of the Holy).* It seemed to be a fitting birthday gift, for the author was then fifty years old. Although it was hailed by Jews and Christians alike as a master work, it did not become an immediate best seller. There were no more than 300 subscribers at a price of 300 marks (about $24.00), an exorbitant amount at that time. By the time it was ready for sale, 40 of the subscribers had died and most of the rest had fallen on hard times.

He traveled from city to city to persuade well-to-do Jews to buy copies for themselves or as gifts for their synagogue libraries. Most of what little money he made, he spent on railroad tickets traveling on night trains, saving the cost of hotel rooms by sleeping on the hard benches of the coaches. He even traveled to America and did manage to sell 100 copies, which barely paid his boat passage and kept him alive.

An interesting event took place in Basle, Switzerland, where he was a delegate at the first Zionist Congress. Mandelkern wanted to introduce a resolution thanking his benefactor Baron von Rothschild for helping to promote the Hebrew language. It was disdainfully turned down by Theodor Herzl and other Zionist leaders who asked, *Wer ist dieser Schnorrer?* ("Who is this beggar?") No one there recognized this sorry-looking old man whose monumental work had appeared at the very moment in history when the foundations of a future Jewish state were being laid.

Mandelkern chose *Hechal Hakodesh* as the title of the book because he was convinced that he was laying the groundwork for *Loshon Hakodesh* (The Holy Language). He was right, for he really could not rely on any other early attempts in this field. He pointed out that in a work so large, there would necessarily be some errors and omissions, and concluded his opening words with the following honest and humble thought: "I am a human being and not a god."

Now, ninety years later, we can say that his opus is the most comprehensive and scholarly work of its kind. It is still the most often used; it is cited as an authority and has been brought to the point of almost absolute accuracy.

Although Solomon Mandelkern did not live to see the enormous success of his work and the realization of his dream—the use of his beloved Hebrew as the official language of the Jews in their own country—his name will forever be linked to the work that is an indispensable aid to the study of the original text of the most widely read book of all ages.—1986

16. The Oldest Known Hebrew Writing Containing the Name of God

After reading the Book of Judges and Josephus, Dr. Gabriel Barkay, professor of archaeology at Tel Aviv University, concluded that the next important find in Jerusalem would be near the Sonol gas station and Liberty Bell Park. This was the southern approach to Jerusalem where five roads intersect. It was just beyond the reach of arrows shot from the wall of the city, and any invader would have to encamp there.

In the early 1970s new construction in that area began to turn up many potsherds of the First Temple, Persian, Hellenistic, early and late Roman, Byzantine, and Turkish-Ottoman periods. Just a hundred yards from where he surmised, there was a small hill next to St. Andrew's Church of Scotland. It seemed to contain burial caves and evidence of several encamped armies.

A few seasons of digs revealed what might be the most important site found in 120 years of exploration in Jerusalem. On the first level of the digs were large pots filled with human ashes. (The Romans cremated their soldiers.) This is where Pompey, the first Roman general to come to Jerusalem in 63 B.C.E., approached the city. It is where Titus built his siege wall and the Tenth Roman Legion was encamped. It was obviously the site of a Roman army crematorium.

Further digging revealed a series of burial caves for Jews of the Second Temple period. This was confirmed by pottery findings. Like most burial areas, it had been looted, yet enough silver, beads, and glass were left behind to indicate that the burials were of wealthy families.

Then, by a stroke of luck, someone struck a loose area and saw a shaft. It turned out that beneath these burial caves were nine more of the First Temple period. They had never been touched and were the family tombs of noble and rich Jerusalemites from around 700 B.C.E.

Two things should be borne in mind. It was the practice of Jerusalemites to bury their dead just outside the city to keep the city ritually pure. This area, known as *Ketef Hinnim* (the Shoulder of Hinnim) was immediately outside the walls of Jerusalem on the road connecting David's birthplace, Bethlehem, and his capital, the City of David in Jerusalem. It was, therefore, a well-traveled road.

In the famous Cave No. 25, the remains of ninety-five individuals and about 1,000 items were found. The pottery definitely dates the cave at the end of the First Temple period (seventh to sixth centuries B.C.E.), to the Babylonian and Persian periods. Included are spectacular pieces of jewelry (six gold and ninety-five silver items). There are glass vessels of the pre-blowing age, cosmetic dishes, objects of bone and ivory. Boat-shaped earrings are particularly prominent.

These finds lead to two conclusions. The jewelry has parallels from Iran in the east to Sardinia in the west, the Kingdom of Ararat in the north to Syria in the south. Jerusalem was already, 2,600 years ago, an international center. Moreover, not all the Jews went into exile after Babylonia destroyed the city. Indeed, some of those who stayed behind were wealthy and powerful.

Also found was a seal with the name *Palta.* This name is found in another inscription in Jerusalem. Now we know the family name. Another important item was a small, worn silver coin. It originated in Kos, a small island in the Aegean. It was struck in the sixth century B.C.E. when coins had just begun to be minted. The dating of the find is now very sure.

It is the deepest wish of every archaeologist to discover inscribed objects. What was found in Cave No. 25 was beyond anyone's fondest hopes. In the course of the excavations two small silver cylindrical objects were discovered. They were rolled into tiny scrolls about half the length of a cigarette. There was a space in the middle through which a tiny string could be inserted, and then the scroll could be worn on the body. The problem was how to unroll the scrolls without damaging them.

Museum experts were consulted all over the world, but they were reluctant to work on the scrolls for fear of harming them. Finally, the Israel Museum laboratories decided to handle the brittle little objects. The backs of the silver scrolls were brushed with acrylic glue to hold the metal together. Then they were slowly and painstakingly unrolled. After they dried, photographs were taken from all angles and blown up. Drawings were made.

Quickly there emerged Hebrew writing of the seventh century B.C.E., and it was almost identical with the biblical verses in Numbers 6:24-26, known as the Priestly Benediction: "Adonay bless you and keep you. Adonay make His face to shine upon you and be gracious unto you. Adonay lift up His countenance upon you and give you peace."

The word for "Lord" is written in the Hebrew YHWH, which is the oldest and most authentic Jewish term for God. Prior to this find the oldest biblical text was from 100 B.C.E. in the Nash Papyrus. Now we have a text going back to the First Temple period or 700 B.C.E.

The object may be an amulet or the forerunner of *tefillin* (phylacteries). The expression "*tefillin* of silver" occurs in the papyri of the Egyptian Jewish community dating to about 300 B.C.E. It is clear that we have here the beginnings of the concept of *tefillin* which, perhaps, arose from simple amulets to more sophisticated concepts. This is the normal progression of religion.

The curator of the Israel Museum collection, Michal Dayagi-Mendels, showed the finds to me in the laboratory before they were opened to public exhibition. I was deeply moved to see all the items but particularly the silver scrolls containing the Priestly Benediction and oldest known Jewish name of God.

By chance, when I returned to our Jerusalem apartment, I noted that the scripture portion for the week was *naso,* which contains the Priestly Benediction. I felt a historical tremor. Imagine saying these words to bless children, marriages, and congregational services, employing the very same words that were uttered 2,700 years ago. I was simply another link in the tradition that is possibly the oldest in the world. Considering this, one might safely assume that despite the vicissitudes of history, Judaism and the human race will not only endure, they will prevail.—1986

17. The Original Words of Jesus

The State of Israel has yielded many extraordinary experiences, but none more startling than the work begun more than twenty years ago by a Jewish scholar and a Christian scholar, each deeply loyal to his own faith. Dr. Robert Lindsey is a Baptist minister who first came to Israel some forty years ago and serves a West Jerusalem Baptist congregation. Dr. David Flusser is an observant Jew who prays every Shabbat at Chovevei Tzion Synagogue and is professor of the history of religion at the Hebrew University.

These men have worked together in a unique and fruitful collaboration. They have gathered about them a group of other scholars, Jewish and Christian, and have created a research project that is challenging some of the basic, traditional assumptions of scholarship centered about the Christian scriptures.

The synoptic gospels of Matthew, Mark, and Luke present parallel accounts of the life and techniques of Jesus. The way that these versions fit together—or sometimes do not fit together—is the most difficult and controversial problem for those studying these texts. David Bivin and Roy Blizzard are among scholars associated with the "Jesus School," and they have just published its first findings under the title *Understanding the Difficult Words of Jesus.* The book presents the background of the research in simple language and then gives examples of problems that arose from lack of understanding of the original Hebrew context. The basic findings are that: the original account of Jesus' life was written in Hebrew; it is possible to reconstruct a large portion of the Hebrew from the Greek text in the same way cities and civilizations are reconstructed from archaeological discoveries; and that, since

Jesus taught in Hebrew to a Hebrew audience, many theological controversies are rendered meaningless when understood against a Hebrew background.

The scholars point out that without understanding the Hebrew idiom some texts are impossible to comprehend. To illustrate, they query: Without understanding English idioms, how would one comprehend (much less accurately translate) phrases like: "Kill time," or "Hit the ceiling," or "Eat your heart out"? According to the authors (and both are devout Christians with strong ties to Christian organizations) the scriptures can only be understood in light of the fact that "the writers are Hebrew, the culture is Hebrew, the traditions are Hebrew, the concepts are Hebrew."

The evidence is overwhelming. Some 5,000 rabbinic parables of that period have come down to us, all in Hebrew. Since extensive excavations in Israel in 1968, numerous scriptures have been unearthed. No Aramaic inscriptions from the Roman period have been found. In studying the Greek text of the Christian scriptures it is clear from the substance, the syntax, and even the mistranslations that it was all written first in Hebrew and then translated into Greek.

This discovery could only have been made by scholars who have lived in Israel. Dr. Robert Lindsey's ear is finely tuned to idiomatic Hebrew. The study of classic Greek, such as Homer, would not enable a modern student to speak Greek. But in modern Israel, if one knows only the Biblical Hebrew of Isaiah, he or she can go out in the street and shop.

Bivin and Blizzard suggest that many translations have far-reaching theological ramifications. One striking example of this can be found in one of the Beatitudes, which is rendered as "Blessed are they who are persecuted for righteousness sake." This statement, attributed to Jesus, greatly contributed to the idea that one could gain religious merit by suffering persecution and martyrdom. Bivin and Blizzard contend that "persecuted" in this context should more correctly be rendered "pursue." "How could 'pursue' be confused with 'persecute'?" the authors ask. They reason, "If one knows Hebrew, he or she can easily understand how this happened." The Hebrew word *radaf* has two meanings: 1) "pursue" or "chase;" and 2) "persecute." It would make no sense, for instance, to translate Isaiah 51:1 as: "Listen to me you who persecute *(radaf)* righteousness." The context forces us to translate, "You who pursue righteousness."

Therefore, the words of Jesus should be read, "Blessed are those who pursue righteousness." Indeed, these are the exact words of the command as found in the Torah in Deuteronomy (16:20).

It is regrettable that the book is flawed in one respect. Jesus never came out and said, "I am the Messiah." The authors try to prove that Jesus implied it, and they use Hebrew texts and rabbinic language in an attempt to justify their conclusion. The fact is simple. If Jesus meant it, he would have said it. The prophets and rabbis were always direct in their teachings. Here one feels a bias, rather than scholarship.

But, be that as it may, the book is a valuable beginning to increase the sensitivity of Christian scholars to the Hebraic mind out of which came Christianity. Jews should welcome a book that publicly acknowledges the great debt that Christians owe to Jews. To truly understand that Judaism is the parent of Christianity would then lead Christians to fulfill the basic command to honor one's mother and father.—1984

18. The Columbus-Jewish Connection

The 1985 television mini-series on Christopher Columbus has awakened our interest in one of the most exciting periods in human history. While this has great interest for those of us in the so-called New World, it is particularly intriguing for Jews.

Before Columbus could even begin to contemplate his voyage, he had to have a map. The most prized map of that period was the Catalan Atlas written by Cresques lo Juheu (Cresques the Jew). The astrolabe that Columbus used was perfected by Abraham Zacuto who not only wrote Hebrew books but also scientific works that had to be translated into Spanish. The astrolabe itself was fashioned after the work of an instrument maker, Tzvi Herz, and is noted for engraved Hebrew inscriptions.

Columbus, himself, deserves the spotlight in a history of Jews in the Western Hemisphere because of a persistent question: Was he a Jew? He was born in Genoa, Italy, and little is known about his origins, which he purposely obscured. Columbo is the name of many Italian Jews, and Columbus had a unique way of signing his name that seems to recall certain Hebrew characters. His son Ferdinand insisted that his father's "progenitors were of the blood royal of Jerusalem." In Columbus' writings he cites the Hebrew Bible and Jewish events with great accuracy. Given the conditions of the time, it was entirely possible that he was a Marrano.

The voyage itself began on the 9th day of Av—Tisha b'Av. There is a record that it was the same day as the edict for the expulsion of the Jews from Spain. In fact, Columbus recorded that as he set out on his journey he could see boatloads of Jews leaving Spain. It is stirring to contemplate that on the day of expulsion from the Old World, a New World of opportunity was just opening up that would one day offer hospitality to Jews.

Eighty-seven of the ninety crew members have been identified. It is not easy to identify the Jews since many of those on the ship were *conversos,* individuals who were forced to give up their Judaism on pain of death. It has been estimated that between ten and twenty percent of his crew were Jewish, most of them fleeing the Spanish Inquisition. We do know for certain that the ship surgeon, Mastre Bernal, was a Jew as well as Louis de Torres, who was to serve as a translator for he knew Hebrew and Arabic.

When Columbus first proposed an exploratory trip to the royal court, he was supported strongly by several friends, among them was Luis de Santangel. Santangel was a Jew who viewed the new vast horizon as a place of refuge for his people. Among Columbus' Jewish friends in court was Gabriel Sanchez, the treasurer of the kingdom. A steadfast Jew, Don Isaac Abravanel, was a powerful friend who upheld him. As one historian wrote: "It was not the jewels of Isabella that made possible the voyage of Columbus but rather the Jews of the court." They helped finance his journey.

An interesting part of the voyage itself is the controversy about who saw the land of the New World first. It was recorded Radrigo de Triana, a *converso* on the *Pinta*, was the first to spy land. Columbus ignored him and claimed that he was first. Radrigo was so angry that after the voyage he left for Africa, renounced Christianity, and returned to his former faith.

The first person to set foot on land was Luis de Torres who, in the words of Columbus, "had been a Jew." He was supposed to deal with the natives because he was proficient in languages. The first European to discover the use of tobacco by the natives, he was also the first Jew to settle in Cuba. He lived out the rest of his life in the New World.

The calendar records that the landfall occurred Friday, October 12, 1492. It happened to be the twenty-first day of Tishre, on which Jews sing *hoshanah* and reverently carry Torah scrolls. According to Jewish tradition, on that day the blessings for the coming year are finally determined. It was a blessing that on that very day Europeans found the New World, which has become a home to millions of Jews.—1985

19. We Will Not Be Silent: Remembering the White Rose

To go against public opinion in your own country in time of victory is a difficult thing to do. Fifty years ago Germans needed only to keep their mouths shut and nothing would happen to them. Interviews with surviving relatives, court records, and diaries tell of the human toll of silence: a German father who detested the Nazis but watched his oldest son become a youth leader in the Nazi movement; a church's response to an order to replace a crucifix with the Nazi symbol; a university whose scholars were gagged, insulted, and forced to listen to a petty bureaucratic denunciation of university women who did not produce babies for the Third Reich. But there were also those who would not be silent. The White Rose, a German student resistance group, spoke out.

For this act of conscience they were executed exactly fifty years ago. For this they must be remembered, honored, and held high as role models for young people—indeed, for all of us. In these difficult times we must recall, pay tribute to, and be inspired by young students who sacrificed their lives on the altar of conscience. They must be our conscience as we commemorate their moral courage. We honor them most not in words, but in deeds.

The moving story of the White Rose centers about a brother and a sister, Hans and Sophie Scholls, who defied Hitler and organized a small group, mainly of medical students, in Munich. In 1942 they bought a press and composed and distributed illegal pamphlets denouncing *Der Führer* and the atrocities of the Gestapo-run society.

Their anti-Nazi leaflets asserted the best in German humanism and religious values with utter clarity. The second leaflet contained this passage: "Since the conquest of Poland 300,000 Jews have been murdered in a bestial manner. Here we see the most terrible crime committed against the dignity of man . . . Every Nazi shrugs off this guilt, falling asleep again with his conscience at peace. But we can't shrug it off. *Guilty, guilty, guilty.*"

Robert Scholl, the father of Hans and Sophie, served as a catalyst when he spoke to his children during long family hikes and around the table. He planted the seeds of doubt when he said bluntly, "This is war. War against the defenseless individual, against the happiness and freedom of children—a terrible crime." Then one spring afternoon while walking along the banks of the Danube, he turned to them and remarked fiercely, "All I want is for you to walk straight and free through life, even when it is harsh."

The leaflets of the White Rose began to appear in Munich in mid-June, 1942. Four of them came out, one after the other, like a staccato burst of fire—filled with rage and brimming with literary citations. The city had seen nothing like it in years. The Gestapo and police were put on full alert to find the authors.

Christoph Probst, Hans Scholl, and Sophie Scholl put themselves in great danger. Alexander Schmorell, Willi Graf, and Professor Kurt Huber neglected their medical studies and other scholastic interests; they, too, placed their families in jeopardy. They found ways to mail their leaflets from surrounding communities and plaster them on the walls of the university.

Meanwhile, the Nazis' fear of denunciation had increased. There were widespread *flüsterwitze* or "whisper jokes." "Do you know that in the future teeth are going to be pulled only through the nose?" one joke went. "Why?" "Because nobody opens his mouth anymore." Hitler became infuriated, and the search for the pamphleteers was intensified. The Gestapo suddenly found itself confronted by what it saw as a massive bombardment of subversive literature from university students.

The White Rose would not stop. Using a portable typewriter, the students pounded out copies of fliers and continued their resistance. They took great risks, even writing slogans on walls at night, such as "Down with Hitler" and "Freedom." Hans went to Salzburg and posted 150 leaflets. Alexander journeyed to Linz and Vienna with a suitcase and mailed the rest on the way home.

In one of their final leaflets they wrote: "We will not be silent. We are your bad conscience. The White Rose will not leave you in peace."

Eventually, they were apprehended. On Monday, February 22, 1943, Hans Scholl (age 25), his sister Sophie (age 21), and their friend Christoph Probst (age 27) were tried for treason by the People's Court in Munich. At five o'clock in the afternoon of the same day, they were beheaded. The others were also subsequently executed.

An opera entitled *Weisse Rose (White Rose)* and subtitled *Wir Schveigen Nicht (We Will Not Be Silent)* was written about them. It is a concentrated expression of the two opposite poles in humans: the incarnations of the absolute, innocent good and absolute, brutal evil. *Weisse Rose* has been performed more than fifty times in European opera houses. I saw it this past summer in Jerusalem. It is an uncompromising opera that moved me deeply. It is painful but necessary and unforgettable.

Dietrich Bonhoeffer, himself executed by the Nazis for his opposition, wrote while he was in prison, "Not in the flight of thought / But in the act alone there is freedom."

On Monday, February 22, the fiftieth anniversary (Yahrzeit) of the execution of the leaders of the White Rose, I shall recite Kaddish (the Jewish memorial prayer) for Hans Scholl, Sophie Scholl, and Christoph Probst. *Yehi Zichrom Baruch,* "May their memories always reside as a blessing." They are true martyrs—witnesses to the nobility, endurance, and triumph of human conscience.—1993

20. In the Year 1096: The Impact of the First Crusade Lingers

In the year 1096 the First Crusade burst onto the European scene. When Pope Urban urged a Crusade in Claremont, France, amidst cries of *"Deus le volt!"* ("God wills it!"), little did he know that its impact and tremors would continue 900 years later.

Indeed, this year conferences have been held all over the world, for the time has come to rethink the First Crusade and the seven that followed. To be sure, those who ignore history and its consequences are doomed to repeat them.

In 1096 led by an enigmatic man known as Peter the Hermit, an army of 20,000 peasants marched across Europe with the goal of recapturing the holy places of Christendom from the Muslims. Peter's band was decimated in what is known today as Turkey, well short of Jerusalem. But his quest began the Crusades, nearly 200 years of war, that left a legacy of magnificent castles, new church orders, and children of mixed parentage.

The Crusaders took home with them innovations as diverse as advanced medicine, mathematics, Greek thought, apricots, scallions, and sugar. They also returned with a muted sense of Christian triumphalism, particularly when Jerusalem was recaptured by Saladin and the Christians were left with just a limited right of access. Saladin rebuilt the city and its walls and became the hero of the Arab world.

To many Westerners, the Crusades are something for the history books. But in the Arab Middle East, they remain much alive, a symbol of European encroachment that still evokes suspicion and comparison to recent events. It is no accident that Khomeini referred to President Carter, a Baptist, as "The great Satan," and Saddam Hussein calls himself "The new Saladin." Last summer, an Islamic group called upon "Crusader forces"—the U.S. military—to leave Saudi Arabia. This year, three Arab countries—Egypt, Syria, and Libya—are producing movies on Saladin.

During the First Crusades, Rhineland Jews suffered devastating attacks. The Jewish communities of Worms, Mainz, and Cologne were virtually wiped out. Eleventh-century Christians believed that the Muslims merely denied Jesus, while the Jews were responsible for his death. A young Jew from Worms named Isaac ben Daniel was told by a man: "You can still be saved. Do you wish to convert?" He signaled with his finger—he was unable to utter a word for he had been strangled—indicating his loyalty as a Jew. They severed his neck. Was this a rehearsal for the Holocaust?

Dr. Robert Chazan, a professor of Judaic Studies at New York University, who wrote the extensive work in 1987 entitled *European Jewry and the First Crusade,* has recently restudied Jewish narratives, personal accounts, eulogies, and liturgical poems of this period. His findings are illuminating, for they show all degrees of good and evil.

Those involved in slaughtering the Jews and pillaging their possessions were Crusaders, burghers, and roving bands with bizarre notions. Negative images of Jews as newcomers, as dissidents, as enemy, as competitor, as baronial ally, were prevalent. These stereotypes plus the era of general lawlessness created the potential for anti-Jewish sentiments.

When possible, Jews resisted. Some took up arms against the Crusaders. Often they withdrew behind fortified walls but to little avail. When given the choice between converting to Christianity or death, overwhelmingly they chose the latter. In Regensberg the burghers brought the Jews to the local river and made the sign of the cross over them, but the "converts" secretly continued practicing Judaism.

The assistance of "righteous gentiles" is deeply moving. The Bishop of Speyer built a strong wall to protect Jews. As a Jewish account testifies, "He pities us as a man pities his son." In Mainz we learn, "Then all of them (Crusaders and burghers) came with swords and spears to destroy us. Some of the burghers came and would not allow them [to do so]." The local German authorities tried to protect the Jews. Many bishops, priests, and friends finally took an oath to save the Jews.

The swearing of protection is not to be taken lightly. Some neighbors hid them. However, most of the population stood on the sidelines. Would this be what Elie Weisel meant when he said, "Indifference is the worst sin"? Is this a lesson for all of us today?

We must be careful to understand the mindset of those centuries. The combination of early Gospel imagery and subsequent ecclesiastical policy created a volatile situation. To Christians, the Jews were simply "Christ-killers." On the other hand, in the eyes of Jews of that era, Christians were polytheistic and worshiped a deity that could live a life of flesh and blood. We are all fortunate to live in a time—particularly the last four decades—when Jews and Christians have come to look upon each other not merely with tolerance but with understanding. We not only accept but truly appreciate each other.

In the First Crusade, when the Jews saw their Torah scrolls trampled in the streets and realized death was imminent, the issue was no longer survival but salvation. They then turned to a unique phenomenon in Jewish history—mass martyrdom. They slaughtered their own families by slashing throats, convinced they were doing God's will. In Jewish chronicles they are portrayed as heroes and honored in *Memorbuchen,* ("memory books") and liturgy.

In one of the Jewish chronicles, Rabbi Moses of Cologne addresses the potential martyrs: "We shall live in Paradise. Each one shall have a gold crown on his head, which is set with precious stones and pearls, seated under the golden tree of life." Interestingly enough, this image almost mirrors contemporary ones of Hezbollah and Hamas in Islam and the Christian beliefs in Jonestown, Guyana, and Waco, Texas. It would seem that extreme fundamentalists are fundamentally alike. When the meanness and shabbiness of this world becomes overwhelming, then the riches, both spiritual and physical, awaiting the martyrs in the world beyond are absolutely overwhelming. Mass suicide becomes the passageway to eternal glory.

Yet during the era of the Crusades great religious theologians produced their most valuable and enlightened works. Rabbi Solomon ben Isaac (Rashi) wrote voluminous commentaries on the Talmud and Bible that have never been surpassed. Moses Maimonides authored the first book of Jewish philosophy and brilliantly organized the Talmud. Ibn Rushd was a scintillating Arab Aristotelian and organizer of Islamic law, and Avicenna wrote original works in philosophy and medicine. Thomas Aquinas stunningly organized Christian theology, and Peter Abelard's analytical thinking and introduction of rationalism in Christianity are still worthy of deep study. It seems that when the nights are darkest the most brilliant stars appear, guiding our way through the ages.

Looking back over the past 900 years, one could say as of every age: "It was the worst of times and it was the best of times." Many things can be learned from reflecting upon these times. But most of all, we must make every effort to be considerate and respect the views of others, and others must endeavor to be considerate and respect our views. This is the only road to a peaceful society.—1996

21. Masada: Message, Myth, or Madness?

The precious articles found at Masada are now on exhibit at the Tel Aviv Museum. In mid-August they will travel to New York's Jewish Museum. Recently, a superb and intriguing book entitled *A Prophet from Amongst You*, a biography of Yigael Yadin, director of the massive explorations of Masada, was published. It was written by Neil Asher Silberman, an archaeologist and historian, who studied under Yadin and worked for the Israel Department of Antiquities.

Reviewing the artifacts of the Masada dig and reading this book raises some thoughtful questions that deserve examining. Yadin's discoveries were "proof" that 960 men, women, and children held off Roman assaults and, rather than suffer the fate of captivity, committed mass suicide. A poem by Yizhak Lamdan captured public imagination with its final image of young Jewish pioneers dancing around a bonfire at the top of the mountain and proclaiming, "Masada shall not fall again."

Since the days of Moshe Dayan's tenure as chief of staff, new recruits of the Armoured Corps of the Israel Defense Forces have hiked up the steep path to the plateau of Masada and have taken the oath of allegiance in that dramatic setting. On one such occasion, Yadin, standing in the flickering torchlight, said to the newly sworn Israeli soldiers: "When Napoleon stood among his troops next to the pyramids of Egypt, he declared, 'Four thousand years of history look down upon you.' But what would he not have given to be able to say to his men: 'Four thousand years of *your own* history look down upon you.'"

The only written account of the Jewish mass suicide is to be found in book seven of Flavius Josephus' *The Jewish War.* Josephus was never at Masada, and his main accounts are based on some of the Roman legion's records, which were read by Josephus after he switched to the Roman side. Two women and five children were hidden in an underground system and survived. Could they have remembered in detail Eleazer Ben-Yair's famous last stirring speech as Josephus reproduced it word by word?

One of the purposes of his polemical work was to ingratiate himself with the Roman court. W. Winston, who first translated the book into English, referred to Josephus as "that notorious liar." Acts of heroism during the first century similar to Ben-Yair's can be found in the works of six classical authors and among at least ten contemporary peoples.

Now to the hard evidence. At the Masada site were found a hoard of silver shekels minted during the revolt, textiles, baskets, keys, arrows, sandals, large fragments of seven ancient scrolls almost identical to the Dead Sea Scrolls, bones of fourteen men, six women, and four children, and the beautifully hand-plaited hair of a woman, as well.

Some nagging questions have arisen. If there were 960 people, why were there not more bones? During the fifth and sixth centuries, Byzantine monks lived there. Where are their bones? Among the animal bones were many from pigs, and this would be unthinkable to Jewish zealots.

The Jewish rebels against Rome were known as *sicarii,* "knife men." Josephus despised them and described them in the blackest terms. Jonathan Price, who teaches history and classics at Tel Aviv, believes that Josephus was trying to show the folly of rebelling against Rome, which would only lead to mass suicide, a futile gesture. David Ilan, a Jerusalem-based archaeologist says: "This is Jonestown, this is Waco. Real Jewish thought values human life and says there's no excuse for mass suicide." Neil Silberman, in a sardonic manner, points out that this might be compared to Custer's Last Stand and the Alamo.

Silberman, in his book on Yadin, patiently sifts through all the evidence and notes that drawing hasty conclusions in absolute terms is uncharacteristic of archaeologists. Phrases like "might have been," "probably," and "possibly" do not exist in Yadin's evaluations. Even when most of the scientists disagreed with his interpretation of the *ostraca* (inscribed pot shards), he published his view as fact. Yadin orchestrated a massive project and seemed intent on the excavation's patriotic overtones gradually obscuring its most scholarly aspects.

In his time, Israel needed to strengthen resolve in order to survive. A myth was badly needed to shore up Israel's feeling of isolation. Here was an intense search and "discovery" of a heroic, defiant chapter in the great Jewish war with mighty Rome. The excavation and Yadin's interpretation firmed up Israel's moral stance and fascinated the world.

While Masada continues to be one of Israel's most popular sites, the grand gestures of bold army ceremonies are gone. While the army holds some modest ceremonies on Masada, the Armoured Corps ceremonies are now held at Latrun, outside Jerusalem. The new exhibit on Masada is straight archaeology and does not address the more mythic implications. Challenging the tale is healthy and part of a maturing nation.

The American columnist Stewart Alsop popularized the term "the Masada complex" to describe what he saw as Israel's emerging diplomatic inflexibility; writing that the image of suicide might someday be a tragically self-fulfilling prophecy. Golda Meir, on a visit to Washington in 1973, confronted Alsop directly about it at a luncheon at the National Press Club. "And you, Mr. Alsop," she said from the podium with righteous indignation, "You say we have a 'Masada complex.' It is true. We do have a 'Masada complex.' We have a pogrom complex. We have a Hitler complex." Alsop and the other critics, for the time being, were silenced.

But times have changed and Masada fever has receded. As recorded in Silberman's excellent book, archaeologists have been questioning the facts for years. The suicide is impossible to prove outside of Josephus' questionable account. Today, it is impossible to imagine Prime Minister Yitzhak Rabin triumphantly citing Masada during a hand-shaking ceremony with PLO-head, Yasser Arafat.

At the time when the earth seems to be moving under our feet, when long-held opinions of enemies on both sides are under serious review, it is perhaps time to reassess our own views of the message and myth of Jewish history.—1994

22. Has the Lost Ark Been Found?

Ten years ago the Hollywood fantasy *Raiders of the Lost Ark* was produced, and it has now become a cult movie. It is an adventurous, hair-raising story of the search for the lost ark. After Mount Sinai, the Ten Commandments were deposited in the Ark of the Covenant, which became the center of Jewish worship. But somewhere along the corridor of history the ark disappeared.

The ark is mentioned more than 200 times in the Bible. It was two-and-one-half cubits long (four feet, two inches) and a cubit and one-half high and wide (thirty inches). It was constructed by Bezalel to the specifications of Moses. It was made of acacia wood overlaid with gold. It accompanied the Israelites in their journey through the desert.

David brought it to Jerusalem. When Solomon built the Temple, naturally it was placed in the center of the Holy of Holies and became the focal point of Temple worship. But then it disappeared, and we do not hear of it again. Where did it go? How was it carried away? And when?

It now turns out that it may be in Axum, Ethiopia. So claims *Kes* (priest-rabbi) Raphael Hadoni of the Ethiopian Jewish community. I met with Hadoni one morning at his home in Mavasseret, a suburb of Jerusalem. He has been in Israel since Operation Moses. His Hebrew is excellent, but when he began to recall parts of the story his father told him in northern Ethiopia forty years ago, he slipped into Amharic. This was translated for me by Ilululi, an Ethiopian staff member of the American Joint Distribution Committee.

The essence of the story he told me is that when the Temple was destroyed in 586 B.C.E., a group of Jews including a priest named Eliezer and Baruch ben Nariyah, the scribe of Jeremiah, escaped with the ark and went to Egypt.

Several hundred years later, the Jewish community moved up the Nile to settle in the Elephantine Island near Aswan. It is a known historical fact that a group of Jews practiced the sacrificial cult there for a long time after the Temple was destroyed. It is hardly likely that they would do so without a priest *(kohen)* and a main relic of the Temple.

After a series of vicissitudes over the next thousand years, the ark came to rest at Axum, which is where Ethiopian Jews have lived for hundreds of years. During this period, the fortunes of the Jews waxed and waned. There was even a powerful Jewish queen. Eventually, the Jews were subdued and the Ark, now known as "The Tabot of Moses," was captured. In the seventeenth century, it was placed in the Holy of Holies of St. Mary of Zion, where it presumably now resides.

This is the legend *Kes* Hadoni told me. It should be remembered that in every legend there is a grain of truth. But there is another legend. According to the *Kebra Negaot,* a thirteenth-century Ethiopian manuscript, the Ark was brought to Ethiopia by Menelik about 1,000 B.C.E. In this view, Menelik I was the son of the Queen of Sheba and King Solomon of Jerusalem. While Chapter 10 of First Kings does record at great length a cordial visit of the Queen of Sheba to the Court of Solomon, and many gifts were exchanged, there is no direct evidence that their meeting was other than a state visit.

However, there is a strong historical rumor that their relationship was more than cordial and that a son was born of that affair. The son was Menelik, and he founded the Ethiopian dynasty. Indeed, Haile Selassie claimed he was the 225th direct-line descendant of Menelik.

Every Orthodox church in Ethiopia has a Holy of Holies, and in every one there is a *tabot* ark. *Teva,* singular, and *tevot,* plural, are the Hebrew names for "ark." It is claimed that these are only symbolic, for only one true ark, known as *Tabota Zion,* was brought by Menelik and is now in the sanctuary chapel in Axum.

Generally, historians dismiss this as a myth. However, a British researcher, Graham Hancock, has spent the past five years tracing the path of the ark from Jerusalem through Egypt and Sudan into Ethiopia. In his recent 500-page book, *The Sign and the Seal,* he concludes that the Ethiopian Jewish tradition placing the ark in the Church of St. Mary at Axum is true and can be substantiated from other sources.

Hebrew University professor Menachem Haran, a leading expert on First Temple times, notes that references to the ark no longer exist after 700 B.C.E. Indeed, the prophet Jeremiah quotes people as saying, "Where is the Ark of the Covenant?" The ark is not listed among the treasures looted from the Temple by Nebuchadnezzar when the First Temple was plundered.

Professor Haran, therefore, theorizes that it was removed during the reign of Menasseh, who ruled the kingdom of Judea from 693-643 B.C.E. Menasseh "introduced an image of Asherah (a Canaanite fertility goddess) into the innermost part of the Temple — the Holy of Holies." Haran suggests some devoted priests would have removed the sacred Ark and hidden it.

The fate of the Ark of the Covenant is one of the most intriguing of ancient puzzles, an historical riddle that has attracted kabbalists, scholars, and Hollywood screenwriters alike.

According to author Hancock and *Kes* Hadoni, the present guardian of the ark in Axum is named Gebral Mikail. Both Hancock and Hadoni have requested to see it. They have been consistently refused permission to do so. The explanation given is that it is so powerful that even to gaze upon it would cause death. This is not unlike the feelings expressed about it in the Bible and the Talmud.

The prophets Amos and Zephaniah make reference to worshipers in Ethiopia. There is a connection somewhere. *Kes* Hadoni is absolutely convinced that this connection lasted throughout the years and their descendants are the present-day Ethiopian Jews who are at this moment coming to Israel.

Kes Hadoni is sure that the Ark is in Axum. His son, David Hadoni, who is a rabbi in Tel Aviv, says of his father's tale and belief, "It's a story that has been passed down from father to son. It's true."

After a long visit with *Kes* Hadoni, I found the story fascinating and the man intriguing. As for the final answer, only the future will reveal it. Perhaps.—1993

23. The Blue Box Exhibition

Recently, the "Blue Box Exhibition" opened at the President's House *(Bet Hanasi)* in Jerusalem. It commemorates the ninetieth anniversary of the Jewish National Fund.

The first blue boxes, distributed almost 100 years ago, were among the earliest practical steps toward the rebirth of the Jewish state. Based on the old *pushke,* charity-box *(tzedakah)* concept, the Jewish National Fund gathered money to purchase the dunams of land for the Jewish people in what was then known as Palestine. Today there are whole forests of trees funded by this concept.

The blue box changed in form many times over the years and, at times, was not even blue. The first boxes, such as Theodor Herzl's, were whitish. Ornamental boxes in Austria in the 1920's were copper-colored. In some areas of Germany they were leather-bound and sometimes black.

Nor was the blue box always a box. In central Europe it was in the form of an envelope which could be pocketed and which was distributed at Zionist Congresses. At times it was a round container. It is only during the past fifty years that it became a metal box. Usually blue and white, it is decorated with a map of Israel and a Star of David and imprinted with the words *keren kayemet l'yisrael* (Jewish National Fund).

Often the boxes contained pictures of hands planting trees. One shows a man with a primitive plow at work in the field. Another contains the phrase, "The Blue Box That Makes Israel Green." A British version pleads, "Please help us by making it up to the nearest pound." A charming box from Jerusalem in the 1960s shows children planting a sapling.

This particular exhibit contains sixty-two boxes. They came from Argentina, other Latin American countries, Sweden, Canada, the United States, France, Israel, Germany, and Poland. The smallest is approximately the size of a matchbox. The largest, which could not be included in this exhibit, is six feet tall. It is a monument in the shape of a blue box made out of stone, located in JNF's Australian Park in the Negev District of Galilee.

Perhaps the most touching item is a crumpled and burned metal box whose blue color is barely distinguishable. It was discovered in the rubble of the Warsaw Ghetto after World War II. It is a gift of Yehuda Silverman. Born in Poland, Silverman served in the Polish and Soviet armies, trying to make his way to Israel while dodging the anti-Semitic elements in both armies.

Late in 1944, with the war almost over and most of the Jews in his homeland either dead or gone, Silverman, as a youth leader in Warsaw, organized the Zionist youth movements to clear out the Warsaw Ghetto and put up a monument. During the work he came upon two items that caught his eye: a gun and the charred remains of what he knew was a JNF blue box. He turned the gun over to the authorities but kept the box. Silverman said when he turned over the blue box to the exhibit in Jerusalem, "It was important because it proved to me that there were Jews in the ghetto who were Zionists and dreamed of a Jewish state." It was a deeply emotional moment for him.

Another special box is one that belonged to Bernard Bucholdt. When deporting Jews from the Lodz Ghetto, the Germans made them leave their suitcases by the train and allowed them to choose just one item for the journey. Many people chose a warm coat, but Bucholdt chose the box. The destination was Auschwitz, and he hid the box under the floorboards in his barracks. Sometimes, at night, he would take it out of its hiding place and hold it.

"It was my *mezzuzah*," said Bucholdt, who presented the box with trembling hands to the JNF. "The entire Jewish people and my entire Jewish heritage were in that box."

The exhibit was organized by Professor Shaul Ladani, who, over the years, collected most of the blue boxes in the exhibition and was the driving force behind the project. Following its stint at the President's House, the exhibit will travel around the country during the coming year.

For many people the blue box is bound up with childhood memories of home and the traditional contribution made prior to the lighting of the Shabbat candles. Author and poetess Yemima Avidar described her experience in this way:

"I taught kindergarten on the outskirts of Tel Aviv, and every Friday the children would arrive with fists clenching a coin (a *'mil'*? a *'grush'*? I can't even remember!). But I well remember the festivity of their dropping the coin into the Blue Box to the accompaniment of the words of the song:

'Here a *dunam,* there a *dunam,* a clod upon a clod, up building the peoples' land, from the Negev to the North.'"

And so the State of Israel came to be.—1984

SECTION V—TRANSCENDENCE

1. Life is Multiple Choice

Two biblical passages frame the scene and set the theme of Rosh Hashanah, the first day of the Jewish New Year. The first describes the creation of the universe and an incident in the life of Adam and Eve. The second, the one that we read on Rosh Hashanah, records the trials and tribulations as well as the thoughts and triumphs of the first Jews, Abraham and Sarah. There is a direct connection between these two, a connection that has immediate relevance to all of us.

In the creation story, God speaks directly to a human being for the first time after the episode in the Garden of Eden. God addresses Adam with but one word. That Hebrew word is laden with tremendous significance that resonates down the centuries: *ahyehka,* "Where are you?"

Long ago, the rabbis recognized the problem inherent in this verse. Didn't God know where Adam was? By definition, God as Creator is all-knowing, so why the question? After thoughtful consideration, the rabbis rendered *ahyehka* to mean: Do you, Adam, know where you are? Are you, the first human being, aware of your station in life? Do you, and by implication, does every human being to follow know what he or she is doing?

It took several generations in the Bible for another human couple, the first Jews, Abraham and Sarah, to come up with the right answer. I think it was placed in the Rosh Hashanah liturgy consciously. To the call of God, Abraham responded—again, with but one Hebrew word—*hineini,* "Here I am." I am ready, willing, and able to accept my responsibility.

The proper response of a Jew to the question "Where are you?" is *hineini,* "Here I am, a responsible human being." The Jew recognizes that responsibility, the readiness to respond to challenges, is the true mark of maturity.

Responsibility means exactly what it says: responding to a situation with a willingness to understand and be involved and a commitment to help. That is what it means to be a Jew and to be created in the image of God. *Hineini,* "Here I am."

I am apprehensive about the condition of American Jews. The survival of people like yourself and myself is by no means guaranteed. We are mobilized and know how to defend Jews against external enemies; however, protection from internal corrosion and disintegration is a more difficult matter. The real threat to the survival of Judaism is in the open society of America, where the danger of destruction is imminent.

I am fearful that the message and meaning of Judaism is being forgotten and distorted among us. Let me bring to your attention some Jewish misperceptions about Judaism that may ultimately result in its decay and disintegration.

There is a pediatric view of Judaism: "It's good for the kids."

There is a cardiac Judaism: "I'm a Jew at heart."

There is nostalgic Judaism: "I love bagel and lox."

There is financial Judaism: "What do you mean? Every year I write out a check to the Jewish community!"

You can add to the list.

While there is some validity to each of these, they will not preserve Judaism. They are expressions of "Jewishness" and not Judaism. Judaism is an articulation of values. Judaism is identity through the regular practice of time-honored traditions. Judaism is continued learning and education. Judaism is binding commitment.

In truth, Judaism is a form of therapy against the illnesses of the world. Judaism is not a problem but a solution.

Here is an interesting example of how Judaism really functions. This summer, one of the leaders of Israel's social services asked Laeh and me to join him in a visit to a yeshiva in Jerusalem. A yeshiva is a traditional study hall of Talmud. I spent a good part of my early education in one, but today I find the old style of learning sterile and vapid.

We joined him as we went into the heart of the Orthodox section of Jerusalem, known as Geula. There we entered the Yeshivah of Machaneh Yisrael. At first glance, it looked like the classic yeshiva; long tables, big books, loud studying, intense discussion of Talmudic passages. Then we learned who the students were: hard-core criminals recently released after serving lengthy terms at such prisons as Ramle. They were former murderers, rapists, arsonists, and armed robbers. A warden was also there studying.

These students spend the first third of the day studying Jewish texts. The second part of the day they learn a trade such as writing *mezzuzahs* or other vocational skills and, if they are so inclined, a phase of art. The last part of the day is given to community service. Then they go home and spend the night with their families. They observe Shabbat and the Jewish festivals together.

The warden told me that the rehabilitation rate was 80%. To anyone who knows anything about criminal behavior, that is an amazing statistic. I did an independent verification and found the figure to be true.

Here is a specific example of the way Judaism provides direction so that we will live in a positive and meaningful way. This is the essence of the function of Judaism as a philosophy and a way of life. With this in mind, I would like to speak to our situation as Jews here.

Jewish observance in the home must be strengthened. Jewish ceremonies, particularly blessing of candles, reciting Kiddush, and saying Motzi on Friday night and festivals must be regularly practiced at the table because the home is literally the cradle of Judaism.

Attendance at services is a reaffirmation of Jewish identity. Those who do not recognize this are weakening the therapeutic effect Judaism can have in their lives. Jewish adult education is not merely an interesting experience but a basic function of learning values that have enabled us not only to survive but to enrich and enlarge our lives.

We have been fed myths by the Jewish establishment, and this has resulted in a weakening of classic Judaism. Preoccupation with the Holocaust, the State of Israel, and anti-Semitism will not save us. These are historical expressions in their own right, but they are not central to the meaning and fundamental purpose of Judaism. Only Jewish learning, Jewish observance, and the Jewish religion will ensure the survival of Judaism in America. Only Jewish identity that is nourished by distinct Jewish practices passed down from generation to generation will preserve our continuity and worth as Jews. For Jewish survival is not survival for its own sake; it is a tradition that helps make our lives worthwhile as human beings.

It is precisely in our Jewishness that we will find a response to the larger moral and ethical problems of our time. It is a mistake to believe that we will achieve justice and advance the human cause by seeing Judaism as narrow. Indeed, Judaism is the opposite. It is a key and a motivating force in trying to keep humanity human.

Natan Shcharansky, in his remarkable book *Fear No Evil,* tells that he became a free person on a day in 1973 when he decided to identify himself as a Jew and commit his life to Judaism. After that, nothing could touch him. His faith was unshakable. Today, Shcharansky has become *the* symbol of dissent in the entire world. Shcharansky, the Jew, is the metaphor for freedom in our time.

Shcharansky concludes his book by pointing out that a shofar has two ends, one with a large opening and one with a small one. Blowing into the large opening produces no sound; however, if one blows through the small end, it produces a mighty blast, a summons to moral battle. Similarly, he notes, neglecting one's Jewishness in pursuit of great ideals will end up in emptiness. But remaining a Jew in every way eventually leads to great ethical heights. The paradox is that through the narrow we come to the greater view, from the particular we come to the universal.

Consider this: There are no greater words and goals for humankind than: "Justice, justice shall you pursue"; "Love your neighbor as yourself"; "Let my people go"; "One law shall be among you, native and stranger alike." These words have toppled empires, steadied the Jew in adversity, and provided the wider vision for a world at peace. For us, then, it begins by being Jewish and it ends up by embracing every man, woman, and child on this planet. This is a proper Jewish response to the world.

We all must, sooner or later, come to God. As Elie Weisel once said, "A Jew may argue with God, debate with God, hurl accusations against God, but cannot ignore God." In the Jewish tradition, wisely, there is no attempt whatsoever to define God. The closest one comes to a description of God is in the Bible, when God says to Moses, *ehyeh asher ehyeh,* "I am what I am." Elijah defines God as *kol demahmah dahka,* "a still, small voice."

What this teaches us is that each of us has his or her own view of God. By God, I mean the highest reaches of morality, the essence of all existence, that which we apprehend when we contemplate the awe and wonder of Creation. Our God may be personal, rational, emotional, natural; an idea, a concept, a set of principles. But the heart of the matter is that greatness summons greatness. There is a force beyond ourselves, pulling at our selves. The call to Adam is a message to all of us.

Ahyehkah. Where are you in life? Where do you stand on those issues that confront us? Does your life matter? What are you doing down here, anyway? Why were you created? For naught? We must answer each question in our own way. *Hineini.* "Here I am."

This we must say: This is my response to the challenges of life. This is my place in the universe. You created me, God, therefore I am a creature of holiness. I am a person of worth. I will not betray You, God, or myself, or my tradition. In whatever I do, God is part of me. In my every achievement, God's presence is felt.

God calls to each of us: *ahyehka,* "Where are you?" If the answer is *hineini,* "Here I am," then we form a partnership with God. Through Jewishness we enhance our choices for doing well and well-being. When you hear the call of conscience, don't put it on hold; answer *Hineini.* Here I am, ready, willing and able. Life is a matter of multiple choices, but the final choice is yours, and yours alone.—1974

2. In the 45th Year of the Bomb—A Ray of Hope

We are beginning the 45th Year of the Bomb. While it is surely not a guarantee for the future, it is nonetheless a ray of hope that this little planet Earth is still here.

Is it too much to ask why? Are we to bow to the altars of luck and determinism? Why does God seem to continue to love us? Why has God not walked off and abandoned us as a bad experiment?

Let's go back to the birth of the bomb. When the first atomic device was exploded in the Los Alamos desert and Dr. J. Robert Oppenheimer, the director of the project, saw the blinding light of a thousand suns and watched the deadly mushroom cloud rise, he was moved to quote from Sanskrit: "I am become Death, the destroyer of worlds."

Those of us who have lived through these past years can certainly sympathize with that statement. After the shock waves of Hiroshima, Nagasaki, Three Mile Island, and Chernobyl, we live in fear and trembling. Will our worst nightmare become true?

But there is another view. Perhaps, with different orientation, Dr. Oppenheimer might have thought of a passage in Genesis: "And there was light and God saw the light was good." This cosmic scene presents another scenario. Millions have benefited from nuclear medicine. The whole science of physics and related disciplines have brought untold benefits to many. The new source of energy, even with its admitted risks, opens whole vistas for humankind.

If anything, the Atomic Age has made us personally, daily, and immediately aware that the whole human race is bound together in life and death, in hope and fear, and in progress and destruction. We are but stewards of whatever goods, possibilities, and potentials that Earth has entrusted to us.

Is it not time, then, that we leave behind our *denominationalist* concepts and begin to think in terms of the planet or the universe? Morning by morning, while respecting our own heritage, should we not also be aware of the universality of matter, spirit, service, and love? Scientists are beginning to talk about the Gaia principle, which derives from the Greek notion that all of nature is bound together in one organism. Environmentalists know this. Students of mythology know this. Students of human nature know this. Everyone knows this.

Yet we are unwilling to live daily with the understanding that we are all part of one another. Touch one of us and we are all touched. Harm one element and the Earth is hurt. Help one aspect of existence and the entire planet is strengthened. We are all bound together in the web of life.

Now the time has come, particularly in religion, to learn anew that God is not Jewish or Christian, Buddhist or Hindu, or any other label we devise. God is God and God is in all of us and above all of us.

Not for one moment should we abandon our own traditions, religious observances, and forms, yet we must enlarge our vision of reality. A true religionist respects the humanity and gifts of all peoples. The idea of God is trans-theological.

Is it not time to understand that that which unites is greater than that which divides us? Is it not time to bring splendor once more into the human experiment?

Is it not time to appreciate and honor the mother of all of us—Mother Earth? Are we not her children?

Science has visually demonstrated to us that the whole planet is a unity. When we see pictures of the Earth taken from the Moon, we do not see any divisions of nations or states. Therefore, when we think about the planet we must no longer think in terms of city or state but rather of the planet—everything and everyone on it and in it. We must learn to think globally before we act locally.

There is a stirring among the people of this physically and spiritually indivisible planet. There can no longer be freedom for some and not for others. We read about this movement in newspapers and see it before our eyes on television, sometimes within milliseconds of each call for freedom. The communications on Earth are now instant, and the globe has shrunk to one city. The heroes of this universal drama are Andre Sakharov, Lech Walesa, Fang Lizhi, and the anonymous human who stood fearlessly in front of the giant tank in Tiananmen Square, who really stands for every person.

The mutual feeling of the unity of all people on Earth is gathering strength and will not be stopped. Even aside from moral, political, or intellectual considerations, it is simply unthinkable to exist otherwise.

I am writing this while sitting in the apartment in Jerusalem where my wife and I have spent the last twenty summers. I am listening to the broadcast of the concluding concert of the Annual Israel Music Festival. The performance is taking place in a valley that was once called *Gehenna* (Hell). Now with a huge stage over thick grass in a setting of giant stones, it is a national amphitheater.

The performance is the *Hallelujah Chorus* from Handel's *Messiah,* sung in Hebrew. The producers of the concert have enhanced this presentation by coordinating it with a magnificent display of fireworks. I stand on my balcony and look over the valley and the Mount of Olives above it. The night is filled with magnificent bursts of light that form flowers, exhibit a range of colors, and create magnificent patterns and designs. The total effect is a feeling of exhilaration and being one with all of existence.

It is truly a Hell turned into a Heaven. Many human beings from many countries cooperated to make this possible. The music was written by a German composer. The chorus is from Jerusalem. The fireworks were made in France. The orchestra is composed of musicians from all over the world. It is as if all the forces of humanity and nature joined in a celebration of creation, if not life itself. I see a bright ray of hope.

Perhaps, then, as we begin the forty-fifth year of the bomb and look to the twenty-first century, our guiding words might be a slight variation of a verse from the Scripture: "You shall love your planet as yourself."

I hope so.—1989

3. Can a Jew Believe in God after the Holocaust?

Can a Jew believe in God after the Holocaust? For a rabbi, this is not only a theological challenge but also an existential problem. It is a matter of religious life and death, a spiritual Rubicon to cross. It is the litmus test of the faith of the contemporary Jew.

Permit me to share with you two episodes that have often shattered my peaceful days and terrorized the landscape of my mind at night. My father was born in America, and his father and grandfather were American citizens. My mother was born in Europe and came to America never to see her family again. Her parents died in the 1930s. During World War II my mother lost all contact with the rest of her family, still in Lithuania, which was invaded by the Nazis. In 1945 we learned that they had been exterminated. We discovered that there was a survivor of the massacre of the Jews of Radun (my mother's home town) by the *Einsatzgruppen,* Nazi murder units. Hidden on the edge of the forest, he was an eyewitness to what happened.

When the murderers entered the neighborhood in search of Jews to kill, my two uncles responded in a somewhat similar manner. The uncle who was a scholar—some said he was pious—declared, "They shall find me doing what I was destined to do." So he went to the synagogue and started to study. The second uncle was a newspaper reporter, a thorough secularist, so he went to the newspaper office and began to write an article describing the event.

The Nazi killers found them and gathered them together with their families at a large pit at the edge of the city, near the entrance to the forest. They stripped them, shot them, and threw them into the pit. To save ammunition, they did not bother to shoot the babies, including my cousins, and instead threw them in alive. Then they covered the pit with earth. The survivor told us that the earth heaved and shook for three days. Then all was still.

The second story was told to me by Elie Wiesel, the messenger of the dead, the symbol of the Holocaust. I think it is recorded in one of his books. It may be factual or apocryphal, but it is true in spirit. One night in Auschwitz several inmates decided to put God on trial. They summoned Wiesel, who was then a child, to bear witness. He was selected because the inmates thought that he would be the one most likely to survive and proclaim the verdict to the world.

The arguments, accusations, and defenses raged back and forth for many days. After the proceedings were concluded and the evidence presented, the judges retired to make a decision. A day later the judgment was rendered on God: "Guilty."

These episodes set the frame for the issue: How can a Jew believe in God after the Holocaust? Is it possible that an omnipotent and just God would permit babies to be smothered? Yet if people are not given choices—to do massive evil as well as massive good—is there such a thing as freedom of choice for human beings? Indeed, if all is predestined, then how is there to be sin, and who is culpable?

If God acts as a checkmate in history against evil, then how, when, and where is evil to be checked? Furthermore, is there a quantitative or qualitative measure of evil?

Let us begin by considering the meaning of the verses describing the Noah episode (Genesis, Chapter 7): "The Lord saw how great was man's wickedness on earth, and how every plan devised by his mind was nothing but evil all the time. And the Lord regretted that He made man on earth, and He was saddened. The earth became corrupt before God; the earth was filled with lawlessness."

Precisely what is "corruption"? Could it have been the 6 million Jews and another 5 million who were beaten, tortured, murdered, gassed, and cremated in the concentration camps by the Nazis? This figure includes 1 million children, which sharpens the meaning of "corruption." What about the complicity of silence? Is that "corruption"? What about the 40 million of all nations who died in World War II? Is that "corruption"?

In Chapter 9 of Genesis (v. 6) we are told, "Whoever sheds the blood of man, By man shall his blood be shed; For in His image did God make man." Here, the main rationale deploring the heinous crime of murder is a diminution of the presence of God in the world. In theology one might term it a form of deicide. In this context, could not mass murder be "corruption" so vast that only God could adequately address it?

It is out of this fear that the Bible reads (Genesis 9:8ff): "And God said to Noah...'I will now establish My covenant with you and your offspring to come...and every living thing on earth...Never again shall there be a flood to destroy the earth.' God further said, 'This is the sign that I set for the covenant between Me and you, and every living creature with you, for all ages to come. I have set My bow in the skies, and it shall serve as a sign of the covenant between Me and the earth.' "

Was this written with a possible Holocaust in mind? The Scripture promises "never again a flood," but it says nothing about a fire. The horrors of Auschwitz were followed by the fires at Hiroshima. Is a nuclear holocaust to be a cosmic punishment for shedding so much innocent blood? Or, again, will God, in an attribute of infinite mercy, extend the meaning of the rainbow?

There is yet another biblical passage that is relevant to our concern. In the *locus classicus* of the biblical value of justice, Abraham confronts God directly. Before the destruction of Sodom and Gomorrah, God informs Abraham of the intended action because "the outrage of Sodom and Gomorrah is so great and their sin is so great" (Genesis, Chapter 18).

Abraham, the first Hebrew, in an unprecedented manner—in a scandalous manner—dares to approach and argue with God with the following challenge that rings out through all times to follow: "Will You sweep away the innocent with the guilty? . . . Far be it from You to do such a thing, to bring death upon the innocent as well as the guilty . . . Far be it from You! Shall not the Judge of all the earth do justly?"

These passages form the parameters of the discussion. Now the issue must be joined.

It is appropriate to begin with Richard Rubenstein's assertion that in the ashes of Auschwitz we see the death of God and the loss of all hope. Rubenstein writes: "Jewish history has written the *final answer* in the terrible story of the God of History." He contends that after the Holocaust "the world will forever remain a place of pain and ultimate defeat."

This approach is intolerable to Jewish history and the facts of contemporary history. In the face of every threat of extinction, the Jew has found a way to restructure theology and life itself and to snatch victory and belief out of the jaws of defeat. Moreover, the establishment of the State of Israel after 1,900 years of exile and only three years after the Holocaust, is demonstrable proof that there was no "ultimate defeat." To the contrary, it may be "an ultimate victory" of the people who have been hounded and pounded for millennia because of their commitment to God and Jewish history.

In the last analysis, the birth of every baby is a denial of the death-of-God approach. The mighty Jewish community in America, now bursting into a Jewish renaissance, and the manner in which more than 2 million survivors of the Holocaust have rebuilt their lives all over the world while remaining loyal to their Jewishness are testimony that Jewish history is not over but may be verging on "a new beginning."

Jewish theological responses may be classified into two positions. The first upholds the God of history. The primary proponent of this view, Emil Fackenheim, has described the commanding voice of Auschwitz, which bids Jews not to hand

Hitler any posthumous victories as they would by repudiating the covenant between God and the founders of Judaism and, retrospectively, declaring Judaism to have been an illusion. There are 613 commandments that are sacred to Judaism. Fackenheim adds a 614th, incumbent on every Jew: "Thou shalt survive."

Eliezer Berkowitz, on the other hand, links the Holocaust to the "suffering servant" concept that was first enunciated by Second Isaiah. It is the Jewish role in history to bear witness to God's presence in the world in spite of (indeed, in the face of) immense suffering and horrendous pain. It is not possible to measure injustice in quality and quantity, for "the Chosen People" must realize that loyalty to God, particularly in the face of guiltless pain and anguish, is required of them. A story (apocryphal or real) arose after the Holocaust that faithful Jews entered the crematoria singing "I believe . . . with perfect faith, I believe." Berkowitz summarizes his conviction with the ringing declaration, "For the Jew, for whom history neither begins with Auschwitz nor ends with it, Jewish survival throughout the ages proclaims God's holy presence at the very heart of his inscrutable hiddenness."

There are variations of this theme in classical and contemporary Jewish literature. Martin Buber, in his *Eclipse of God,* advanced the view that there are moments when God withdraws from this world. This is hardly new; the concept of *Deus absconditus,* a "hidden God," is most ancient. Buber argues that faith is living life in the presence of the Redeemer, even when the world is unredeemed. There is an ebb and flow of the presence of God in history. Auschwitz was a time when there was a lessening of the divine. But "faith" means a constancy in attitude, knowing that in time the divine presence will be strengthened.

There is also a school of thought that God's ways are beyond human understanding. Indeed, Isaiah (55:8) says: "My ways are not your ways." For a human mind to try to grasp the ways of God is quite impossible, an attempt by the finite to measure the infinite, which cannot be. Again, Isaiah (40:25) expresses it very clearly: "To whom, then, can you liken Me, to whom can I be compared?—says the Holy One." Kierkegaard describes it well when he uses the phrase "Wholly other." Perhaps this is the "out of the whirlwind" answer of God to Job. God is a *mysterium tremendum* which we humans simply cannot penetrate, much less grasp.

Yet, with all this, Jewish theologians do not exonerate God of all the suffering of the innocent in history. They may explain it, place it in context, attempt to diffuse it, but in the end they are baffled and pained by it. The strain of pillage and persecution was expressed in the rabbinic formula *tzadik verah lo,* "why must the innocent suffer?" Or, as moderns would say, "Why do bad things happen to good people?" Yet, despite the times of testing, historically and presently, the Jew has stood beside his/her faith.

Judaism is a religion of redemption. It is affirmation of human faith out of the central events of history. The basic orientation of the Jew is the Exodus. Out of the overwhelming experience of God's deliverance of His people came the judgment that man is of infinite value and will be redeemed. This is the authentic faith of the Jew.

In the end, perhaps the question is wrong. Should it not be: "After the Holocaust can a Jew have faith in humanity?" The Holocaust was mainly carried out by Germany, which was considered the twentieth century's height of intellectualism and sophistication. Is the Holocaust a moral failure of liberalism, democracy, and universalism? If German officers could listen to Beethoven and then go out and gas people, can one ever trust culture again? If German soldiers could play with their children and then go out and burn babies, can we ever trust human beings again? The accusation is hurled against God but, in all honesty, should we not also place people on trial?

The other side of the coin can be highlighted by the work of the "righteous Gentiles" who saved Jews. True, their numbers were not overwhelming, but those who dared to help exposed their lives and the lives of their families—and some even paid the supreme price. They shine like a beacon in the dark night of despair. There is an Avenue of the Righteous in Jerusalem near Yad Vashem (the Holocaust Memorial) on which trees are planted in honor of noble Christians (both clergy and lay) who endangered themselves to protect Jewish men, women, and children. These acts of bravery, compassion, and the religious expression of responsibility must never be forgotten.

We can now close the circle by asking the obvious question: Was the Holocaust a unique event in Jewish history? Or was it just another catastrophe on the long list in Jewish history? This question was thoroughly examined in a scholarly and balanced manner by David B. Roskies in his book, *Against the Apocalypse: Responses to Catastrophe in Modern Jewish Culture.*

One answer can be found in the story of Gershon Levin, a medic serving in the tsarist army in 1916. He came upon the ruins of Husiatyn, a town that straddled the border between Galicia and Poland. The Russians had destroyed the Jewish village, house by house. Levin records his feelings in the following words: "Only then did I grasp the Destruction of Jerusalem, for whenever I had read the Book of Lamentations in Hebrew school, or heard the dirges chanted on the anniversary of the destruction of the Temple (the Ninth of Av), the scene seemed grossly exaggerated. But, on seeing what the Russians did to Husiatyn in the twentieth century, I could easily imagine what the Romans might have done to Jerusalem some two thousand years ago."

Here we see an analogy that triggers a leap across history to the oldest record of Jewish disaster, which serves as an archetype of later catastrophes. The destruction of the First Temple in 587 B.C.E. and the Jewish response sets the guideline for Jewish history, for if Jews could survive the destruction of a Temple, a culture, and a land, they could survive anything. Jews are the survivors of history.

But even beyond that, Jews respond in a positive and creative manner to tragedy. Theologically, they renegotiate their Covenant with God. After the destruction of the First Temple in 587 B.C.E., the synagogue was born. Following the leveling of the Second Temple in 70 A.D., the Bible was canonized and rabbinic Judaism was born. The survivors of the Crusades reshaped the liturgy of the Jewish prayer book. The Khlenitsky massacres (1648-49) resulted in the Hasidic movement. Even though it is too early yet for the Holocaust to make a definitive statement, there is one expression that must be thoughtfully considered.

There is a direct connection between the Holocaust and the State of Israel that has yet to be fully explored. Israel is a legitimate heir to the tradition of the Jews of Europe. It is no accident that after some 1,900 years of exile, Jews reestablished the ancient homeland. The Holocaust provided the thrust, the energy, the desperation, and the determination that resulted in Israel. The response to Jewish powerlessness had to be Jewish power with all of its hazards.

Recently, Israel produced a medallion entitled *yetziat europa,* "the exodus from Europe," commemorating the fortieth anniversary of the transfer of the survivors of the Holocaust to Palestine, which soon became Israel. There is a line that links the medieval ghetto of the European village to the Jewish settlement in Palestine—Israel. Each phase is an expression of collective survival and each is built upon the other.

Yet in the long view of Jewish history, the Holocaust was still different. The sheer weight of the numbers killed, the fiendish-scientific experimentation, the length of time, the sadistic torture, the cruelty, the gleeful degradation, the use of science and technology in the killing, the bureaucracy of destruction, the complicity or at least the silence of an entire continent, if not the whole world, pushes the theologian to madness—if not beyond.

The meaning of the Holocaust and where it is to be placed in the realm of theology and history may never be resolved. We can study the Holocaust, ponder it, react to it, talk about it, and write about it but, in the last analysis, there can be no definitive explanation or answer to the question, "Can a contemporary Jew believe in God after the Holocaust?" There is ample precedent for this in Jewish literature. In the Talmud, when an issue is not resolved, the passage ends with the initials that are pronounced *tayku.* It stands for "The *Tishbite* (Messiah) will resolve all questions and dilemmas."

In the end, it may all come down to the ancient issue of theodicy, which has never been resolved. The essence of the problem is how to reconcile our notion of God, *theos,* with our concept of justice, *dike.* Or, how can we justify the ways of God to humans? Indeed, the problem of Auschwitz may be said to be the problem of Job magnified six million-fold.

Abraham Joshua Heschel, one of the great theologians of our age and himself a survivor of the Holocaust, once said: "Religion is the art of living with unsolved problems." Judaism and Jews have lived for centuries with unsolved problems. They will continue to do so for centuries to come.

Job, after having thoroughly considered his sufferings, says: "I will lay my hand on my mouth and I am silent."—1988

4. How Could Maimonedes Know More than Moses, Who Met God on the Mountain?

Shavuot is celebrated as *zman matan torahtaynu,* commemorating the giving of the Torah—namely the meeting between God and Moses on Mount Sinai. In theology this is known as revelation; that is, revealing God's will to human beings.

Revelation is the problem of God's communication with men and women. Specifically, what did God communicate on Mt. Sinai? Historically there have been two approaches among believing Jews. One is that God gave the *torah shebektav,* "the written Torah," and *torah baal pey,* "the oral Torah" (i.e., all future interpretations) at the same time on the top of the mountain. The other is that the Ten Commandments and other parts of the Bible were given on high but their subsequent interpretations were in human hands. Indeed, the Talmud records *torah lo bashamyim hi,* "the Torah is no longer in Heaven" (Baba Metzia 59a). This means the Torah was given to us to interpret and amplify.

Which view is correct? Of course, it depends on one's beliefs, feelings, and convictions. I am willing to respect both positions as long as neither side forces its views on the other. Who can be so sure as to impose his or her will on others? Indeed, if they do try—as we see in Israel, Iran, and America—it only results in strife, contention, and eventually blows and blood.

But I would like to give you my interpretations and its implications. I do this with ample Talmudic and rabbinic precedent. A very important passage in the Talmud (Menakhot 29b) tells us that God transported Moses to the classroom of Rabbi Akiva in the second century. Moses was bewildered by the teachings of Rabbi Akiva. He never imagined, according to the passage, that there were such meanings in the words that he was given on Sinai. But God reassured Moses that it was meant to be that way, for the Torah is an evolving, active, developing process.

If we met God today as Moses did at Sinai, would we receive that same Torah? Think about it: revelation must depend in part on the listener. Our ancestors heard at Sinai what they were capable of hearing.

If revelation ended at Sinai, then all later experience—Isaiah's, Akiva's, Maimonides', ours—is repetitive, and the accumulated learning of civilization is pointless. But revelation continues. It builds. The interpretation of one generation becomes part of the text for succeeding generations.

We can hear a little better and learn more all the time, if we are listening. Sinai was not our final list of commandments. We have always taken new mitzvot upon ourselves: the holiday of Hanukkah, wearing a kipah, reciting the Kaddish and observing Yizkor to honor our departed, establishing congregations and writing prayers, ordaining women as rabbis and cantors, supporting the State of Israel. The list goes on.

The growth of understanding is God's gift to us. If study led merely to making ourselves into the image of our ancestors, we would be denying the growing body of human knowledge, the expanding conscience of the sensitive, and our own contemporary insights. We would be practicing a form of idolatry, enshrining the past. Nostalgia alone is not enough.

We can understand God's message better than Maimonides could. We have history, archaeology, literature, philosophy, and psychology, as well as Talmud and the thinking of great scholars—both Jew and non-Jew, men and women—the accumulated wisdom of Judaism and all humanity. We have to use it all. We have constantly to rethink what is expected of us as people and specifically as Jews.

This is not a task for rabbis and scholars alone. It never has been. It is the responsibility of the whole Jewish community. We have always been a community of thinking, caring, studying people who increase the power of God's words by living them and growing with them.

Painting did not stop with Michelangelo. Sculpting was not over with Rodin. Composing was not concluded with Mozart. Physics was not finished with Einstein. New vaccines were not terminated with Salk. And Judaism did not end with Maimonides. To the contrary, because they were giants, we can stand on their shoulders and see farther.

Arthur Rubenstein, the great pianist, was once listening to a student playing one of his favorite sonatas, but with some variation. When he finished everyone waited to hear the master's comment. Then, thoughtfully, Rubenstein said, "Ah, so it can be played that way, too!"

Every experience in life challenges us to open ourselves again to revelation and to listen, to learn, to do. As the Psalmist (119:18) prayed: *Gal aynai vahbitah neflaot metoratehcha,* "Open my eyes that I may see the wonders of God's teachings."—1979

5. Out of the Whirlwind

God: A Biography by Jack Miles. New York: Knopf.

Moses requests to see God. The reply is, "No human can see my face" (Exodus 33:20). Indeed, how can the finite mind grasp the infinite? How can a created object understand its creator?

All references to God, of necessity, have to be metaphors. If God can be perceived as creator, father, friend, lover, redeemer, king, mother, warrior, shepherd, or gardener, why not as a literary character? This is exactly what Jack Miles has brilliantly done in *God: A Biography.*

Miles is a former Jesuit priest, totally familiar with critical biblical scholarship, linguistics, and the commentators. His career has taken him from the Pontifical College in Rome to the Hebrew University in Jerusalem and finally to Harvard University, where he earned a doctorate in Near Eastern languages. He has written a postmodern, stimulating work on the Hebrew Bible, a.k.a. The Old Testament.

The book is for believers and nonbelievers, atheists, and those convinced of the inerrancy of scripture. It is exciting because it gives us inventive and startling ways to look at the texts. Though many in the West no longer believe in God, like a lost fortune the idea has effects that still linger. This volume is a remarkable tool to probe one of the greatest concepts ever woven into the texture of civilization, allowing us to view it in new ways.

A rabbi was once meeting with his students and discussing God. One student asked, "Where does God dwell?" The rabbi replied, "Wherever we choose to permit the Divine Presence to enter."

Miles finds new ways for God to enter our lives and new ways to examine texts and narratives. He sees God as a divine antagonist, a sort of Deus Agonistes.

From the earliest rabbinic commentators up to Kierkegaard, all have assumed that God asked Abraham to sacrifice his only son, Isaac, as a test of faith. (Of course, at the last minute, a ram is provided as a substitute.) Miles, however, asks: What if Abraham is feigning? Abraham seems to be complying with God's request, but perhaps he is seeing how far God will really go. Would a God of compassion really ask a man to sacrifice his only son as an act of faith without a peep of protest?

As in all literary accounts, the protagonist goes through many changes of mood, feeling, and attitude. This forces us to ask, "What is it that makes God godlike?" This scintillating work of literary scholarship traces God in various roles. At what point do we apprehend what God is all about?

In the semantic shifts in the search for a name for God, there is a term that is extremely useful. Moses is told that the term for God is *yahweh* (YHWH). Through a series of historical-theological circumstances, this has been rendered as "the Lord." Wrong. Yahweh is a verb. In Miles' text, the term *ehyeh asher ehyeh* (Exodus 3:14) has been translated as "I am that I am"; "I am who I am"; "I will be what I will be." Using pronouns for God is simply irrelevant.

Ethical monotheism is commonly named as Judaism's greatest contribution to Western civilization. This concept deserves the honor it has received, but it is time to reconsider. Hinduism is polytheistic to this day. Are Hindus less ethical than monotheistic Muslims, Bible-reading Jews and Christians? Aren't theirs alternative paths to an equivalent outcome? What counts is that, in one way or another, moral values be placed above all other values.

In the literary, if not theological, study of the Bible, we read that God inflicted plagues and destroyed Sodom, Gomorrah, and the generation of the flood, for example. Is God a destroyer? In Deuteronomy (11:13-21) we are told that if we do not listen to the word of God, terrible natural disasters will befall us. Is God a terrorist? Here we see the darker side of God.

We read that God is "compassionate, merciful, gracious, forgiving" and we feel like a newborn babe wrapped in a warm blanket. We learn that God is "a still small voice," and the revelation is like a gentle breeze on a hot summer's day. We are commanded "to let justice flow down like the water and righteousness like a mighty stream," and a moral rush comes through our veins. God's response to Job "out of the whirlwind" is like Stravinsky's *Rite of Spring* in its surging, crashing power. This is the bright side of God.

What are we to believe? Is our view of God distorted and ever shifting, like the reflection in a curved mirror at the circus? What are we to make of a cryptic revelation of imminent destruction that is stayed by divine intervention? What about the sufferings of the innocent? What shall the postmodern age make of the literary view of God?

One of the great Jewish commentators of the Bible, Don Isaac Abravanel, flourished in the last half of the fifteenth century in Lisbon and Venice. He began each passage of commentary by asking between five and twenty questions. Then he proceeded to answer them.

We have always assumed that the study of religion is the search for right answers. Perhaps, Miles suggests, the purpose of religion is to seek to ask the right questions.

The ancient memory of God in whose image we were created is buried deeply in us. God is the restless breathing we hear in our sleep, inspiring thoughts like the ones in Jack Miles's book.

Read it, for it is a dazzling guide to help us reflect anew.—1996

6. Elijah is Coming

At our Passover Seder tables when it comes to filling the fourth cup of wine, we place an additional cup in the center of the table and fill it for Elijah the Prophet. At that point in the ritual we open the door so that our legendary guest can enter and take a sip, then leave for the next Seder. Why, of all the characters in the length and breadth of Jewish history, is it only Elijah for whom we pour a cup of wine and set a place at our Seder table?

The explanation is fascinating. Elijah, known as the *Tishbite,* was active politically, socially, and morally in Israel in the ninth century before the regular calendar. The following are some interesting experiences recorded in the Bible.

The first is that he gathered all of Israel upon Mount Carmel and he challenged them. The worship of the idol Baal had begun to grow in Israel, and this disturbed Elijah greatly, for it implied abandoning the traditional Jewish belief in God and turning to idolatry. So Elijah placed 850 priests of Baal on one side of the mountain and he stood on the other side of the mountain. Then he turned to the people and said: "How long will you keep hopping between two opinions? Choose between God and the idols" (I Kings 18:21). Then the people shouted as one: "Adonoy, He Alone is God!" (I Kings 18:39). This is the phrase that we repeat seven times at the conclusion of the great Yom Kippur service, emphasizing the Jewish belief in monotheism. So Elijah symbolizes the concept of the unity of God.

Another episode reveals the nature of Jewish thinking about God. Elijah sits alone in a cave and yearns for communication with God as he prays for God's presence. "And the voice of God came to him saying, 'Stand in front of the cave.' Suddenly a great, strong wind came rending mountains and shattering rocks before him, but Adonoy was not in the wind; and after the wind there was an earthquake, but Adonoy was not in the earthquake; and after the earthquake, fire, but Adonoy was not in the fire; and after the fire a still small voice and God was in the quiet" (I Kings 18:11, 12).

Here we learn from Elijah that the presence of God does not come to us through violence or fire or even shattering moments but rather in quietness, in calmness, and in thoughtfulness.

But the real reason that we invite Elijah to the Seder is his mystic association. This belief originates in the Bible in the Second Book of Kings. Elijah is walking with his disciple Elisha. They sense that soon Elijah will pass from this earth. As they are walking and talking, suddenly there appears a chariot and horses of fire. Elijah steps into the fiery chariot and suddenly disappears from view as he ascends to heaven.

This episode left a deep impression on Jewish history. Hence, Elijah became associated with mysticism and with legend. As time passed Elijah came to be considered as the forerunner of the Messiah. Before the Messiah actually comes, Elijah will appear and announce the time and place of the Messiah.

In the Talmud Elijah became a defender of the Jewish people when they are in trouble. He is concerned with Israel's safety and appears when the people are in dire distress. Moreover, there are many legends, both written and oral, about Elijah being the defender of the poor, the wretched, and the unfortunate. He is always concerned that people not be hurt.

One legend about Elijah is really very contemporary. Elijah is walking across a crowded street with a certain rabbi. The rabbi asks, "Who among these people are destined to go to heaven?" The rabbi thought it surely would be a pious person—a scholar or someone like that. Suddenly Elijah points to two clowns and says, "They are destined for an eternal reward." The rabbi is very puzzled and asks, "Why is that?" And Elijah answers, "For when people are sad, they cheer them up; when they are depressed, they make them feel good; and when they are anxious, they relax them."

Now we begin to understand why Elijah is such a welcome guest at the Seder table. Passover is the first festival of our people, and it contains the great miracle of the exodus. Elijah himself is a miraculous person. Since Elijah will announce the Messiah, since Elijah is the symbol of the belief in one God, since Elijah stands for religious experience through quiet thought, since Elijah is filled with compassion for the unfortunate, it is appropriate that he appear at our Seder table. He stands for the many values of Judaism, including faith and hope and charity.—1979

7. Their Brothers' Keepers— The Other Side of the Holocaust

The Holocaust is a shocking tale of brutality, torture, murder, and systematic savagery on a grand scale. It pains us deeply to recall it. But, on the other hand, we should also remember some inspiring moments of those tragic years. Those include the actions of the non-Jews who risked and sometimes gave their lives to save Jews. We talk about the six million who perished but we do not discuss the more than one million who were saved.

Many of these people survived because of non-Jews who defied the sternest edicts and threats of the Gestapo and sheltered Jews in their homes, churches, orphanages, barns, factories, schools, and similar places. These Christians proved that they were their brothers' keepers. These Christians, though limited in number, should be singled out and remembered for the highest honor and the deepest of praise. These Christians were people like the following:

Jozefek, the cattle dealer in Lwow, who sheltered thirty-five Jews even though it led to his being hanged in a public square.

The Mother Superior and the Benedictine nuns at Vilna who hid imperiled Jews in their convent and clothed them in their own garb to hide them from the would-be murderers.

The Protestant minister, Pastor Vergara, who hid seventy Jewish children in his church.

Edoardo Focherini, the editor of the daily *Avvenire d'Italia,* who rescued Jews until he was caught. It cost him the lives of his seven children in a concentration camp.

One could quote many verses from the Torah, but it would be more appropriate to quote a verse from John (15:13): "Greater love has no man than this, that a man lay down his life for his friends."

We really ought to understand the situation in which these noble Christians operated. Hiding a Jew was not an easy matter. It required more than willingness, courage, and readiness to imperil the lives of one's family. A proper place was necessary, as were the ability to camouflage the hide-out and contact with like-minded individuals who would risk taking the Jew in the event of an imminent raid. Experience had taught the host as well as the one hiding that frequent changes in hiding places were essential for survival. Thus, the saving of one Jew or a whole family often involved the cooperation of many Christians. Often Jews were hidden in a reconstructed house, false closets, cemetery graves, or pig sties. The children had to be taught to be silent.

The Gestapo was constantly on the alert for the thousands of Jews who seemed to burrow into the ground like moles. Among the Nazi allies were collaborators, professional informers, anti-Semites, drunks, and prattlers. The terms for turning someone in were absolutely absurd. The Gestapo usually paid one quart of brandy, four pounds of sugar, and a carton of cigarettes or a small amount of money. The prices varied at different places and times. Anyone caught helping a Jew was usually executed on the spot or hanged in a public place as an object lesson to "Aryans" who entertained the notion of hiding a Jew. Now, one can appreciate the real sacrifices of these extraordinary and sainted human beings who risked so much to help other human beings because it was right. There are thousands of such stories, too many to tell.

However, there is one name that has become the symbol of the nobility to which a human being can rise. That name is Raoul Wallenberg. His story is well known. He is responsible for saving the lives of thousands of Jews. His end is a mystery. He was captured by the Russians and disappeared in their prisons. Last year, someone from Russia testified that he saw him in a Russian jail cell. Recently, he was designated an honorary citizen by the Congress of the United States, an honor accorded to few.

A minister at the University of Oregon has begun an interesting project. He asked why it was that certain Christians volunteered to help the Jews. He studied seventeen biographies for more than two years in the archives of Yad Vashem in Jerusalem and narrowed his study down to this: at the exact moment of intervention, when the Christian said, "Now I will act," what motivated him or her? All the Christians who helped had a strong religious background with powerful religious values. They attended Sunday School regularly as children, or they went to church and listened to the sermons, or they read the Bible. In other words, as children or adults they had a strong, definable set of values.

At the moment of intervention, each person said that a role model appeared as their guide to action. In other words, someone said, "I will do this because this is something my pastor would want me to do." Or, "My mother and father always helped people, so how can I stand by now?" Or, "My Sunday School teacher told me that one day I would be tested in my religion." Or, "I had a friend (or a relative or a public school teacher) who represented the very best, and I would like to be the same way." It was always a personal role model who triggered the action. The implications of this ought to be very clear to those who work in the field of religious education.

Many consider "Love your neighbor as yourself" as the most important verse in the Torah. It does not say: "Love your neighbor the Jew," or "Love your neighbor the Catholic," or "Love your neighbor the intellectual," or "Love your neighbor the artist." It just says, "Love your neighbor." Love your neighbor because he or she is a person, because he or she was created in the image of God. Love him or her because that is right, decent, and the only way to live.—1986

8. If You Know One Religion...You Don't Know Any

The Search for God At Harvard, by Ari Goldman. New York: Random House.

"If you know one religion . . . you don't know any" were the words Ari Goldman heard on the first day of classes at the Harvard Divinity School. This planted a seed in his mind that eventually flowered into a book. But all the while his deep faith as an Orthodox Jew was a firm stem, and its roots grew deeper.

For more than a decade, Goldman has been a reporter for *The New York Times,* most lately as a distinguished religion correspondent. Much to his surprise and delight, as well as challenge, he was given a sabbatical to enroll in the Harvard Divinity School for a year. This book is a record of that experience as well as an *apologia pro vita sua.*

Rabbinic teachings frame the chapters of his well-written journal (after all, he is a wordsmith by trade) that includes an account of his own stormy childhood. One quickly understands that religious Orthodoxy is the main, stable force in his troubled life, yet at Harvard Divinity School he slowly learned that understanding the words and followers of the New Testament, the Koran, the Upanishads, and other texts would enable him to develop a richer and fuller appreciation of himself and Judaism.

The book is essentially brought to life by a Hindu story. The gods Vishnu and Brahma meet and argue over which of them is the ultimate Creator. A fight ensues. Brahma enters Vishnu's body to consider the validity of his opponent's view. Vishnu enters Brahma's body to do the same. So impressed are they by their new perspective that they give up the fight and decide to honor each other as the Creator. Which God created heaven and earth? It depends on your point of view.

Goldman provides a valuable guide to what it means to take religion seriously in our secular society. He found that his fellow students at Harvard did not fit the old stereotypes. There was Ann, who wore fishnet stockings and wanted to become a Unitarian minister. Robert, a banker, had seen his bank collapse into insolvency and his wife deteriorate into alcoholism. Diane, "an apple-cheeked, all-American kid from suburban Detroit, was the leader of the school's Gay and

Lesbian Caucus." As the author records their conversations, the all-too-human side of doing God's work is revealed.

Ari Goldman is very much taken with Gandhi's book entitled *All Religions Are True.* And rightly so. For Gandhi writes: "It is idle to talk of winning souls for God. Is God so helpless that He (She) cannot win souls for Himself (Herself)?" Gandhi further notes: "God will ask, asks us now, not what we label ourselves, but what we are, i.e., what we do."

From African faiths, Goldman learns the difference between "natural religions" and "revealed religions." Natural religions stem from the basic experiences of humans: seeing one's shadow, having a dream, watching the death of a loved one. Revealed religions begin with stories, which become sacred. One has its origins in natural phenomena, the other in ideas. It would do us well to keep this in mind, for they are both sides of the same coin.

Goldman uses the term "religion," from the Latin "to bind," and infers that it means "to bind back" to the past. This meaning is usually derived from "tradition," from the Latin *traditio,* "to hand over." In Hebrew, the same concept is called *mesoret,* which also means "tradition" and is the handing over of heritage from one generation to another.

It appears to me that religion binds our life into meaning and gives it integrity. Its practices bind our lives together during rites of passage from the womb to the tomb. Its ceremonies bind our year through the celebration of the seasons. Its values and system of morals bind our behavior and give us guidance. Its wisdom binds us, holds us, and stabilizes us in times of adversity, distress, and suffering. In this sense does religion bind and sustain us.

Goldman's book is filled with many insights. Spirituality is hidden under a thick layer of intellectualism and politics but is revealed in the connections between people. Religion is what we do; what others do is superstition. The use of candles in many faith systems is a bond with the way we use fire for religious celebration. God made a piece of clay come to life in each of us and enabled that clay to transcend life.

His penetrating observations on Islam and Christianity are worth pondering for their striking originality. In addition, I was surprised to learn that Lord Krishna is mentioned in the Hebrew Book of Esther. I must have read this book sixty or seventy times and never noticed this.

Ari Goldman also records his struggles to preserve his Orthodox Judaism in both the secular and spiritual world (if one can indeed separate them). He is thoroughly honest as he is confronted and tested by ideas and life's experiences. But he wisely concludes, "Judaism must be probed, studied, questioned and challenged, for it is in the struggle that it comes to life."

There is the lovely story of a mother who took her child to the circus. Suddenly, they were separated in the vast crowd. The child began to shout, "Sarah! Sarah!" Immediately, the mother found the boy. Whereupon she asked him, "Why did you call me Sarah, when you always call me mother?" The youngster replied, "There are lots of mothers here, but I wanted my mother."

In *The Search for God At Harvard,* Goldman teaches us that there are many mother faiths that we must respect, learn from, and regard. But, at the same time, we can and must deeply love our own mother faith. This understanding is a part of the search for God everywhere and at all times.—1991

9. Can One Be Loyal to One's Faith and Still Respect the Beliefs of Others?

I am honored to speak at the Annual Interfaith Program and Tea sponsored by the B'nai B'rith Women of St. Paul, Church Women United, and the Council of Catholic Women. Since its inception some four decades ago, it has been a bright star in the firmament of our community, guiding us in the right direction.

The fact that this tea always takes place in a House of God inevitably leads to a discussion of perceptions of God, what they mean to us, and how we should handle them in the context of community. In this mood, I would like to raise a fundamental issue—call it a dilemma or paradox—that goes to the heart of the matter of interfaith dialogue. That is: "Can one be loyal to one's faith and still respect the beliefs of others?"

I would like to discuss this in a thoughtful, serious, and responsible manner. After all, if one believes in a code of morals or a faith system that is good and rewarding, shouldn't one try to convince others of a good thing? If one is convinced that one's belief system is not merely the right way to salvation but the only way, is it not an obligation to save others, to convert others, to convince others of the truth?

If this be so, then how can we relate to others? If you hold one "truth" about religion and I hold another, are we to be perpetually in conflict? If there are many religious approaches in a society and each is based on deep commitment—for after all, that is what religion is all about—then how can that society endure? Will it not degenerate into conflict, ultimately to disintegrate?

All religions have struggled with this problem in one form or another. This dilemma is known as the tension between the universal and the particular. How are we like everyone else and how are we different? What do we have in common and what is it that makes us individual?

It is interesting to note that even though Christianity at times may express its exclusiveness, there is a classic passage in John 14:2 in which Jesus says: "There are many rooms in my Father's house." For all of its claims to absolutism, Islam includes Moses, the Patriarchs, and Jesus among those to be revered. Even though at times the Jews thought of themselves as the Chosen People, we find this remarkable passage in first-century rabbinic literature: "I [God] call heaven and earth as witness. The spirit of holiness rests upon each person according to the deed that each does, whether that person be non-Jew or Jew, man or woman, employer or employee" (Seder Eliahu Rabbah 34:8).

Before theologians begin to erect their particular edifices, there is the universal acceptance of the concept that each and every human being is created in the image of God. We all carry within ourselves a spark of the divine. Logically, then, it is our responsibility to respect others, for as we are holy, so are they. This foundation, upon which most belief systems are built, might be expressed in a bit of serious humor.

Once a stranger approached a local citizen and asked, "Were any great men or women born in this town?" The citizen answered with a straight face, "No, only babies." We are born, and then chance and circumstance determine toward which religion or lack of religion we will gravitate. First we are human, then we acquire doctrines. That is the essence of the classical biblical commandment to respect others, encapsulated in the words: "Love your neighbor as yourself" (Leviticus 19:18). For as you were born in the image of the Holy One, so was your neighbor, who therefore is holy and merits reverence even as you do—and for the same reason.

Indeed, this concept was secularized into the thought of political democracy. Was it not written in the Declaration of Independence: "We hold these truths to be self-evident; that all men (and of course, women) are created equal; that they are endowed by their Creator with certain inalienable rights; that among these are life, liberty, and the pursuit of happiness."

Unless there is respect for an individual's life, how can a society function? Unless there is liberty for each person, how can a society be just? Unless there is an opportunity to pursue happiness as each person views it, how can a society be called free? Rights, implying respect for other beliefs, are the very keystone in the arch of democracy and its spiritual drive.

Having said that, how do we deal with the strong faith that so many of us hold is essential to a meaningful life? We need a religion that will give us a system to integrate ourselves into the universe, endow our lives with spirituality, and be a guideline for values and a code of morality. We need a source of inspiration and a way to make life transcendent. We have to have a tradition that will carry us through the rites of passage from birth to death. We need a religion to hold us during the terrifying moments of moral bewilderment, disorientation, and personal anxiety. We need a religion as a steadying and stabilizing force when faced with loss, reversal, disillusionment, disappointment, and despair. We need a way to cope with the mystery of the world and the majesty of creation. In short, we need God.

That is why religions have found paths to the Divine, created a system of beliefs, assembled sacred literature, formed customs and ceremonies, and developed myths—in short, evolved a tradition. These are holy paths, for they lead us to the sacred. As human beings, we can think in the abstract, but we must act in the concrete. Religion links heaven to earth. Each of us has a need to walk in a specific path toward salvation and the good life. Our way, created by our ancestors, our particular language of faith, our special traditions are holy and sacred to us. We grow up with these traditions or we choose them, and they become the essence of our being. Eternity is what we are born into, but time and place gives it meaning.

We all want our own religions. Through great loyalty and love of our own religion we can learn to respect the importance of other religions. There is no need to judge, to evaluate, to use terms like "superior" or "inferior" in dealing with religion. But there is every need to respect, to regard, to understand, to appreciate other religions. My religion is right for me and your religion is right for you—period.

We are speaking, mainly, of Western religions. However, in the study of Eastern religions one learns that there is a much easier acceptance of beliefs other than one's own. We have a great deal to learn about tolerance from religious systems far from our own.

My wife and I have owned a condominium in Jerusalem for twenty years. Each year we go there for the summer. There I have the opportunity to pursue one of my hobbies, which is archaeology in the Holy Land. Once, standing in an excavation in the ancient city of David near the holy sites of the religions of the Western world, I noticed an archaeologist examining a bone. I asked him what he could learn from the bone. He replied, "From this bone I can fairly accurately tell you the age, sex, height, and some other significant details of the person's life." Then he paused and added, "But the one thing I can't tell from a person's bones is his or her religion. That I can only do from the cultural context." He looked up at the Holy Sepulcher, the Dome of the Rock, and the Western Wall and concluded, "That depends on where the individual chose to worship."

We know in our bones that all people are equal. We feel in our very depths that our own religion gives us meaning and is a matter of our life and death. We know that cancer, Alzheimer's Disease, and a broken heart are not Catholic, Protestant, or Jewish—they are human. We know that when a hungry person is fed, a homeless person is sheltered, and an injustice righted it doesn't really matter whether the help comes from a church, a mosque, or a synagogue. Open-heart surgery is not sectarian, treating a tumor is not theology, and creating employment is not a matter of catechism.

Surely, religion is a crucial force in motivating the healing process. While spirituality inspires us to cure and care, doctrine, dogma, and declarations do not help in specific, definable ways. The spirit of God moves mysteriously to heal and to inspire, but can we truly say it is the monopoly of any specific denomination?

I am reminded of the story of Sir William Osler, the great British surgeon. A student observing him in an operating theater remarked, "What a wonderful healer you are, Dr. Osler." Osler replied, "I merely dress the wound. God heals." God is the healer of us all. And, it seems to me that to claim exclusivity with God is an ungodly act.

We all look forward to the times of the Messiah, however we choose to define that term. Times when there will be justice, sustenance, environmental safety, and peace for all. The only difference is that in Jewish theological thinking about the Messiah the time is known as "the First Coming," and among Christians it is known as "the Second Coming."

I would like to conclude with a personal account. About twenty years ago I was walking across the Ford Bridge with Abraham Joshua Heschel, who is considered one of the foremost Jewish theologians of the last half of the twentieth century. We paused halfway and looked at the little island in the middle of the Mississippi River. Then we walked to Temple of Aaron. He excused himself and went into the study that we provided for him during his two-month stay.

He emerged an hour later and this is what he wrote: "No Religion Is an Island."

No religion is an island;
there is no monopoly on holiness.
We are companions of all who revere the Holy One
We rejoice when God's name is praised.
No religion is an island;
we share the kinship of humanity,
the capacity for compassion.
God's spirit rests upon all, Jew or Gentile,

man or woman, in consonance with their deeds.
The creation of one Adam and one Eve promotes peace.
No one can claim: my ancestry is nobler than yours.
There is no monopoly on holiness
there is no truth without humility.
We are diverse in our devotion and commitment.
We must be united in working for the reign of God.
There can be disagreement without disrespect.
Let us help one another overcome the hardness of heart,
opening minds to the challenges of faith.
Should we hope for each other's failure?
Or should we pray for each other's welfare?
Let mutual concern replace mutual contempt,
as we share the precarious position of being human.
Have we not all one Creator? Are we not all equal children?
Let us not be guided by ignorance or disdain.
Let lives of holiness illumine our paths.
God is open to all who seek the Holy One.
Let our deeds reflect that we share the image of God.
Let those who revere the Holy One speak one to another,
leading everyone to acknowledge the splendor of God.—1991

Backword

This is my fiftieth year of association with the Temple of Aaron in St. Paul, Minnesota. I started as student rabbi, then became the assistant rabbi, associate rabbi, rabbi, senior rabbi, and, now, rabbi emeritus. During these years I have published columns, articles, and book reviews. Recently, out of curiosity, I asked for copies of these articles and saw, to my surprise, that there were close to two hundred.

For fifty years I have not only served the congregation but have been active in Jewish affairs locally and overseas. I have been intensely involved in many communal and national issues and have reflected on Jewish history. These interests found expression in the articles. Syndicated by the J.T.A., Seven Arts Features, and other agencies, these articles have been published in 30 papers reaching the Anglo-Jewish community. Articles have also appeared in *Sh'ma, The Reconstructionist, The United Synagogue Review, Women's League, The Hungry Mind Review,* the *Minneapolis Star and Tribune,* the *St. Paul Pioneer Press, Hadassah Magazine, Reader's Digest, The Catholic Digest, Conservative Judaism,* the *Jerusalem Post,* the *Jerusalem Report,* and others. I have received inquiries, critiques, comments, and compliments from all over the world. It is impossible to cite the source of each article, but the original publication date has been noted.

It was suggested that an anthology of the most interesting articles be published in a book to record one person's thoughts about the last half of the twentieth century, one of the most powerful periods in history—certainly Jewish history. Moreover, since the writing was done in Minnesota, the book also represents events and a point of view from this perspective.

I am grateful to Cecelia Rose Waldman, my associate for 40 years, who has great ability and deep commitment. She has been invaluable in all phases of my rabbinic work. Much credit and heartfelt thanks are due her.

Anne R. Kaplan has edited several of my books and articles and has been especially devoted to this book. Her skill, talent, and wisdom have helped to shape it and added immensely to it.

Bruce E. Kuritzky not only typed some of the original articles but this entire book—indeed, several times. He is not only a superb typist but offered suggestions and observations that helped shape its style.

I want to especially thank Harry and Sandy Lerner, who helped this book to see the light of day, and Zach Marell for sharing his great talent.

During the past decade I have served on the faculty of Macalester College in St. Paul. There I am surrounded by some of the best minds in the world. The faculty and staff have broadened my understanding and deepened my knowledge. I am grateful to them for having stretched my mind and enriched my understanding of religion, Judaism, and life itself. The library staff of Macalester has been most helpful.

But most of all I offer deepest gratitude and all my love for more than fifty years to Laeh Raskas for her constancy, companionship, care, counsel, and abilities as a gourmet chef. We were married when I entered the seminary as a raw potential rabbi. She helped me develop social skills and sensitivity and opened up avenues that have helped me appreciate others, value the arts, and enrich my life. Her work with the American Jewish Joint Distribution Committee opened my eyes to the vastness of Jewish service. We have traveled together all over the world. For two months annually during the past twenty-five years we have summered in our condominium in Israel. We have beautiful memories of that as well as the golden years of our love.

During all of my life in St. Paul I have lived one block from the Mississippi River. As a Minnesota rabbi, a river of friendship broad and deep has run through my life. Perhaps, then, it is appropriate to conclude with a paraphrase from a rabbinic statement:

"I have learned much from books, more from my teachers, but most of all from my students."

Shalom - Peace.

Bernard Solomon Raskas

St. Paul, Minnesota Jerusalem, Israel

2000/5760

Bernard Solomon Raskas

Rabbi Bernard Solomon Raskas attended the University of Chicago and received a Bachelor of Arts degree with Final Honors from Washington University in Saint Louis. In 1949 he was ordained by the Jewish Theological Seminary of America, where he won the Bible Prize with a dissertation on "Deutero-Isaiah" and the Talmud Prize. He received his M.H.L and was conferred a D.D. in 1975. He also did postgraduate work in comparative religion and anthropology at Western Reserve University in Cleveland.

Raskas is currently Rabbi Emeritus at Temple of Aaron Congregation in Saint Paul, where he served for 38 years as senior rabbi. Under his leadership, the congregation doubled in size and built the new synagogue on Mississippi River Boulevard. He is also Distinguished Visiting Professor of Religious Studies at Macalester College in Saint Paul, where he was the first Associate Jewish Chaplain.

Rabbi Raskas has been an active leader in Jewish and civic affairs. He is a member of the Board of the United Israel Appeal and annually attends the Jewish Agency meetings in Jerusalem. He was campaign chairman of the St. Paul United Jewish Fund and Council for two years, served as a member of many committees, and has been a consultant to the campaign cabinet for the past six years. A founding member of the United States Holocaust Memorial Council, he was also a member of the board of the Jewish Museum in New York, the board of the Minnesota Psychoanalytical Foundation, and board of advisors of the Hill Monastic Manuscript Library at St. John's University in Collegeville, Minnesota. He helped to found the Minnesota Chapter of Religion and Mental Health and has served on almost every community board of directors, ranging from the St. Paul Chamber of Commerce to the Human Rights Commission and the American Cancer Society.

Rabbi Raskas writes a regular column for the Anglo-Jewish press and is the author of 200 published articles on Judaism. In addition, he has written a trilogy, Heart of Wisdom, a volume, Over The Years, and has edited A Son of Faith, Beacons of Light, and Living Thoughts. His other publications include twelve different editions of the Passover Haggadah, A Rabbinic Commentary on the New Testament, The Jewish Experience in America, Contemporary Ethics from a Jewish View, The Evolution of the Jewish Mind Source Reader, Universal Values as Reflected in Jewish Literature, and many liturgical programs in commemoration of Israel Independence Day, Holocaust remembrance, and major events in Jewish and American life, and High Holy Days services. He has also taught many popular adult education programs over the years.

In 1985 Rabbi Raskas received the Agus Award, which is given by the Rabbinical Assembly to "a pulpit rabbi who has distinguished himself in scholarship." Three years later he received the Distinguished Alumnus Award from the Jewish Theological Seminary of America. In 1997 Raskas received the Service to Humanity Award from the United Hospital Foundation.

In addition to his involvement in community and religious affairs, Raskas enjoys pursuing interests that range from contemporary art to anthropology, psychiatry and promoting literacy. All proceeds from the sale of this book will be donated to literacy programs.

To commemorate his 50th year with the congregation, the Temple of Aaron Board designated Raskas as Rabbi Laureate, marking his half-century of distinguished work and contributions to Judaism and human welfare.

In Appreciation

Publication of this volume is made possible by grants from The Harris Foundation, Otto Bremer Foundation, Stanley S. and Karen Hubbard, David & Jane Berg, Frank and Toby Berman, Reuben and Corrine Birnberg, Arnold and Rae Divine, David Feinberg, Gerald and Gail Frisch, William L. Frost, Lillian Geller, Loren and Rosie Geller, Harry and Rivoli Golden, Dean and Marilyn Greenberg, Leo and Doris Hodroff, Lynn and Gloria Johnson, Scott and Sally Johnson, Dr. Yale and Jean Kanter, Elliot and Eloise Kaplan, Ted Kuller and Betty Marshall, Stephen E. and Sheila Lieberman, Harold and Sylvia Liefschultz, Harvey Lubov, Donald and Rhoda Mains, Stanley and Joyce Malmon, Michael and Polly Saxon, Sandra Schloff, Richard and Rossy Shaller, Bruce and Linda Singer, David and Dede Smith, Milton and Evelyn Smith, Sheldon and Maxine Stewart, The Saint Paul Foundation, Alex and Mollie Tankenoff, David and Sally Toushin, Joe and Sandra Wolkowicz, Millie Wolkowicz and Dr. George Chaitkin, William and Jody Weisman, Ronald and Lynn Zamansky,

To these organizations and individuals, I offer my heartfelt thanks.

Rabbi Bernard Solomon Raskas

Colophon

Seasons of the Mind was composed by Interface Graphics, Inc. in the Times typeface with display lines in Hiroshige, printed by the John Roberts Company and bound by Muscle Bound Bindery, Inc., in Minneapolis, Minnesota.